The Government and Politics of France

Dr Wright was reader in French politics at the London School of Economics before taking up his present post as Fellow of Nuffield College, Oxford. He has also taught at several European and American universities and at the European University Institute in Florence. He has written extensively on modern French history and French and European politics in British, American and French journals. He has been, since its creation in 1978, joint editor, with Gordon Smith, of *West European Politics*, and was a member of the editorial board of *Political Studies*. He is the author of a book on the French Council of State, and joint author of one on the French prefects. Dr Wright is also the editor of several books on French and on European politics.

The Government and Politics of France

Third edition

Vincent Wright

London

First published 1978
by Hutchinson Education
Second edition 1983
Third edition 1989 published by Unwin Hyman
Reprinted 1990 (third impression)

Reprinted 1992, 1994
by Routledge
11 New Fetter Lane, London EC4P 4EE

Typeset in 10/11 Times
Printed and bound in Great Britain by
Biddles Ltd, Guildford and King's Lynn

British Library Cataloguing in Publication data

A catalogue record for this book is available from the British Library.

ISBN 0–415–09078–4

To
Dorothy and William Pickles

Contents

Preface to the third edition

All books which claim to describe "The Government and Politics" of a country are presumptuous, and short books are doubly so. All suffer, too, from being out of date the moment they are written (and even more so by the time they are published), but those on France are in a particularly hazardous position, for every national election – and they are all too frequent – may produce a political and constitutional crisis which damages or even destroys the assumptions and arguments of the book. Furthermore, the nature of the present régime has not remained static since its creation some twenty five years ago: since the early 1980s, for instance, important new decision-making bodies have been created, the Constitutional Council and the Senate have become notable political actors, and the party system has been significantly changed.

No book can pretend to capture in any detail the immensely rich and complex interplay of social, economic, political and psychological forces which comprise the political process. The author of a book on politics is like the practitioner of the art: he is constantly squeezed into unpleasant choices, and in ordering his priorities he betrays his idiosyncrasies and prejudices, and reveals his indolence and ignorance. The priorities of this book centre upon an examination of the stages of, and the reasons for, the growth of presidential government in France. It also analyses the obstacles to, and the limits of presidentialism. Its general theme is that, compared with the previous régime, there is now a closer focus of authority on the office of the presidency. However, the power of the presidency may be radically reduced in certain circumstances, notably when an unfriendly majority exists in the National Assembly – a situation which prevailed between March 1986 and June 1988. Moreover, political power continues to be highly fragmented and subtly suffused among a vast number of public, semi-public and private bodies whose relationships – when they exist – range from contented co-operation to bilious antagonism.

I am aware that the organization of the book leaves something to be desired: the need to be brief frequently competes with the desire to be coherent, and clarity of presentation often does disservice to highly complex truths. But, on the whole, I hope that I have not over-sacrificed either coherence or truth in seeking a framework which allows a logical development of the main theme of the book.

Needless to say, this book owes a great deal to my present and former research students and to my colleagues and friends on both sides of the Channel and of the Atlantic, many of whom commented critically (if charitably) on the book when it first appeared. They will find their ideas pillaged and perverted in this short book, so may I take this opportunity of thanking and apologizing to them in advance. Finally, I should like to thank Eileen Gregory, my ex-secretary, and Trude Hickey, my present secretary, whose patience, good humour and efficiency greatly facilitated the writing of the book.

Vincent Wright
August 1988

Introduction: the Fourth Republic and the Gaullist critique

It is easy to sneer at the Fourth Republic; most Frenchmen did and, if they remember it all, continue to do so. Yet its defects should not be exaggerated nor its achievements belittled. Indeed, recent historical work looks kindly on the régime: credit is now being given to the rulers of the Fourth Republic – honest and talented men who had to tussle with formidable problems, a defective constitution, and bitter party divisions. During the period 1945 to 1958 France was geared to meet international economic competition and was firmly linked to Europe through the Coal and Steel Community, Euratom and, finally, by the Treaty of Rome, the European Common Market. The country was also firmly integrated into the NATO alliance, and relations with Germany, the traditional enemy, were improved (the settlement of the Sarre problem in October 1955 greatly helped). Diplomatically, France of the Fourth Republic may have been weak, but it was not isolated. Even in the colonial field, progress, although slow, begrudged and often achieved at a terrible price, was made with the granting of independence to Indo-China (1954), Morocco (1956) and Tunisia (1956). In black African states, measures taken by Gaston Defferre in 1956 were to help smooth the path to the independence achieved during the Fifth Republic. And if the Algerian problem proved intractable, it should be remembered that it was to take all the ruthlessness, the courage and the guile of General de Gaulle to impose a solution upon an army, part of which did not hesitate to resort to rebellion and assassination. Moreover, the first President of the Fifth Republic was able to count upon the massive support of a war-weary public, a support which had been denied his predecessors.

On the domestic level, too, the record of the régime is far from dishonourable. It was during the Fourth Republic that the social gains of the Popular Front government of 1936 and the family welfare schemes of the Vichy régime were consolidated and extended. The foundations of the much vaunted French "economic miracle" were also laid during this period. The achievement was all the more remarkable in view of the economic situation of the

1

country in 1945 after five years of war, invasion and enemy occupation. Large areas of France, it must be recalled, were a battlefield not only in 1939-40 but also in 1944-5, and by the time of the Liberation, about a fifth of all French real estate was destroyed or seriously damaged. More than half a million houses and three-quarters of a million farms, half the country's railway engines, a third of its merchant navy, and three-quarters of its harbour installations and freight yards were affected. Key mines had been put out of action and innumerable bridges blown up, and those factories which had survived the holocaust were geared to the war effort. An acute food and fuel shortage was not helped by a widespread and highly lucrative black market. By 1958, the situation had been transformed by what was arguably the most revolutionary period in French economic history. It is true that economic progress was accompanied by financial instability and fragility (with occasional bouts of excessive inflation and a humiliatingly weak franc), thus giving substance to the Gaullists' oft-repeated accusation that the politicians of the Fourth Republic had left the country bankrupt. It is equally true, however, that French financial policy was, in some measure, deliberate, and that a large part of the problem lay in the financial strain of the colonial wars and heavy defence commitments, both of which were applauded and encouraged by the same Gaullists.

Even on the purely political level, it is to the credit of the régime that it repulsed determined and often violent onslaughts from the extreme Right and the extreme Left, and that by 1958 France was still a parliamentary and pluralistic democracy and not a dictatorship. Furthermore, like so many of its predecessors it was defeated by forces outside France: if Wellington helped to destroy the First Empire and Bismarck the Second Empire and if Hitler smashed the Third Republic, it was left to the French army in Algeria to overthrow the Fourth. For twelve years the régime took France through a period of unprecedented social and political tension and disruption, which was due to the consequences of the Second World War and military occupation and of the Cold War, to momentous economic changes and to the colonial wars. It should also be added that among the régime's most virulent critics were those who were partly responsible for its defects: the extreme Right demanded "order", yet flirted with disruptive and disorderly minorities; the moderate Right clamoured for greater political stability, yet by its undisciplined and irresponsible behaviour in parliament ensured instability; the Communists appealed for greater social justice, but by their intransigence and short-sightedness helped to sabotage any effective means of achieving it. The Gaullists were no less culpable of this fatal ambivalence:

they agitated for stronger authority, yet many of them made it difficult to impose such authority by encouraging dissidence in metropolitan France and by fanning rebellion in Algeria.

In spite of its real achievements, the Fourth Republic remained unloved – *la mal aimée*. The régime, like the present Italian régime, could probably have survived, lurching from one ministerial crisis to the next, but it was clear by 1958 that the very legitimacy of the régime – that intangible yet essential ingredient of any political system based on consent – was seriously undermined. Already by 1951 nearly half the electorate was voting for parties that rejected the parliamentary system as it prevailed. Faced with the challenge of May 1958 the régime simply could not call upon the loyalties of its citizens. Even those politicians who defended the régime regarded the system with a mixture of resignation, lassitude, exasperation and even despair. In January 1958, barely four months before the *coup* which resulted in the downfall of the régime, the President of the Republic solemnly reiterated his warning that "our basic institutions are no longer in tune with the rhythm of modern times". It was a view shared by many but especially by General de Gaulle, the régime's most persistent and bilious critic, and by Michel Debré, his faithful lieutenant whose vehemence outstripped that even of his master.

Shortly after his return to power, General de Gaulle, in a radio broadcast of 27 June 1958, told the nation that the country was facing three pressing problems: Algeria, the financial and economic situation, and the "reform of the state". In fact, he was faced with five distinct, yet related problems. He had to:

- Put an end to the war in Algeria;
- Challenge the political power of the army which had become a "state within a state";
- Remedy a disastrous financial situation and strengthen a promising yet precarious economic position;
- Re-establish French power and prestige abroad;
- Forge new political institutions which were effective, "republican", democratic and respected.

For de Gaulle and his political and constitutional advisers, those problems were inseparable one from the other, and all sprang from a common source. That source was the chronic weakness of French political institutions which paralysed state authority, and which, in turn, led "infallibly" (to use de Gaulle's own word) to trouble in the colonies and the army, to social disruption and to the loss of national independence. General de Gaulle's main constitutional ideas had been outlined in his celebrated speeches at Bayeux and Épinal in June and September 1946. He attributed much of the weakness of the Fourth Republic to the lack of executive authority which was prey to a divided parliament. During the Fourth Republic there were no fewer than twenty-five governments and fifteen prime ministers (during the same period in Britain there were only four); only two prime ministers, Henri Queuille and Guy Mollet, lasted for more than a year. Associated with ministerial instability were ministerial crises – those periods between the fall of one government and the successful investiture of another. Such crises were not only frequent (an average of two a year) but they were also increasingly difficult to resolve: in the year before the collapse of the Fourth Republic France was ruled by a caretaker Government for one day in every four. While the extent and impact of instability and crises should not by exaggerated (there was a surprising degree of continuity in personnel and policies throughout the period) both undoubtedly brought the régime into disrepute (both abroad and with its own citizens) and occasionally paralysed badly needed action.

De Gaulle saw the fault of the régime in its defective constitution, which gave too much power to parliament, which was itself at the mercy of the many and divided parties. For the Gaullists, political parties were, by their very nature, the spokesmen and defenders of sectional interests, and they reflected, articulated and perpetuated the basic divisions of French society. They argued that since France was so bitterly divided over many issues there could only be many bitterly divided parties. And with many bitterly divided parties government could only be unstable. Parties had, therefore, to be kept firmly in their subordinate place. The logic was implacable, yet faulty: the problem of the Fourth Republic was not that it was dominated by the parties but rather that those parties which formed successive coalition governments were so internally divided and so undisciplined in their parliamentary behaviour.

Two other important premisses underpinned Gaullist constitutional ideas. The first related to the precariousness of the French national fabric: for many Gaullists the unity of the nation itself was under constant threat. This was scarcely surprising, given the diversity of the country: the cultural and historical links between the inhabitants of Picardy, Provence and Normandy, of Lorraine, Roussillon and Savoy, of Brittany, the Basque Country and Auvergne, to mention but a few of the many provinces which compose France, were seen to be very tenuous. It was, therefore, scarcely surprising that the concern for national unity was an obsession of the chauvinistic Gaullists. Certainly, the past activities of separatist movements were never forgotten and rarely forgiven. The second basic premiss of Gaullist constitutional thinking related to the view of the French as being not only diverse and divided but also as being somehow "ungovernable". It was claimed that, compared with the regimented Germans or the socially virtuous British, the French, that "effervescent" and individualistic people, were socially undisciplined, and only too ready to defy established authority. The claim was made with a mixture of despair and pride: de Gaulle was both fascinated and appalled by the fissiparous nature of his compatriots. The Gaullist response to the divisions, the diversity and the "perpetual effervescence" of the French was the need to construct a strong, centralized and respected state based on an executive authority capable of governing and of eliciting obedience. And that was what the Fourth Republic had failed to do; for Michel Debré, it was "a régime of chaos and confusion". The terms *crise de l'État, crise de l'autorité, carence de pouvoir* (power vacuum) figure prominently in the Gaullist critique of the Fourth Republic. With sufficiently strong institutions such problems could have been avoided. In other words, the Gaullists proposed a series of constitutional and political reforms which would serve to compensate for certain defects or inadequacies of political behaviour, themselves rooted in the nature of French history and society. But constitutional reforms designed to strengthen the authority of the state (by reinforcing the executive against a parliament dominated by the despised parties) were insufficient. They had to be accompanied by resolute action against those groups whose actions were undermining the state. Those groups included not only the political parties and the pressure groups whose intrinsic role was to further sectional interests, but also comprised the administration (especially that in the colonies) and the army, who were supposed to be obedient custodians of the national interest but whose autonomy threatened the very integrity of the state.

The most striking exercise of autonomous and uncontrolled authority took place in the French colonies, where initiatives were often taken by local civil servants, themselves prisoners of other local forces whose sole concern was the maintenance of the colonies in French hands. Representatives of the French government in the colonies such as General Leclerc and Admiral Thierry-d'Argenlieu in Indo-China, Jean de Hautecloque in Tunisia and General Juin in Morocco played crucial parts in shaping French policy, often in defiance of instructions emanating from Paris. Successive prime ministers and foreign ministers complained that they were unable to get any orders obeyed or that they were constantly faced with embarrassing *faits accomplis*. Thus, in March 1952, it was the French Resident-General, Jean de Hautecloque,

who took the initiative in having the Tunisian prime minister
arrested. Similarly, in August 1953, the deposition of the Sultan
of Morocco was much more the inspiration of colonial officials
than French politicians. Indeed, in both cases, the government was
unhappy and embarrassed about the decisions but did nothing to
prevent them.

The Algerian "cancer" which was to undermine and eventually
to destroy the Fourth Republic was contracted in Indo-China
and spread unchecked in Morocco and Tunisia. The dreadful
tissue of lies, evasion and irresponsibility which characterized the
Algerian war had already been evident in the six and a half years
war in Indo-China, which had ended in the military humiliation
of Dien-Bien-Phu and which cost the French 92,000 dead and
114,000 wounded. The cost of the Algerian war, which began
in November 1954, was even more appalling, and may, in some
respects, be likened to that of the Vietnam war for the United
States: it sacrificed many men; it was a cause of governmental
and financial instability; it weakened the country's already feeble
diplomatic position; it sapped the moral probity of the régime;
it eroded some of the very bases of the state – the loyalty of its
army, of its administration and of its citizens. In short, it slowly
undermined the legitimacy of the régime. It was in Algeria that
the authority of French governments was most acutely contested.
Residents-general who were sent from Paris to Algiers with
the task of introducing liberal measures were quickly seduced
or intimidated either by the French settlers or by the army.
Soustelle, a Left-wing Gaullist, Lacoste, a Socialist, and Salan, a
"republican" general, were among those residents-general whose
liberal intentions were quickly transformed into illiberal practices.
More dangerously, civil authority gradually relinquished power to
the army, often (as was the case with Lacoste in 1957) only too
willingly. In the development of the relationship between Paris
and Algiers there were thus two distinct yet related stages: first,
decisions were increasingly taken in Algeria, and second, power
within Algeria was gradually transferred from civilian to military
hands. A multitude of incidents served to illustrate the inability
and unwillingness of Paris to impose its will on a suspicious,
obdurate and rebellious local administration and army. In October
1956, for example, Ben Bella, one of the leaders of the Algerian
independence movement, who was flying from Morocco to Tunisia,
was forced by the French airforce to land in Algeria where he
was immediately arrested. The government in Paris, which was
in highly secret and sensitive negotiations with the Algerian
"rebels", was horrified: Savary, the Minister for North African
Affairs, resigned in protest (a singularly effective gesture). But

Prime Minister Mollet, although stupefied by the action, accepted and then justified it. Another example of governmental impotence and cowardice, no less revealing and certainly more tragic, was the Sakhiet incident of February 1958. Prime Minister Gaillard had no foreknowledge of the French bombing of the Tunisian village of Sakhiet, which was suspected by the French army of harbouring Algerian independence fighters. Sixty-nine Tunisians (including twenty-one children) lost their lives, the Tunisian government was outraged, the French government was astonished and angry, international opinion indignant. But the prime minister, fearful of army reactions, was forced to condóne the bombing. Such acts of defiance by the army were clearly intolerable to General de Gaulle – once in power.

The creation of a strong, centralized, democratic and respected state, based on a powerful executive headed by the president and protected against a previously omniscient and omnipotent parliament, served by an obedient and efficient administration and army, and willing and able to resist the particularist demands of the groups and of the parties – such were the aims of the Gaullist reformers. They were a response to a pressing situation but they also corresponded to a deeper political philosophy. For the first President of the Republic, those aims had to be carried out "within the context of republican legality": there could be no recourse to vulgar dictatorship, which de Gaulle abhorred for reasons based on historical experience and on a tactical reading of contemporary French politics. How the Gaullists attempted to fulfil their aims and how successful the régime they founded has been in achieving them serve as two of the underlying themes on this book.

1 The basis of presidential government: constitutional powers, political instruments and personal agents

In his *Conduire le changement*, published in 1975, Michel Poniatowski, Minister of the Interior, intimate friend and political adviser of President Giscard d'Estaing, advocated "a further push towards presidentialism". The reaction of some observers was to ask whether such a push was possible, since the régime had already become so ostentatiously presidential. Those observers could be excused their reaction, for the emergence of the presidential office as the major centre of political decision-making was perhaps the most important single institutional change after the collapse of the Fourth Republic in 1958. This chapter will briefly examine the presidency under the Third and Fourth Republics and then consider the powers invested in the president by the 1958 Constitution. It will then examine more closely the instruments and agents of presidentialism.

The Presidency of the Republic before 1958

When de Gaulle decided to stand for election to the presidency of the Republic he was making clear that the office was destined to become the real power-house of French politics. It was, in many senses, a surprising choice, for its image had been somewhat politically tarnished during the Third and Fourth Republics. Occupants of the presidency before 1958 were depicted, at best, as distinguished yet colourless figures or, at worst, as harmless nonentities. They were seen as the creatures and prisoners of the members of parliament who had elected them and who, when choosing the president, had sought to avoid the election of a strong personality – a man who might prove a danger both to the privileges and prerogatives of parliament and to the Republic itself. The successful *coup d'état* of 2 December 1851 which ended the Second Republic and the abortive one of 16 May 1877 which threatened the Third Republic were both carried out by incumbent Presidents of the Republic. Those two dates (*le deux décembre* and *le seize mai*) remained anchored in the parliamentary consciousness: a strong-minded and popular choice, such as Clemenceau, for the presidency was to be avoided. In order to be elected President of the Republic by a highly divided parliament a candidate had to project himself as a man of no decided views. Occasionally, parliament was so divided that it took much bargaining before a compromise candidate could emerge. René Coty, the second and last President of the Fourth Republic, was elected in December 1953 after thirteen time-consuming and somewhat humiliating ballots: it was a system which seemed designed to ensure the survival of the weakest. The nondescript were preferred to the brilliant, the safe to the adventurous, the cautious to the ambitious, and of the long list of Presidents of the Republic only Thiers, Grévy, Poincaré, Millerand and possibly Auriol emerged from the ranks of obscure worthies. Among de Gaulle's predecessors at the Élysée were: Sadi Carnot, who secured his place in French history by his assassination (an unkindly contemporary remarked that Carnot's life had been unworthy of his death); Félix Faure, who was remembered for his romantic yet compromising death in the arms of his mistress; Paul Deschanel, whose nocturnal and half-naked perambulations and other bizarre activities finally led to his forced resignation; Gaston Doumergue, who is remembered for his bitter complaints about his own powerlessness; and Albert Lebrun, whose reputation was sullied by his procrastination during the terrible events of 1939-40. It was small wonder that the office was the object of a derision and contempt which was summed up by Clemenceau's famous jibe that the presidency was as superfluous as the prostate gland. Yet to depict the presidential office during the Third and Fourth Republics as a constitutional superfluity is seriously to mistake the nature of the post, since its power depended to some extent on the personality of the incumbent. And however discreet, that power could be considerable. This was true during the Fourth Republic even though the framers of the Constitution of 1946 had deliberately created a weak presidency.

During the Fourth Republic there were two presidents: Vincent Auriol (1947-54) and René Coty (1954-8). Neither may be described as entirely impotent. It is a point worth emphasizing, since the powerful Presidents of the Fifth Republic are all too frequently contrasted with their apparently powerless predecessors of the Fourth. The two Presidents of the Fourth Republic exercised their power in several ways. First, both were always intimately involved in the delicate negotiations which preceded the formation of any new government and also in marshalling parliamentary support for that government once it presented itself to the Assembly for investiture. Both Auriol and Coty took their duties seriously in that area, and both made controversial interventions: the appointment of the very conservative Pinay as prime minister in 1952 owed much to the wily manoeuvring of President Auriol, while the choice of the Socialist Guy Mollet after the elections of January 1956 was engineered in part by President Coty, who was said to dislike Mendès-France, the man many assumed the obvious candidate for the post. Second, both Auriol and Coty gave constant advice and warnings to successive governments and they represented continuity during periods of great ministerial instability. They were constantly informed of all major decisions, especially in the area of foreign, colonial and defence policy, and they had highly developed political antennae sensitive to the ever-changing moods of parliament. Third, Auriol and, to a lesser extent, Coty directly intervened in the formulation of policy. The former's antipathy towards German rearmament was public knowledge (his public utterances frequently made clear his disagreement with governmental policy), while the latter's support for the cause of *Algérie française* was certainly no secret, especially to the army. The importance of the role played by Auriol in foreign affairs and in certain controversial domestic issues (the breaking of the communist-inspired political strikes of the winter of 1947-8, and the problem of church–state relations) should not be underestimated, and it is only now beginning clearly to emerge. President Coty was more discreet, but it should not be forgotten that his attitude and activity in the troubled days of May 1958 were to be a vital factor in easing de Gaulle's path to power. Naturally, in the face of a resolute and hostile prime minister the president could not insist on having his way. On the other hand, a determined president could try to block proposals and wait for the ineluctable collapse of the ministry: the succeeding prime minister might prove sympathetic or more pliable.

While the power of the presidency during the Fourth Republic should not be underestimated, it should be emphasized that presidential power was exercised only so long as it was tolerated by parliament and the government. It was not rooted in constitutional texts, in time-honoured conventions or in strong party backing. It was highly personalized and its exercise hinged upon the tenacity, discretion and patience of the president and the good-will (or tolerance) of the government and parliament. Moreover, as an ex-member of parliament of long-standing, the President of the Republic was all too aware of the limits of his own power. To that extent, the office was clearly an unsatisfactory power base for General de Gaulle, a man who had no parliamentary experience, who disliked being ignored and who hated being overruled. Why, then, choose the presidency, a traditionally weak force, as his power base? Several factors seem to have influenced him. First, it was an office which would enable him more easily to take his distance from the despised politicians. In his conception of his role, de Gaulle wished to be 'above politics and politicians', and as prime minister running a government he would inevitably be dragged into the tawdry business of day-to-day bartering and bargaining. The presidency was an office which better ensured a certain aloofness which suited both his temperament and his view of his role. Moreover, the office may have had a politically tarnished image, but it was not morally compromised. Previous incumbents may have been grey mediocrities, but no neurotic liar had ever disgraced the office as was shortly to be the case in the United States. But the French presidency, although strategically well-placed, had to be reshaped and strengthened. The fulfilment of that task was commenced by de Gaulle in the Constitution of 1958 and pursued by him for the following ten years. His successors were no less assiduous in pursuing the same aim, and there is no doubt that less than twenty years after the collapse of the Fourth Republic the presidency had been radically reinforced in a way that even General de Gaulle could not have envisaged.

The constitutional arrangements of 1958

The text of the present constitution was adopted by the government on 3 September 1958 and presented to the nation the following day. It was the first republican constitution not to have been drawn up and debated in parliament. The constitution was accepted by the nation on 28 September 1958 in a referendum in which only 15 per cent of the electorate abstained. Four out of five voters accepted the proposed constitution, and there was a majority for acceptance in every one of the then ninety *départements* of metropolitan France. The electorate appears to have been moved by mixed motives. Some electors were voting against the Left, some for a solution to the Algerian problem, some for de Gaulle: the constitution itself was regarded with supreme indifference. This did not prevent the government from claiming that the new constitutional arrangements were firmly rooted in public assent: this contrasted sharply with the two previous republican constitutions, since that of the Fourth Republic was accepted by a small margin in a low poll and that of the Third was never put to the nation.

If the decision of the electors in September 1958 seemed clear it was more than could be said for the text they had accepted, for it was the result of unhappy compromises between men who held basically conflicting views on the future distribution of political power. Directly involved in the drafting of the constitution was a small group of members of parliament (who enjoyed a consultative role and who wished, not unnaturally, to preserve the prerogatives of parliament), Michel Debré (the recently appointed Minister of Justice who was clearly determined to strengthen the executive branch of government in its relations with parliament), and General de Gaulle (who was intent on reinforcing the presidency to which he was shortly to accede). Since General de Gaulle was at that time still currying parliamentary favour and since parliament was keen not to displease the General, both sides were prepared to make concessions, yet the result of those concessions was not a happy compromise but a constitutional mess. The unfortunate constitutional experts of the Council of State were called upon to juxtapose and superimpose conflicting ideals, and in the resulting lengthy text confusion competed with contradiction and ambiguity with obscurity. In essence, the lawyers were trying to fuse two ultimately incompatible notions: on the one hand, the separation of powers with a strong head of state (which smacked of presidentialism); and on the other, the principle of governmental responsibility to parliament (which implied a parliamentary régime).

The central question of any consitution – who rules? – is fudged. Is it the President of the Republic who is given certain potentially important powers, including that of appointing the prime minister? Or is it the prime minister who is put "in general charge of the work of government" which "decides and directs the policy of the nation" (Articles 20 and 21 of the constitution) and which is responsible to parliament? Certain articles of the constitution clearly suggest that the prime minister governs, while successive prime ministers until 1986 and Presidents of the Republic have so far claimed that the president rules: with the French Constitution of 1958 we enter the world not of Descartes but of Lewis Carroll. Ambiguity shrouds key areas of decision-making. Thus, Article 15 reads: "The President of the Republic is Head of the armed forces. He presides over the Higher Councils and committees of National Defence." Yet Article 20 clearly indicates that the government "has at its disposal....the armed forces", and Article 21 notes that the prime minister is "responsible for National Defence". Article 13 gives the president the right to appoint to certain military posts while Article 21 empowers the prime minister to appoint to others. In other words, in the crucial area of defence, powers are shared but power is ill-defined. The constitution clearly establishes a dyarchy at the top, a twin-headed or bicephalous executive, but it does not clarify the respective roles of president and prime minister. Such clarification was left to the interplay of personality and political circumstance.

Two major facts emerge, however, from the constitutional morass of 1958: first, the role of the presidency was undoubtedly enhanced, and second, the executive was strengthened *vis-à-vis* parliament. The second fact will be considered at some length in Chapter 7, and it is the first fact that must now be examined. If the constitution of the Fifth Republic does not create a presidential régime, it does, undeniably, confer new powers and an enhanced prestige upon the presidential office. In the first place, the constitution changes the electoral source of presidential power. Presidents of the Third and Fourth Republics were elected in a joint session of the two Houses of Parliament, a system which was clearly intolerable to General de Gaulle, whose opinion of parliament was not always very flattering. Initially, both he and Debré, his constitutional *alter ego*, also rejected the idea of electing the President of the Republic by direct suffrage. The result was that in the 1958 text of the constitution the president was to be elected by an electoral college, comprising some 80,000 political *notables*. But this method of electing the president was changed by the referendum of October 1962: henceforth, the President of the Republic was to be elected by universal suffrage.

The change accepted in October 1962 conferred no new functions, privileges or prerogatives upon the presidency. But Professor Duverger rightly argued that if it granted no new *powers* it did afford him an important new *power*. From 1965, the date of the first presidential election, successive presidents could claim (and have claimed) that their mandate came directly from the people, that the source of their authority was impeccable, that their democratic legitimacy was at least equal to that of the National Assembly, which was also elected by universal suffrage. The president was, in the full sense of the term, the *élu de la nation*, and exercised his functions as the result of the sovereign decision of the electors. The political significance of the October 1962 reform cannot be overestimated, for it upset, in favour of the president, the uneasy and ambiguous balance established in the 1958 Constitution. As President de Gaulle claimed in his January 1964 press conference:

we behave in such a way that power...emanates directly from the people, which implies that the Head of State, elected by the nation, must be the source and holder of power...that is what was made clear by the last referendum.

Apart from strengthening the source of his authority, the constitution confers upon the president all the powers traditional to the office. The traditional rights he inherited as head of state and commander-in-chief of the armed forces include those relating to the presiding over the Council of Ministers and important councils, the negotiating and ratifying of international treaties, the appointing of the prime minister and important officials, the signing of decrees in the Council of Ministers, the promulgating of laws and the granting of pardons. In the exercise of these powers, many of which are purely formal, the President of the Republic, according to the constitution, must act with the agreement, and on the initiative of the prime minister together with that of any other appropriate minister. This stipulation was included to underline the constitutional myth of the political irresponsibility of the president. And it led to the claim of Michel Debré that the president was essentially a *solliciteur*, a word with unfortunate connotations in English but which implied that the president had to "solicit" the intervention of the prime minister before he could act.

A number of new powers are given to the president in the 1958 constitution, and in order to exercise them he does not need to solicit ministerial intervention. These powers were included to enable him to fulfill the presidential role, as defined in Article 5 of the constitution. That article is one of the most important and most controversial of the constitution, and it is worth quoting in full:

The President of the Republic sees that the constitution is respected,ensures by his arbitration the regular functioning of the organs of government and the continuity of the State. He is the protector of national independence, of territorial integrity, and of respect for agreements with the [French] Community and for treaties.

The concept of *arbitrage* contained in Article 5 has excited the minds of some constitutional experts and stimulated the imagination of others: the most extraordinary ingenuity has been employed to rationalize the prejudices (often political) of the lawyers in the interpretation of the notion. Incorrigible supporters of parliamentary supremacy insist that the notion requires the president to be an objective referee, an impartial observer, an olympian arbitrator, while Gaullist lawyers (and notably Marcel Prélot) have unearthed the ancient Latin sense of *arbitrium* which involves the right of the president to make decisions on the basis of his own judgement. This Gaullist interpretation naturally attributes a much more dynamic and interventionist role to the President of the Republic. In truth, Article 5 is sufficiently vague to enable successive presidents to interpret it as they wished.

In order to carry out his role as arbiter, the president receives certain powers not accorded to presidents of the Fourth Republic:

● He may ask Parliament to reconsider a law or specified articles of a law which has been submitted to him for promulgation (this happened only twice between 1959 and 1988 – on both occasions by Mitterrand).

● He has the right to submit a Bill or a treaty to the Constitutional Council for judgement on its constitutionality. He also has the right to appoint three of the nine appointed members of the Council.

● He may have a message read out for him in either or both houses of parliament (this power was invoked eleven times between 1959 and 1986).

● He is empowered to grant or refuse a request of either the government or the two houses of parliament jointly for a referendum.

● He has the right to dissolve the National Assembly before the official end of its term of office, although he is prevented from dissolving the Chamber again in the following twelve months (the President dissolved the National Assembly four times between 1959 and 1988).

● Article 16 of the constitution enables the president, after consultation with the prime minister, the presidents of the National Assembly, the Senate and the Constitutional Council, to take whatever measures he sees fit, "when there exists a serious and immediate threat to the institutions of the republic, the independence of the nation, the integrity of its territory or the fulfilment of international obligations, and the regular functioning of the constitutional public authorities has been interrupted". This so-called emergency-powers provision gives the president total and unchecked power in circumstances defined by himself. In the early years of the Fifth Republic it caused a storm of controversy, for many observers were rightly concerned about its possible abuse. It was included on the insistence of General de Gaulle, who had in mind the traumatic events of May 1940 when, in the face of an advancing German army, political authority was completely paralysed. Since 1958, the article has been used only once, by General de Gaulle, between 23 April and 30 September 1961, following a military *putsch* in Algeria.

The President of the Republic is given, therefore, three fairly distinct sets of powers: one to carry out his normal duties as head of state, one to act in a politically charged situation, and one to take complete control in very exceptional circumstances (Article 16). But these fairly wide-ranging powers were clearly insufficient to meet the demands of the first President of the Fifth Republic, who not only fully exploited the constitutional powers given him but did not hesitate to violate the constitution and even, in October 1962, to change it (by means deemed by many to be unconstitutional). It has been said that the 1958 constitution was "tailor-made" for General de Gaulle, but since it was so frequently abused by the General one must conclude either that the tailor was totally incompetent or that the statement is untrue. Before examining, in the next chapters, the functions and the extension of the powers of the presidency, it is worth briefly examining the instruments and agents at the president's disposal.

The instruments and agents of presidentialism

The tentacular growth of the presidency during the first twenty five years of the Fifth Republic was both the cause and the consequence of a growth in the number and the use of the instruments and agents at its disposal. In order that the presidential will may prevail many means (some of highly doubtful constitutional validity) were employed, and in the pursuit of his policies each president acted by either communicating directly with the nation or through his many aides – the president's men.

Presidential direct links with the nation

President Mitterrand, like his predecessors of both the Fourth and Fifth Republics, regularly visits the French provinces: General de Gaulle claimed that during his first seven-year period of office he made eighty visits outside Paris, going to every *département* and to more than 2500 towns. It is the most striking example of the president's direct contact with the people and a means of ensuring the physical presence of state authority. Giscard d'Estaing even underlined the latter point by holding a small number of meetings of the Council of Ministers in provincial towns. The present president, also like his three predecessors, regularly uses television and radio to convey, over the heads of the "intermediaries", his personal message to the nation or to explain government policies.

The differences in the style of the four presidents of the Fifth Republic may be seen in their press conferences. Giscard d'Estaing oscillated between a nervous ponderousness and a relaxed conversational style, while Pompidou after an early informality gradually lapsed into heavy solemnity. Their press conferences certainly lacked the sense of theatre which infused those of de Gaulle. To the English observer they could verge dangerously on Dr Johnson's view of opera – "an exotic and irrational entertainment" – in which the listener was expected to suspend belief, sit back and simply enjoy the spectacle. But they were more than that. They were great didactic exercises (it was said that de Gaulle's *conférences de presse* were really *conférences à la presse*), massive acts of presidential egoism, and some were major political moments of the régime. President Mitterrand's press conferences are not totally dissimilar, for although they are more relaxed in tone they arc organized in a way which is designed less to inform the world's press than to impress his fellow citizens.

The need for President Giscard d'Estaing to communicate directly with the people was highlighted by the publication in October 1976 of a short book, *Démocratie française*, which outlined his basic philosophy, ideals and ideas. Nearly a million copies were distributed or sold (it is not known how many were read), and the publication of the book was accompanied by an unparalleled propaganda campaign on television and radio. A president is not only interested in establishing a direct link with the people but always displays a keen interest in the shape of that link. Like his predecessors, Mitterrand closely supervises any major policies affecting the television network (this was certainly true of the 1981-2 reforms), and he has a full-time press officer who is in permanent contact with the political journalists. Between 1959 and 1986 the president was also kept well informed of the prevailing state of opinion through prefectoral and police reports (analysed by the minister of the interior). The president also receives summaries of the press (prepared by his press officer) and of current opinion polls (analysed by an expert on the Élysée staff).

The final method by which the president establishes contact with the people is through elections. Presidential election campaigns are occasions for the candidates to give detailed accounts of themselves and their future programmes. The president sees his election as the basis of his legitimacy and a mandate for him to carry out his programme. Elections to the National Assembly have also been considered by successive presidents as judgements upon themselves and their programmes, and Mitterrand, like de Gaulle, Pompidou and Giscard d'Estaing, did not hesitate to intervene in a general election campaign to exhort the voters to back friendly candidates.

The third type of electoral consultation which has been used by the president to make a direct and personal appeal to the nation is the referendum – the most Bonapartist weapon in the presidential armoury. There was a tendency to exaggerate the significance of the referendum in the functioning of the present régime: Professor Prélot, for example, went as far as to describe the Fifth Republic as "a plebiscitary democracy". It is true that every general election and referendum has been turned into a plebiscitary appeal by the President of the Republic. Nevertheless, it should be emphasized that the referendum itself (the object of so much apprehension and criticism) has been used only six times since the beginning of the régime and only three times since October 1962. President Pompidou used the device only once and Giscard d'Estaing never used it. Mitterrand's first attempt to resort to it, in 1984, was thwarted by opposition from the Senate. In theory, the president cannot take the initiative in calling a referendum: that intiative lies with the government or parliament. Nor can he call a referendum on any reform which would be in conflict with the constitution. In practice, however, de Gaulle and Pompidou both took the initiative in calling for the five referenda and at least two involved major changes in the constitutional structure (Table 1).

Table 1   Referenda of the Fifth Republic

---

8 January 1961
    Related to the Algerian war.
8 April 1962
28 October 1962   *Direct election of the President.*
27 April 1969   *Creation of regions and restructuring of Senate.*
23 April 1972   *Ratification of the treaty relative to the entry of Denmark, Ireland, Norway and Great Britain into the European Community.*
6 November 1988   *Statute for New Caledonia*

General de Gaulle once claimed that the referendum was "the clearest, the most honest and the most democratic" of political practices. But the experience of the Fifth Republic suggests that, while it may be democratic (by inviting the people to make a sovereign decision), it is also unclear and singularly dishonest as an instrument of government. The public's sentiments on matters of great moment he should not have been so selective in the subjects he chose. Pompidou and Mitterand held their referenda on policies which manifestly commanded massive parliamentary and public support. The profoundly dishonest nature of the referendum also emerged in the presentation of the issues. The first two referenda on Algeria involved one reply to two distinct questions, while the fourth (that of April 1969) required a single response to a wide-ranging and complex package deal which included major innovations in local government, a radical reform of the Senate and a change in the interim presidency (in the event of the incumbent president). The opinion polls showed that the electorate had different responses to each of the proposals: the regional reforms were popular, those involving the Senate were not, and those concerning the interim presidency were largely unknown. Furthermore, it was clear that, as in the three previous referenda, the electors when casting their votes were motivated less by their views of the proposals than by their assessment of General de Gaulle and his government. In a sense, this was perfectly understandable, since de Gaulle had deliberately turned the referendum into a vote of confidence in himself. Each of his referenda was proceeded by a stern warning that in the event of a negative vote he would resign, a threat (or promise) he carried out after the failure of the April 1969 referendum.

The dubious nature of the referendum emerged clearly in the April 1972 referendum: according to a British observer (Michael Leigh) the president's motives for holding the referendum were fourfold:

● *To claim credit for European policies which differed somewhat from those of his predecessor.* He was attempting to mobilize opinion to strengthen his position against the hard-line Gaullists, just as de Gaulle, in January 1961 and April 1962, had mobilized opinion behind his Algerian policies to demonstrate the political isolation of the extremist supporters of *Algérie française.*

● *To increase the prestige of the government and his power over it.* This had also been a motive of de Gaulle in April 1969 when he attempted to buttress his own personal authority which had been so seriously undermined during the events of May 1968.

● *To exploit the conflicts of opinion on a subject which clearly divided the opposition Left-wing parties* at a time of negotiations (for greater unity of action) between those parties.

● *To underline the extent of his popular backing* for future diplomatic negotiations.

In other words, the President of the Republic was not attempting to sound public opinion on a contentious issue, but rather was bolstering his own domestic and diplomatic position.

The use of referenda under the Fifth Republic has not only been dishonest (and unconstitutional – a peccadillo in the catechism of the régime); it has also proved dangerous to the president. The failure of the April 1969 referendum led to de Gaulle's resignation, and the exceptionally low turn-out in the April 1972 referendum (the electors "bristled with indifference", to use Michael Leigh's felicitous phrase, and only 67.7 per cent bothered to vote) damaged Pompidou's image as an effective political manager. Equally, the result of the November 1988 referendum on New Calendonia, which was technically a sucess for the government (80 per cent of those who voted did so in favour of the proposals),was interpreted as a severe embarrassment for President Mitterrand and his prime minister because 63 per cent of the electorate did not turn out to vote – a record abstention rate for any consultation since the introduction of universal suffiage in 1848. The lesson of the last three referenda will not be lost on future Presidents of the Republic, and for that reason the referendum is likely to be used only sparingly – if at all – in the future.

The president's men

Presidential councils and counsellors

The president stands at the head of an extensive and complex network of political counsellors and executants, some official and others less so, who enable him to carry out the task of deciding and implementing the major policies of the nation. The widening of the web of aides has been both a cause and a consequence of the growth of presidential government. The nature of the relationship between the president and his aides may be institutionalized and formal or purely personal and informal, and it may be permanent or very transitory. The president may appoint a person to carry out a particular task or mission which, once accomplished, may put an end to the relationship. Thus, in 1975, President Giscard d'Estaing appointed Arpaillange, a judge, to study the reform of justice: Lecanuet, the minister of justice, was merely informed of the presidential decision. In the same year, he gave Pinot, another judge, the task of looking into the lot of French prostitutes, he asked Guichard, a Gaullist ex-minister, to prepare a report on the problems of local government, he requested Monguillan, a financial expert, to report on the consequences of introducing a capital gains tax, and he invited Raymond Barre, not then a member of the government, to examine the vexed problem of housing subsidies. In May 1977, he appointed Poniatowski, ex-Minister of the Interior, as a roving ambassador, and in the following month he invited Madame Pelletier to draw up a report on the increasingly controversial subject of drugs. President Mitterrand has continued the practice: one of his first acts was to ask his brother to visit the Middle East in order to reassure political leaders who were anxious about a change in French policy towards Israel. Later, he sent his close friend François de Groussouvre on delicate assignments to the Lebanon and Morocco.

The president also acts through a network of councils and committees, the more important of which are mentioned in the constitution. These include the powerful Higher Council and Committees of National Defence (it is there and not in the Council of Ministers that defence policy is decided). The president may also establish permanent councils or committees which are either presided over by him or directly accountable to him. These include the Higher Committee for the Environment (created in 1970 by Prime Minister Chaban-Delmas but enlarged by President Giscard d'Estaing in 1975), the Central Planning Council (created in 1974 with the task of laying down the guidelines of the French five-year economic plan and of ensuring co-ordination between government departments in the implementation of the plan), the Council for Nuclear Foreign Policy (founded in September 1976 with the task of examining all the international implications of French nuclear policy, including any proposed exports of nuclear equipment) and the Council for the South Pacific (set up in December 1985 to coordinate French policy in that troubled area). *Ad hoc* committees may also be created by the president to examine specific problems. One such committee was the Committee for Algerian Affairs which was established after the revolt in Algeria in January 1960 and which functioned until the end of the Algerian war in 1962. Other *ad hoc* committees include the Commission for the Reform of the Tourist Industry which was created in January 1977, and the council established in September 1986 to coordinate the battle against terrorism. Finally, there are a number of *conseils restreints* – a small group of advisers brought together to deal with a specific issue – education, energy, the preparation of a Franco-German summit. Under Giscard d'Estaing there were four such councils a month. They increased sharply in number with the election of Mitterrand to the presidency, but decreased sharply after 1984 – an indication of presidential withdrawal from many policy areas. These major instruments of presidentialism are accountable to him alone and their importance cannot be overestimated, but they do not give the kind of continuous advice afforded by the next category of advisers – the Élysée staff.

The Élysée staff

The most immediate collaborators of the president belong to his personal staff who work at the *Château*, the name given familiarly to the Élysée Palace. Under the Fourth Republic this staff was very small (President Auriol never had more than eleven and President Coty never more than twelve), weak and concerned essentially with administrative tasks. This situation has changed under the Fifth Republic: the *services* of the Élysée have become bigger (by 1986 over seven hundred people were working for the presidency) and more influential, thus reflecting and helping to perpetuate the power of the presidency. The size and nature of the Élysée staff depend on the tastes and personality of each president, for it is his team, accountable to him alone and disbanded when he leaves office. It is not mentioned in the constitution and has no formal status: its size, shape and membership are entirely dependent upon the will and whims of the president.

Since the beginning of the Fifth Republic, the *services* of the Élysée have comprised three basic elements, even though the nature of the relationship between them has varied according to the wishes of each president: the three elements are the General Secretariat, the *cabinet* and the Military Household. A fourth element – the General Secretariat for French Community and Malagasy Affairs which was responsible for relations with countries of the French union – was created by de Gaulle and maintained by Pompidou but was abolished, in May 1974, by Giscard d'Estaing. For the entire period 1958-74 it was headed by the influential and shadowy Gaullist "baron" Jacques Foccart.

Of the three present elements, the most important is the General Secretariat. The Military Household has a specific and limited sphere of competence, and the *cabinet* is mainly involved in administrative chores (although individual members of the *cabinet* may be influential): it regulates the domestic arrangements of the Élysée, organizes presidential trips to the provinces, is responsible for the clerical and secretarial side of the Élysée, and arranges presidential audiences. The General Secretariat is the centre of decision-making at the Élysée. It is composed of a small group of people (never more than forty since 1959, and at one point only seventeen) who are drawn mainly, but not exclusively, from the upper ranks of the civil service, and most are the products of the *grandes écoles* (the highly competitive schools which provide the nation's administrative elite). At the head of the General Secretariat is the general secretary of the presidency of the republic (not to be confused with the general secretary of the government). The organizational structure of the General Secretariat has been modified several times since 1959 in order to suit the working habits and political requirements of the president of the Republic. A majority of its members is recruited from the *grands corps* and has thus proven ability, administrative experience and extensive contacts with the administration. More than half the Élysée staff under Giscard d'Estaing had belonged to his private staff (*cabinet*) when he had been Minister of Finance, and a select few were known to be personal or political friends of the president. Mitterrand's Élysée team comprises three distinct elements (long-standing personal friends, close political allies in the Socialist Party, and politically sympathetic bureaucrats and technocrats) and is more *overtly* political than the one it replaced. Most members of the Élysée staff have specific tasks to perform or a specific field to cover and their duty is to provide ideas for the president, advise him on the political impact of his projects and keep a general eye on the work of the ministries. Their work is coordinated by the general secretary who makes a daily report to the president of the Republic. Between 1959 and 1988 eleven men held the post of general secretary; the longest serving were Burin des Roziers (February 1962 to July 1967) and Biancho (June 1982—) and the shortest was Bérégovoy (May 1981 to June 1982).

The general secretary is not only an administrative co-ordinator. He may represent the president at official ceremonies or deputize for him at certain inter-departmental meetings. He enjoys a privileged position, since he meets the president daily and acts as the final screen between the president and the outside world. He is, in the words of J. Gicquel, "the eyes, ears and arms" of an absent president. Yet the influence of the general secretary depends a great deal on his willingness and capacity to use it. Under de Gaulle, successive general secretaries, although influential, were diplomatic, discreet and self-effacing, and had a largely administrative view of their role. Of the two general secretaries who served Pompidou, the first, Michel Jobert, was interventionist and political (he left the post to become Foreign Minister) while his successor was a quiet and efficient technician. President Giscard d'Estaing first appointed Pierre Brossolette, a close friend and collaborator of long-standing, but personal and political differences between the two men led to the resignation of Brossolette and to his replacement, in July 1976, by Jean François-Poncet, another personal friend of Giscard d'Estaing who was also known to be more sympathetic to the president's proclaimed reformist ideals. When François-Poncet was appointed Foreign Minister in November 1978 he was replaced, as general secretary, by Jacques Wahl who, like Giscard d'Estaing, was a product of the ENA and the financial inspectorate. François Mitterrand's first choice for the post of secretary general was Pierre Bérégovoy who was a very powerful figure in the Socialist Party and spent part of his time as general secretary as the link between the President of the Republic and the Socialists. He was to leave the Élysée to become the head of a greatly enlarged Ministry for Social Affairs. He was replaced in June 1982 by a member of the Council of State, Jean-Louis Biancho who through his many administrative contacts, his discretion and his competence was greatly to facilitate the transition to *cohabitation* after the March 1986 elections.

The general secretary may not be the only or even the most powerful man on the presidential staff: the official hierarchy gives little clue as to the influence of each of its members. Under President de Gaulle the most powerful man was Jacques Foccart, who, from 1959 to 1974, was officially in charge of France's relations with her colonies and ex-colonies in Africa, but who frequently intervened on the president's behalf in governmental and Gaullist Party matters. The *éminence grise* of Pompidou's personal staff was the arch-conservative Pierre Juillet, who was the president's principal political adviser. Under Giscard d'Estaing several men were reported to be as influential as the general secretary: Hunt, the official spokesman of the Élysée, Riolacci and Sérisé who were political counsellors, Chapot who was a *chargé de mission* for political matters, Journiac who was responsible for African policies, and Lecat who was responsible for contacts with the president's political party. Similarly, the general secretary of the Élysée under Mitterrand has to compete with several other very influential personalities, some of whom have known the president for many years: these have included or include men such as André Rousselet, the first director of the *cabinet* of the president who gave constant advice on delicate political matters, Jacques Attali, the brilliant if erratic "ideas man" of the Élysée, Guy Penne who is the counsellor for African questions, and is known as *Monsieur Afrique*, and François de Grossouvre, an intimate friend of the president for more than thirty years.

The power of the Élysée staff is difficult to assess. It has certainly been claimed that they exercise power without responsibility, and it is true that they are strategically placed, through their direct access to the president and their contacts with the administration, to exercise great influence. It is equally true that certain members have exerted considerable power in particular circumstances:

Foccart (under de Gaulle) and Journiac (under Giscard d'Estaing) bypassed, and Penne (under Mitterrand) bypasses ministers in shaping French policy in black Africa, while Juillet undoubtedly played a key role in the downfall of Prime Minister Chaban-Delmas in 1972. Similarly, Sérisé was influential in determining the political strategy of Giscard d'Estaing and was one of the president's firmest supports in his conflict with Prime Minister Chirac. It is also true that Mitterrand's style of government – inviting advice and ideas from several sources before deciding – adds to the potential power of the Élysée, or more accurately to individual members of the Élysée, since the Élysée does not work (again as a reflection of the president's style) as a *team*. Unlike Giscard d'Estaing, Mitterrand never organizes regular meetings of the private staff to discuss general policy but prefers to keep direct contact with his staff to a minimum.

Members of the Élysée staff generally exert a discreet yet pervasive influence by presenting the president of the Republic with advice on policy options which may confirm, differ from or even conflict with those of the ministers. President Mitterrand, like his predecessor, has not infrequently asked both a member of his staff and of the government to write reports on the same subject, and reserves the right to make the final choice and decision. Members of the Élysée staff have neither the time nor the facilities effectively to supervise all the activities of the ministers and their civil servants. They also lack the political weight and the legitimacy to meddle too openly, too directly, too closely or too frequently in decision-making. It would be wrong to conclude that members of the presidential staff have become *véritables super-ministres* and represent "a technocratic parallel government" or even "the occult government of France". President Giscard d'Estaing described them as his "grey cells", as members of his brains trust, and insisted that they should not become a screen between him and his ministers, who were his principal collaborators.

Conflicts between the Élysée staff and members of the government were commonplace between 1959 and 1986, even though all were serving the president. It is well known that relations between Chaban-Delmas's government and Pompidou's private staff were far from cordial. In his memoirs (*L'Ardeur*) the prime minister recounts how he fell foul of the "terrible tandem" of Pierre Juillet and Marie-France Garaud of the Élysée staff: he was accused of "bringing socialism to France". The *rapports* between the Leftist-leaning staff of Giscard d'Estaing and Prime Minister Chirac were characterized by mutual suspicion. The public wrangle in 1975 over the purchase of telephone equipment for modernizing the French network and which opposed the industrial counsellor of the Élysée and the Minister of Posts and Telecommunications was noticeable because of its acrimony, not because of its exceptional nature.

Mitterrand's style of government also lends itself to conflictual relations between his advisors. It is closely modelled on the divide and rule methods he had perfected as First Secretary of the Socialist Party. There is an inner circle – the *chouchous* and *favoris* as Régis Debray described them in his book *Les Masques*, or the *visiteurs du soir* as prime minister Mauroy ironically depicted them. This inner circle has direct and constant access to the president. It has varied in composition (the characteristic of all courts) and may include members of the *cabinet*, the general secretariat, and close friends. There is also a group of close personal friends to whom he turns sporadically for advice or who may act as his *missi dominici:* Maurice Faure, Mayor of Cahors, senator and political boss of the *département* of the Lot; Roland Dumas who was one of Mitterrand's international trouble-shooters before he was made Foreign Minister in 1984; Jean Riboud a close friend of the president and a wealthy industrialist with useful contacts in the industrial and financial worlds. Finally, between 1981 and 1986 and after the May 1988 elections there were members of the government who belonged to the inner charmed circle. But it is clear that, in the eyes of the president, some ministers were infinitely more equal than others. From 1981 to 1984, for example, Charles Hernu (Defence), Laurent Fabius (Industry) and Jack Lang (Culture) were all part of the court, and were able to appeal to the president against prime ministerial decisions. Alliances between members of the government and the Élysée staff could be struck, causing great prime ministerial resentment: this was the case, for example, in 1984 when Industry Minister Fabius gained the support of the general secretary of the Élysée and the presidential adviser on industrial affairs in his battle with Prime Minister Mauroy over the major restructuring of the steel industry. Interference from the Élysée staff (especially in African affairs and in matters of state security) could provoke ministers' anger, and in one case, in 1982, led to a resignation. There is some evidence that from 1983-1984 Mitterrand discouraged the Élysée staff from interfering in ministerial decisions: indeed, he claims to have dismissed one member of his staff for having done so. But tension between the various agents of executive authority is inevitable, given their overlapping jurisdictions, personal ambitions, and Mitterrand's methods of government.

2 The functions of the presidency

Whatever the intentions of the framers of the constitution, by 1986 presidential supremacy had clearly been established by the practice of successive presidents. Practice transformed the nature and scope of the office. The President of the Republic came to assume five basic functions: he was the ceremonial head of state, the guardian of the national interest, the fountain-head of patronage, the country's most prominent politician and, finally, the head of the executive. The priority given to each of these functions, their interpretation and their execution depended on the taste, the temperament and the ability of the incumbent, but under successive Presidents of the Republic the office was much more powerful, more interventionist and more political than the constitutional texts appeared to imply. Nevertheless, in analysing the functions of the presidency it is possible to distinguish between the first four, which are constitutionally embedded and have remained constant, and the remaining function – the executive one – which was been shaped by personal preferences and political pressures and which has changed over time. As will be made clear, with almost tedious regularity throughout the following three chapters, the executive role of the president was shaped not only by constitutional provisions and personal predilections but also by favourable political circumstances. Those circumstances no longer prevailed between March 1986 and May 1988 when a Left-wing president had to contend with a Right-wing prime minister supported by a majority in parliament.

The first function of the President of the Republic concerns his role as head of state, which involves him in a great deal of time-consuming ceremony. Like Presidents of the Fourth Republic, he receives foreign heads of state, makes courtesy visits abroad and accredits ambassadors. The president is also expected to make frequent visits to the French provinces. These visits, which are a veritable ordeal for local officials (particularly the local prefects who are responsible for the smooth running of the visit), are seen as a useful means of keeping the president in touch with the people. In the performance of these ceremonial duties there have been marked contrasts in the style of the four presidents of the Fifth Republic.

The second main presidential function relates to his role as the guardian of the national interest, the leader of the nation, the

physical embodiment of its traditions and its continuity and the
guide to its future actions. As Mitterrand told an assembled crowd
at Mulhouse in November 1984, 'the President of the Republic
incarnates the nation, the state, the Republic. Everyone should
remember that more. In any case, I do not forget it.' After the
1986 elections which saw the victory of his opponents he stayed
on as president: 'My only duty' he proclaimed, 'was to ensure the
continuity of the state and the regular functioning of institutions.
I carried it out without delay'. The president has become the
nation's principal pedagogue, using this role to emphasize the
essential unity and harmony of the nation, constantly calling for
effort and sacrifice. The presidential New Year message always
stresses these themes. In moments of crisis, the president attempts,
not always successfully, to rise above the political fray and to
perform the role attributed to him by the constitution – that of
the ultimate arbiter of the national interest. The role was assumed
with superb aplomb by the first President of the Fifth Republic:
at his best, de Gaulle was unsurpassable: his television appeal to
the nation after the army revolt in Algeria in April 1961 was as
moving and as resolute as it was effective, a rare combination
of high drama and deep sincerity. The role of national leader
was assumed less convincingly but no less readily by de Gaulle's
successors. Thus, during the economic and financial crisis of the
spring of 1982 Mitterrand gave a (televised) press conference in
which, in sombre tones, he exhorted his countrymen to greater
efforts, criticized the selfish attitude of certain sectional interests
and appealed for national consensus in dealing with the country's
problems. Unfortunately, such appeals have often a hollow ring:
patriotism, the last refuge of the scoundrel, is often the first device
of the cornered politician.

The president's third main function relates to his constitutional
pov. . ˉ of appointment to key posts in politics, in the armed forces,
in t   top ranks of the civil service and in the judiciary. His most
imp :tant appointments concern the choice of prime minister and
his government. According to the constitution (Article 8):

> The President of the Republic appoints the Prime Minister.
> He terminates his period of office on the presentation by
> the Prime Minister of the resignation of the Government. He
> appoints and dismisses the other members of the Government
> on the proposal of the Prime Minister.

There is no doubt that presidential interpretation of this article
has been exceedingly elastic. With the exception of the nomination
of Jacques Chirac in March 1986 (when the president had no
alternative but to appoint), all prime ministers have owed their

office to the president. Many have been far from obvious choices: Pompidou in 1962, Messmer in 1972, Barre in 1976, Fabius in 1984 were devoid of any power base save that provided by the president. Furthermore, prime ministers have not only been appointed but also dismissed (although the dismissal always took the form of a forced resignation) – often in summary fashion and to the astonishment of at least one prime minister (Chaban-Delmas in 1972). Moreover, presidents have not been reluctant to meddle in the choice and removal of ministers and have also protected ministers who did not enjoy the confidence of the prime minister. Generally, and with the notable exception of 1986-1988, the choice of ministers has been the result of agreement between the president and the prime minister, although there is evidence to suggest that for some appointments the president has merely consulted or informed the prime minister. He has also ignored prime ministerial advice and overruled his objections. Even the composition of the Chirac government in March 1986 was partly decided by Mitterrand who vetoed two appointments. Until 1986, by his liberal interpretation of the constitution, the president increasingly turned the government into an instrument of his own ascendancy. He became the principal dispenser of political rewards and revenge, able to make or break the career of the aspiring and the ambitious. This distribution of patronage is an important component in the president's political armoury, since by his choices he determines the political complexion of the government.

In other spheres, too, the president has an important source of patronage. He appoints, in the Council of Ministers, to key posts in the judiciary. He nominates all members of the Higher Council of the Judiciary (a body which makes recommendations to the government on appointments to top judicial posts, advises the president on the exercise of his right to pardon, and acts as a disciplinary court for judges) and also appoints three of the nine members of the increasingly influential Constitutional Council (the body which is called to give judgement in constitutional disputes). The President of the Republic also appoints, in the Council of Ministers, ambassadors, councillors of state, prefects, rectors of academies, senior members of the Court of Accounts, the civil service heads of the divisions in the ministries and senior posts in broadcasting. Unofficially, he may, of course, propose candidates for other posts, and few people are likely to refuse presidential requests. Again, the only exception was between 1986 and 1988 when the Right-wing government used all its powers to block and even undo President Mitterrand's appointments. Generally, however, there is no doubt that the power of patronage has been used to good effect by successive Presidents of the Republic, and when Mitterrand carried out his purge of Giscardian personnel between 1981 and 1983 he was merely emulating his predecessor who, during his presidency, had replaced Gaullist sympathizers by his own supporters: hence, 'the Gaullist state' was replaced by 'the Giscardian state', which, in turn, gave way to 'the Socialist state', to use the fashionable but somewhat simplistic epithets. It should be stressed that in many areas presidential patronage of a political nature is quite severely restricted: there is no highly developed spoils system in France, for it is limited by law, by well-rooted conventions (such as the seniority rule) and by the need for continuity and experience in top posts. It is revealing that the Socialist purge of 1981-2 spared many key men (to the fury of some Socialists who demanded at their party congress that 'more heads should roll') and many of the new appointments were dictated by the need for proven ability and not by political favouritism.

Furthermore, politically inspired appointments are certainly not peculiar to the Fifth Republic. Nevertheless, posts at the discretion of the president can be, and have been, used to reward the faithful, to tempt the waverers, to punish the recalcitrant and the hostile, and to get rid of the embarrassing. The presidential right of appointment was skilfully exploited by de Gaulle when he was cleansing the army of its dissident elements and purging the French Foreign Office of diplomats suspected of being too pro-American or too pro-European. President Pompidou displayed no reticence in rewarding loyal political and personal friends: several young members of his private staff enjoyed meteoric promotion. President Giscard d'Estaing was not overscrupulous in the exercise of his power of patronage and several top civil servants with a history of *anti-Giscardisme* fell victim to his rancour.

The fourth function of the president is purely political. The constitution of 1958 proclaimed the principle of the political irresponsibility of the President of the Republic, and it may well be that the first President of the Fifth Republic had no intention of sullying his hands by playing politics: he wished to be, as he so frequently declared, 'above politics'. But whatever the pious implications of the constitution or the intentions of General de Gaulle, each President of the Republic has been obliged to descend into the political arena. Indeed, in January 1976, President Giscard d'Estaing could openly admit that politics were 'part of his mission', a confession which would never have been made by General de Gaulle. Presidential intervention in political matters takes three basic forms. First,

● as the effective (if not the constitutional) head of the government for most of the Fifth Republic (except for 1986 to 1988), the president has constantly to defend governmental policies and to criticize those of the opposition. He appears on television to explain, comment upon and justify the government's record. In one important respect Presidents Giscard d'Estaing and Mitterrand differ from their predecessors: unlike de Gaulle and Pompidou, they meet frequently, officially and openly representatives of important pressure groups. Such contacts had always been expressly refused by General de Gaulle who disliked and despised the 'intermediaries', the representatives of sectional interests.

● The second area of presidential political activity concerns his relations with his own supporters, for the president increasingly intervenes to marshal party and parliamentary support for his policies. General de Gaulle was content to leave most of that activity to his willing prime minister or to Foccart, a 'Gaullist baron' who exercised great influence behind the scenes. But both Pompidou and Giscard d'Estaing were quickly drawn directly into this area, although the former was generally (though not always) more discreet in his methods. Among Pompidou's political acts were his interventions in the choice of the general secretary of the Gaullist Party in January 1971 and in the election of the speaker of the National Assembly in 1973. President Giscard d'Estaing regularly met leaders of the parties which composed the governmental coalition in order to ensure some co-ordination between them, to iron out differences, or to mobilize support behind a minister in difficulty. In November 1974, he had to back his Minister of Health in her battle over the abortion bill, which was being given a rough passage by the government's own supporters. He intervened again in June 1976 to support his Minister of Finance, who was struggling to push through parliament a capital gains tax in the teeth of fierce opposition from members of the governmental coalition, and in November he tried to impose on the government coalition his own candidate, Michel d'Ornano, for the local elections in Paris. President Mitterrand has been particularly interventionist at this level, and this is not surprising since he has a special relationship with the Socialist Party which he helped to found, to nurture and to bring to victory. Regular links between the Socialists and the president are ensured by the general secretary of the presidency and by the first secretary of the party (a very firm Mitterrand supporter between 1981 and 1988). Mitterrand also holds regular lunches and breakfasts with the 'barons' of the party.

● The final and most obvious area of presidential political action is electoral. In the first place, like the British prime minister, he has to time the general election in a way most favourable to his supporters. The power of the president to dissolve the National Assembly is now considered to be an important political weapon at his disposal, although it was felt by some constitutional experts at the beginning of the Fifth Republic that the power of dissolution was unlikely ever to be used. In fact, it had been invoked only once since May 1877 when the royalist President MacMahon dissolved a National Assembly dominated by the Republicans. The ensuing elections were won by the Republicans, and a year later the President of the Republic was forced to resign. The dissolution of 16 May 1877 was a perfectly valid constitutional act, yet for good republicans it was considered to be a *coup d'état* against them, and for that reason no subsequent president ever used the power. It was not until October 1962 that a President of the Republic, General de Gaulle, dared dissolve a hostile National Assembly. He was to do so again in May 1968 when the government's majority was both small and precarious. On both occasions, the desired result – an increased majority for the government – was achieved. One of the very first acts of President Mitterrand after his election in May 1981 was to dissolve a National Assembly dominated by his political adversaries: in the subsequent elections the voters gave the president a vote of confidence by electing a friendly majority. Similarly, shortly after his re-election in May 1988, Mitterrand dissolved the National Assembly which housed a Right-wing majority. The electors were not, however, as obliging as they had been in 1981: whilst they deprived the Right of its majority they did not give the president's party a working majority. The new Socialist government could survive however thanks to a divided opposition and to an array of constitutional devices (see below). It is revealing that the president's right to dissolve the National Assembly is now accepted by everyone: the weapon is not only constitutionally theoretical but is now rooted in convention. Nevertheless, however effective it may be (and has proved to be), the right to dissolve is also, as Wilson and Heath in Britain were bitterly to discover, a double-edged weapon: an error of judgement may be very costly indeed.

Presidential electoral action has also been extended to the choice of governmental candidates in the general elections. Under de Gaulle and Pompidou pressure was exerted on the government coalition parties to present only one candidate at the first ballot of the elections. This naturally gave rise to fierce disputes in the constituencies, and arbitration at national level was needed. During General de Gaulle's period of office, this duty of arbitrating between the conflicting claims was left almost exclusively to the prime minister who, for the general elections of 1962, 1967 and 1968, was Georges Pompidou. When Pompidou became the President of the Republic he was unable or unwilling to relinquish this task which he had performed so well. President Giscard d'Estaing's power in this domain was drastically reduced, because the major party of his coalition, the Gaullist Party, rejected his right to arbitrate, and the task was carried out by representatives of the various parties of the coalition. Nevertheless, Giscard d'Estaing asserted his power over his own party in the 1979 European elections when he imposed the leadership of Simone Veil on the pro-Giscardian candidates and directly intervened in the choice of the others. President Mitterrand, ex-leader of the Socialists, certainly played an arbitrating role in the choice of candidates in the 1981, 1986 and 1988 elections.

The final area of presidential electoral intervention is in marshalling support for friendly candidates. Both General de Gaulle and President Pompidou appeared on television openly to support their candidates and to attack the opposition. In the June 1968 general elections, for example, de Gaulle unscrupulously exploited a non-existent communist menace, while in the March 1973 elections, Pompidou denounced the opposition in terms which gave the lie to his claim to be 'the president of all the French'. His successor at the Élysée, obsessed with the prospect of a Left-wing victory at the polls in March 1978, started his election campaign as early as 1976, following severe governmental defeats in the local elections. President Mitterrand's direct intervention in the general election campaign of June 1981 was brief yet pointed: sensing that the electorate was sympathetically inclined he gently asked it 'to confirm its verdict' of the previous month when it had elected him. In both the 1986 and 1988 elections Mitterrand intervened on television to ask the electorate to support politically sympathetic candidates.

The President of the Republic has, therefore, three major political roles: first, he is the general spokesman of the government and its principal pedagogue (again, the exception of the 1986-1988 period must be noted); second, he is the guardian of the unity of the coalition which supports him; finally, he is the coalition's principal electoral guide and agent. This politicization of the presidential function was inevitable, since the president became the effective head of the executive during the Fifth Republic, and that function could be carried out only if accepted or tolerated by parliament. Yet presidential entanglement with domestic politics and involvement in the polemics of his supporters, while inevitable, are dangerous, for the president is bound to become a main target for opposition attacks and his supporters' disgruntlement. In such circumstances he is led inevitably to defend himself, thus inviting further political attacks, and possibly tarnishing his image as 'the president of all Frenchmen'. The vicious circle is established and closed. There was once a fiction of the president being 'above politics', of his being the statesman who stands aloof from party polemics, parliamentary strife and electoral warfare. That fiction was quickly eroded under de Gaulle and Pompidou and was shattered under Giscard d'Estaing. The style of President Mitterrand after 1986 partially restored the image, but the president is constantly having to choose whether he is 'the president of all Frenchmen' or the president of that half of France which generally supports the Left.

The fifth and final major function of the President of the Republic is policy-making, for, whatever the constitutional texts may declare, the President of the Republic has emerged as the effective head of the executive. He does not 'solicit'; he commands: the prime minister and the government are not his equals but his servants. The president's role as chief policy-maker in France is examined in detail in the following chapter.

In extending the powers of the presidency, successive presidents did not hesitate to exploit all the powers given them by the constitution. For most of the Fifth Republic (1986-88 excluded) when the President of the Fifth Republic 'presides over the Council of Ministers' he has done so in a way totally different from his predecessors of the Third and Fourth Republics, for he fixes the timetable and the agenda and generally decides who may or may not speak. Similarly, the constitutional power 'to negotiate and ratify treaties' has not been viewed in any narrow or formalistic manner but has been seen as signifying presidential primacy in the field of foreign affairs: the French president is fully in charge of the conduct of foreign policy and, in that field, enjoys an independence far greater than the American president, who is constantly having to keep a wary eye on the reactions of Congress.

Successive presidents of the Fifth Republic have also shown a remarkable facility for interpreting loosely (and advantageously) certain ambiguous articles of the constitution. If French constitutional lawyers discuss with theological intensity the exact meaning of the term 'arbitration' contained in Article 5, Mitterrand, like his three predecessors, has always acted as though it involved much more than a purely representative, consultative and advisory role for the presidency. General de Gaulle argued that it gave him 'supremely important responsibility for the destiny of France and of the Republic', which meant, in effect, that it empowered him to govern the country. None of his successors demurred at that interpretation. Finally, the first President of the Fifth Republic did not hesitate to act unconstitutionally to strengthen his position. There were a number of celebrated examples: his refusal to convoke a special session of parliament in March 1960 even though a majority of the National Assembly had requested it; his abuse of Article 16 in June 1961 (its use was extended well beyond the time required to crush the army *putsch* which had provoked its use in the first place); his method of amending the constitution in October 1962 and his attempt to amend it in April 1969 by use of a referendum instead of by the means outlined in the constitution.

The steady violation of the spirit and the occasional infringement of the letter of the constitution in order to strengthen the presidential office caused little stir among the French. They belong to a country which has never displayed undue respect for the prevailing constitution. And whereas in the USA the constitution is regarded as a quasi-sacred text and as binding upon the president as upon the most humble citizen, in France the constitution was always regarded, to use Professor Goguel's phrase, as 'a mechanism, a rule in the game'. It was not the foundation of the political and social system but an elaborate device for trying to make the system work. If it did not appear to work it could be discarded. Furthermore, anchored in the memory of Republicans was the notion that the source of democratic legitimacy lay in the people and in their representatives and not in constitutional texts: a law found its authority in the will of the people expressed by legislators, and that authority could not be constrained by judicial review. The first President of the Republic exploited, sometimes in spectacular fashion, this indifference to the status of the constitution. Only in the 1970s and 1980s have the French, under the proddings of the Constitutional Council, come to accept the over-riding legitimacy and authority of the legal framework of the régime. The Council, in a celebrated decision of 23 August 1985, declared that 'the law expresses the general will only when it respects the constitution'. This is a break with French political tradition and constitutes a major step in the creation of a legally constrained polity. But there were no such constraints in the early years of the régime.

Like his three successors, de Gaulle was also able to exploit political circumstances to assert presidential pre-eminence. President Pompidou carefully played upon the fears of the Right, anchored in anti-communism and heightened by the events of May 1968, to forge a powerful electoral and political coalition under his leadership. President Giscard d'Estaing skilfully exploited the fatal ambivalence of the position of the Gaullists (who could cause him trouble), because while many of them had no particular affection for him they had (and retain) a deep-rooted respect for his office and recognized (albeit ungraciously) his position as *de facto* leader of the anti-Left forces. The greatest expert in seizing the chances offered by propitious political circumstances was the first President of the Fifth Republic, de Gaulle. He brilliantly manoeuvred himself back to power during the confusion and fear of May 1958; his admirers claim that he came to power perfectly legally, but the fact remains that he did so by exploiting an illegal situation – an armed rebellion against the authority of the French state. He later used the attempt against his life at Petit-Clamart in August 1962 to propose the introduction of universal suffrage for the election of the president. In September 1962, when the National Assembly passed a motion of censure against the Pompidou government, he immediately dissolved the chamber, and the ensuing election gave his supporters a comfortable majority. Similarly, in May 1968, he exploited the existing chaos to dissolve a troublesome National Assembly where his majority was only wafer-thin: the chamber which had been elected only a year previously, had, in de Gaulle's memorably arrogant phrase, 'the vocation to be dissolved'.

It was in Algeria that de Gaulle was fully to exploit political circumstances in order to strengthen his office. Indeed, it is probably the case that without Algeria de Gaulle would never have come to power at all or might not have survived the first four years of his office. General de Gaulle once noted that '*l'Algérie bloque tout*'. By 'everything' he really meant the pursuit of a more active and independent French foreign policy. But the Algerian war also blocked something else very important: the political opposition to himself. That opposition was hostile to many of his other policies, but it recognized that only de Gaulle could 'solve' the Algerian problem. Lack of space precludes a detailed account of the war which broke out in November 1954 and which dominated the life of the last three years of the Fourth Republic and the first four years of the Fifth. It was no manichean affair although it was viewed as such by extremists on both sides. All the major groups involved in the war – the government, parliament, the political parties, the white settlers, the army, the Algerian population and the independence fighters--were divided both between and within themselves over ends and means, over motives, strategy and tactics. It was an immensely complex war rendered poisonous by all the instruments of modern war: military might and urban guerrilla warfare, political persuasion and moral blackmail. The war consumed French manpower, money and diplomatic energy and was punctuated by bloody and dramatic incidents (notably in January 1960 and April 1961), some of which appeared to threaten the very existence of the Fifth Republic. De Gaulle had neither sentimental attachment for, nor aversion towards, *Algérie française*. Nor had he any pronounced doctrinal penchant for Algerian independence, but he saw it as the only means of ridding France (and himself) of a huge economic, political and diplomatic millstone. By a mixture of brutal cynicism, prudent opportunism, calculated idealism and characteristic audacity, he imposed not a solution (there was no solution, since the participants were so irreconcilably opposed) but an end to the war. In order to do so he exploited the divisions of his opponents, the loyalty of his own supporters (Michel Debré, the prime minister, was notably lukewarm about Algerian independence) and the war-weariness of a frustrated French population. Nowhere was the skill of the General more evident and nowhere was his achievement more resounding: by mid 1962, the war was over, the political power of the army was destroyed, the extremists were crushed, and his popular support was high. The opposition parties had been reduced to silent disapprobation of many of his acts, but their silence was more significant than their disapprobation. For the four formative years of the Fifth Republic they had been content to stand back and allow the General to violate the constitution, to consolidate his personal position and to strengthen his office. They could do little else, since to bring down de Gaulle involved their being once again saddled with the Algerian problem – a problem which had caused their own demise and provoked their ultimate downfall. Thus, for those four key years Algeria prevented the opposition from acting against the president of the Republic: the Algerian war, noted Raymond Aron, was an effective substitute for a parliamentary majority. And it is revealing that less than six months after peace was restored in Algeria, the opposition parties passed their only successful motion of censure against the government.

The first three Presidents of the Fifth Republic exploited not only specific and shortlived political circumstances, they were also able to take advantage of the continuing unpopularity of the previous régime. That unpopularity emerged from all the opinion polls. A constant theme of Right-wing propaganda after 1958 (and, indeed, long before that date) was that the Fourth Republic was a chaotic and unstable régime, and the very considerable success of such propaganda must be explained by the fact that it coincided with a widely held perception: when General de Gaulle intoned his dark and frequent warnings about the dire consequences of returning to the disorder of the Fourth Republic he touched a responsive chord in the electorate. The French yearned not for dictatorship but for governments which at least gave the appearance of governing. They not unnaturally resented the reputation of their country as the sick man of Europe (the Americans and the British were prolific in wounding and condescending sneers), and while they may not have liked some of de Gaulle's acts they appreciated his efforts in restoring their sense of national pride. Even twenty years after the fall of the Fourth Republic, President Giscard d'Estaing could still exploit a potential threat of a return to the 'disastrous régime of parties'.

Finally, until 1986 successive presidents of the Republic were able to exploit the increasing acceptance of presidential government. The prime minister, the government, parliament, most of the parties and the pressure groups came to recognize the dominance of the presidency, and to focus their attention and energies in that direction. So, too, did the electorate. The exceptionally high turn out at the presidential elections was an eloquent affirmation of the importance that the voters attached to the office. Moreover, opinion polls clearly revealed that a great majority of people, when casting their votes, considered that they were voting for the man who was going to govern the country.

That people saw the presidency as the real powerhouse of French politics was confirmed in small but revealing ways, such as the number of letters received at the Élysée: de Gaulle received an average of 50,000 letters a year, Pompidou 180,000, while Giscard d'Estaing received over 200,000 letters, and the number was steadily increasing: by 1980 there were seventy members of the Élysée staff to deal with the 209,000 letters which arrived.

The power of the presidency may be traced to the 1958 constitution and the October 1962 constitutional reform. But it was undoubtedly reinforced by the activities of successive occupants of the office, who did not hesitate to exploit propitious political circumstances in order to increase the scope of each of their functions. The most remarkable extension of presidential power was in their function as one of the heads of the executive, which is the subject of Chapter 4.

3 The presidency: the personal factor

If the old adage that office maketh man is arguable, the Fifth Republic provides irrefutable proof that man also maketh office. The French presidency, its powers, power and its functioning owe a great deal to the will, the style and the personality of the incumbent president. For that reason it is worth briefly looking at the four men who have so far occupied the office under the Fifth Republic.

The importance of General de Gaulle, the first President of the Fifth Republic, in shaping the presidential office cannot be over-estimated. Elected president, 21 December 1958, by 78 per cent of the 80,000 electors who comprised the presidential electoral college, he was re-elected for a further seven years in December 1965. But on the latter occasion he was elected by direct suffrage, beating François Mitterrand, the Left-wing candidate, but only at the second ballot. He occupied the presidency until April 1969, when he resigned after the defeat of his proposals in a referendum. He was thus President of the Republic for ten years. General de Gaulle intervened both directly and indirectly in the framing of the constitution, and later, by his actions, he secured the supremacy of the office he occupied. He came to the presidency with clear ideas about the need for strengthening the state and reinforcing executive authority. Those ideas emerged from a long and anguished historical experience, for de Gaulle had witnessed the steady decline of his beloved country and had participated in some of its greatest tragedies. His long life was marked by bitter personal and political memories: the impotence of squabbling politicians in the 1930s; the cowardice of the political elite in the black days of May 1940; the humiliation of his country's occupation and his self-imposed exile; his acrimonious relations in the provisional government after the liberation of France; his withdrawal from government in 1946 and his long and lonely 'crossing of the desert' until 1958. He had witnessed the total collapse of his country once and had experienced the progressive degradation of the state, and he was determined to prevent the former and reverse the latter. For de Gaulle, strong governmental authority was required and he was determined to provide it. Yet such authority would have to be legitimate, republican and democratic: General de Gaulle may have had dictatorial tendencies but he was no vulgar dictator, and some of his finest lines dissect the moral and political bankruptcy of dictatorship. There were thus limits which de Gaulle refused to transgress in the means he employed to extend presidential power. But within those limits, he felt free to act. Authoritarian pronouncements, impassioned and emotional outbursts, extremely moving exhortations, paternal jocularity and a natural charm were all weapons in his considerable personal armoury.

In this extraordinarily rich and complex character, in this monarch who destroyed one republic and founded another, certitude competed with paradox, faith with scepticism, high principles with brutal cynicism. He was at once a Jesuit and a Jansenist, a Florentine and a Venetian, a man of world vision and a carping chauvinist. This mountain of insensitivity (who could crush his close associates with his ingratitude) could also display a profound, touching and tragic concern for his mentally handicapped daughter. He disdained politicians and despised 'politics' yet he proved himself a consummate practitioner of the art. He was a profound realist who nevertheless took up his sword against diplomatic windmills: Cervantes would have done him proud. This intense nationalist accelerated the process of decolonization, and this army officer broke the army as a powerful political force – perhaps his greatest political achievement. There were, in truth, the elements of several folk-heroes in de Gaulle: like Don Quixote he defied the inevitable, like Till Eulenspiegel he cocked a snook at traditional authorities, like William Tell he frequently displayed great physical and intellectual courage.

A man of action, de Gaulle was also a philosopher and writer with a highly developed (if tendentious) view of history. He was a born pedagogue who used the public platform and the television screen to great effect, and his elegant writings all profess those eternal truths he so cherished. His mastery of the French language was proverbial ('*il gouverna par le verbe*', noted one critic) and he could use words, often simple in appearance, to disguise obscurity: verbal decisiveness often masked profound equivocation. De Gaulle also had a finely attuned sense of theatrical moment. His sense of theatre and the dramatic found expression on several occasions: on 18 June 1940 when he fled to England to lead the Free French in a continued struggle against Germany; on 29 May 1968 when he suddenly disappeared from a Paris which was in political turmoil to visit high-ranking army officers in Germany. Yet allied with the taste for striking gestures were an empiricism, a prudence, a capacity for improvisation and an occasional calculated prevarication, all of which he displayed during his accession to power in May 1958 and in his conduct of the Algerian war between 1958 and 1962. Furthermore, if circumstances demanded, he would resort to silence, secrecy and even deceit.

General de Gaulle lived at several different levels: as the personification of the values and virtues of French civilization; as the living embodiment of the state; as the man of providence defying the elements; as the author conscious of writing his own place into world history; as the Cassandra who foresaw the collapse of his own country in May 1940 and as the prophet who forecast the inevitable defeat of Germany; as President of the Republic resolutely constructing a strong executive authority; as a bilious politician constantly marshalling support for his dreams and schemes; as an anguished and perceptive spectator of his times. This extraordinary man, who could refer to himself in the third person, was partial prisoner of his own myth. As a national leader, General de Gaulle elicited both deep-seated hatred and also an admiration which bordered occasionally on adulation: the political magic of the man was sufficient to create a fervent and sometimes fanatical following. And if that support declined during his long period in office, it must be remembered that in the referendum which led to his resignation he was still backed by a percentage of the voters greater than that enjoyed by any British prime minister since the war. Intelligent and powerful men accepted without question his moral authority – however illegal or unconstitutional his activity. In his genius for communication he displayed an uncanny ability to touch a responsive chord in the national consciousness. When he resigned in 1969, after ten years in office, he handed over to his successor a presidency which enjoyed both power and prestige.

The successor to General de Gaulle was Georges Pompidou, who was elected to the presidency in June 1969. His rise to the presidency was, in many senses, spectacular. When de Gaulle appointed him prime minister in April 1962 he was totally unknown to the general public, and his appointment was interpreted by many as an act of defiance by de Gaulle towards the Gaullist Party and towards parliament, since he had never been a member of either. That he was to become undisputed master of both was a measure of the man's uncanny ability. Pompidou had not rallied to the call of 18 June 1940, he had fought no battles for the Resistance, he had taken no part in the heroic episode of the RPF (the first Gaullist Party) from 1947 to 1951, he had played no part in the Gaullist conspiracy in Algiers and Paris which helped to pave the way to de Gaulle's return to power in May 1958, he had suffered none of the many setbacks of Gaullist diehards such as Michel Debré and had taken no active part in Gaullist Party propaganda. During the Fourth Republic, after a brief spell as a school teacher and then as a collaborator of General de Gaulle, he enjoyed a short yet distinguished career in the Council of State and a longer and infinitely more lucrative one in Rothschild's bank in Paris. It was during that period that Pompidou acquired his business contacts, a certain financial security and a taste for modern art (with which he was to desecrate certain rooms of the Élysée after his election to the presidency). He made money, read poetry and lived the good life. His background seemed less suited for the battlefront of politics than the salons of the well-heeled, the well-bred and the well-read. But Pompidou was an able and trusted confidant of General de Gaulle who appreciated his discretion, his fidelity, his literary ability and his managerial efficacy. And while he had played no active role in politics, his Gaullist credentials were well established: he had been a member of de Gaulle's private office in 1945 and was recognized as one of the Gaullist 'barons' (together with men such as Chaban-Delmas, Foccart and Frey) who met weekly to discuss political tactics. He was known to be in frequent contact with de Gaulle from 1946 to 1958 (and gave the General financial advice), and from 1958 to 1962 carried out several confidential missions for the president.

Pompidou remained prime minister for six years – for the longest period in French republican history – and by 1968, when he 're-signed', he had created for himself a very powerful political base. He had nursed his parliamentary constituency with the assiduity of an old-style politician, he had emerged as a skilful parliamentary debater and a powerful public speaker, he had established himself as the undisputed leader of the Gaullist Party, he had been successful in forging unity of action (if not of attitude) between the parties which composed the governmental coalition (which he led to electoral victory in 1962, 1967 and 1968) and he proved himself a remarkably effective prime minister, especially during the disorders of May 1968. More dangerously, he had emerged as the *dauphin*, the legitimate and apparently inevitable successor to de Gaulle. For de Gaulle it was an intolerable situation. In June 1968, Pompidou was gracelessly replaced as prime minister by the lacklustre Couve de Murville. Then began his personal *traversée du désert*, a short but painful period marked by a total breach with de Gaulle and by ugly rumours, as scurrilous as they were unfounded, of his being involved in an underworld scandal. With de Gaulle's resignation in 1969 Pompidou immediately declared himself a candidate for the presidency, and, after an unexciting campaign, was elected at the second ballot against Poher, an avuncular mediocrity whose political opinions were as colourless as his personality.

De Gaulle's apocalyptic prophecy of the political deluge which would engulf France after his departure was to be disproved by Pompidou's presidency. Until he was undermined by his appalling illness he was a strong and effective president who considerably extended the presidential sphere of government. Rumours of Pompidou's illness were circulating long before his death: this was scarcely surprising, since he was literally dying a public death. In his last two years, in spite of terrible suffering, he clung tenaciously to office and continued to make and shape the major policies of the régime. He made frequent visits abroad and to the French provinces and continued to preside over the weekly Council of Ministers. But he had neither the will nor the strength closely to control the activities of his ministers or even his own personal staff. Increasingly, both his personality and style of government changed. His well-known ability to take quick and decisive decisions was replaced by a disquieting procrastination, his personal joviality by lassitude, his enthusiasm by indifference, his opportunism based on acute political sensitivity by an over-prudent conservatism, his good-living by the introspective piety of the recently converted, his worldly scepticism by a deepening religiosity which bordered on mysticism: Pompidou, a prize product of the secular Republic, ended his days firmly in the embrace of the church.

Pompidou, as president, was a firm political and social conservative. His profound scepticism about men and the world was expressed in his highly personal *Noeud gordien*, published in June 1974 but written when he was out of office in 1968-9. This son of a socialist primary school teacher from one of the poorest parts of France (the Cantal in the Massif Central) reached the top through his local *lycée* and the *École Normale Supérieure*. Talented, intelligent and ambitious, Pompidou made good, and like many of his kind, had little understanding of those unable or unwilling to do the same. In one important respect, however, he was a radical: he was obsessed by the need economically to transform France, by the need to make his country a great industrial power. And to that end a great deal was sacrificed: the environment and greater social justice were among the victims. When Pompidou died, 2 April 1974, he must have been satisfied with his work, for France had become one of the greatest economic powers in the world.

The third President of the Fifth Republic, Valéry Giscard d'Estaing, comes from the same region – the Auvergne – as his predecessor. But here end all similarities in origins. Giscard d'Estaing hails from an old and distinguished family of political and industrial *notables*: indeed, ingenious genealogists, encouraged by the president, trace part of his ancestry to the French royal family.

He is the great-grandson of a minister of Marshal MacMahon and a vice-president of the Senate, the grandson of an influential deputy and the son of an *inspecteur des finances* who became a director of several banks and a member of the French *Institut*. Many of his relatives are prominent in banking, industry and the higher reaches of the civil service. His wife is the grand-daughter of Eugène Schneider, the immensely wealthy industrialist and ex-speaker of the lower House of Parliament during the Second Empire.

Giscard d'Estaing inherited from his family great wealth, many political contacts and a ferocious intelligence. This last quality was admirably displayed in the highly competitive examinations to and within the *École Polytechnique* and the *École Nationale d'Administration* (ENA) – the two schools which together form so much of the present French elite. His performance at the ENA enabled him to follow his father in choosing a career in the highly prestigious financial inspectorate. In 1953 he had his first taste of politics when he entered the private office of Edgar Faure, then Minister of Finance. Thereafter, his political ascension was meteoric: Deputy of the Puy-de Dôme in 1956 at the age of 30 (his grandfather discreetly retired from his parliamentary seat to make way for his ambitious grandson); junior minister in the Ministry of Finance in the Debré government from January 1959 to January 1962; Minister of Finance from January 1962 to January 1966. In the meantime he was building a secure political base for himself – both locally as Deputy and as Mayor of Chamalières (a wealthy suburb of Clermont-Ferrand) and nationally as leader, after 1962, of the newly formed Independent Republican movement. His dismissal as Minister of Finance in January 1966 came as a humiliating shock to him (he was dismissed like a common servant, he later bitterly claimed). De Gaulle, who had performed relatively badly in the December 1965 presidential elections, attributed part of his failure to his Finance Minister's unpopular economic policies.

Relations between Giscard d'Estaing and de Gaulle deteriorated from that moment, with the former making increasingly pointed remarks about the authoritarian aspects of the régime and the Gaullists responding by refusing to elect him to the chairmanship of the Finance Committee of the National Assembly. In the referendum which led to the resignation of General de Gaulle in April 1969, Giscard d'Estaing publicly announced that 'regretfully' he would vote against the presidential proposals. This act of *lèse-majesté* was to earn him the lasting enmity of the diehard Gaullists who nicknamed him *Judas Giscariot*. In the presidential elections of June 1969, after some hesitation, he finally declared his support for Pompidou. His reward after Pompidou's election was the Finance Ministry; he kept this key post, without interruption, throughout Pompidou's presidency (22 June 1969 to 2 April 1974). When Pompidou died, Giscard d'Estaing was not the inevitable successor but he was an obvious candidate. He was elected to the presidency after one of the most exciting election campaigns in recent history, trouncing Chaban-Delmas, his Gaullist rival, at the first ballot, and going on to beat Mitterrand, his Left-wing opponent, by a wafer-thin majority at the second.

As President of the Republic, Giscard d'Estaing displayed many admirable qualities. He was, by all accounts, an immensely nice man (in this respect, he contrasted sharply with the first president), and clearly lacked neither intelligence nor courage. He was also no less aware than de Gaulle of his own image, and constantly projected himself as a high-powered and technically competent leader. If de Gaulle was a slightly strict father and Pompidou a jovial uncle, Giscard d'Estaing was the clever brother. In the early years of his presidency, he also cultivated another image – that of the dynamic, easy-going, youthful and accessible Kennedy figure. To that end he was photographed behind the wheel of his car, shaking hands with the inmates of a Lyons prison, dining with a garage mechanic and receiving dustmen at the Élysée. He was even seen in swimming-trunks (the mind reels at the very idea of de Gaulle in such apparel). Furthermore, for personal and political reasons, this scion of the upper classes had to demonstrate his sensitivity to the needs of the ordinary Frenchman. But there was something rather sad and pathetic about this impeccably well-bred man displaying his aristocratic knees on the sports field of his home town of Chamalières or his musical talents on the accordion to his local electors, or dining with garage mechanics and firemen. But for the president these latter antics were part of his campaign to change the style of the presidency: a more relaxed atmosphere replaced the previous stifled formality of the office. In the later years of his presidency, however, Giscard d'Estaing became 'devoured by the office', and the easy-going informality of the early years was gradually replaced by a stultifying pretentiousness: the 'monarchical' activities of the president and his family were regularly chronicled in the satirical *Canard Enchaîné* and the censorious *Le Monde*.

In his *Démocratie française*, published in October 1976, Giscard d'Estaing declared his ambitions to create 'a peaceful and thought-ful democracy' untainted by 'the timidity of conservatism and by revolutionary confrontations'. He was especially disturbed by the 'gratuitously dramatic' nature of French political controversy, and argued that the source of that controversy was no longer sociological but ideological: he rejected the idea of his country being divided into two warring classes – the bourgeoisie and the proletariat – but rather discerned the emergence of 'an immense central group' capable, eventually, of integrating the whole of French society. The president's ideas were not free from contradiction, since he praised the principle of pluralism yet rejected one of its most eloquent expressions, class conflict. Giscard d'Estaing's second ambition, as expressed in *Démocratie française*, was to modernize and to liberalize French society without anguish or torment, and in certain important respects (the lowering of the voting age to 18, penal reform, the introduction of divorce by mutual consent, the easing of legislation on abortion and contraception) he made an important impact on French society for some time. Yet the president of the Republic oscillated between a certain audacity and a prudent realism: he wished to reform French society but was all too aware of the political constraints imposed by his supporters and, in that respect, he sometimes gave the impression of being rather like a London street busker, with one eye on the crowd and the other anxiously peering over his shoulder for the reactions of the forces of order. By the end of his presidency, however, Giscard d'Estaing came to betray the reformist ideals he had earlier enunciated: his policies became much more conservative, particularly in the fields of economic policy and law and order. The change in policies corresponded with (and are partially explained by) a modification in the general outlook of the president who became more pessimistic, and whose view of the world and of France's place in it became increasingly bleak, almost tragic. Giscard d'Estaing's abandonment of his reformist ideals was to cost him dearly in the presidential elections of May 1981: it was certainly a contributing factor in his defeat.

The third ambition of Giscard d'Estaing, as expressed in his *Démocratie française*, was to render French society 'more pluralistic', and this in all spheres. Yet his concentration of power in presidential hands, his berating of the political parties (among the major instruments of political pluralism), his discrimination against certain politically unsympathetic pressure groups, his obsessive surveillance of the state media and his interference in certain press matters, all suggested a less than total commitment to the pluralistic ideal.

When Giscard d'Estaing stood in the presidential elections in May 1981 most observers and the majority of the electorate were convinced that he would be re-elected. He was beaten. And by his long-standing adversary whom he greatly underestimated, François Mitterrand. Giscard d'Estaing lost the election for a number of reasons: the disastrous economic record of his government, particularly in the election year when all the major indices (but particularly those on unemployment and inflation) were very poor; the extraordinary unpopularity of his prime minister, Raymond Barre, whose insensitive and cantankerous behaviour antagonized many; the hostile activities of the Gaullists who were increasingly critical of his policies; the absence of a reforming programme which he had promised in May 1974 when he was elected; his inability to construct a powerful party base; the impact of a series of scandals affecting himself and his entourage in the late 1970s; his own complacency reflected in a lacklustre election campaign. He also lost because in May 1981 there was a viable and attractive 'alternative' in the person of François Mitterrand.

The victory of François Mitterrand in May 1981 was a personal triumph for a man who had been dismissed as the 'eternal loser' by Michel Poniatowski, an intimate friend of Giscard d'Estaing. Before his election to the presidency, Mitterrand had enjoyed a long and varied career. Brought up in a middle-class (his father was a railway official) Catholic family, Mitterrand began his professional life at the Paris bar after studying at the Paris Law Faculty. His brief legal career was cut short by the war: he was conscripted, captured and, after two unsuccessful attempts, eventually escaped. He joined the Resistance movement and in spite of his youth played an important role under the name of Morvan. After the war he entered politics and during the Fourth Republic established himself as an able administrator and an influential parliamentarian. He was Mayor of Château-Chinon (a post he held until his election to the presidency in 1981), president of the departmental council of the Nièvre and Deputy of that *département*, and he enjoyed a meteoric rise in Paris: he held ministerial office no fewer than eleven times, his last post being that of the Minister of the Interior in 1956. During the Fifth Republic he consolidated his local power base in the Nièvre, and rapidly became one of the leading opponents of the Right. In the National Assembly he proved a formidable figure: he was a brilliant, incisive and caustic critic, using irony and malice with frequent and telling effect. From the mid 1960s Mitterrand began to organize the political forces which were to bring him to power. His strategy was twofold: to claim the leadership of a rejuvenated non-communist Left (then in disarray) and, from a position of strength, to negotiate an electoral agreement with the Communists (see Chapter 10). By 1981 Mitterrand had achieved his first aim (with the creation of a powerful and popular Socialist Party) and had largely established his credentials as the leader of the entire Left. (In the 1965 and 1974 presidential elections he stood as the unsuccessful candidate of the Left, never ceased to root his strategy in the need for Left-wing unity, and was the recognized principal critic of governments of the Right.) After the 1978 general election, which resulted in a rather unexpected defeat for the Left, Mitterrand gained another reputation, that of the dignified and disinterested elder statesman, whose active political career was over. He cultivated this image as well as that of being the legitimate heir to the other great figures of republican and socialist France: Jules Ferry, Jean Jaurès and Léon Blum. In spite of his successive defeats (particularly those of 1974 and 1978) he had established his place in French history and the knowledge of this seemed to give him an inner self-assurance. Mitterrand also acquired a reputation in literary circles with his many books, all written in a thoughtful, highly literary, ironic vein. Therefore, when Mitterrand entered the election campaign of 1981 he had behind him a solid party base (the Socialist Party, of which he was the first secretary, was the most popular in the country), a great deal of sympathy in the Left as a whole, the reputation of being the Right's most biting and effective critic, and an image of being the calm and measured elder statesman. To win the presidency he had first to outwit his rivals within the Socialist Party (which he did with consummate skill) in order to become the party's candidate, and then to beat Giscard d'Estaing. He ran a very good campaign, exuding reassurance and promising reform – the combination which had won Giscard d'Estaing the presidency seven years earlier. In the event, he won the election at the second ballot with a comfortable margin: the 'eternal loser' had confounded his critics.

During his first term in office Mitterrand's popularity reached record highs and record lows in the polls. The immense popularity of the first few months evaporated quickly under the impact of recession and austerity, and from April 1983 his unpopularity was greater than that of any of his predecessors. By November 1984 only 26 per cent of those polled by IFOP declared themselves satisfied with the president compared with 57 per cent dissatisfied. However, from 1985 his popularity ratings began slowly to improve, and after the victory of the Right in March 1986 they improved spectacularly: from May to July 1986 the proportion of people satisfied with the president rose from 39 to 59 per cent. It was to remain above 50 per cent throughout the period of Right-wing government and until and beyond his triumphant re-election in May 1988. Two factors appear to explain the dramatic change in the fortunes of the president after March 1986. In the first place, he consolidated his popularity among Left-wing voters who disliked the policies of the new Right-wing government. Second, his open acceptance of the electors' verdict in the legislative elections and his efforts to avoid a constitutional crisis by appointing a Right-wing government attracted centrist and moderate voters. Throughout the period of *cohabitation* with the Right-wing government of Jacques Chirac he succeeded in projecting an image of being both the *pater familias* and the defender of the underprivileged. By reassuring moderates and his own constituency he revealed his tactical genius.

President Mitterrand is a strange mixture. As an orator he is outstanding, lacing his lyricism and brooding romanticism with literary allusion and acerbic wit, gentle irony and bitter sarcasm. As a debater, however, he is weak, hesitant, defensive, over-personal and sometimes gratuitously wounding. Mitterrand is also the teacher, the poet, the author and the prophet. He is a man who exudes a sense of his own inner self-assurance, who seems secure in his achievement of having reconstructed the party of Jaurès and Blum, and who is aware that he has already achieved an honourable place in the history of his country. Yet, at critical moments, he can prevaricate (as did de Gaulle in May 1968) as was evident after the dramatic sinking of Greenpeace's *Rainbow Warrior* in 1985, when agents of the French secret service decided that environmental protest required a violent response, when the government wavered, when the international community demanded action and when the Defence Minister had eventually to resign. His vacillation was equally apparent in his agonizing over the austerity programme of March 1983. There are touches of de Gaulle in Mitterrand – the isolation, the obstinacy, the ambition, the aloofness, the haughtiness, the ingratitude towards his friends, the ruthlessness towards his rivals, the disdain for his enemies, the moral distaste for great wealth, the pretension to be 'above politics' while carefully and even cynically indulging in them, the skilful manipulation of language, the vision, and the quiet taste for publicized martyrdom. Like de Gaulle, he evokes respect and admiration but little affection: he may have earned the familiar nickname of *Tonton*, but no-one outside his small circle of intimate friends indulges in *tutoiement* with the president. Like de Gaulle, too, he has a court, and a fanatical following – 'Tontonmania' it was called in 1988. Finally, in true Gaullist fashion, Mitterrand appears to be forging his own biography, ever aware of his own impact, ever sensitive to his own image.

President Mitterrand differs greatly from his predecessors in social background, in his education, his professional training and also in several other important ways:

● He differs in his working methods: unlike Giscard d'Estaing who worked closely with his team at the Élysée, Mitterrand works very much alone or with particular individuals, and

unlike all his three predecessors he has much closer institutionalized links with the principal party of his coalition--
links which are provided by carefully chosen friends within
the party.

● His *style* of governing is somewhat reminiscent of that of
General de Gaulle – distant, autocratic, olympian – but
contrasts sharply with that of Giscard d'Estaing who by 1981
had become coldly didactic, technocratic and haughty.

● He differs in temperament and personality: de Gaulle and
Giscard d'Estaing, in later years, were imbued with a profound scepticism and pessimism rooted either in a tendentious reading of history (de Gaulle) or in an appreciation
of the contemporary scene (Giscard d'Estaing); Pompidou
was pervaded by a sense of peasant caution, although his
rumbustious and earthy perception of his fellow citizens was
later tinged with fatalism; Mitterrand combines a largely
optimistic view of mankind with a cautious, often suspicious,
view of men.

● He has a different view of French society. De Gaulle
was obsessed with its deeply divisive nature and attempted
to create political institutions to soften the divisions and
ensure that they did not tear the nation apart. Pompidou
believed that, beneath the tensions, the bases of the nation
were sound and healthy and should not be disturbed by
political and social reforms. Giscard d'Estaing's views clearly
changed during his seven years' office: an optimistic view of
a society which he saw evolving rapidly (a view expressed
in his *Démocratie française*) gave way to a much gloomier
assessment, and the breezy reformism of the early years
changed to a narrow and prudent conservatism. President
Mitterrand has an ambivalent attitude towards French society, for he has a clear insight into its inner strengths and an
almost arrogant view of France's rule in the world, yet he
has become increasingly sensitized to its many political and
social defects.

● The present President of the Republic is neither a Gaullist
like de Gaulle and Pompidou nor a moderate conservative
like Giscard d'Estaing. If he is not a Marxist he is certainly
a man of the Left: a humanitarian, humanistic, universalistic
socialism vies with an attachment to the French republican
tradition. Mitterrand's heroes are not Marx, Engels and
Lenin, but Jules Ferry, Jean Jaurès and Léon Blum.

● Mitterrand differs from his three predecessors in the ends
he is pursuing. President de Gaulle's peculiar and somewhat
archaic obsession was national unity and France's place

in the world, Pompidou's passion was the modernizing of the French economy, and Giscard d'Estaing's declared aims were to liberalize and render more pluralistic French society, even if those aims were not always wholeheartedly pursued. Mitterrand's programme retains an ambitious role for France in the world, includes a preoccupation with France's industrial strength, and maintains the Giscardian plan to liberalize and render more pluralistic French society. Indeed, the first years of the Socialist government after 1981 were characterized by frenzied reform activity designed to ensure or at least to facilitate the emergence of a more liberal and pluralistic France. But Mitterrand's initial ambitions went much further, and there was talk of the creation of 'a new model society' and 'a new citizenship' based on greater social justice and equity. An unrepentant demand for greater fraternity and equality continues to underpin many of Mitterrand's pronouncements, although the pressure of events has limited the process of implementation.

The four men also have much in common. Mitterrand shares his predecessors' qualities of intellectual ability, political sensitivity and personal courage. Like his three predecessors he has undoubted stature. He also shares their aversion to political instability and to collectivist political ideals and practices. Like his predecessors, too, Mitterrand is an inveterate pedagogue and careful image-builder. And part of both the pedagogy and the image-building is directed to stressing the primacy of the presidential office. Only a few days after his election in December 1958, General de Gaulle could declare that 'as the guide of France and Head of the Republican State I shall exercise the supreme power in as wide-ranging a manner as necessary'. When he resigned in 1969 it was clear that he had certainly carried out his wish. President Pompidou was no less specific about his role, and very few of his major political speeches failed to insist upon the supremacy of his office. Giscard d'Estaing made it clear during the 1974 election campaign that he wished 'to push the régime further in a presidential direction' and all the evidence suggests that by 1981 he had done so. Indeed, he was so successful that even Gaullists had joined the chorus of critics who pointed to the 'excessive' presidentialism of the régime. The case of Mitterrand is more interesting. Until his election in May 1981 he was the most consistent and persistent critic of the political institutions of the Fifth Republic and denounced with genuine anger the presidential drift of the régime which he considered to be 'anti-republican'. Yet in his very first utterances as President of the Republic he confessed that 'the [political] institutions were not made with me in mind. But they are well made for me'. He insisted that he would exercise presidential powers to the full (*dans leur plénitude*), and told *Le Monde* that 'as for the President of the Republic, he exercises supreme power, particularly in the fields of foreign affairs and defence'. Moreover, the experience of government after May 1981 eloquently demonstrated that presidential power had not been diluted. The emergence, strengthening and consolidation of presidential authority corresponded, therefore, to the expressed wish of successive incumbents. So, too, did the scope of the presidential sector.

4 The presidential policy-making sector

The presidential sector of policy-making is accordion-like: it expands or contracts according to changing requirements. In the case of the presidency those requirements are essentially three-fold: the constitution and its interpretation; the political circumstances; the personal wishes of the incumbent president. Nonetheless, the first thirty years of the Fifth Republic have been characterized by a gradual extension of the presidential sector well beyond the intentions of the framers of the constitution followed by a contraction of the sector as the result of political and personal pressures. At only one stage – between March 1986 and May 1988 – was the central decision-making role of the presidency contested and partially undermined. But at no stage has presidential supremacy in defence matters been disputed. Nor have presidential prerogatives in foreign and European affairs ever been in dispute, although between 1986 and 1988 the government clearly intervened in these fields. It is, therefore, the area of domestic affairs which has undergone most change since 1958, expanding and contracting according to political circumstances and presidential calculations.

The presidential sector 1958-1986

In 1967 Valéry Giscard d'Estaing, then an embittered and ambitious ex-Finance Minister, made a celebrated attack on General de Gaulle's methods of government: the President of the Republic, he alleged, was concentrating too much power and too many decisions in his own hands. Ten years later, the same accusations were being made, with greater justification, by the Gaullists against Giscard d'Estaing, then President of the Republic. Such attacks were inevitable, for the steady and uninterrupted growth of the presidential domain constituted one of the more striking characteristics of the present régime.

In November 1959, Chaban-Delmas, then president of the National Assembly, in a speech to the Gaullist Party congress, defined the so-called presidential 'reserved domain' as encompassing foreign affairs, defence matters, questions relating to the

French Community and Algeria. This restrictive interpretation was rejected by the president both by his practice and in his speeches. On 31 January 1964, de Gaulle insisted that it was the president himself who defined his own field of responsibility. De Gaulle, however, did not interfere in all areas of decision-making: he was content to leave a great deal of discretion to his prime minister and his ministers. His main interests were foreign policy, defence policy (especially after 1962), colonial and French Community questions (with Algeria dominating all else until April 1962) and European questions. But as shall be made clear, de Gaulle would not hesitate to intervene in any policy area he considered of importance or interest.

When Georges Pompidou became president in June 1969 he inherited the presidential domain as defined by General de Gaulle, and added to it his own field of interests (mainly economic and political) which he had acquired during his long premiership (1962-68). The presidential domain was further extended with the election of Giscard d'Estaing in May 1974: he was unwilling to relinquish any of the established fields of presidential policy-making and was keen to add to them his own interests in financial, social and environmental questions. The steady accretion of presidential power in the 1960s and 1970s was rather like the accumulation of geological strata, with each president bequeathing to his successor a new layer of responsibility. Thus, paradoxically, the power of the present Left-wing president is the result of the tentacular designs of his three Right-wing predecessors.

At the beginning of 1976, President Giscard d'Estaing claimed that there were only two areas in which he would never intervene – justice and information – so presumably any other area was vulnerable to presidential interference. However, both the areas he mentioned had already been invaded. The president makes key appointments to the judiciary and to the Constititutional Council General de Gaulle, during the Algerian drama, had several altercations with members of the judiciary, a celebrated clash with the Council of State in 1962, and established special courts to deal with offences arising out of the Algerian crisis. The media had also received a fair share of presidential attention. Moreover, untrue to his word, President Giscard d'Estaing showed more than a passive interest in the relationship between the state and television: certainly the 1974 Act which completely reorganized the French television network was carefully supervised from the Élysée, and the president was careful to award key positions in the networks to political sympathizers. Furthermore, the affairs of the Paris press were also closely watched by the presidency.

François Mitterrand inherited, therefore, a presidential sector in which anything was, or could be, included. From the outset he made it clear that his electoral platform would be the basis of governmental activity and that he was '*le premier responsable des affaires publiques*'.

The presidency had apparently become omnipresent – a phenomenon which was all the more surprising since it had little basis in the constitution.

There were essentially five components of the presidential domain:

● *Foreign and European affairs, defence matters, and colonial and French community matters.* This was the area defined by Chaban-Delmas in 1959 as constituting the presidential 'reserved domain', and may be described as the traditional domain.

● *Economic, financial and industrial matters*, which became increasingly important after the election of Georges Pompidou to the presidency in June 1969.

● *Social and environmental issues* which figured prominently in the presidential domain after May 1974 when Giscard d'Estaing was elected to the presidency.

● *Questions which suddenly appeared on the political agenda because they were politically delicate or explosive.*

● *Matters which attracted presidential attention for purely personal reasons.*

The last two categories involved presidential intervention of a sporadic nature.

The traditional domain

The supremacy of the presidency was quickly established in this area since it was during the Algerian crisis that General de Gaulle took decisions with little regard to either the government or parliament. The Council of Ministers was consulted only once (in August 1959) throughout the crisis which more than once threatened the stability of the régime, and Prime Minister Debré, who was known to be unhappy about aspects of the president's policies, was constantly by-passed. By a combination of tenacity, guile, mendacity and courage he imposed his policies towards Algeria on a rebellious army, a discontented prime minister, a divided parliament and an unhappy Gaullist Party. Time and again he stressed the personal nature of his policies. In his direction of French policy towards French colonies and ex-colonies he was equally autocratic: his decisions in the Bizerta affair of July 1961 and his sending of troops to Gabon in February 1964 were never discussed in the Council of Ministers. Presidential interest in these areas continued: Presidents Pompidou and Giscard d'Estaing both extensively visited ex-French colonies in black Africa, the latter for both official and less official reasons (big game hunting): his personal interest in black African affairs may be seen in the friendship he struck up with Bokassa, the dictator whose career he furthered and financed (the friendship was eventually to damage the president's image and reputation), and more dramatically in his decision in 1978 to send French troops to Kolwezi. President Mitterrand visited Africa in his first year of office, and like his three predecessors, has a full-time political councillor for African affairs – a testimony to the importance attached by the president to this area. Certainly the French intervention in Chad in 1982 was the decision of the president and was not previously discussed by the government. Similarly, the French bombing of the main airport in Chad in February 1986 followed a decision by the president.

The supremacy of the president in foreign affairs was unquestionable and unquestioned, and foreign ministers were generally chosen simply as faithful executors of presidential policy. The policy of *rapprochement* with Eastern Europe, the recognition of China, the decision not to sell arms to Israel, the outrageous proclamation about Quebec were among the many personal acts of the first President of the Fifth Republic. President de Gaulle's decisions to take France out of NATO and to order the Americans to withdraw their troops from French soil were discussed in the Council of Ministers three days after the American president had been informed. The presidency clearly retained its supremacy in foreign affairs after de Gaulle's resignation in 1969. For instance, among President Giscard d'Estaing's personal initiatives were the offer to act as mediator in the Lebanese crisis (an offer he made while he was in the USA and which surprised many ministers), and the much criticized visit to Warsaw to meet the Soviet leader to discuss the Afghanistan crisis. President Mitterrand's early personal contributions included a hardening of French attitudes towards the Soviet Union (over the Soviet invasion of Afghanistan and the military crackdown in Poland) and towards Chile, the controversial dispatch of aircraft to Iraq in 1983, the sending of French troops to the Lebanon as part of the international peacekeeping force in the same year, and an attempt to improve French relations with Israel. Like their predecessors, Giscard d'Estaing and Mitterrand were prepared to ignore governmental sensitivities: in 1980, the Foreign Minister learnt about Giscard d'Estaing's visit to Warsaw only after a personal emissary of the president had settled all the details. The South African prime minister was invited to Paris in May 1984 in spite of Prime Minister Mauroy's opposition (Mauroy even refused to receive him, thus causing one of his rare conflicts with Mitterrand), and in December 1985, Prime Minister Fabius learnt of the visit to Paris of General Jaruzelski, the Polish leader, from a press agency. The publicly expressed unhappiness of Fabius about the visit did nothing to prevent it, and it is significant that no one denied Mitterrand's right personally to define French policy. French foreign policy is not only highly personal, it is also highly personalized. President Mitterrand, like his three predecessors, has travelled abroad a great deal (too much, according to his critics), and has had personal meetings with representatives of foreign powers at the Élysée and has represented France at major international conferences. In 1984 he even made a secret journey to Crete to meet Colonel Kadhafi, and in the same year made an equally secret trip to Morocco to meet Hassan II.

In European affairs the supremacy of the president was equally manifest. De Gaulle had the disconcerting habit of making pronouncements on European affairs at press conferences where apprehensive ministers learnt, at the same time as the rest of the world, of changes in French policy. On 15 May 1962, for example, European-minded ministers sat in grim-faced disapproval as de Gaulle attacked their cherished ideas: some were to resign immediately after. President de Gaulle's two vetoes of British entry into the Common Market were also highly personal decisions, and neither enjoyed the unanimous support of his ministers, who were informed of his decisions at the same time as the rest of the French public. President Pompidou's decision to lift the French veto on British entry was equally highly personal, a fact readily admitted by Pompidou himself: it has been claimed that the prime minister learned of the decision at the same time as television viewers. Giscard d'Estaing was no less determined to assert presidential supremacy in European affairs: when Britain was renegotiating the terms of its entry into the Common Market, in Dublin in March 1975, the French president made concessions without first consulting or informing the Council of Ministers. Similarly, the decision in the early summer of 1976 to press ahead with the direct election of the European Parliament was taken at Brussels by the president and announced to the Council of Ministers on his return. Prime Minister Chirac, who was known to be less than lukewarm about the pro-European ideals of the president, was later to reveal that he was informed only at the same time as his ministerial colleagues, and that at no stage was he consulted or kept informed on the issue. Mitterrand's hand in European affairs may be seen in the number of initiatives he tried to implement in the first year of his presidency: these included attempts to change the financial structure of the Common Agricultural Policy, to stimulate industrial investment (through the European Investment

Bank) and to give new impetus to European regional policies. It was President Mitterrand, too, who informed the apprehensive Spanish in 1982 that their entry into the European Community was likely to take longer than they anticipated. And it was the same president who later informed them that France would do everything to ensure that entry.

As in the general field of foreign policy, European policy-making became highly personalized. De Gaulle attended the important Rome meeting of the six European members of the European Common Market in May 1967; Pompidou represented France at The Hague summit conference of 'the Six' in December 1969; Giscard d'Estaing personally conducted French negotiations at the Dublin meeting in March 1975. At all the European and the industrialized nations' summit meetings it is President Mitterrand who (like his predecessors) represents France. French presidents also struck up profitable relationships with individual European statesmen: de Gaulle's friendly and fruitful relationship with Konrad Adenauer, the German chancellor, was followed by a similar relationship between Pompidou and Edward Heath and then between Giscard d'Estaing and Helmut Schmidt (this was temporarily to sour after the chancellor was reported to have made some very uncomplimentary remarks about the French president).

Defence has always fallen within the presidential domain, although when General de Gaulle was preoccupied with the Algerian problem during the first three years of his presidency the Prime Minister, Michel Debré, took many important decisions. The President of the Republic plays three key roles in defence policy: as effective head of the executive, as official commander-in-chief of the armed forces and as chairman of the National Defence Committee. He may determine the main lines of French defence policy as was demonstrated by de Gaulle's decision to withdraw from NATO or by successive presidents' pursuit of an independent nuclear deterrent. He may also shape the strategy to be employed: for instance, President Pompidou effectively opposed the Military High Command's desire to reorganize French territorial forces, and defended his predecessor's ideas on the size and role of French conventional forces. Or the president may recommend specific courses of action: hence President Giscard d'Estaing's insistence in December 1974 on maintaining a fleet of conventional strike and reconnaissance aircraft and his arbitration on the type of aircraft to carry out that task, and his decision, in mid 1978, to press ahead with the construction of a new nuclear submarine. Hence, too, Mitterrand's decisions taken shortly after his election, to develop the French independent nuclear deterrent, to continue the work on the neutron bomb, to retain the length of military service at one year (in spite of an election promise to reduce it to six months), to replace the old generation range of ballistic missiles by a new one, and to build a seventh nuclear submarine. All these decisions were presidential decisions and announced from the Élysée.

The President of the Republic also defends the defence budget in the Council of Ministers (it was on President Giscard d'Estaing's insistence that the defence budget was raised in 1976 from 17 to 20 per cent of the total state budget), appoints to key military posts, arbitrates between the conflicting claims of the various branches of the military establishment and between the various sections within each branch, and arbitrates between his ministers and the Military High Command. Presidential supremacy in the area of defence was highlighted in May 1976 when the president personally amended the Defence Long Term Plan proposed by the Minister of Defence and when he presented the government's defence proposals on television. In the following month he insisted before an assembly of high-ranking officers that defence policy should be imbued with his own conceptions and ideas, and reminded them that the President of the Republic was responsible both for the guidelines of policy and the means for implementing them. He ended his speech by quoting Louis XV before the battle of Fontenoy in 1745: 'Gentlemen, I invite you to keep quiet. The battle plan has been drawn up, the Commander has been chosen. It is up to him to take charge of the action'.

Economic, financial and industrial matters

In this area, presidential power gradually increased. Initially, General de Gaulle intervened only occasionally in this field and generally to emphasize the main lines of policy. It was de Gaulle who, at an inter-ministerial council on 23 December 1958, took all the important decisions which were to define the main lines of French economic policy for several years. And from the mid 1960s he showed increased interest in economic affairs, possibly as the result of the influence of Jacques Rueff, that arch-apostle of pre-Keynesian economic and financial orthodoxy. In August and September 1963 he presided over several inter-ministerial councils devoted to the economic stabilization plan, and in June 1964 he took an active part in the discussions in the Council of Ministers on the problem of rents and prices in the public sector. Nor would President de Gaulle hesitate to intervene directly and personally if he felt a problem to be critical. In autumn 1968, on the advice of Raymond Barre, then a little-known economist in Brussels, he astounded the financial world, his Prime Minister and Finance Minister, by refusing to devalue the franc (reputable newspapers had already reported the decision to devalue as certain). On the whole, however, General de Gaulle tended to leave economic and financial matters to his Prime Ministers and finance minister.

President Pompidou was initially very interventionist in this domain; this was scarcely surprising, since this ex-banker had, as prime minister, exercised considerable influence in shaping French economic and financial policy. It was he who was mainly responsible for the decision to devalue the franc in 1969. Furthermore, as a sensitive politician, President Pompidou kept a keen eye on the state budget and would occasionally arbitrate between the conflicting claims of the spending ministries on the one hand, and, on the other, between the spending ministries and the Ministry of Finance, the protector of the public purse. And his constant defence of the agricultural budget was an open secret. Most of the time, however, President Pompidou left the role of budgetary arbiter to the prime minister. In his last year of office, when Pompidou was seriously ill and when the prime minister was the ineffectual Pierre Messmer, the minister of finance gained more and more power. That finance minister was Giscard d'Estaing who, when he became President of the Republic, was unwilling to surrender his financial prerogatives. As expected, when he became president he retained tight control over economic and financial policy. His first finance minister, Fourcade, was a personal and political friend who was happy to bend to presidential directives. The reintegration of the French franc into the European monetary snake in July 1975 and the decision to leave it in March 1976 were both presidential decisions. In May 1976 the president publicly committed the government to rejecting an incomes policy, and in the summer of the same year he pushed his reluctant finance minister into pressing ahead with a controversial capital gains tax: he corrected the first draft of the bill, demanded that it be introduced as quickly as possible in parliament and defended it throughout its passage against the hostility of many of his nominal supporters. With the appointment of Raymond Barre as prime minister and finance minister in September 1976 direct presidential economic and financial power weakened somewhat. Nevertheless, the prime minister's resolution in October 1976 to reject a timid wealth tax was first motivated by presidential hostility (the resolution was later reinforced when the Paris stock exchange almost collapsed at the thought of such a revolutionary measure). In the following month, the President of the Republic announced on radio his intention of asking the prime minister to introduce measures to protect people with small savings by a system of indexation. It was perfectly clear that Premier Barre could pursue the main lines of his liberal economic strategy only with presidential approval.

It was felt that with the election of Mitterrand in May 1981 presidential control over economic and financial affairs would weaken: it was certainly thought that the Socialist leader's grasp of complex economic issues was not always evident (he displayed an 'encyclopaedic ignorance of economics' according to one wry observer) and he had always been visibly uncomfortable when discussing them. Yet the evidence was at variance with the expectation. The devaluations of October 1981 and June 1982 were certainly decided by the president. Mitterrand also sternly 'invited' the government to restrict the size of the budget deficit in 1981, and decided in 1982 that the reduction of the official working week from forty to thirty-nine hours should involve the workers in no loss of pay. In 1983 Mitterrand was once again in the centre of economic policy-making and had to arbitrate in the debate which divided the advocates of the open market and those who favoured greater protectionism. After initially supporting the latter he backed the former. It was arguably Mitterrand's single most important economic decision. From 1983 to 1986 the president threw his full weight behind the 'modernizers', the liberalizers, the deregulators such as Prime Minister Fabius and Finance Minister Bérégovoy, although his unilaterally decided policy statements could cause both some discomfort. Such was the case in 1984 when he announced a reduction of one per cent in the overall tax burden for the following year.

French industrial policy-making also reflected presidential ideas. The first two presidents of the Fifth Republic actively pursued policies for the restructuring of French industry: massive subsidies and tax incentives were given to encourage the formation of giant industrial complexes which were equipped for European and international competition. President Giscard d'Estaing, on the other hand, seemed to be keener on helping small and medium-sized industries, and in March 1976 announced several measures to help them. The first two presidents also had a penchant for projects which they assumed would add to French prestige: their support for massive and prestigious projects such as the petrochemical complex at Fos (an industrial, social and ecological disaster), their attempt through large-scale office-building in the Défense area of Paris to make the French capital the business centre of Europe, and their obstinate defence of projects such as Concorde and the Channel tunnel reflected this preoccupation. President Giscard d'Estaing had a healthy disregard for such considerations, and his decision to scrap several prestige projects (including a particularly expensive and nasty aerotrain which was axed almost immediately) was helped by the changed economic circumstances when the folly of such projects became more apparent. The differences in policy between General de Gaulle and President Giscard d'Estaing were most clearly marked in their approach to the computer industry. It was de Gaulle who personally decided in 1967, for political reasons, to create the *Compagnie Internationale pour l'Informatique* (CII), an exclusively French computer complex which he protected against its own inefficiency and savage American competition by subventions and guaranteed orders. The purpose of the move was to protect the home computer industry, since de Gaulle was rightly convinced that an independent defence policy was dependent upon the existence of a national computer industry. Eight years later, in May 1975, after months of tergiversation, President Giscard d'Estaing personally decided to authorize the dismantling of the CII in its existing form and its merger with the American-dominated firm of Honeywell-Bull. The personal nature of the decision was underlined in the *communiqué* which accompanied the announcement of the measure.

It was not at all surprising that President Mitterrand should take a close interest in industrial policy-making, for he had expressed constant concern at the de-industrialization of the French economy which had taken place in the 1960s and the 1970s and had insisted that his predecessor's purely financial strategy for improving the economy should be replaced by an 'industrial strategy'. His interest has been expressed in many ways. In the nationalization debates of 1981 it was the president who took the final decision over which private banks had to be nationalized, over the nature of compensation to be paid, over the decision-making structures of the newly nationalized industries and over the appointments to their top management posts. It was Mitterrand who decided that the state should take over the nationalized firms completely, and not by a 51 per cent stake, as was being urged by moderates in the government. Such concern was not unexpected, since the president attached great importance to the role of the extended state sector in renovating the French economy. Similarly, the increase in the research budget of the state must be seen as one of the president's priorities in his ambition to make France 'the Japan of Western Europe' (a task, it must be recognized, which would be much easier if the French were Japanese). Further examples of presidential industrial policy-making include Mitterrand's decision to push ahead with the particularly costly restructuring of the steel industry in April 1984 ('I shall accept the particular consequences of this choice', he told the Council of Ministers), his arbitration in

December 1985 over the restructuring of the telecommunications industry, and his support for the Channel tunnel.

Political, social and environmental questions

President Giscard d'Estaing was elected in May 1974 on a programme of reforms (although not *for* a programme of reforms, since the great majority of his supporters were for the *status quo* and voted for him because he was likely to do less damage than François Mitterrand, his Left-wing opponent). In three areas at least – the political, the social and the environmental – he kept some of his promises, and it would be churlish to deny his early achievements in that area. Among the political reforms introduced after May 1974 were the reduction in the voting age to 18, and a no less welcome reduction in telephone-tapping, which had become very widespread in the last years of Pompidou's presidency. Political asylum was made easier, the police were told to make their presence less felt in the streets of Paris, and Left-wing newspapers were allowed into army messes (*Charlie-Hebdo*, an extreme Left-wing satirical newspaper, celebrated with a provocative and indelicate headline: *Merde à l'Armée*). Of greater significance was the presidential decision to provide access to the Constitutional Council to members of parliament who are concerned about the constitutionality of an act. The president also announced that no one would be pursued in the courts for politically motivated attacks upon him. The general effect of these early political reforms was to give a more liberal hue to the régime.

Giscard d'Estaing's record in the social field was somewhat less impressive. Presidential *intentions* were made clear when he appointed ministers for prison, immigrant and feminine affairs and nominated Jean-Jacques Servan-Schreiber, a vociferous political maverick, to the post of Minister of Reforms. Although the latter was to survive less than a fortnight (he publicly denounced government nuclear defence policy) some reforms were quickly forthcoming. Female contraception was legalized, abortions legally authorized, divorce made easier. Limited but unpopular measures were also taken to make life a little more bearable in French prisons. In all these measures, the President of the Republic took a keen and courageous interest: he annotated and amended the first divorce bill sent to him by the Minister of Justice, and he had frequently to back the Minister of Health in her struggle against conservative members of parliament. However, it was the same president who was to change the image of the régime, particularly in the last two years of his office. For a variety of reasons he pursued a much more conservative line, especially in the field of law and order: one bill, for example, was rejected by the Constitutional Council for infringing individual rights, while another, the infamous *Sécurité et Liberté* Law of June 1980 (which tightened up penalties, restricted the powers of the judiciary and singularly limited the rights of the defence) was steam-rollered through a reluctant parliament and in the teeth of vociferous opposition from large sections of the legal community.

President Giscard d'Estaing's concern with environmental issues was dictated both by electoral pressures and by personal taste. He shared with a growing number of his compatriots an anxiety about the insensitive damage being inflicted on large parts of France. The beauty of major cities such as Lyons was being destroyed by massive building programmes in which good taste was not always the most striking characteristic. Uncontrolled industrial expansion had turned the outskirts of most major French towns into dreary, ill-equipped and crime-ridden dormitories. Paris and the Paris region were specially badly affected and the wave of speculative building was so uncontrolled and often so flagrantly illegal that one critic could describe the region as 'a Far West without a sheriff'. Elsewhere, building permits allowed the construction of barbarisms such as Basque villas on the Brittany coast and Alpine chalets in the Auvergne. Areas such as the Mediterranean coast became the particular targets for speculative and frequently illegal horrors. The President of the Republic acted quickly in this domain. In June 1974, barely a month after his election, he effectively sabotaged the extension fo the Left-bank motorway in Paris by withdrawing state aid for the project (the area affected is now being turned into gardens). This especially outrageous piece of urban vandalism had enjoyed the active encouragement of President Pompidou. Two months later, in August 1974, Giscard d'Estaing scrapped the plans for an International Commercial Centre in Paris, a huge slab of concrete nastiness which was scheduled to replace Les Halles, the old fruit and vegetable market in the heart of Paris. Later measures revealed the president's continuing concern for environmental issues. In two open letters to the prime minister in September 1974 and January 1975, he clearly defined his objectives and priorities for Paris and the Paris region. In April 1975 an interministerial council, chaired by the president, decided to limit the growth of the Paris region, to reduce the urban motorway programme and to develop the public transport system. The 1975 Land Act and the Law on Nature Protection of the same year (a project which had been gathering dust on the shelves of the Ministry of Environment for the previous five years) were both presidential initiatives to limit environmental damage and to ensure greater public control over, and participation in, urban development. Later, in July 1975 and in June 1976, in open letters to the prime minister, the president clearly indicated his preference for a new urban policy and insisted on the introduction of new measures (such as limiting the height of new buildings) to prevent France from becoming 'uglier' (*l'enlaidissement de la France*). In a similar letter in October 1976, he insisted that twenty hectares of La Villette be made into a public garden and in February 1977 he launched his 'ecological charter' in which he reasserted his concern for environmental issues.

Presidential interest in political, social and environmental matters was even intensified with the election of François Mitterrand, who was committed to a policy of *changement*. In his first term of office he supported his governments through a programme of reform which involved a distinct liberalization of the régime: increased powers were given to the localities; the rights of immigrant workers were strengthened; the state-run media were reorganized and a more impartial watch-dog body created; French citizens were given the right to go directly to the European Court of Justice; the death penalty was abolished; political asylum was ensured and extradition made difficult; the bitterly disliked Court of State Security was abolished; the plan to introduce computerized identity cards abandoned; and two particularly repressive law and order measures of previous Right-wing governments were repealed. In all these measures the hand of the President of the Republic could be perceived, often by the process of publicized arbitration: for instance, he publicly backed the liberals of the government against his Minister of Justice on the issue of the abolition of the Court of State Security (the minister merely wished to modify its functioning, not abolish it).

Interventions of a sporadic nature

Apart from the above-named areas in which presidential interest was pervasive and constant, and intervention frequent, there were other areas in which the president might intervene on specific occasions. This occurred in a number of cases. The first case was when ministers reached deadlock, as was the case in 1967 when de Gaulle decided to introduce paid advertising on state-run television. Since the Socialist government between 1981 and 1983 proved divided on a number of important issues President Mitterrand had to intervene to impose a decision: the abandoning of the vast military camp at Larzac (the great battlefield for the environmentalists during the 1970s) was decided by the president who backed his Prime Minister against his minister of defence; he backed a junior minister against the Minister of Industry over the vexed issue of abandoning the nuclear power station at Plogoff in Brittany (another target for the environmentalists); he supported the Minister of Culture against the Minister of the Interior over the control of subsidies to local and regional cultural initiatives; in November 1985 he imposed on a divided government his own choice of companies to take over the new privately run television channel.

The second case of sporadic presidential interventionism arose when the problem proved particularly intractable because of the interests at stake. It was President de Gaulle who swept aside the objections of a powerful network of pressure groups in 1959 and decided that the wholesale meat and vegetable markets should be moved from the centre of Paris to the wind-swept wastes of Rungis in the suburbs, and it was President Giscard d'Estaing who, in October 1975, personally took the final decision to move an unwilling *École Polytechnique* out of Paris to the suburbs. Mitterrand's decision to locate a major nuclear research installation at Grenoble and not Strasburg provides another example of sporadic policy-making. Such questions may seem minor, but decisions had been held up by powerfully entrenched groups (in the case of the renovation of Les Halles for nearly forty years!) and presidential authority was required to impose them.

The third case in which the president was likely to intervene in an area not normally belonging to his domain was when an issue became politically explosive. General de Gaulle's decisions, during the stormy events of May 1968, to reform the higher education system and to introduce regional reforms both fall within this category. In both cases de Gaulle was responding to what he considered to be a widespread yearning for greater participation in decision-making – a yearning he discerned in the protests, the demands and the slogans of those troubled days of May 1968. In the passage of the educational reforms the President of the Republic had to throw all his personal authority and support behind Edgar Faure, the Minister of Education, who was under constant attack from the government's own parliamentary supporters. The regional problem plagued successive presidents of the Republic. President Pompidou sabotaged his own prime minister's ambitious regional plans, and the conservative and prudent regional law of July 1972 reflected the president's own sceptical views on the subject. His successor was no more adventurous, and in spite of promises made during the election campaign, Giscard d'Estaing continued his predecessor's very conservative policy. President Mitterrand, on the other hand, encouraged a fairly radical programme of regionalization as part of a much wider decentralization programme. The best example of Mitterrand's intervention to defuse a politically explosive situation was in July 1984 when he personally withdrew a bill on private education that had brought thousands of Catholics on to the streets. Alain Savary, the minister responsible for the bill, and Prime Minister Mauroy were informed of the decision less than one hour before the rest of the nation. The minister resigned. But the situation was defused.

The fourth area of presidential intermittent intervention concerned issues which *threatened to become* politically explosive. Thus Giscard d'Estaing interfered in detailed fashion in the drafting of the June 1975 Secondary Education Act, even though, according to the Minister of Education, the President of the Republic was responsible only for the general guidelines of the bill: in a nation where students can and do paralyse universities and where school children have a penchant for rowdy and sometimes violent street demonstrations, the country's chief political leader can scarcely afford to ignore what is going on in the field of education. Smaller yet no less revealing examples of presidential intervention in politically delicate situations occurred in 1976 when Giscard d'Estaing personally prevented the building of the controversial toll booths on the A4 motorway, and in 1981 when Mitterrand publicly rebuked a minister who had fixed the day for the official commemoration of the end of the Algerian war on the date which angered the electorally influential *pieds noirs* (the French who lived in North Africa, most of whom returned to France after independence was granted to the various North African countries): the rebuke was followed by a change of date. In the following year Mitterrand met leaders of the FNSEA, the major farmers' union, after several minor riots and a major demonstration, to 'dissipate the farmers' malaise, and to establish the bases for a group–state dialogue'.

The personal domain

The fifth and final category of presidential interventionism involved issues related to the personal predilections of the president. Often the president wished to satisfy a whim, and the fact that he could do so was the ultimate proof of his authority. Examples abound: President de Gaulle had the convicted murderer Gaston Dominici released from prison after seeing the sad old man on television, while Georges Pompidou protected the study of Latin and Greek in French *lycées*. Giscard d'Estaing's many whims included an insistence on a change of tempo of the Marseillaise, the French national anthem, when it was played on official occasions (his successor personally insisted on reverting to the traditional tempo). Giscard d'Estaing also raised such vital questions as the type of trees to be planted in the Place des Vosges, one of the capital's most beautiful squares, the need to modernize the French telephone directories, the type of evening dresses to be worn by women generals, and even the kind of uniform suitable for the female traffic wardens of Paris – a relentless and unforgiving breed, worthy heiresses of the *tricoteuses* of the revolutionary period. President Mitterrand's personal tastes have been given concrete expression on several occasions. Perhaps the most revealing example occurred in October 1981 when he successfully intervened to exempt all art objects from the scope of the wealth tax then going through parliament, even though the minister, the *rapporteur* of the Budget Committee and the chairman of the Socialist Party parliamentary group were opposed to such an exemption. The cultural tastes of successive presidents have always been evident: Pompidou, for example, had the Centre Beaubourg (now renamed the Centre Pompidou) – that immensely successful architectural perversion – built in the heart of revolutionary Paris, while Giscard d'Estaing, a man of quieter taste, personally insisted on the transformation of the disused Orsay railway station into a museum devoted to nineteenth-century art. Mitterrand insisted – eventually successfully – that the Ministry of Finance vacate those parts of the Louvre it occupied to make way for an extension of the museum, and he personally chose the architect Pei to design the controversial glass pyramid for one of the courtyards of the Louvre. He also gave the go ahead for the building of an opera house at the Bastille and a major new museum at La Villette. At the time of his re-election in 1988, the *chantiers du président* in Paris were the increasingly visible manifestations of his first *septennat*.

A generation after the foundation of the Fifth Republic the presidency had clearly established itself as the main centre of decision-making in France. The president might not be, as was asserted by one French writer, 'omniscient, omnipresent and omnipotent', but his power was considerable and his influence all-pervasive: he was head of state, the *de facto* head of the government, the unofficial leader of a party coalition and the nation's ultimate policy-maker. Presidential intervention affected all areas of public and private life, as roles assigned to others were gradually usurped by the president, aided by his personal staff and his ministers. Successive presidents did not hesitate to impose their policies on their prime ministers or publicly to contradict their ministers. It was presidential encroachment upon the prime ministerial domain which eventually provoked the resignation of Prime Minister Jacques Chirac in the summer of 1976.

Presidential power was rooted in many factors: in the constitutional texts and in their pro-presidential interpretation, in his direct election by the people, in his patronage, in the loyalty of his lieutenants, and, in some instances, in a popularity which transcended the boundaries of his political party support. Yet the power of the presidency, whilst very considerable, rested on precarious constitutional and political foundations and it also depended on the president's willingness to extend his power. In the mid-1980s, political events and personal calculations were to redefine the nature of the presidential office.

The curtailment of presidential power

At about halfway through his first *septennat*, Mitterrand began to redefine the presidential role. He became increasingly absorbed in the areas of defence, foreign affairs and Europe, and withdrew somewhat from direct involvement in domestic questions. A combination of factors contributed to this redefinition. First, he became genuinely more interested in the 'regalian' functions of the state: its independence, integrity and place in the world and in Europe. Second, he became increasingly aware of the centrality of the 'Matignon machine' (the prime minister's office) in terms of policy coordination and implementation and disliked the electorally harmful bickering between the staffs of the executive dyarchy. Third, after an initial period of highly publicized divisions, the Mauroy government became progressively more cohesive: presidential arbitration was, therefore, less essential. Fourth, with the implementation of the major Socialist reforms in the first two years of office there were fewer contentious issues to attract presidential arbitration. The final – and perhaps most important factor – was that he was aware that too close an identification with domestic policy in a period of recession was electorally damaging. The result was that the prime minister and the government were given increasing freedom in domestic matters: the Fabius government of 1984-86 particularly was accorded a degree of autonomy rarely enjoyed by its predecessors. There was, in the phrase of Olivier Duhamel, 'a governmentalization of politics', and this may be seen in a number of ways: in the president refusing to arbitrate in matters that, he claimed, had to be left to the prime minister, and in the number of inter-departmental councils chaired by the president (they became increasingly rare under Mauroy and virtually disappeared under Fabius). Furthermore, from 1984 Mitterrand in his public speeches emphasized that many problems had to be dealt with by the government. Of course, the ultimate authority remained the presidency, but that authority was now being exercised in a more limited and discreet fashion. The period of *cohabitation* which opened after May 1986 did not, therefore, constitute as radical a break as many observers contend. It did, however, signify that the weakening of presidential power was no longer voluntary.

After the victory of the Right-wing coalition in the March 1986 elections, President Mitterrand honoured his declared intention of retaining his office, and, after some discussion with Right-wing leaders, called on Jacques Chirac, the leader of the Right, to form a government. So opened the period of so-called *cohabitation*. It was to last two years, until the re-election of Mitterrand and the appointment of a Socialist prime minister in May–June 1988.

Cohabitation was neither *cogestion* (joint management) nor peaceful co-existence which assumes mutual tolerance and a degree of good-will. Rather, it was a system of conflictual collaboration, based on a sharing of responsibilities for different policy areas. Collaboration was essential since it was embedded in a number of constitutional provisions and because policy areas inevitably overlap. Yet constitutional provisions could be vague, and overlapping policy areas provided the potential for conflict. Conflict was probably inevitable, too, since the president and the prime minister were from opposing political parties and had been rivals for many years. Nevertheless, collaboration was eased by the fact that in some policy areas there was a high degree of consensus. Moreover, during the first year after the March 1986 elections *cohabitation* was highly popular with the French: neither the president nor the prime minister could afford to be seen as willing to destroy it. Finally, conflict was somewhat muted because the president, for reasons of political self-interest, withdrew from too direct an intervention in domestic affairs (a withdrawal which had been taking place before 1986) and because the prime minister could not radically undermine the office of the presidency – a post to which he aspired. However, competition for the presidency also heightened tensions between Mitterrand and Chirac. There was, thus, an uneasy balance: mistrust, wariness and suspicion were the key characteristics of the period.

When Chirac became prime minister and formed a government he made it clear that he had a democratic mandate to govern, that the electors had chosen the programme of the Right and had rejected the policies of the previous five years. And he pointed to articles 20 and 21 of the constitution which gave him authority to govern. Yet it was quickly made clear that the president was not going to be reduced to a purely symbolic or ceremonial role. From the outset he declared that he would respect the choice of the nation and would let France be governed. But he would not remain 'inert', and would try to prevent any measures which called into question the unity of the French and the harmony of France. In a speech on 17 March 1986, he declared that, 'in the task which you have conferred upon me and which I exercise, I shall firmly defend, both inside France and abroad, our freedom and our independence, our commitment to Europe, our place in the world'. For Mitterrand the constitution had invested him with certain powers and he was determined to deploy them. '*La Constitution, rien que la Constitution. Mais toute la Constitution*' he declared. Moreover, there was no question of unravelling *all* the constitutional conventions of the preceding twenty-seven years.

What form, in practice, did *cohabitation* take?

In the first place, constant contact was maintained between prime minister and president through their respective *directeurs de cabinet*, and through regular meetings of experts from the Elysée and Matignon. Important political issues were discussed directly either by telephone or at the meeting that took place between the two men before every council of ministers.

Second, a *modus vivendi* was established on the respective spheres of influence. In domestic affairs the president became a constitutional monarch, with the right to advise, to warn and to be consulted. In foreign and European affairs there was some sharing of responsibilities. And in defence matters, he remained supreme.

In domestic affairs, the President fully exploited his constitutional powers: he negotiated the composition of the government with Chirac and ensured that Jean Lecanuet did not become Foreign Minister and that François Léotard did not get the defence portfolio (both posts were given to technicians); he presided at all councils of ministers (the atmosphere could be frigid on occasions); he appointed his political allies to the Constitutional Council, and did not hesitate to submit to it bills which he considered to be unconstitutional; he slowed down certain civil service appointments (notably in the Interior Ministry) by refusing to give his signature; he invoked Article 13 and refused to sign *ordonnances* on privatization (July 1986), on the redrawing of constituency boundaries for parliamentary elections (October 1986), and on the introduction of more flexible working hours and practices (December 1986); in December 1987 he refused a government request to allow parliament to discuss changing the legal status of Renault, the public sector car group, at an extraordinary session which had been called to debate the financing of political parties;

finally, he invoked his ultimate power, and in June 1988 dissolved a hostile National Assembly.

President Mitterrand could, and did, criticise the Right-wing government over a wide range of issues which included the privatization of one of the state television channels, plans to privatize part of the prison service, government policy in New Caledonia (which, he claimed, favoured the settlers and not the indigenous population), the broadcasting policies of the Right (he questioned the impartiality of the watchdog body which was created by the government), and the planned higher education reforms of 1986-87 (the president made a public appeal for the reforms to be withdrawn). Yet, in domestic matters, Mitterrand could criticise and delay governmental measures, but he could not block them completely. *Cohabitation was to demonstrate that a government with a friendly majority in parliament could displace the president as the centre of domestic decision-making.* Indeed, between March 1986 and May 1988 most major domestic decisions were made either by bilateral discussions between the prime minister and the minister concerned (this was notably the case for macro-economic and financial policy) or in ministerial meetings (*réunions des ministres*) which excluded the president: thus, in 1986, there were ministerial meetings on unemployment (July), drugs (July and September), communications satellites (July) and the financing of Disneyland (August). The Council of Ministers became even more of a rubber stamp than before. Matters were somewhat more complicated in other policy areas.

In foreign and European matters, the president kept a high personal profile, and represented France at international summits and European Council meetings, although the prime minister also attended international gatherings together with the president (they arrived and left separately). The prime minister also had a foreign policy adviser on his staff and was well briefed on foreign and European affairs by a 'diplomatic cell' based on the Matignon. Although the president was an active diplomat there were some decisions which suggested that the major initiative lay with the government and not the president: such was the case of the freeing of the French hostages in the Lebanon in April 1988. Other foreign policy decisions suggested a sharing or a blurring of responsibilities. For instance, both the president and the prime minister claimed responsibility for the refusal, in April 1986, to allow American aircraft to overfly French territory on their way to a bombing raid on Libya. On most major foreign policy and European matters there was little conflict between the president and the government: the 'Gaullist consensus' remained essentially intact.

In October 1986, at the military camp at Caylus, the president told the assembled officers that defence matters remained firmly under presidential control. Any attempt to encroach upon presidential prerogatives in this domain was quickly and firmly resisted. It was the president who decided to withdraw French troops from the Lebanon in April 1986, and to order the sending of French troops to Togo in September of the same year, although in both cases the prime minister was in full agreement. In November 1986 it was the president after a series of meetings of the Defence Council who imposed his views on the Council of Ministers in favour of the underwater element of the French nuclear deterrent. Later, in February 1987, on a visit to the plateau d'Albion – the site of the eighteen ballistic missiles of the French nuclear force – Mitterrand revealed that in discussions with the government he had insisted that the new generation S4 missiles should continue to be sited there (and not mounted on mobile carriers): 'I came down on the side of Albion' [*j'ai tranché en faveur d'Albion*'] he noted. It was, finally, the president who, in the Council of Ministers of 4 March 1987, defined the French position on Soviet proposals on nuclear disarmament in Europe.

During the period of *cohabitation* Mitterrand succeeded in reconciling the irreconcilable. On the one hand he projected himself as the father figure of the French, a man above the political fray, the protector of national unity and harmony, interested only in the higher interests of the nation and resolved to defend them. Thus, in July 1986 he refused to sign the *ordonnance* on privatization on the grounds that French industry was insufficiently protected against foreign domination. On the other hand, Mitterrand clearly intimated his sympathies for the *peuple de gauche*: his refusal, in December 1986, to sign the *ordonnance* on greater flexibility in working hours and practices was motivated by his declared wish not to destroy the *acquis social* (the acquired social rights) of the workers; his highly publicised statement in the same month, that he was 'in tune' with the students who were demonstrating in the streets of Paris against proposed government legislation and his visit, as an act of solidarity, to the family of Malik Ousseline, a young student who was killed during the demonstrations; his reception of a delegation of striking railwaymen in January 1987. He also manifested his attachment to certain humanistic values and freedoms which, he claimed, were essential elements of the Republic. For instance, he criticised, in November 1986, the brutal expulsion by the Interior Ministry of a hundred Mali nationals who were without proper immigration papers. And in the same month he openly attacked draft legislation to reform the rules governing French citizenship. Throughout the period of *cohabitation*, Mitterrand combatted the government's policies in New Caledonia and clearly revealed his sympathies for the FLNKS, the representative of the indigenous Kanaks.

Cohabitation was not a particularly happy episode in the history of the Fifth Republic. It was described by a spokesman of the prime minister as 'rather like a scar – one has to live with it': *cohabitension* was how the ever-inventive *Canard Enchaîné* redefined it. Its popularity with the French waned quickly, and there was widespread relief when it came to an end. Yet the *cohabitation* interlude was to demonstrate the flexibility of the constitutional arrangements: the political crisis that most feared in the event of a Left-wing president being confronted with a Right-wing National Assembly (or vice versa) did not come to pass.

The *cohabitation* interlude also confirmed Mitterrand in his belief that a certain distance from domestic politics and policy-making was essential to the maintenance of the mystique and prestige of his office. After his triumphant re-election in May 1988 he expanded the Élysée staff somewhat, and ensured that some of his allies were given suitable rewards. He also, after the June legislative elections, interfered – successfully – in the choice of the leadership of the Socialist party group in the National Assembly and – unsuccessfully – in the leadership struggle for the Socialist Party (he favoured Fabius, who was beaten by Mauroy). The choice of prime minister was unquestionably that of Mitterrand: Rocard the controversial leader of a minority faction within the Socialist Party owes his office to the president – a fact recognised by all, including the president and the prime minister – and in the choice of ministers, since the president made clear his preferences for the Defence and Foreign Ministries. But he left Rocard great freedom for other portfolios. After the formation of Rocard's second government following the June 1988 elections he let it be known that he disapproved of the appointment of a prominent Centrist to the Labour Ministry, but in other respects Rocard was given a free hand. The early signs suggest that Rocard will be allowed great autonomy in domestic policy – but within the general parameters set by the president. The president may criticise (it was leaked that on the issue of the rate for the new wealth tax he preferred a rate higher than that proposed by the prime minister) and advise (hence his early exhortation to the government to base itself on its own Left-wing constituency) but he is unlikely to become involved too closely in domestic affairs. Throughout his election campaign he had insisted on the need for a better balance between the two arms of the executive: the presidency, he declared, was 'a place for arbitrating major conflicts'.

By June 1988 President Mitterrand had established himself as the ultimate source of authority, supreme in defence, foreign and European affairs and watchful in domestic matters. His party, led by the disciplined and faithful Mauroy, dominated the National Assembly and his close lieutenants were well placed to transmit the presidential will: Claude Estier, chairman of the Socialist group in the Senate, Louis Mermax, chairman of the group in the National Assembly, Robert Badinter, head of the Constitutional Council, were simply the most prominent in a wide network of people faithful to Mitterrand. The 'excessive' presidentialism of the late 1970s and early 1980s was diluted, but its very dilution hinted at greater effectiveness.

5 The "other executive": prime minister and government under the Fifth Republic

The constitution of the Fifth Republic, as already noted, created a twin-headed executive, apportioning powers and responsibilities between president and prime minister in an often vague and potentially conflicting manner. Until 1986 the constitution was interpreted in favour of presidential dominance because political and personal circumstances conspired to do so. Nevertheless, even during this period prime ministerial and governmental subordination to the president did not signify powerlessness, since both enjoyed autonomy and exerted influence in some domestic policy areas. Moreover, towards the end of this period there was a clear tendency towards the "governmentalization" of executive decision-making in domestic affairs. During the period of *cohabitation*, between March 1986 and May 1988 the president retained his supremacy in defence, but had to share his powers in European and foreign affairs, and concede the running of domestic matters to the prime minister and the government. Yet it must be emphasised that the smooth transition from presidential supremacy to prime ministerial dominance in domestic affairs was facilitated by the changes that had already occurred in the latter half of Mitterrand's first *septennat*. It was greatly eased, too, by the existence of the "Matignon machine" – the vast and sprawling administrative empire that co-ordinates and implements policy. The post-1988 balance between president and prime minister is based on a return to the last years of Mitterrand's first term of office: defence, European and foreign affairs to the president; domestic policy to the "other executive". It is within this context of the changing balance within the executive "dyarchy" that the following analysis must be understood.

The prime minister

The prime minister has been described as the chief of the presidential headquarters (René Capitant), as a vice-president (Raymond

Aron), and as the principal executive officer of the president (Marcel Prélot). Other observers have been less charitable. François Mitterrand, when he was an opposition leader, likened the prime minister to a political strip-teaser who, under the greedy eyes of the president, steadily shed the prerogatives clearly conferred upon him by the constitution. He was, of course, not speaking about the period 1986-1988 when the prime minister insisted – successfully – on exercising those prerogatives.

According to the 1958 constitution "the Prime Minister is in general charge of the work of the government": and to that end he is given an impressive list of powers, which include the right to appoint and dismiss ministers, to make appointments to certain top-ranking military and civil servant posts, to replace, in certain circumstances, the President of the Republic as Chairman of the council of ministers and other important committees, to be consulted by the president before the dissolution of the National Assembly or about the application of Article 16 (emergency powers), to ask the Constitutional Council to judge the constitutionality of a law or treaty. He also countersigns measures of the president (except for those expressly requiring no countersignature). In practice, many of the constitutional powers of the prime minister were usurped by the President of the Republic. Nevertheless, even before 1986, the importance of the prime minister should not be underestimated: in public press conferences, successive Presidents of the Republic stressed the significance of the office.

The office of prime minister under the Fifth Republic was initially criticized by defenders of parliamentary government as being weak and ineffectual. Professor Duverger in a celebrated article could even ask whether Michel Debré, the first prime minister, existed. Furthermore, ex-Prime Minister Chirac could declare (in a speech of 16 September 1977) that "when I was Prime Minister I learnt that it [the role of Prime Minister] was very humble [*fort modeste*] and basically called into question [*contesté*]". Yet these were the words of an embittered man whose role as prime minister, though constantly called into question, had been far from humble. In some important respects the prime minister of the Fifth Republic is much more powerful than his predecessors of the Fourth Republic. First, the choice of a Fourth Republic prime minister was often as arcane, as subtle and as mysterious as the election of a modern Pope, with the role of the Holy Ghost being assumed by the very earthly President of the Republic. But the analogy goes no further. Even the present Pope can count upon the loyal support of most of his followers, the unquestioning backing of some and the querulous acceptance of the rest, whereas a prime minister of the Fourth Republic was always the prisoner of the forces that had brought him to power (or rather to office). He was the broker of often violently conflicting interests and of personalities who were united only in their desire for portfolios. He was viewed with envy by all, with suspicion by many (even by members of his own party), and with dislike or contempt by some. Rarely had any prime minister of the Fourth Republic any genuine following in the country: the exceptions were Pinay and Mendès-France. Moreover, gathering popular support could be construed as demagogy, and to the republicans, creatures and victims of their own history, the demagogue inevitably concealed the future dictator. A prime minister of the Fifth Republic is stronger than his predecessors of the Fourth, for he is not constantly absorbed and even exhausted by the task of keeping his government together, and can spend more time on policy-making. Compared with his predecessors before 1958, a prime minister of the Fifth Republic is less plagued by the persistent harassment of his ministerial, party and parliamentary colleagues. Edgar Faure, premier from January to February 1952, claimed he lost four kilos in forty days in his struggle with the Deputies. He is in a stronger position, too, because he enjoys a much longer tenure of office: under the Fourth Republic, a prime minister survived, on average, only six months, whereas since the beginning of the Fifth Republic there have been only ten prime ministers (see Appendix 4). The shortest-lived prime minister of the Fifth Republic survives much longer than the average prime minister of the Fourth, and each has been able to take a longer-term view of his task.

The role of the prime minister under the Fifth Republic has been the subject of a great deal of debate and controversy. When President Giscard d'Estaing declared that the president was responsible for what was "permanent and essential" while the prime minister was in charge of "contingency problems", he was clearly violating the letter and the spirit of the 1958 Constitution. But he was reiterating a doctrine preached and practised by his two predecessors and also by his successor. President Mitterrand, in an interview with the BBC in September 1981, declared that the prime minister was responsible "for the problems of daily life and even for a certain number of big problems" while the president "acts or intervenes for what could be called the major guidelines, the main orientations". In practice, the tasks of the prime minister under the Fifth Republic have been essentially five-fold. The importance of those tasks has varied over time. They are:

● *To ensure the overall co-ordination of government policy.*

- *To provide a constant liaison with parliament to ensure the smooth passage of governmental legislation.*
- *To maintain friendly contact with the biggest party of the government coalition.*
- *To arbitrate between the conflicting claims of the parties of the ruling coalition.*
- *To become the central policy-maker in domestic affairs.* This was, of course, especially important during the period of *cohabitation*, but even during other periods the prime minister has been left great latitude in those numerous areas in which the president has been unable or unwilling to intervene. Moreover, the prime minister has always enjoyed a general influence in the formulation and implementation of presidential policies. Prime Minister Debré took a direct interest in all areas of policy: his tenacious, hard-working, authoritarian and meddlesome methods led to the resignation of at least two disgruntled and exasperated ministers, but they facilitated the pushing through of badly needed reforms in subjects as diverse as state aid to church schools, the transfer of the Paris wholesale meat market from the centre of the capital to a more salubrious site in the Parisian suburbs, the reduction in the brewing of home-made alcohol, and the thorny problem of ex-servicemen's pensions, all subjects which had confounded previous administrations. Prime Minister Pompidou was more discreet, but he insisted on seeing all files, and, like Debré and Raymond Barre, played an important (arguably predominant) role in shaping French economic and financial policies during his premiership: it is revealing that the economic policies of France during the period 1976 to 1981 were known as *barrisme*. Prime ministers showed a keen interest in particular areas of policy. Chaban-Delmas, in the name of his "new society", took a direct interest in forging better relations with the unions, and was directly responsible for the introduction of workers' educational and training schemes. Jacques Chirac always kept a keen eye on agricultural matters, and on at least one occasion (in June 1975) was able successfully to oppose the Minister of Agriculture who enjoyed the support of the president. Raymond Barre coupled his direct – and influential – interest in economic policy with a constant interest in university matters, while Prime Minister Mauroy was known to be particularly interested in local government matters and his successor, Fabius, in industrial problems.

The prime minister thus provides a two-way channel between the president on the one hand and, on the other, the government, parliament, the ruling party coalition and the administration. In short, he initiates, co-ordinates, arbitrates, conciliates and implements. It is the prime minister who heads France's vast administrative machine: his power over the *implementation* of policies is very much greater than that of the president of the Republic. He is also at the centre of an extensive network of patronage which adds singularly to his power, and he chairs countless inter-ministerial committees which are increasingly more important that the inter-ministerial councils (chaired by the president) as the major decision-makers at political level. The figures are telling. In 1974 there were fourteen permanent inter-departmental committees chaired by the prime minister. By mid-1986 this number had risen to thirty-three (nine were created in 1983). The prime minister also chairs a number of *comités restreints* which are convoked to deal with a specific problem: there were 118 in 1961, 121 in 1971, 120 in 1982, 57 in 1983, 51 in 1984 but only 20 in 1985. However, the main co-ordinating work of the Matignon takes place through the *réunions interministérielles*, which are *ad hoc* meetings of high-ranking civil servants from the ministries affected and which are chaired by a member of the prime minister's staff or by the general secretary of the government. There were 142 such meetings in 1961, 356 in 1965, 592 in 1971, 778 in 1975, 1,129 in 1980, 1,163 in 1981, 1,836 in 1982, 1,500 in 1983, 1,356 in 1984, 1,307 in 1985 and 970 in 1986. The peaks in the numbers of all these meetings in 1982 to 1984 reflect the major reforming activity of the newly elected Left-wing government.

The political and administrative role of the prime minister has always been important, time-consuming and exhausting: Chaban-Delmas described his period in office as "two hundred weeks of work six days a week, fifteen hours a day". It is also fraught with difficulties and it requires great mental and physical stamina to predict and deal with them. The administrative work of the government is left to the General Secretariat of the Government, which was founded in 1935 and which is headed by a secretary general and manned by about forty other civil servants. The secretary general, a high-ranking and politically neutral (but not hostile) civil servant (normally from the Council of State), prepares all ministerial meetings (even those chaired by the President of the Republic), assists at such meetings and ensures that the decisions taken are translated into administrative action, guides their administrative passage into law and ensures their implementation. He also prepares replies to parliamentary questions on government legislation. Between 1945 and 1988 there were only six holders of the office, thus ensuring a high level of continuity in government business. Only once, in 1986, has an incoming government removed a secretary general.

The prime minister is also assisted by a number of junior ministers (whose numbers have varied greatly since 1958) who are attached to his office, and by the heads of a vast array of administrative agencies which are under his control. Finally, the prime minister is provided with the backing of a private staff – his *cabinet*, composed essentially, but not exclusively, of young and able civil servants who act as the eyes and ears of the prime minister. The *cabinet* is usually small – about thirty members, although those of Chaban-Delmas and Mauroy were much bigger. Within the *cabinet* there are always several distinct elements: the purely political element (to look after parliamentary, party, electoral and constituency matters), the policy-making element (to initiate policies or merely supervise those of other ministers), the technical element (for instance, there is always a legal expert, normally from the Council of State, who advises on the legality or constitutionality of the proposed measures), and the secretarial element (which carries out all the clerical work and organizes the prime minister's timetable). Co-ordination between the various elements is ensured by the head – the *directeur* – of the *cabinet*. Prime ministerial *cabinets* have varied greatly in their activity, style and reputation, and they have tended to reflect the personality and tastes of the prime minister. The *cabinet* of Debré was overtly and often ruthlessly interventionist and reformist in certain areas, while that of Pompidou was more conservative and more discreet but equally ubiquitous and reputedly very influential. Messmer's *cabinet* was a lacklustre affair and thus truly reflected the personality of the prime minister. Chaban-Delmas recruited a *cabinet* which quickly gained the reputation of being brilliant, creative, innovatory, active and reforming, and as such was regarded as dangerous, incompetent, meddlesome and socialistic by the president of the Republic and his private staff. By 1972 the prime minister's *cabinet* had grown in both size and prestige, and the emergence of this powerful group constituted a major institutional innovation of the Fifth Republic. Since the dismissal of Premier Chaban-Delmas, however, the power of the prime ministerial *cabinet* appears to have declined. The *cabinets* of Chirac and Barre, although undeniably very competent, were largely administrative and rarely innovatory. Prime Minister Mauroy modelled his *cabinet* on those of his immediate predecessors, although he politicized its composition somewhat by including in it some people who had previously belonged to his powerful local base in the north of France. Chirac's *cabinet* from 1986 to 1988 was dominated by politically sympathetic civil servants but also contained an influential group of *parisiens*, recruited from the Paris town hall which Chirac runs. Apart from his official *cabinet* a prime minister may also be assisted by a group of *officieux* – unofficial aides who are attached to the *cabinet* and specialize in particular policy areas. There were said to be more than a hundred aides in the *cabinets* of Chaban-Delmas and Mauroy. The Matignon is thus an immense machine, "*un gros village*" in the words of Thierry Pfister who worked there for Prime Minister Mauroy. It is the central co-ordinating and implementing instrument of executive domestic policy-making on which both president and prime minister depend.

The power of the prime minister rests not only on political circumstances, on his strategic administrative position or on the ability and activity of his *cabinet* but also on a number of other factors. The first is his own political stature. He must have sufficient force of personality and prestige to enable him to impose his views or judgements upon his ministerial colleagues and his parliamentary and party supporters. He has occasionally to conciliate and arbitrate between the conflicting forces that compose his political backing: this task may involve him in delicate and difficult situations. For most of the Fifth Republic, he has had, for instance, to arbitrate in choosing candidates in the national and local elections, and he has had to define both the strategy and tactics of that coalition. Even Barre, who had openly declared his intention of devoting himself exclusively to economic and financial matters, was quickly drawn into the electoral arena, although with singular lack of success, as the Gaullist Party rejected his political leadership. To succeed, a prime minister requires a good relationship with the dominant party of the government coalition (the Gaullists from 1959 to 1981 and from 1986 to 1988 and the Socialists between 1981 and 1986 and after 1988), and a good working relationship with the other coalition parties: Pompidou and Mauroy had both; Debré and Chirac the latter but not the former; Couve de Murville, Messmer and Fabius had neither, and Barre appeared to have the latter but clearly lacked the former. Rocard may find that he has a more harmonious relationship with his centrist allies than with the Socialist "barons" who dominate his government.

The second main factor which explains the power of a prime minister is the political situation prevailing at the time. Prime Minister Chirac's power between 1986 and 1988 rested on the fact that he, and not the president, was the leader of the dominant party of the victorious coalition in the National Assembly. But he was constantly plagued by sniping criticisms from some of his allies, notably ex-Prime Minister Barre. Before 1974, while the prime minister, the majority of the government and the dominant party of the *majorité* were all Gaullists, political friction between them, although sometimes real, was nonetheless limited. This situation changed when a non-Gaullist president appointed a Gaullist prime minister to head a government dominated by non-Gaullists and to impose its policies upon a parliamentary group still dominated by Gaullists. The prime minister, Chirac, who was the unquestioned leader of the Gaullist Party, was quickly torn between his dual and conflicting loyalties, and resignation was eventually the only way out of the dilemma. The situation after the appointment of Raymond Barre remained conflict-ridden, with ex-Prime Minister Chirac leading a Gaullist Party which, until 1981, was the biggest single party in the National Assembly and which was increasingly hostile to President Giscard d'Estaing, unhelpful in its dealings with the prime minister who was not a member of the party, and deeply suspicious of a government which it no longer dominated. With the appointment of Pierre Mauroy as prime minister in May 1981 and the election of a Socialist-dominated National Assembly in the following month, relations between the executive and the legislature improved, particularly as Mauroy had always been a popular, powerful and respected figure in the Socialist Party. Mauroy's successor, Laurent Fabius, was powerfully helped by three factors in maintaining some cohesion within the government and between the government, the legislature and the Socialist Party: the unswerving support of the President of the Republic; the setting of a less contentious agenda; the unifying effect of impending elections. The position of Michel Rocard, appointed premier in 1988, is an intrinsically difficult one: he has some following in the country and leads an important minority faction within the Socialist Party, but many of his ministers are wary of him, and the bulk of the Socialist Party suspicious of him.

The final factor which has determined a prime minister's powers for most of the Fifth Republic (the period of *cohabitation* must be excepted) has been the extent of the support given to him by the President of the Republic. The prime minister is, in conformity with the constitution, chosen by the president, and the choice of prime minister has always been a highly personal affair: de Gaulle chose as his prime ministers an unpopular Senator (Debré), an unknown banker (Pompidou) and a professional diplomat, who had been foreign minister for the previous nine years (Couve de Murville). None had any previous experience in the National Assembly to which they were constitutionally responsible. President Giscard d'Estaing, in his appointment in August 1976 of Barre, a university teacher and high-ranking civil servant with no parliamentary experience and no party links, publicly emphasized the personal nature of his choice. With the exception of the nomination of Chirac in March 1986 when the president had no real choice, Mitterrand's selection of prime minister has been a politically dramatized and personal event. Each has been preceded by a period of orchestrated rumour and counter-rumour and calculated suspense. Mauroy, Fabius and Rocard all owed their appointments to the president and all were made aware of the fact. In spite of the constitutional provisions and the early assertions of General de Gaulle, the prime minister is also dismissed by the president. Indeed, the dismissals of Prime Minister Pompidou (who had just led the government forces into a landslide victory at the polls) in June 1968 and of Chaban-Delmas (who had just received an overwhelming vote of confidence by 368 votes to 96 in the National Assembly) in July 1972 were brutal reassertions of presidential supremacy.

For most of the Fifth Republic, the executive has functioned smoothly as the result of a good working relationship between the president and the prime minister based on mutual confidence and what Pompidou described as "a wide-ranging identity of views". This does not mean that the president must always take the prime minister into his confidence: Debré was invariably kept in the dark over President de Gaulle's intentions in Algeria; Pompidou was not warned at all about de Gaulle's mysterious and dramatic trip to Germany in May 1968 when the country appeared to be on the verge of anarchy; Chirac was always kept by Giscard d'Estaing in complete ignorance over foreign policy and European policy; Mauroy was not informed of the withdrawal of the controversial bill on private education in July 1984 until only one hour before Mitterrand broadcast the news to the nation; Fabius publicly confessed his "*trouble*" (upset) on learning – through a news agency - of the visit to Paris of Polish dictator Jeruzelski. Nor, as shall be seen, does a good working relationship signify that there can be no differences of opinion on particular subjects. But if presidential support of the prime minister is seen to be *generally* lukewarm or hesitant the latter's position is seriously weakened and ultimately untenable. The suspicion felt by the highly conservative President Pompidou towards Chaban-Delmas's reformist ideas was public knowledge, and was exploited both by the Élysée staff and by the prime minister's party adversaries. The resignation of Chirac in 1976 was motivated by his feeling that the president was "depriving him of the means of carrying out his functions" (Chirac's own phrase) and was giving him insufficient backing in his struggle with his ministers: in the six months before his resignation, the president had reshuffled the government without fully consulting him, had rejected his request for an early election and had backed the finance minister against him in a number of budgetary disputes. Rocard's past record of troubled relations with the president does not augur well for his premiership: from the outset a certain mutual wariness has characterized the relationship.

Generally, the president has been able to assert his ultimate supremacy over the prime minister, but the situation altered between 1986 and 1988 when the prime minister, backed by a majority of the National Assembly, had views which radically conflicted with those of the president, and insisted on his constitutional right to impose them. Such a situation may well recur if the Left wins a general election during a Right-wing presidency or the Right during a Left-wing presidency. The relationship between the president and the prime minister, even if they do enjoy a "wide-ranging identity of views", is, in the very nature of things, complex and troubled. The *Canard Enchaîné*, a Left-wing satirical weekly, put it nicely:

> A Prime Minister must have no merits....He must take responsibility for all errors, especially if they are those of the President. He must not fail, otherwise he runs the risk of being sacked or being forced to resign for incompetence. Still more, he must not succeed, for to do so would be the ultimate impertinence, and his disgrace would then be even more terrible....A Prime Minister must maintain himself as an honest, active and competent mediocrity, half-way between obvious failure which would harm the President and striking success which would put the President in the shadows.

The prime minister faces a number of dilemmas: if he succeeds and is popular he may be seen as a rival but if he fails he will be considered incapable; if, like Pompidou or Chirac, he is a strong personality (which is required for him successfully to carry out his many duties) then conflict with the president may prove chronic and even acute; on the other hand, if, like Couve de Murville or Messmer, he is a weak personality he will avoid clashes with the president but may lack the forcefulness successfully to pursue his many demanding duties. For the President of the Republic, the ideal prime minister must be omnipresent but self-effacing, powerful but discreet, forceful but conciliatory, acceptable but not too popular. In short, he must combine strength with subordination – a combination more readily found in saints than in ambitious politicians. What is clear is that an unpopular prime minister can be a serious liability. The unpopularity of Raymond Barre, prime minister from 1976 to 1981, was certainly a factor which contributed to the defeat of President Giscard d'Estaing at the polls in May 1981, for instead of becoming a political shield for the president (one of the essential functions of any prime minister), screening him from public disgruntlement, he became an added source of presidential unpopularity: he aggravated rather than attenuated public resentment towards the president. The experience of Barre suggests that a president must know not only whom to appoint as prime minister but also when to dismiss him.

The government

Nowhere is the gap between constitutional theory and presidential practice greater than in the formation and functioning of the government. According to the 1958 constitution, the government "decides and directs" the policies of the nation, and has at its disposal the administration and the armed forces. Its members are proposed by the prime minister to the President of the Republic, who appoints them. In principle, the government is a collective body of ministers, responsible to the National Assembly which is empowered to force it out of office. In practice, for most of the Fifth Republic the government has been yet another instrument of presidential government, with its members reduced to the role of presidential advisers. In that sense, the French government came to resemble the cabinet of the American president. The control of the president over the government between 1959 and 1986 may be seen in several ways:

- *The president appointed and dismissed its head, the prime minister.*
- *The president openly fixed the agenda and timetable of the Council of Ministers and determined the programme of the government.* This was done during the presidency of Giscard d'Estaing by way of "directive letters" to the prime minister: twenty-five such letters were sent, seventeen relating to specific questions, twelve to the general lines of the policy to be pursued. President Mitterrand abandoned this practice, but between 1981 and 1986 he constantly reminded the French that his election pledges – and they alone – constituted "the charter for governmental action", and both he and his ministers acted upon that understanding.
- *The president determined the size and shape of the government.* Thus, the shape of the government formed under Giscard d'Estaing reflected the preoccupation of the president: in May 1974 he appointed junior ministers for penal reform, feminine affairs and immigrant affairs, three areas where he hoped to introduce reforms. In December 1976, without informing the prime minister, he created a post of junior minister for industrial affairs in order to relieve the minister (a political

friend who was totally absorbed in the Paris elections) of his heavy departmental duties. The creation of new ministries after the election of Mitterrand in May 1981 reflected some of the new priorities of the president.

- *The president intervened directly and increasingly in the choice of individual ministers*. President Giscard d'Estaing made no attempt to disguise his direct interference in ministerial appointments and even went so far as to comment upon them on television. But he merely extended and made more open the practice of his two predecessors. There were several instances of the president nominating ministers who were viewed with frank disapproval by the prime minister: the most striking cases include those of Jean-Jacques Servan-Schreiber, the *enfant terrible* of French politics, who was appointed to a newly created Ministry of Reforms in May 1974 against the better judgement of the prime minister; of Jean Françoise-Poncet, a well-known anti-Gaullist, who was made junior minister at the Quai d'Orsay in January 1976 and minister of Foreign Affairs in November 1978. The choice of individual ministers in the Mauroy and Fabius governments was very clearly determined after direct and close consultation with President Mitterrand who insisted on the inclusion of his close allies such as Hernu and Fabius and the exclusion of others such as Georges Marchais, the Communist leader, in 1981.
- *The president determined the political balance of the government*. President Pompidou always insisted on the political predominance of the Gaullist Party, while his successor clearly worked to reduce Gaullist representation in the Council of Ministers: in the first government formed under Giscard d'Estaing's presidency, only a third of the members belonged to the Gaullist Party, compared with two-thirds in the last government formed under Pompidou. In the Barre government, formed in August 1976, the Gaullist Party not only lost the premiership but was given only five of the eighteen portfolios, and only four of the eighteen junior ministers were members of the party. The president also clearly attempted to displace the political axis of the government towards the centre Left. The political balance of Left-wing governments under the Mitterrand presidency was openly dictated by the president. The Mauroy governments were composed of representatives of the political coalition which brought the president to power: it was certainly Mitterrand who, in 1981, decided to include Communists in the government and who determined the representation of the various factions of the Socialist Party in it.

● *The president treated the government not as a collective body responsible to the national Assembly, but as a group of individuals responsible to himself.* Indeed, General de Gaulle in his *Mémoires* was specific on that point: "when one is a minister, it is to de Gaulle and to him alone that one is responsible". And Pompidou, Giscard d'Estaing and Mitterrand never failed to act upon that unconstitutional assumption.

Two studies of the ministers of the Fifth Republic before the election of Mitterrand to the presidency, by Pascale and Jean-Dominique Antoni and by William Andrews, noted that they were predominantly male, married, middle-aged, bourgeois (with a sprinkle of aristocrats), northern French and well-educated (generally at the Paris Law Faculty and/or the Institute of Political Sciences), and they had many links with established political, administrative, financial and economic elites. Socialist ministers after 1981 have been strikingly similiar in many respects, although they tend to be less wealthy, more southern and less connected with the financial elites. Compared with ministers of the Fourth Republic those of the Fifth have lacked parliamentary experience: indeed, several had no parliamentary experience at all before becoming ministers. The first governments of the Fifth Republic had a high proportion of non-parliamentary ministers, although by 1974 such appointments had become very rare. The practice was revived by President Giscard d'Estaing: in the Barre government, formed in August 1976, six of the eighteen ministers and six of the eighteen junior ministers were chosen from outside parliament. Successive Socialist governments have also contained relatively large numbers of non-parliamentarians (see pages below). Another interesting fact to emerge from the studies is that before 1981 half the ministers had started their careers in the civil service, a proportion which dropped somewhat thereafter but still remained high. Hence the complaints of the *fonctionnarisation du pouvoir politique* which have frequently been made during the Fifth Republic.

Under the Fifth Republic, it would be misleading to refer to the power of the government, since, in practice, it exercises no *collective* power at all. This had led certain commentators to dismiss ministers as "the little toy soldiers of the President", and as sycophantic executants of presidential whims. Such a view would be equally misleading, since certain ministers exercise considerable power, and the extent of that power depends upon the interplay of several factors:

● *The degree of interest displayed by the President of the Republic or the prime minister in the affairs of the ministry.* As already noted, the interest of the President of the Republic in certain areas is intense and continuous and precludes any initiative on the part of ministers. President de Gaulle could even keep a minister in the dark about matters concerning his own department: the Minister for Algerian affairs learned through the newspapers of the details of a secret deal which de Gaulle had concluded with the Algerian liberation fighters. As previously indicated, some prime ministers (such as Debré) meddled in all governmental matters, some (such as Pompidou and Chirac) were interested in specific areas of governmental policy while others (Couve de Murville and Messmer), by taste or necessity, left a great deal of discretion to ministers. Prime Minister Barre was too absorbed in economic and financial matters to have time to interfere too much elsewhere, although he was reputed to have intervened on several occasions in university matters. His successors Pierre Mauroy and Laurent Fabius left a great deal of initiative to individual ministers, but because the government was divided on many issues their role as inter-ministerial arbitrator was strengthened.

● *The support of the president of the Republic or prime minister*. Some ministers have clearly enjoyed a privileged relationship with the president. It was said by Prime Minister Pompidou of Malraux, who was Minister of Culture for ten years, that he was so little gifted for action that he was incapable of posting a letter without tying himself in knots. Malraux spent all his time in the Council of Ministers scribbling immensely elaborate and psychologically revealing doodles. Yet with the active and unflagging support of President de Gaulle Malraux was able successfully to pursue his policies of creating *Maisons de Culture* (cathedrals of enlightenment in the French provincial desert), defending ancient monuments and cleaning Paris. Successive presidents of the Republic seem to have had a *faible* for their minister of culture: Jean-Philippe Lecat had a close relationship with Giscard d'Estaing (he had worked previously in the president's private office), while Jack Lang clearly enjoys the powerful protection of Mitterrand. Chirac, as Minister of Agriculture and later as Minister of the Interior, enjoyed a warm and close personal relationship with President Pompidou (who referred to him as his bulldozer) while Poniatowski – *le Prince* – enjoyed similiar *rapports* with President Giscard d'Estaing. The latter also protected the unrepentant and pugnacious minister responsible for university affairs (Alice Saunier-Seïté) against the wrath of the prime minister and enabled her to pursue most of her highly controversial policies. Presidential support may be vital: according to Michel Jobert in his *Mémoires d'avenir*, it enabled the finance minister to get his way against the prime minister in 1965. It also helped Edgar Faure to push through his much contested Education Act of 1968, and was essential to the ministers of justice and of health in 1974 and 1975 when the government parties were clearly unhappy about their proposed reforms of the divorce and abortion laws. Mitterrand has always had several *favoris* to whom he has given undue influence: they have included not only Jack Lang as Minister for Culture but also Charles Hernu, his first Defence Minister, Pierre Bérégovoy at Social Affairs and then as Finance Minister, Laurent Fabius as Industry Minister, and Gaston Defferre as Interior Minister. Defferre's vast programme of decentralisation and Fabius' major projects for restructuring French industry were greatly facilitated by presidential backing. When Chirac ran the government between 1986 and 1988 he had an inner cabinet which included notably, Edouard Balladur the Finance Minister, Alain Juppé Junior Minister at the Finance Ministry and Charles Pasqua, the over-active Interior Minister.

●   *The minister's conception of his role.* Some ministers view their role as essentially technical and managerial, and become the faithful and faceless executors of the presidential will. Since 1958 several professional diplomats have been promoted to the post of minister of foreign affairs. Each, with the exception of Claude Cheysson, Mitterrand's first Minister of Foreign Affairs, was noticeable by making himself unnoticeable, carrying diplomatic discretion to the lengths of total self-effacement. Other ministers, however, have left reputations as able and active reformers: Edgar Faure at Education, Debré at Defence, Chalandon at Public Works, Ségard at Foreign Trade, Pisani at Agriculture, Defferre at Interior, Badinter at Justice, Fabius at Industry. A determined and skilful minister with an ambitious programme can easily establish a reputation for himself. The case of Gaston Defferre, the ambitious, brutal and resolute Minister of the Interior who was appointed in May 1981, is very revealing in that respect: his wide-ranging proposals for decentralization were pushed through in a way which won him no love but great respect.

●   *The political weight of the minister.* Some ministers, especially the non-parliamentary ministers, lack the political influence and "punch" of their colleagues. Much of Giscard d'Estaing's influence as minister of finance (a post he occupied for many years) sprang not only from his technical and financial expertise but also from his leadership of one of the parties of the governing coalition. Many ministers buttress their position (particularly within their own ministries) by acquiring political positions. And one of the more interesting political phenomena of the Fifth Republic has been the number of ministers of purely technocratic background who have sought local political office and party positions. It is eloquent testimony to the need for a minister to acquire political credibility and stature.

● *The minister's tenure of office.* The longer a minister remains in office the more likely is he to be able to carry out his own policies. Malraux, Minister of Culture from 1959 to 1969, was clearly in a happier position to initiate policies than any of his successors, who have survived, on average, for little more than a year. Under the Fifth Republic, certain ministries (notably Defence and Foreign Affairs) have been "stable" while others have been much less so: during de Gaulle's presidency there were only two ministers of foreign affairs but twelve ministers of education and eleven ministers of information. During the period of the seventh five-year plan there were no fewer than four ministers of labour, and during the critical years 1981 to 1983 the Industry Ministry changed hands four times. Several ministers have spent remarkably little time in a particular ministry: in 1974 Jean-Jacques Servan-Schreiber was dismissed after only eight days as minister for his criticisms of the French nuclear deterrent, and in 1988 Léon Schwartzenberg was removed after less than one week as Health Minister for his remarks about drug addiction and AIDS. Ministerial instability during the Fifth Republic may be seen in the fact that reshuffles are so frequent: more than sixty between January 1959 and June 1988.

● *The prestige and power of the ministry.* Certain ministries, notably Industry, Interior and Finance, enjoy a very high reputation and confer upon their political head an undeniable prestige. Other ministries, such as Education and Agriculture, are considered as "the graveyards of political ambitions", while others, such as the short-lived Ministry for Feminine Affairs, suffer from a weak administration, lack of adequate financial resources, an ill-defined scope of action and the scepticism of other ministries.

● *The strength of the administrative services of the ministry.* This factor raises the question of the autonomy of the administration and its power to resist the will of politicians. The administrative services of the Quai d'Orsay are known to be fairly weak while those of Education, Finance and Industry have the reputation of being very powerful. It requires a minister with ambition, ruthlessness and longevity to impose his policies upon these latter ministries.

● *The efficiency of his own private staff (cabinet ministériel)*. The minister's *cabinet* is composed of a small group of individuals, drawn mainly from the civil service, whose task is to provide the link between the worlds of politics and administration. The *cabinet* is the minister's brains trust, adviser and negotiator. It ensures that the ministry is sensitive to the political exigencies of the minister and that the minister is not impervious to the requirements of the ministry. It also looks after the minister's local responsibilities, provides a permanent liaison with parliament and ensures a constant link (often through their personal relations) with other *cabinets*. *Cabinets* vary enormously: some are timid, self-effacing and dominated by the administration, while others are dynamic, interventionist and highly effective. Some see themselves as the provider of ideas while others view their role as essentially managerial. There is, in truth, an infinite variety of *cabinets* and it is difficult to generalize about them, but a well-organized, determined and sensitive *cabinet* may be a powerful support for a minister.

The power of individual ministers depends, therefore, on a number of factors. Some ministers may justifiably be described as "little toy soldiers" while others are powerful and highly susceptible political figures. The president's view of the government is profoundly ambivalent: Mitterrand, like his three predecessors, insists that the government is a team and he places a premium upon its "unity, cohesion, and harmony", yet he persists in treating it as an assembly of individuals, all beholden to himself alone.

The president of the Republic meets his ministers in a number of circumstances, and often in ways which appear designed to emphasize their non-collective nature. For although he meets them at official Councils of Ministers, these tend to be formal and ritualistic occasions for rubber-stamping decisions made elsewhere. This was especially true during the period of *cohabitation*. Between 1981 and 1986 President Mitterrand allowed a freer flow of discussion than under his predecessors, but a minister still generally spoke only when invited, and normally only on his ministry's affairs. The president also meets ministers at inter-ministerial councils held at the Élysée (*conseils restreints*) which are chaired by himself and attended by the prime minister and a selected number of ministers and their top civil servants. These *conseils restreints* were often seen as the real decision-making bodics of the Fifth Republic, and they were certainly used with great frequency: President Pompidou presided over one inter-ministerial council a month while Giscard d'Estaing presided over one a week when Chirac was prime minister (1974-6) and one every two weeks during Barre's premiership (1976-81). Many of the major decisions of the Fifth Republic were taken in these *conseils restreints* and then later presented to a Council of Ministers for formal accept-ance. However, as noted above the number of inter-departmental meetings chaired by the president during Mitterrand's presidency dropped off very sharply after 1984. During the period of *co-habitation, all* important decisions on domestic affairs were taken before the Council of Ministers by various committees chaired by the prime minister or a member of his staff.

The president also meets his ministers at working lunches, at the many ceremonies at which he has to preside, and on his provincial, European or foreign travels (there is always an important contingent of ministers in the presidential delegation). President Giscard d'Estaing also held a number of governmental seminars with his ministers in "an exercise of collective reflection" on the major policies to be pursued. Finally, the president meets members of the government individually: he meets the prime minister at least every week (Giscard d'Estaing had 210 têtes-à-tête with Prime Minister Chirac and 560 with Barre), and once a week he has a working session with the foreign minister, the finance minister and the minister of the interior. President de Gaulle in an impressive calculation noted that in his first term of office (1959 to 1966) he held 320 Councils of Ministers, 420 inter-ministerial councils, he met the prime minister 605 times and other ministers, individually, on nearly 2000 occasions. A breakdown of President Giscard d'Estaing's timetable in 1975 shows that he held 53 Coun-cils of Ministers, 72 *conseil restreints*, 77 working lunches and 195 individual audiences with ministers. President Giscard d'Estaing frequently used the telephone directly to contact his ministers (a device rarely resorted to by his predecessors or his successor). The president is also normally represented (generally by the general secretary of the Élysée) at inter-ministerial committees held at the Matignon, and a member of his personal staff is present at any other important gathering of ministers. Thus the president is informed either directly or indirectly of the activities of all the ministers, and is thus well placed for supervising their work and judging their ability.

The "other executive": some concluding remarks

It is questionable whether the numerous advisers of the executive constitute in any real sense, a team. Indeed it may be argued that

there has emerged around the executive a system of institutionalized tension, a system encouraged, either actively or tacitly, by
successive presidents and prime ministers. This tension manifests
itself at different levels:

● *Between the president and the prime minister.* Even outside
the troubled period of *cohabitation* there have been several
well-publicized differences between the two men. The ever
faithful Debré was known to be hostile to President de
Gaulle's Algerian policy, and voiced private disquiet about
the president's somewhat cavalier interpretation of the constitution (in March 1960 and August 1961). Prime Minister
Pompidou, who, in de Gaulle's own publicized phrase, practised "the art of temporizing", had a quiet and effective
capacity for shelving some of General de Gaulle's "wilder" schemes, such as workers' participation. He successfully
prevented the execution of a general involved in the 1962
army putsch in Algeria, and in May 1968 he dissuaded
the president from holding a referendum on participation.
Later, as president, Pompidou clashed with Chaban-Delmas,
his prime minister, over the latter's proposals to reform the
regional and communal structure of France, to liberalize the
French television network, to introduce limited measures of
worker participation, to restructure the social security system,
and to negotiate a limited incomes policy which guaranteed
an automatic increase in the standard of living. On all these
issues the president took a prudent, sceptical and very conservative line. The differences between Prime Minister Chirac
and President Giscard d'Estaing revolved round policy (the
prime minister disliked the president's flirtation with social
democracy and his pro-European ideas), strategy (Chirac
wished to reassure the traditional conservative electors of
the *majorité* while Giscard d'Estaing was intent on attracting
the votes of the moderate Left) and tactics (the president
refused the prime minister's request for an early election).
The differences were such that one observer (Viansson-Ponté)
could describe the prime minister as "the chief of staff of
a general of whose strategy he disapproves". Between President Giscard d'Estaing and Prime Minister Barre there was
the occasional well-leaked difference of opinion – followed
invariably by a denial of such a difference – yet on the whole
the two men enjoyed a good working relationship. A similiar
relationship emerged between President Mitterrand and the
hard-working, able, conciliatory and faithful prime minister,
Pierre Mauroy. Although, for some time in 1983 there was

a clear difference between the two men over the economic strategy to be adopted.

● *Between the prime minister and the ministers.* The history of the Fifth Republic has been punctuated by unseemly squabbles between the prime minister and his "subordinates". When at his last Council of Ministers in August 1976 Prime Minister Chirac accused certain ministers of not having made his difficult task any easier, he was merely making known the sentiments that must have been felt by many of his predecessors. The disputes take place over three sorts of problems. First, there are conflicts over defining respective spheres of competence: this is especially true over settling budgetary disputes, with the finance minister disputing the prime minister's right to exercise (normally with electoral considerations in mind) an ultimate control. Second, there are frequent altercations over specific policies: even the mild-mannered Messmer was moved in January 1974 to rebuke Charbonnel, the industry minister, whom he accused of showing too much leniency towards the workers who were then occupying the Lip watch factory. Finally, disputes may take place over the political line of the prime minister: the last year of Chirac's government of 1974 to 1976 was marked by real friction between the prime minister and some of his more "reformist" ministers. Prime Minister Barre appears to have exercised tighter control over his ministers, but this did not prevent highly publicized disputes between him and some of them. His successor, Mauroy, was faced with the problem of the presence of four Communist ministers, who, although invariably loyal, occasionally intimated their reservations about his policies. Mauroy was also confronted with powerful Socialist Party "barons" whose entrance into the government did not still their public squabbles. Under Fabius, the cohesion of the government was once again established: imminent parliamentary elections were a powerful cement.

● *Between individual ministers.* As has been previously underlined, the government under the Fifth Republic has not created any tradition of collective solidarity and responsibility. Clearly, if a minister disagrees with an official major policy of the government he will resign (several ministers resigned over de Gaulle's Algerian and European policies) or will be dismissed (the most dramatic example was the sacking of Servan-Schreiber in June 1974 after he had publicly exposed the folly of French nuclear policy). But there is a surprising amount of latitude allowed to ministers in airing their quarrels in public: in 1975, for example, it was no secret that the minister of the interior and the finance minister disagreed over the reform of local finance, that the minister of finance opposed the views of the minister of labour over the financing of the social security system, and that the industry minister and the foreign minister were at loggerheads over the restructuring of the French computer industry (or what remained of it). The disputes in 1959 between the ministers of education and of defence over national service deferment and in 1960 between the industry and the finance ministers over the freedom of industry and trade were matched by much later squabbles between the ministers of justice and of feminine affairs in 1975 over proposals to pay salaries to mothers with very young children, and between the finance and the justice ministers in 1976 over the latter's reluctance to start judicial proceedings against unnamed petrol companies suspected of illicit price-fixing. Between the minister of the interior and his colleagues at justice friction is endemic: as early as 1959 the two ministers clashed over the seizing of *La Gangrène*, a book which depicted the spread of torture in Algeria. Sixteen years later their successors were indulging in a bout of public mutual recrimination: in November 1975, the minister of justice, in a public speech, rebuked his colleague for his attacks on the country's judges (whom he had accused of pusillanimity). In December 1976 another public dispute broke out between the two ministers over the expulsion of the workers who were occupying the offices of the *Parisien Libéré*, a Right-wing newspaper, and in 1980 there was a major disagreement between the two ministers on the issue of computerized national identity cards. The advent of the Mitterrand presidency did little to curb the disputes between the two ministries: in April 1982, for example, there was a public argument between the two ministers over identity controls. After May 1981, the cohesion of the Left-wing government was strained on many other occasions, and on issues such as the pace of implementing the president's reformist programme, the extension of the military camp at Larzac (a bitterly contested decision of previous Right-wing administrations), the politically difficult major restructuring of the steel industry which involved massive job losses, the building of a nuclear energy plant at Plogoff in Brittany, there was a public debate in which some ministers took part – often on opposite sides. Given the heterogeneity of the government (which ranged from Communists to mild social democrats) public disputes were perhaps inevitable and came to the surface most visibly over issues such as social security coverage and financing the scale of nationalization

(51 per cent state control was advocated by the moderates, 100 per cent by the hard-liners), the reduction in the working week (whether or not it should be accompanied by a corresponding reduction in wages), the successive wages and prices freezes, the de-indexation of public servants' pay, and the issue of France remaining in the European Monetary System. Such disputes impaired the effectiveness of the government and damaged its image, and the president made several requests for greater unity. Divisions within the Right-wing government of Jacques Chirac from 1986 to 1988 were *exacerbated* by imminent elections, because they were for the presidency: the parties of the ruling coalition were constantly manoeuvring for political advantage and the resultant tensions were inevitably felt at governmental level. Thus, François Léotard, the leader of the Republican Party who had presidential ambitions, found himself very marginalized within the government over his handling of the reform of the state-controlled media. Charles Pasqua, the controversial Minister of the Interior and close confidant of Jacques Chirac, attracted the public wrath of several ministers: they included Léotard, who protested over the proposed banning of a number of alleged pornographic magazines, Claude Malhuret, the Minister for Human Rights, who denounced the high-handed expulsion of a hundred Mali nationals, and his own junior minister Pandreau, who disagreed on the means of handling the public sector strikes in January 1987. Other major conflicts were those between Philippe Séguin, Minister for Social Affairs, and Edouard Balladur, the Finance Minister, over the financing of the social security system, and between Albin Chalandon, the Justice Minister, and Michèle Barzach, the Health Minister, on the issue of criminalizing drug addiction. But the most spectacular display of internal governmental disagreement was over the handling of the students' revolt of November–December 1986, with some ministers openly requesting the withdrawal of the bill which triggered off the demonstrations, some advising the abolition of certain clauses and others urging the retention of the entire bill.

- *Between ministers and their junior ministers.* There have been several well-publicized disputes at this level. Among the most sharp were those which involved the minister and junior minister of agriculture (all contacts were carried on by laconic notes) in 1974-5, the minister of infrastructure (*Équipement*) and his junior minister for housing in the same period, the minister of education and his junior minister for university affairs in 1975 and in 1976. One junior minister was criticized by the President of the Republic for opposing the project of his minister during a Council of Ministers: "the role of junior ministers is to defend the position of their minister, even if at the drafting stage they can make their objections known".

The disputes within the executive have revolved around differences of personality, of policy or over the vexed question of their respective areas of competence – the political demarcation lines. It may be that this institutionalized tension or even friction between the agents of the executive enables either the president or the prime minister better to control them, on the age-old principle of dividing and ruling. Yet constant tension and dissension may easily produce vacillation and even paralysis. It is certainly detrimental to the cohesion and to the image of the governing team as well as damaging to policy co-ordination – one of the major problems of public decision-making in the Fifth Republic.

6 The administrative state: foundations, myth and reality

In popular demonology, the administration looms as large in France as the trades unions used to do in Britain. The French administration is seen as a modern Leviathan condemning man to an existence which is becoming more nasty and more brutish because it is getting longer. Its "dictatorship" was described as both "arrogant and inhuman" by President Pompidou, who added his voice to the all-party chorus of vilification. By the end of the presidency of Giscard d'Estaing, it was argued that the Fifth Republic had become "a technocrat's state": the deputy-centred regime of the Fourth Republic had been supplanted by the civil servant-dominated regime of the Fifth. The criticism of the role of the administration had become widespread, persistent, strident. The election of the less technocratic Mitterrand to the presidency and the appointment of Mauroy to the premiership (the first non-ex-top civil servant to hold the post during the Fifth Republic) momentarily stilled the hostile clamour. With the elections of June 1981, which saw the entry of scores of school teachers into the National Assembly (34 per cent of the total membership and 59 per cent of the Socialist and Left-wing Radical group), the merchants of generalization (and they are legion in political science) assured the French that the "Republic of civil servants" had been replaced by the "Republic of teachers". But the administration was not to be spared for long, and within six months of the May 1981 presidential election the chorus of invective had recommenced: the administration was too powerful, too autonomous, too secretive, too insensitive, too independent, too obstructive. Increasingly, the Right and, more especially, the extreme Right of Jean-Marie Le Pen, demanded a diminution in the role of the State and a reduction in the number and influence of its agents who were presented as the self-interested protectors of social and economic egalitarianism. One of the first decisions of the Chirac government in 1986 was to investigate the means of abolishing certain administrative bodies. Recommendations were made (the Belin-Gisseret Report) but by 1988 when the Right lost

99

office none had been implemented. The government did, however, reduce the number of full-time civil servants (by 19,000 in 1987) and cut by half the number of students studying at the *Ecole Nationale d'Administration* (see below). With the return of the Left to power in 1988, ideologically inspired government attacks on the administration ceased, but it remains the object of popular suspicion and even dislike.

The foundations and myth of administrative power

Several arguments have been forwarded to buttress the claim that the Fifth Republic is an "administrative state".

- *The power of the State has increased under the Fifth Republic.*
- *The present regime had the declared intention of expanding the role of the administration.*
- *The civil service has permeated all levels of decision-making.*
- *The ruling coalition has politicized the civil service in a sense favourable to itself.*

Let us look at each argument in turn.

The power of the French state has been further strengthened under the Fifth Republic

The state has become omnipresent, invading all areas of private and public life. Already in the nineteenth century there were eloquent denunciations in France of "the all-invading" nature of the state, and these were multiplied as state intervention increased with the impact of three major wars (1870-1, 1914-18, 1939-45), with the increased demands of social welfare and for full employment, and with the increasingly technical and costly nature of economic policies. Since the advent of the Fifth Republic, the economic and social transformation of France has been accelerated, and massive state intervention and aid have been required to coax France into "marrying her century", to use President de Gaulle's phrase. More than ever, the state has become an employer of men, an owner of property, a manager and modernizer of the economy, a protector of the nation's boundaries, a guarantor of its social welfare: its two million agents now constitute more than a tenth of the total work force and their salaries and social security costs amount (in 1986) to nearly 20 per cent of total public expenditure. Between 1956 and 1980, and again between 1981 and 1983, the number of non-military state employees increased by some 40,000 a year. Since 1984 an attempt has been made to reduce this number (although in not always a coherent manner), but the reduction in full-time employees has been more than compensated by an increase in the number of part-timers and of people working on short-term contracts. Civil servants regulate the citizenry from before the cradle to beyond the grave. The state's share of gross domestic product reveals the extent of increased interventionism: it rose from 33 per cent in 1960 to 43 per cent in 1981 (higher than in Great Britain and West Germany, and much higher than in the USA and Japan), and peaked in 1985 at 44.5 per cent, a proportion which remains obdurately stable in spite of successive government's efforts to reduce it.

Interventionism is particularly apparent in the economic sphere where the state has been described as "tutor, patron, and main risk taker": at present, the state controls, either directly or indirectly, almost all credit facilities and more than half of all French industrial investment. Outside neo-liberal intellectual circles and a small but increasingly influential group of Right-wing politicians the principle of interventionism elicits no primitive or instinctive antagonism (although its implementation by the administration frequently does) either from the public, the major political parties or the business community. It is exercised through a variety of methods and mechanisms.

The directives and "indications" of the national plans

The plans (there have been nine since the war) are elaborated by the Planning Commissariat (*Commissariat au Plan*) which is headed by a planning commissioner, the best known of whom was Jean Monnet, the first to hold the post. It is a small and high-powered brains trust of civil servants, a permanent, administratively autonomous and intellectually independent body which forms an integral part of the present machinery of government, and has access to all levels of government from the presidency (through the Central Planning Council) to the local administration. Its task is to form committees which associate business, trade unionists, civil servants and other industrialists and economic experts: the membership of various committees is nearly 5000 and a half to two-thirds are appointed by the pressure-groups. By linking the groups within the state, it is able, in theory, to transmit the state's general directives, by providing, through a national plan, a framework which "indicates" the medium-term economic and social priorities of the government: hence the term "indicative planning". Traditionally, plans were destined to cover a five-year period, but since the mid-1970s several have been abandoned and replaced by interim plans. The Socialist government in 1988 announced a four-year plan to take France up to 1992, the date at which trade barriers within the European community are scheduled to be totally dismantled. It is within the plan's framework that the social and economic "partners" (a word frequently employed) are asked to collaborate. Pierre Massé, a previous planning commissioner, described the objectives of the plan as reducing the areas of economic uncertainty (by issuing forecasts of the likely evolution of various economic sectors) and as providing a "framework of social justice".

During the 1960s and 1970s the French plans became increasingly ambitious, technical, complex – and ineffective. The planning process was clearly under a shadow and lost a great deal of its prestige: it encountered the jealousy and hostility of the Finance Ministry (which even established "parallel" functions such as its own Forecasting Division): the main unions boycotted its work because they felt, not unjustifiably, that they were under-represented; the Left-wing parties emphasized the timidity of its proposals in key areas such as income distribution, suspected it as a tool of governmental propaganda and claimed that it was insufficiently discussed in parliament. Its reputation for political neutrality and impartiality – one of the props of its influence – was, therefore, badly shaken. Moreover, its vulnerability to outside events (such as the Algerian war, the May events in 1968, the explosion in petrol prices after 1974) had been all too apparent. It was twice sacrificed to short-term anti-inflationary packages; it was abundantly clear, for example, that the Barre anti-inflation plan of 1976 basically destroyed the seventh plan (1976-80). Perhaps the most serious blow to the plan was that few people believed in it: even most of the planners were plainly discouraged about its inefficacy. The fate of the eighth plan (1981-5) was characteristic: it was very imprecise (it was said by the wags that the only figures in the plan were the page numbers), very unambitious (a far cry from the early plans), was drafted with scepticism and greeted with boredom, and was abandoned when the Socialists won the 1981 elections. The election of a new President of the Republic in 1981, and the appointment of a new Socialist government, a new planning minister (Michel Rocard) and a new planning commissioner (Hubert Prévot) were expected to breathe new life into the plan. It was hoped that planning would be more ambitious, more precise and more democratic. However, the events of the first two years of Socialist government (with three reluctant devaluations, a lower than expected rate of growth and of investment, and a higher than expected inflation rate and balance of payments deficit) had a sobering effect on the new administration. With the departure of Rocard from the Planning Ministry and the reduction in the status of the Ministry itself, together with the enhanced position of the Finance Ministry after 1983, national planning was relegated under the Socialists to its largely symbolic and exhortatory role. The Right which came to power in March 1986 placed more (but not total) faith in market forces and did not even indulge in the rhetoric of planning. However, after the 1988 elections, the appointment of Michel Rocard to the Premiership and the appointment of a new planning commissioner (Pierre-Yves Cossé) gave heart once more to the demoralised planners. But the early indications suggest that planning is unlikely ever to regain the prestige and influence it enjoyed in the years after the war. For a variety of reasons, planning is simply much more difficult in the 1980s than it was in the 1950s and 1960s.

Policies and general level of activity of the public sector

Following the nationalizations of 1981-2 this sector became one of the biggest in the western world and the one which was most directed to industrial activities of a purely competitive nature. The extension of the public sector was a very long process: the monopoly on postal deliveries and on the manufacture of tobacco and matches go back a very long way, as does the state's involvement in the munitions industry. But the real growth of the public sector came in three major waves: in 1937 the Popular Front government nationalized the Bank of France, most of the railway network and the Compagnie Générale Transatlantique; the period just after the liberation of France saw the nationalization of the four main banks, thirty-four insurance companies, most of the coal mines, the electricity industry, the Renault car firm (accused of collaboration with the Germans) and part of the aeronautics industry; the Socialists in 1981-2 virtually completed the nationalization of the banking sector, extended state control over the armaments industry, formally took over the steel industry, and also nationalized five major industrial groups and a number of foreign-owned companies or companies in which foreign holdings were substantial. The state's share in industry after the 1981-2 measures may be seen in Table 2.

Table 2   State share of industry in 1982 – by turnover

	Before Nationalizations (per cent)	After (per cent)		Before Nationalizations (per cent)	After (per cent)
Steel	1	80	Capital goods	3	1
Metalworking	13	63	Heavy engineering	0	5
Base chemicals	23	54	Arms	58	75
Synthetic textiles	0	75	Computer and		
Plastics	4	15	office equipment	0	36
Fine chemicals	5	14	Power generating		
Pharmaceuticals	9	28	equipment	0	26
Glass	0	35	Electronics	1	44
Construction			Consumer durables	0	25
materials	1	8			
Cardboard	0	9	Shipbuilding	0	17
Foundry	4	22	Aircraft	50	84
Machine tools	6	12	All industry	18	32

But Table 2 gives only part of the picture, for the state also controlled (if that is the appropriate word) a network of firms as the result of secondary shareholding. The reports of Édouard Bonnefous and of Jacques Feron both revealed the scale of "creeping" or "backdoor" nationalization which took place during the period of Right-wing governments because of the diversifying activities of state-owned companies. In the period 1955 to 1975, when the number of state-owned holding companies declined from 170 to 130, the number of their subsidiaries multiplied from 266 to over 650. As a result, the number of state employees increased by more than 300,000, and in industries as diverse as pharmaceuticals and cosmetics. It was highly revealing that the state already had shares in many of the industries or groups before they were nationalized in 1981-2: the state owned, directly or indirectly, 76.9 per cent of the capital of Sacilor and 64.7 per cent of that of Usinor (the two groups which together produced four-fifths of French steel production).

The neo-liberal government of Jacques Chirac, elected in March 1986, promised a far-reaching programme of privatization: the 1986 Privatization Act listed sixty-five state companies to be sold off to the private sector. These companies comprised, with subsidiaries, a total of 1,454 firms, with some 755,000 employees. They included 19 insurance companies, 289 financial institutions and almost 350 companies in the industrial sector. The victory of the Left in 1988 put a stop to the privatization drive. Nevertheless, the Right succeeded in organizing twelve major flotations, and carried out almost half its promised programme.

As a result, nearly 300,000 employees were transferred from the public industrial groups to the private sector, and over 100,000 bank employees moved from the state to the private sector. Yet, it must be emphasized that even if the entire programme had been implemented the state sector would have remained very extensive. There was never any question, as was the case in the United Kingdom, of denationalizing the public sector monopolies, gas, electricity and coal. And industries which were perceived as "strategic" (the state airline, steel, the aerospace industry) were left firmly under public control. It is also highly revealing that the state retained a variety of controls (potential and real) over the privatized firms and banks, appointed their managers, and structured their shareholdings (often in highly political fashion). The privatization programme of the Right, ambitious in conception and significant even in partial implementation, did not seriously weaken the state's industrial and financial leverage within the economy.

The state sector also includes a host of semi-public corporations such as the giant petrol groups Elf and Total. It directly controls investment for exploration, their share of the domestic market, their pricing policies and their crude oil importing policy, and it exercises its control in a way which would have caused a revolt in BP if a British government had done likewise. The state also plays a dominant role in the CFA-COGEMA, the massive and highly integrated electro-nuclear power holding which has private partners both at home and abroad.

The weight of evidence suggests that most of the public sector enjoys a great deal of autonomy (the investment and borrowing policies of some French public concerns would shock British politicians), but there is no doubt that successive governments (as in Great Britain) have not hesitated to impose their views on reluctant state industries and banks. They complain about the defects of the nationalized industries and about the huge subsidies they feel obliged to pour into the public sector, but have insisted, for example, that Air France continue to use the loss-making Concorde and the unpopular Roissy airport, have told the mining industry to work old and unprofitable mines in areas of high unemployment and have insisted that the electricity industry give preferential rates to industry. The state sector is an immensely useful instrument in the hands of the government. It was, for example, public sector investment which boosted the economy after 1974 when private investment was collapsing. The Socialist administration of 1981 initially saw the extended public sector as a major instrument of a more voluntaristic industrial strategy: President Mitterrand, in a press conference, referred to the nationalized industries as an instrument of "the next century" (although some of his more sceptical ministers viewed them as an instrument of the last century), and envisaged a dynamic role for them in restoring French industrial might. However, economic circumstances and effective pressure from the nationalized industries' chairmen ensured that they increasingly acted not as instruments of state *dirigisme* but as semi-autonomous baronies.

The powerful grip on credit through the Bank of France, the Conseil National du Crédit, the nationalized banks and insurance companies

Even before the nationalization measures of 1981-2 state control of credit was described by Jean-Maxime Lévéque, chairman of the then private *Crédit Commercial de France*, as "barbaric". The French pursue a policy of *encadrement du crédit*: the expansion of the money supply is controlled directly by limiting increases in loan volume. Rather than controlling the banks' sources of funds, the French regulate their use through a ceiling on the volume of loans (governments also, of course, attempt to control their own budgetary deficits – the other major component of the money supply). Credit control has always been used by French governments, which have never hesitated to employ the wide range of punitive weapons at their disposal in order to impose such a control: the economic policies of the Barre government (1976-81) and of the Mauroy and Fabius governments (between 1983 and 1986) were certainly characterized by an attempt rigorously to control credit.

The far-reaching but generally ineffective system of price-control and price-fixing

This is regulated by the ordinance of 30 June 1945 (although price control by the state has much longer antecedents). Attempts have been made since the Barre government of 1976 to 1981 to dismantle the mechanisms of price control as part of a more liberal economic strategy, but no one doubted that they would be brought into play again if economic circumstances so require. The Socialist government of Pierre Mauroy first declared its intention of not restoring price controls, but events were more powerful than desire, and the austerity packages of 1982 and 1983 included a prices and incomes freeze. Nevertheless, there is increasing evidence that governments, of whatever political hue, seem determined to dismantle the system.

Loans, investment and research grants

These are facilitated by bodies such as the *Crédit National* (a semi-public organ which is the principal dispenser of long and medium-term loans to private industry), the *Caisse des Dépôts* and the *Caisse de Crédit Agricole* which have branches in the provinces.

State purchasing policy

State orders are now massive and they can effectively protect an industry over a number of years. The French have always preached the liberalization of purchasing policies in the European Community but have practised a policy of protecting home industries.

The sectoral investment funds and committees

These include the FDES (the Economic and Social Development fund), and the FIAT (the Regional Intervention fund used for promoting industrial decentralization). A local firm may call upon not only the FDES or FIAT but also the FNAFU (the urban and landbuilding fund), the FAD (another fund for helping industrial decentralization), the FAC (a special crisis fund), the FNE (a fund available for helping "restructure" industry and which provides, for example, subsidies for early retirement), and the FSAI (a special fund for industrial adaptation, used to help regions such as the Nord and Lorraine which were badly hit by the decline of the steel, coal and textile industries). The rural areas may exploit the Rural Renovation Fund, the FORMA (used for restructuring the agricultural marketing system) and the FIDAR (a rural development fund). The above list is by no means exhaustive: there is an absolutely bewildering array of investment funds organized by the state.

Involved in the process of state economic intervention is an army of officials from the nationalized banks, industries and insurance companies, the semi-public corporations, the INSEE (the National Institute of Statistics), various specialized divisions and subdivisions of the Finance Ministry (notably the Budget Division, the Forecasting Division and the Economic Intervention Service which vets requests for loans and whose advice on marketing prospects may be decisive), the Planning Commissariat and the DATAR and from the sponsoring ministries (which may intervene in the siting and detailed regulations of an industry). Mention should be made, too, of bodies such as the National Employment Agency (created in 1967 and reorganized in 1980) and the National Research Development Agency (founded in 1979), which are financially and administratively autonomous public law bodies operating under government supervision. To co-ordinate the work of these many bodies several inter-ministerial committees have been established and they are now among the most powerful organs of state economic interventionism. They include the Codis (the committee for the development of strategic industries), which was created in September 1979 and was replaced by the FMI (the industrial modernization fund) after 1981 to channel money into "the industries of the future", such as electronics, robotics, bio-technology; the Ciri which, after 1981, replaced the Ciasi (the committee for industrial restructuring), founded in 1974 to help firms in difficulty and often referred to as "the red-cross of French industry"; the Cidise (committee for investment development and maintenance of employment), which helps expanding firms; and the Cepme, which is a kind of soft loan bank for small companies. Public money has been poured into private industry and will continue to be so whatever the political complexion of the government.

There is no doubt that the French government has fully exploited all the means at its disposal: the *Plan Calcul*, of 1967, designed to create a powerful independent French computer industry; the creation of the vast petro-chemical complex at Fos; the policy of encouraging industrial mergers in the 1960s; the massive loans to restructure and modernize the motor car industry and the iron and steel industry of Lorraine; the vast telecommunications and electro-nuclear programmes in the 1970s; the reshaping of the textiles, toys and paper-making industries, and the major industrial restructuring operations of the Mitterrand presidency. These are the more striking examples of direct state interventionism.

State intervention has not only increased quantitatively but it has also changed qualitatively, and in ways that invariably strengthen the administration. Nowadays, the state is involved in imparting a certain sense of direction to groups, firms and individuals: this is especially true in urban and industrial planning. The increasingly complex nature of decisions places a premium upon technical expertise and esoteric knowledge, and the administration, imbued with the sense of its own competence and permanence, has the time, the stability and the facilities for acquiring both.

The present régime had the clearly declared intention of expanding the role of the administration

The founders of the Fifth Republic, in their search for a strong and respected state, stressed that political and constitutional reform had to be complemented by administrative reforms. The constitutional and political reinforcement of the executive led to a corresponding reduction in the powers of parliament, and the regulatory power and discretion of the administration was increased by Articles 34 and 38 of the constitution which severely restrict the realm of law-making (areas where parliament is necessarily involved). Moreover, many of the important laws passed in parliament are so-called *lois d'orientation*, laws which present the general outlines and guidelines of legislation and which leave the details to the administration. Under the Fifth Republic, civil servants are also much less harassed by prying Deputies (pursuing a constituency or pressure-group interest) and their projects are more likely to survive unscathed. The administration may exercise its influence *before* a piece of legislation is presented when it helps in drafting, *during* its presentation when it advises ministers on the desirability of concessions to members of parliament, and *after* the passage of the legislation when it supervises its implementation. Its obstructionism can be very powerful: for instance, the Nature Protection Act of April 1976 emerged from the *bureaux* of the Environment Ministry only after five years of savage mauling. Obstructionism is generally most evident at the stage of implementing a law – and especially if parliament has had the temerity to insist on concessions. The Agricultural Act of December 1968 was still waiting full implementation by the end of 1977. After 1981 some of the difficulties of implementing the Socialist government's policies were ascribed to the obstructionism of the administration, and more than one Socialist Deputy demanded a purge of the administrative "wreckers". The administration's powers in the formulation, the drafting, the passage, the implementation and the supervision of legislation are traditional: under the Fifth Republic they have been constitutionally extended to encompass a greater number of subjects.

The views of the founders of the present régime on the administration involved not only a strengthening of its traditional powers, but also another related objective – the increasing of its efficiency. This objective emerges from the utterances of Michel Debré, the first prime minister of the Fifth Republic and the constitutional *alter ego* of President de Gaulle. Debré was one of the few politicians to recognize the importance of the administration, and in 1945 had been responsible for the creation of the *École Nationale d'Administration*. In his book, *La Mort de l'État Républicain*, written in 1947, he insisted that "a new type of political power must be accompanied by a new kind of administration". Underlying the need to strengthen the administration was the desire to "rationalize" decisions, to "depoliticize" them, and to reject the incrementalism practised by the politicians of the previous régime. Since 1958, the efficiency of the administration has been the object of countless and constant reforms. In 1963, a Ministry for Adminstrative Reform was created to complement (the critics said duplicate) the work of older bodies such as the Central Committee on the Cost and Efficiency of the Public Services, and later a Permanent Mission for Administrative Reform was founded. New bodies at national, regional and local level have mushroomed forth with astonishing regularity, all intent on solving the crucial problem of administrative co-ordination, but most resulting in rendering the original problem that shade more intractable. Economic decentralization was placed essentially (but not exclusively) in the hands of the National Employment Agency, created in 1967, while the problems of atomic energy were dealt with by the *Commissariat à l'Énergie atomique* and the co-ordination of scientific and technical research by the DGRST (the *Direction Générale de la Recherche Scientifique et Technique*). The role of the Agency for the Development of Computer Processing Applications, created in 1979, is clear from its name. The economic development of certain regions was confided to horizontally organized *missions,* those of the Languedoc-Roussillon and Aquitaine are the two best known, and the tackling of specific problems, such as the growing threat to the Côte d'Azur from pollution and property speculation, or the encouragement of a solar energy programme, was confided to other *missions* which were to cut through the entanglements of the traditional administrative jungle. Typical of these *missions* was the *Mission de la Mer* founded in 1978 after the *Amoco Cadiz* shipping disaster led to the pollution of large tracts of the Brittany coast, a pollution which had spread because of the ill-coordinated efforts of the various services involved. *Missions* were to be "specialized, dynamic and creative" in the words of their early inspirer, Edgard Pisani, then a Gaullist minister who was exasperated with the ponderousness of the traditional administration. On other occasions, *ad hoc* commissions have been given the role of co-ordinating administrative activity in a specific domain: the Barre commission on housing finance of 1975 was one such commission. At the local level, new regional institutions have been created to co-ordinate the social and economic policies of the provinces, and an attempt has been made to ensure some degree of policy co-ordination in the growing urban conglomerations through the creation of urban communities and districts (see pages below). The régime's obsession with administrative co-ordination and efficiency also explains the major restructuring of the Paris region, the creation of super-ministries, the founding of new ministries, the appointing of co-ordinating general secretaries in certain ministries, the internal reform of almost all ministries, and the increase in the number of inter-ministerial committees. This constant flurry of administrative reform has been motivated by the régime's desire for greater efficacy. So, too, was the introduction of RCB (the French equivalent of PPBS) in the mid 1960s which also attempts to introduce "rationality" into public policy making.

The civil service has permeated all levels of social and economic decision-making, both public and private

Civil servants, the agents of state control, have infiltrated all aspects of public and private decision-making through their membership of:

- *The presidential staff, and the private staffs of the prime minister and other ministers*: they now constitute between seventy and ninety per cent of those staffs. The Left tends to recruit fewer civil servants, and particularly from the *grands corps*, to politically sensitive posts: only seven per cent of the Élyseé staff were not civil servants during de Gaulle's presidency, 27 per cent under Pompidou, 11 per cent under Giscard d'Estaing but as many as 44 per cent under Mitterrand.
- *The numerous inter-ministerial committees* which bring together ministers and their civil servants concerned with particular policy areas or specific policies.
- The *ad hoc* and *permanent specialized bodies*, which have proliferated since the war. It was calculated that already by the mid 1960s there were no fewer that 500 councils, 1200 committees and 300 commissions linking the organs of state with the major pressure groups. These "instruments of administrative pluralism" have been increasing at all levels, both national and local, giving rise to mounting disquiet about "government by commission" and the accompanying effacement of the traditional representative institutions.
- *The French Planning Commissariat* which, although seriously weakened, is considered by some as a key element in the French system of *concertation*.
- *The boards and management of many private firms and public industries* through the process of *pantouflage*: top civil servants often take up lucrative posts either in the public or private sector. As a consequence of *pantouflage*, almost all major French firms have ex-civil servants on their boards of directors. The result is to establish a widespread network

of personal relations which enables the state to transmit, on a purely informal basis, its wishes.

There has been increasing politicization of the civil service, and in a sense favourable to the ruling political coalition

Under the Fifth Republic there has been an increased tendency for civil servants to colonize politically sensitive positions and even the major political institutions of the country. As already noted, the presidential staff, the prime minister's staff and other ministerial *cabinets* comprise many civil servants. These posts invariably involve – and often directly – some of those civil servants in areas which are intrinsically political: party, parliamentary and constituency affairs are all sensitive and overtly political, and all are dealt with by members of presidential or ministerial private staffs. The politicization of the administration may also be seen in the number of civil servants who stand in parliamentary elections and who are elected: in 1946, 23.5 per cent of the Deputies were ex-civil servants, in 1951, 20 per cent, in 1956, 22 per cent, in 1958, 19.5 per cent, in 1962, 22.7 per cent, in 1967, 29 per cent, in 1968, 26 per cent, in 1973, 33 per cent, in 1978, 38.8 per cent, in 1981, 53.2 per cent, and in 1986, 47 per cent. These figures, however, include school teachers who are civil servants in France. Nevertheless, if school teachers are excluded, the figures, though less spectacular, are still high and show constant progress. In local politics, too, the influence of civil servants (especially of those based in the capital) is quite astonishing. In 1987, 5 of the 22 chairmen of regional councils and 33 (including 20 teachers) of the 96 departmental council chairmen were civil servants, as defined by the French. Among the 38,000 mayors of France, members and ex-members of the *grands corps* and the central administration are well represented, particularly in the big towns.

What has also struck many critical observers is the increasing identification of some civil servants with the ruling political coalition. The contact of the régime's top politicians with the civil service appears to exemplify this. Between 1959 and 1988, the great majority of Foreign Ministers (80 per cent), Defence Ministers (80 per cent), Finance Minsters (75 per cent) and Education Ministers (70 per cent) hailed from the civil service. Even more strikingly, during the same period all the prime ministers had spent part of their career in the civil service; Debré, Pompidou and Fabius had been members of the Council of State, Chaban-Delmas, Couve de Murville and Rocard started their careers in the Financial Inspectorate, Messmer emerged from the colonial administration, Chirac started his professional life in the Court of

Accounts, Barre, after teaching, became a prominent "Eurocrat", and Mauroy left the teaching profession to become a full-time politician. A study of the ministers of the Fifth Republic shows that more than half those who served de Gaulle and Pompidou were recruited directly from the civil service or had been civil servants. This compares with a figure of 32.8 per cent for ministers of the Fourth Republic. The proportion of ex-civil service ministers increased during the presidency of Giscard d'Estaing: 62 per cent of the 1974 Chirac government, 64 per cent of the 1976 Barre government. By May 1981, the president of the Republic, the prime minister and two-thirds of the ministers had had previous experience in the administration. With the election of Mitterrand, an ex-lawyer, to the presidency, the appointment of Mauroy to the premiership and the appointment of fewer ex-civil servants (though more ex-teachers) to the government, the image of the governmental team changed somewhat: it was no longer seen as a group of technicians trained in the civil service. Yet civil servants were still very prominent and numerous: for example, six ministers of the June 1981 government – and by no means the least important – had been students at the *École Nationale d'Administration*. The number of *Énarques* increased in the Chirac government of 1986: thirteen of the forty one (or a third) were ex-students of the ENA. It is not surprising, therefore, that it is contended that there has been a clear *fonctionnarisation du pouvoir politique* under the Fifth Republic. It is difficult to know where the civil service starts and the government ends, and all the more so because the *fonctionnarisation du pouvoir politique* has been accompanied by a *politicisation de la fonction publique*.

Evidence of the politicization of the civil service in a pro-governmental sense may be gleaned from a study of the appointments to the key posts of *directeurs* (who head the divisions of the central administration) and to ambassadorial, top police and prefectoral posts (which are among the 500 posts at the discretion of the government). Even the *grands corps* have been penetrated by political appointees through the judicious use of outside appointments: the government has the right to appoint a certain proportion – usually about a quarter – and it has used this right to place politically sympathetic people. The first two years of the Mitterrand presidency was marked by a fairly radical purge of the top posts in the administration; notably in the Interior Ministry, the Finance Ministry, and the Education Ministry. *All* the members of the private staffs of the president, the prime minister and the ministers were replaced, many of the university rectors were sacked, most of the prefects were transferred to different *départements*, the police were shaken up, seventy per cent of the *directeurs* in the central administrations were transferred or demoted, and political sympathizers were placed in other strategic positions in the state machine. The *État Giscardien*, it was argued, had been replaced by the *État Socialiste*, and the tradition of the interpenetration of political and administrative elites continued. With the election of the Chirac government in March 1986 many Socialist sympathizers in the top posts of the administration, the police and the nationalized industries were evicted to make place for friends of the Gaullist Party – to the irritation of the Gaullists' allies. Once again the "spoils system *à la française*" became the subject of bitter recrimination, this time by the Socialists who, when re-elected in 1988 resorted to the same tactics.

The reality of administrative power

The growing power of this ubiquitous and apparently highly politicized civil service has caused grave disquiet in all circles: *L'Administration au pouvoir* was the title of a popular book, a title which contained a warning, confirmed a popular prejudice and purported to state a fact. But to claim that the administration is running the country is grossly to oversimplify the real situation. It is true that it exercises considerable influence: that influence is ensured by its strategic position in the drafting, the passage, the implementation and the supervision of legislation. It is equally true that certain parts of the civil service and certain civil servants exercise a discretion which borders on the autonomous exercise of power: such civil servants would include Jérôme Monod, head of the DATAR from 1968 to 1975; Pierre Massé, the planning commissioner from 1959 to 1966; Pierre Dreyfus of the nationalized Renault company until his appointment as industry minister in 1981; Bloch-Laîné, the head of the *Caisse des Dépôts* from 1952 to 1967; Pierre Guillaumat, managing director of the state-owned petrol empire; Jacques Calvet, the head of the private office of Giscard d'Estaing when he was finance minister; Pierre Laroque of the Council of State and "the father of the French social security system", Gérard Théry, director-general of Telecommunications during most of Giscard d'Estaing's presidency; Jean-Pierre Souviron, director-general for Industry in the last years of the same presidency; Albin Chalandon, ex-Gaullist minister who became the assertive boss of Elf-Aquitaine and whose clashes with André Giraud, the industry minister, more than once provoked presidential intervention. The power of certain *corps* such as the Financial Inspectorate and the state mining engineers, and certain *directions générales*, is well-known and well-founded. And there are well-documented studies of the exercise of civil service power or influence during the passage of the regional and departmental reforms of the 1960s (by Catherine Grémion) and in the development of the French electro-nuclear programme (by Nelkin and Pollack). The autonomy of certain parts of the state apparatus (especially in the industrial sector) has also been revealed on several occasions. It was ironical that on the day that Prime Minister Mauroy was justifying the nationalization of the remaining private banks in terms of the need to tighten the state's grip over credit the finance minister was denouncing the policies of the heads of the nationalized bank (because they had the impertinence to act like private bankers...).

Parts of the administration do, therefore, enjoy power, influence, initiative, yet a close look at the French administration raises nagging doubts about its so-called omnipotence.

If, as is commonly asserted, the adminstration is all-powerful, why do so many of the more able and more ambitious civil servants forsake it for politics? Why do so many depart so precipitously for posts in the private sector? For so many to deny themselves the exercise of power would constitute a collective act of self-abnegation rarely paralleled in French history. If the civil service is omnipotent why are so many civil servants so disgruntled and disenchanted? Why do so many complain of their omnipotence? Why *"la crise de la fonction publique"*? The picture of the Fifth Republic as an "administrative state" requires serious reservations, and for the following reasons.

The founders of the Fifth Republic were intent not only on strengthening the administration but also on ensuring its subordination

They were determined not to tolerate what they thought to be the administration's unchecked exercise of power during the Fourth Republic. It was one of the axioms of students of the Fourth Republic that the administration was the real centre of decision-making, but like most axioms in politics, the claim represents but a half-truth, and half-truths on close examination are rarely even half-true....According to the claim, there lay behind the chaotic and pusillanimous behaviour of short-lived governments the unchanging, the omnipresent and omnipotent administration. This *sottogoverno* was the steadfast guardian of the national interest against the politicians and the pressure groups. For the Gaullists, this "administrative state within the state" clearly had to be dismantled, and the loyalty and subordination of civil servants ensured.

The government's determination to ensure the subordination of the administration was emphasized in the 1958 constitution, in the 1959 revision of the civil service charter and in the 1964 decree regulating relations between the state and the French radio and television network personnel. Limitations were placed on the right of state employees to strike, governmental control of the nationalized industries was tightened, the police were brought into line, and the prefectoral corps' professional association was informed that its open complaints about working conditions would no longer be tolerated. In attempting to ensure the subordination of the civil service, conflict with the civil servants was inevitable. The latter, imbued with a keen sense of their own permanence, their stability, their technical competence and their disinterested guardianship of the national interest, view the politicians as transient and personally ambitious, their vision of the national interest frequently blurred by parliamentary, party, pressure-group or purely electoral considerations. The politicians, keenly aware of their democratic legitimacy, of their responsibility for decisions taken, and of their self-importance, see the administrators as antediluvian, lethargic and generally obstructive, with their guardianship of the national interest normally manifested in an implacable and unhealthy attachment to the *status quo*. For the politician, the administration is a kingdom where precedent reigns supreme, where habits are sacrosanct, where innovation is frowned upon and where imagination is treasonable. In such circumstances conflict is always near the surface. There have been some epic struggles under the Fifth Republic between the civil servants and politicians: the ferocious clashes between Debré, when minister of defence, and his officials led to the "resignation" of the naval chief of staff in March 1970. In the late 1970s there were several conflicts between Albin Chalandon, the chairman of Elf-Aquitaine, the state-controlled petrol company, and his minister. They came to a head over the crude oil purchasing policy of the company: the public row was calmed only after the president of the Republic had intervened. The Ministry of Education has also been the scene of many quarrels between politicians and civil servants. The conflict between Quermonne, director of higher education, and the junior minister responsible for higher education in 1975 and 1976 was occasionally infused with all the intense academic malice of which those two ex-university teachers were capable, and was settled only by the resignation of the civil servant. In fact, there was a constant battle between the administration of the Ministry of Education and Alice Saunier-Seïté, the minister of higher education, whose methods were denounced as those of "a Gauleiter in occupied territory". The advent of a socialist government did not put an end to the battles between the politicians and civil servants. Indeed, many were intensified as the Socialists pursued their policy of reform, and there were several highly publicized clashes, notably between Delors, the finance minister, and the managers of the nationalized banks and between Defferre, the minister of the interior, and his police. Throughout the Fifth Republic there have been several instances of the civil servants resorting to their favourite blocking tactics to combat unpopular policies. The obstructionism of the *ingénieurs de l'équipement* of the Environment Ministry is legendary; the minister who first held the post described it somewhat dolefully as the *Ministère de l'Impossible*. The role of the prefects in cooling the reforming zeal of successive ministers who wished to reform the local government system is also well-known.

Yet relations between ministers and civil servants under the Fifth Republic generally conform neither to the Gaullist wish nor to the popular stereotype. First, there are often areas of broad agreement between the administration and the politicians: for example, the financially orthodox Giscard d'Estaing, when finance minister, ruled over a ministry whose members were mostly dedicated to financial orthodoxy. Similarly, the power of certain top civil servants in the Industry Ministry was due to the backing they enjoyed from their ministers. Secondly, there are areas where the administration has been passive, weak or largely managerial and has not actively opposed the minister: the civil servants of the Quai d'Orsay were often opposed to French foreign policy but they were unable or unwilling to modify it. Third, a skilful minister will always get his own way even against a powerful administration: Edgar Faure imposed his mildly liberal educational reforms upon an administration which considered them as positively Maoist; the construction of the Rhine–Rhône canal was given the go ahead in spite of the animosity of large parts of the Ministry of *Équipement*; France withdrew brutally from NATO even though the Defence Ministry was violently opposed to the policy; an aggressive and insensitive Socialist minister of the interior (Gaston Defferre) was able to impose a liberalization and decentralization programme upon a sceptical and reluctant administration. Finally, many ministers enjoy a symbiotic relationship with their civil servants a strong minister may be a nuisance but for whom is more likely than a malleable minister to fight for some of their projects at the political level. Among the factors that shape the relationship between the civil servants and ministers are the determination, skill and political weight of the minister, the strength of his private staff and the cohesiveness of the administration.

The régime has been inconsistent in its administrative practice

No one would dispute the quantity of administrative reforms under the Fifth Republic. But the lack of internal logic and coherence of those reforms has frequently struck observers. Indeed, it would be no exaggeration to say that there has been a total lack of system, since the reformers have sought to reconcile or to juxtapose or even to superimpose basically conflicting ideals. The reformers could not make up their minds whether the fundamental purpose of their measures was to render the administration more efficient, more subordinate or more democratic. By some mysterious alchemy it was hoped to fulfil all three objectives. Nowhere was the confusion more apparent than in the "reform" of the local administration in the 1960s and 1970s. Ministers involved in the reforms were divided among themselves about their nature and even their desirability. Michel Debré, the first prime minister, viewed any concession to the provinces as the thick end of the wedge, as a dangerous step in the dismemberment of a fragile nation, while Pompidou, first as a prime minister and then as president of the Republic, continually cast a prudent electoral eye on the reaction of the established local *notables*. Jeanneney, a Left-wing Gaullist, who was responsible for the ill-fated regional reforms proposed in the 1969 referendum, was primarily concerned with the problem of increasing public participation in decision-making. The administrative advisers of the ministers were no less divided in their attitudes, with some (notably in the prefectoral administration) becoming the vociferous defenders of the interests and the privileges of the *corps* to which they belonged. The consequence of the divisions of opinion was a series of compromises which were ill-digested, incoherent, unhappy and uninspiring, designed to satisfy everyone but failing to please anyone.

Contradictions emerge in other reforms of the administration. The declared intention of Louis Joxe, the minister of administrative reform, was "to simplify, to co-ordinate the structure of administration, to reduce duplication and to reorganize the already too numerous public services". Certain reforms have undoubtedly achieved that end: the "harmonization" of local public services within the context of the regions and the "rationalization" of administrative services within the regions, the restructuring of certain ministries and the creation of new ones must be counted as successes. There are many areas, however, where the problems of co-ordination and of duplication have not been tackled and have even been made worse. For instance, the policy of industrial decentralization was confided to a newly created *délégation* – the DATAR – but other administrations which continue to be involved include the staffs of the president of the Republic and of the prime minister (for electoral reasons), the appropriate officials of the Ministry of the Interior (since its implementation involves the local prefects), of the Finance Ministry (since it has financial implications), of the Ministry of *Équipement* (which analyses any technical aspects) and of any other affected ministry (for example, Housing or Transport). The DATAR has thus become yet another cog in a very large and badly functioning machine. Nor has the creation of *ad hoc missions* solved the problem of administrative co-ordination: they tend to establish themselves as a permanent part of the machinery of government and, like the DATAR, often complicate rather than expedite business: the *mission* for the Languedoc-Roussillon region was established in 1963 and survived for nearly twenty years, while the *mission* for Fos (the vast petrochemical complex in the south of France) which was established for six months was still, ten years later, very much alive and kicking (mainly against the rest of the administration).

The power of the administration is weakened by its internal divisions

Much of the critical literature on French "technocracy" rests on the assumption that the administration is one coherent entity, whereas it is vast and complex (with over 900 *corps* and over 10,000 different grades). Most of the evidence points to its diversity and fragmentary nature (François Dupuy and Jean-Claude Thoenig have written an excellent book with the revealing title *Administration en Miettes*) and suggests that it is especially prey to internal tension and dissension. Moreover, the interplay of divergent interests is often open, unlike in Britain where differences are masked behind a screen of courteous yet apprehensive anonymity.

Internal divisions are manifested in various ways. First, like most large organizations, the administration is not spared personal and generational conflicts which sometimes transcend professional and ideological similarities. One of the distinguishing characteristics of the French administration is the existence of rival networks, often organized by or around a powerful personality. These *clans* often spring from friendships created at the Paris *Institut d'Études Politiques* (or *Sciences Po* as it is familiarly known), the *École Nationale d'Administration* (or ENA) or the *École Polytechnique*, and may structure and further the career of civil servants. Second, there are deep-seated ideological cleavages within the administration, even within the top elite. Most studies emphasize that top civil servants come largely from the Paris bourgeoisie, tend to be the sons of civil servants, are generally educated in the better state schools (often in the select group of Paris *lycées*) and then either attend *Sciences Po* to prepare for the highly competitive examination to the *École Nationale d'Administration* or they prepare for the no less competitive examination to the *École Polytechnique*. Students form the ENA (often referred to as *Énarques*) take another competitive examination at the end of their studies at the school, and the result of that examination determines the student's career prospects. The well-placed *Énarques* choose the highly prestigious *grands corps* (the Financial Inspectorate, the Court of Accounts, the Council of State and to a lesser extent the prefectoral and the diplomatic *corps*). Students from the *École Polytechnique* also have a competitive examination at the end of their studies, at which time many go to a specialist technical school – *École des Mines* (for mining engineers), the *École des Ponts-et-Chaussées* (for highway engineers), the *École de Génie* (for military engineers) are three of the better known – before entering the appropriate state technical corps which are no less prestigious than the administrative *grands corps*. Members of the state administrative and technical elite issue, therefore, from a narrow social and educational base, and their exclusiveness is heightened by their belonging to the small yet powerful professional *corps*. It is frequently contended that family, educational and professional socialization produces an administrative elite which is remote, cut off from the bulk of the nation and insensitive to its aspirations: hence the critical allusions to its "arrogance" and "inhumanity". It is further contended that socialization tends to produce among the elite certain shared attitudes, a common language and technocratic outlook, a widely accepted mystique. A profile of the typical French civil servant emphasizes his attachment to the values of pragmatism, efficiency, scientific rationalism and apoliticism. He believes in the strong state, the purveyor of social justice and of progress, and lauds the virtues of state interventionism which prevents public poverty amid private affluence.

Such generalizations must be treated with scepticism, for it is questionable whether the top civil servants share a common *weltanschauung*. Social and educational backgrounds may be powerful socializing agents, but they may push towards diversity as well as uniformity: the essence of the training at the ENA and the *École Polytechnique* is that it fosters among the students both a certain uniformity of approach (if not of outlook) and a sense of rivalry (if not of enmity) which is rooted in the mercilessly competitive nature of the schools. Moreover, social and educational influences may be offset by professional pressures: the *Énarques* tend to become generalists while most "X" (as students of the *École Polytechnique* are called) become technical experts (at least initially) and they are distributed among the *corps*, each of which has its own peculiar rites, norms and prejudices. Other variables also complicate the picture. The attitudes of a one-legged Protestant transvestite bourgeois *Énarque* may be shaped as much by his physical deformity, his religion or his sexual abnormality as by his social origins or his professional training. Furthermore, even if it were possible to extrapolate from an analysis of social, educational and professional background to the construction of a syndrome of shared beliefs, it would still be necessary to demonstrate that shared *beliefs* lead to shared *behaviour*. There may be no relation between the two, because top civil servants (like members of every other group) differ in courage, ambition, assiduity and a whole range of other personal characteristics. Sociological determinists too readily confuse backgrounds, beliefs, attitudes and conduct in a comforting, yet dangerously misleading, general equation. Ezra Suleiman has shown that attitudes among top civil servants *do* differ, and that one of the determining factors is the function or role they perform. Furthermore, a change of function may lead a top civil servant to adopt different attitudes: a member of a *grand corps* who takes up a position in a ministry frequently adopts the norms and prejudices of his new home (indeed it may be an essential prerequisite of success to do so); prefects who are promoted to the Council of State are often zealous – and knowledgeable – critics of the administrative malpractices of their erstwhile colleagues; a member of the litigation (*contentieux*) section of the Council of State who joins a ministerial private staff may shed his professional obsession with legal niceties to become usefully inventive in circumventing the tiresome supervision of the Council (he is often recruited to the *cabinet* to do precisely that). In short, the *role* played by the civil servant may be as important as his family, class, educational and professional background in fashioning his behaviour and conduct. Finally, it should be added that too often top civil servants are seen as representative of the whole administration. In fact, they represent a small (some 12,000–13,000) and admittedly decisive part of the administration, but there are many influential civil servants further down the hierarchy who come from totally different social and educational backgrounds.

In truth, the French civil service is riddled with cleavages, which is scarcely surprising given its highly fragmented nature. It is possible to discern four main groups involved in decision-making: the *grands corps*; the technical *corps*; the top-ranking civil administrators; the middle-ranking bureaucrats. Members of the *grands*

corps and the technical *corps* are often very mobile: they move in
and out of their *corps* to key posts in the ministries and ministerial
cabinets. Members of the other two groups generally remain in one
ministry, frequently in the same division, forming veritable administrative closed shops. While it is generally possible to pinpoint
the level of *responsibility* for decisions it is not always possible to
identify the *effective* points of decision-making. Top-ranking civil
servants are often like politicians: they are absorbed in presiding
over the work of others, in arbitrating between the ideas and views
of subordinates, and in time-consuming ceremonies. They are also
like politicians in that they tend to spend only relatively short times
in particular posts: divisions are seldom headed by the same man
for more than three years.

Cutting across hierarchical divisions are the differences between
the generalists and the specialists, the bureaucrats and the technocrats. The four main decision-making groups are distributed
among different ministries (and different divisions within those
ministries) and their local field services, the *grand corps* and the
technical *corps*, and the so-called missionary administrations such
as the Planning Commissariat and the DATAR. Between the various administrative organs there is plenty of scope for conflict, and
the evidence suggests that such conflict exists. Conflicts *between*
the ministries are inevitable, since in any policy area a number
of ministries is necessarily involved, and each naturally tries to
defend its own interests and departmental viewpoint. For example,
industrial policy-making involves the Ministry of Finance, the
Industry Ministry, the DATAR, the Planning Commissariat, the
nationalized banking and industrial sector and, at the level of
arbitration, one or more inter-ministerial committees and the
offices of the president of the Republic and the prime minister.
To this long list of administrative agents must be added the local
representatives of the ministries who are involved in the process of
implementation. Conflicts between ministries are endemic. There
is continuous struggle between the Finance Ministry, the watchdog
of the nation's wallet, and most of the spending ministries.
Conflicts between other ministries arise over specific issues which
crystallize deeper commitments. The Ministry of the Interior has
clashed with the short-lived Ministry of Penal Reform (which it
accused of wanting to build "three-star hotels" instead of prisons
to house delinquents), with the Ministry of Justice over the use
of the law as an instrument of political repression, and with the
Ministry of Health over the treatment of drug addicts. There
have also been conflicts between the Ministries of Education
and of Defence over the deferment of national service for *lycée*
students and the reform of the *École Polytechnique*, between

the Ministries of *Équipement* and of Cultural Affairs over the destruction of ancient monuments, between the Ministries of the Environment and Industry over river pollution. Disputes between the ministries can paralyse action: the law of 30 December 1968 on the exploration of the continental shelf emerged only after two years of acerbic wrangling between the Ministries of Posts and Telecommunications, of Transport and of the Navy.

Conflicts *within* the ministries are no less frequent, for most ministries resemble the Education Ministry which has been likened to a highly compartmentalized and hierarchical "monstrous machine" (Catherine Arditti) but where the official hierarchy is sometimes bypassed. The Ministry of Industry is said to be "a juxtaposition of independent and compartmentalized divisions" (Friedberg and Desjeux) while the Finance Ministry with its 170,000 employees has been described as "a federation of autonomous divisions" (in June 1978 there were no fewer than 102) often physically separated (there were no fewer than thirty-four annexes of the ministry in Paris): "it is easier to turn a soldier into a sailor than it is to transfer from one of the Finance Ministry's divisions to another" (Jean Monthen). Conflicts within a ministry may be muted and polite, disguised by affable courtesy: such is normally the case in the Foreign Office which for many years is said to have been divided between a pro-Gaullist "clan" – nationalist, favouring *rapprochement* with the Soviet bloc and pro-Arab – and an anti-Gaullist "clan" – more Atlanticist, pro-American, pro-European and pro-Israel. Or the conflicts may be less than courteous: in the area of urban planning the constant friction between the planners and the engineers has been known to boil over into vicious confrontation within the ministry. Conflicts between the *grands corps* and the technical *corps* and the rest of the administration often spring from resentment when the latter see the former being appointed to key administrative posts outside their *corps*. The administration also dislikes the pettifogging supervision (and condemnation) of its activities by the Council of State, the Court of Accounts and the Financial Inspectorate. Between the "missionary" administrations and the rest of the administration there is frequent dissension. Many of the missionary administrations were formed originally to solve specific problems requiring urgent action, but they have tended to become permanent bodies and have taken on many of the characteristics of traditional administrations. The latter not unnaturally resents having lost many of its interesting tasks to the missionary administrations, and professional rivalry is often compounded by policy differences. The Finance Ministry has always cast a jaundiced eye on the work of the Planning Commissariat, whose policies it suspects as financially dubious and intrinsically inflationary. It has done much to undermine the faith in the five-year plans, and where it has been unable to beat the planners it has duplicated their work: the Economic Intervention and Forecasting Services were founded at the *rue de Rivoli* (the home of the Finance Ministry) to parallel those of the Planning Commissariat. The work of the DATAR also elicits an obstructive animosity in certain administrative quarters.

Rivalries between the *corps* are a normal feature of French administrative life, and they sharpen when there are disputes over respective areas of influence and competence. Particular *corps* believe that certain sectors or posts or policy areas are their "reserved domains" (for instance, the financial inspectors view the banking sector and the *corps* of mining engineers the energy and the steel industries as preserves), and "driven by the monopolistic logic" (Jean Claude Thoenig) do all they can to extend or to protect their domain against the marauding activities of other *corps*.

The French administration is, therefore, fragmented and stratified and is riddled with internal tensions and dissensions. Some co-ordination is introduced by the highly mobile *grands corps* and technical *corps* which, through their corporate links and personal friendships, overcome some of the compartmentalization of the administration. Co-ordination is also attempted by the ministerial *cabinets*, by the horizontally organized missionary administrations, by the "giant ministries" which have merged several smaller ministries, by the numerous inter-departmental meetings (*réunions*) which involve only high-ranking administrative officials, and by the inter-departmental committees which bring together politicians and their principal administrative advisors. But such methods are clearly inadequate, and their inadequacy has often been demonstrated: the notorious inability to control the money supply or the equally notorious ability to build science faculties for non-existent students are but two examples. Corporate, functional and ideological friction often hampers effective co-ordination, prevents the administration from acting as a corporate entity, and singularly diminishes its collective power.

The weakness of the administration is accentuated by its inability to carry out its many tasks

Paradoxically, the greater the area and depth of administrative intervention the more difficult may it be for the administration effectively to intervene. It is not only the poor *administrés* but also the administrators who are inundated with endless streams of laws, decrees, directives, circulars and instructions: between 1971 and 1980 these numbered 126,516! The local social security services, for example, receive no fewer than ninety to a hundred detailed texts from the ministry in Paris every month: like the rest of the administration it is overworked and undermanned. In theory, the implementation of laws and decrees gives the administration wide discretionary powers. In practice, however, the administration is often so overwhelmed by the sheer magnitude of its tasks that it is incapable of doing anything but keeping a minimum of administrative order. Erhard Friedberg has shown that the economic intervention service of the Finance Ministry, which is at the very centre of French economic decision-making, is so overburdened with work that it is materially impossible for it to deal in any depth with the mass of matters which clamour for its attention. The rest of the Finance Ministry – the favourite target of the administration-haters – is so weighed down by its purely managerial and administrative tasks that it has little time to take initiatives or think creatively. And Thoenig's perceptive study of urban development policies in France confirms that, while the state administration has numerous weapons at its disposal, it is often physically incapable of wielding them. Contrary to popular mythology, important parts of the administration are *undermanned*: this is true of many of the supervisory services: parts of the labour code are rarely implemented because of the lack of inspectors, and illicit price-rings in industry flourish because of inadequate supervision. Similarly, one of the reasons tax avoidance is so rife in France is because the tax inspectorate simply cannot cope with the problem. The administration – the modern Leviathan - on closer analysis resembles a land-locked whale: impressive, yet more dangerous in appearance than in reality.

The French civil service is undoubtedly very politicized but the nature of that politicization has been over-simplified

The civil service in France has always been more overtly "political" than those of other European states. It is equally true, as Guy Drouout shows in his study of the *député-fonctionnaire*, that there has been a steady increase in the number of Deputies issuing from the civil service – from 17 per cent at the end of the Third Republic to 20 per cent at the end of the Fourth to 53 per cent at present. But his study also reveals that the proportion had been higher in earlier régimes: a *majority* of the Deputies of the July Monarchy (1830-48) held civil service appointments.

The phenomenon of politicization is not peculiar to the present régime. Nor should its extent be exaggerated: many Deputies may be ex-civil servants, but the vast majority of civil servants never become Deputies. Nor is it true that the politicization always works in favour of the government: the administration is no docile creature manipulated by an unscrupulous government. It may be conceded that a government appoints no declared political opponents to politically sensitive civil service posts (such as prefect or ambassador), and it has never hesitated to replace key civil servants who are suspected of hostility by the politically sympathetic. But the political opinions of civil servants are as diverse as those of the population at large. During the period of Right-wing domination (1959-81) prominent Left-wingers held posts in the central administrations and in the *grands corps*. And even among those who were amicably disposed towards the Right, sympathy was tempered by prudent scepticism. In a country which has seen so many political upsets (and administrative purges) it is scarcely surprising that an expectant opportunism suffuses the entire civil service. It is revealing that when the Socialists came to power in 1981 they left many top officials in their posts (these included the governor of the Bank of France, the secretary-general of the government and most of the top officials in the Ministries of Defence and Foreign Affairs), they merely transferred some to other posts of equal standing (this was the case notably with the Finance Ministry and the prefectoral administration) and they even promoted some who had played prominent roles under the previous government (for example, one of the main *directeurs* in the Finance Ministry was appointed to the chairmanship of a nationalized industry). Furthermore, the Socialists had no problem at all in finding Left-wing sympathizers to man those posts left free by resignations or dismissals. Civil service sympathy for the Right-wing governments which dominated the first twenty years of the Fifth Republic was not always apparent. The leaking of confidential and damaging reports (the Lamoureux Report on the Côte d'Azur, the Albert Report on Paris, the report on the progress of the five-year plan which was leaked during the 1974 presidential election) and of ministerial tax returns revealed a degree of animosity on the part of certain civil servants. The Council of State opposed General de Gaulle's unconstitutional referenda of October 1962 and April 1969, and added insult to injury by leaking its hostile – and "secret" – comments to the press. As a result it earned the reputation in opposition circles of being "a bastion of republican defence", a severe and televised rebuke from the irritated President of the Republic, an official government protest, two venomous paragraphs in General de Gaulle's *Mémoires* and the lasting enmity of diehard Gaullists. Right-wing suspicion of the Council of State has continued throughout the

Fifth Republic: in 1986 Gaullists were accusing it of harbouring *"une armée rose"* because of its numerous socialist sympathizers. Sympathy and even support for the Left was widespread in the top civil service and predominant in the lower echelons (where the decisions are often made and where the scope for obstruction is unlimited). Jean-François Kesler showed that the *Énarques* were more likely that the rest of the population to vote for the Left, while a poll taken just before the second ballot of the 1974 presidential elections among 600 students of the *École Polytechnique* gave Mitterrand a slight majority against Giscard d'Estaing (an ex-student of the school). While the Communist Party attracts few top civil servants the Socialist Party of Mitterrand draws widespread and often active support: among Mitterrand's close lieutenants is a bevy of young, able and ambitious civil servants who now occupy key posts in the Mitterrand presidency.

Government supporters have constantly complained about the political malevolence of the civil service. A Right-wing Deputy, Destremeau, claimed that during the early years of the Fifth Republic there was a "semi-sabotage of governmental decisions in several ministries", and in 1976 several ministers, including Poniatowski, the minister of the interior, denounced politically motivated tax inspectors who were wrecking the government's electoral chances by excessive zeal in collecting taxes. The Left, when in power, took up the chorus, and the administration was now accused of being the enemy of reform. It was revealing that the Council of State, once a "bastion of republican defence" for the Left became the object of Left-wing criticism because it insisted on changes in several government bills. And since the purge of the administration by the Left was not complete, government supporters harboured the gravest doubts about the political reliability of the administration. Yet such paranoia, which underpins most politicians' assessments of civil servants (and not only in France) is largely unjustified. Any government will find political sympathizers in the administration as well as a vast majority of officials who, motivated by careerism or imbued with the notions of service to the state, will offer their services.

Controls on the administration of the Fifth Republic have remained intact and in some respects have been strengthened

The barrage of internal control mechanisms includes a network of Administrative Tribunals, headed by the Council of State and the Mediator's Office (founded in the autumn of 1972 and a pale version of the Ombudsman), which are judicial bodies with the task of judging alleged administrative abuses against the citizen. The Court of Accounts and the Financial Inspectorate look into the financial irregularities of the administration. The efficacy of some internal controls has frequently been called into question. The Court of Accounts, for example, has displayed extreme timidity in inquiring into politically explosive affairs. Concorde, the creation of the petrochemical complex at Fos, the *Plan Calcul* which was supposed to give France an independent computer industry, and the building of the giant meat-marketing complex at La Villette in the Paris outskirts were all examples of extraordinary financial profligacy: Concorde is a commercial disaster, Fos is an economic and ecological catastrophe, the *Plan Calcul* collapsed completely, and La Villette – one of the great scandals of the régime – cost the state ten times the original estimate and is now being transformed into a museum. Yet the Court of Accounts contented itself with criticism only after the scandals broke: like the army of Offenbach, its courage was restored when it was clear that it could reach the battlefield only after the battle was over. The Council of State is also under a cloud because many civil servants treat its judgments with casual disdain: at present a third of its decisions are never executed by culpable officials. Nevertheless, the significance of internal controls should not be understated. The average civil servant dislikes the quibbling inquiries of the *corps de contrôle* and fears the adverse publicity given to any administrative peccadillo.

Perhaps even more important than the *post hoc* internal control mechanisms are the external political controls over the administration. Parliamentary control of the executive has undeniably weakened, but members of parliament still keep a keen eye on the activities of the administration. It may also be argued that with the reinforced ministerial power of the Fifth Republic the power of the civil servants should, logically, decline. Governments of the Fifth Republic, unlike those of the previous régime, can count on a strong and disciplined majority in parliament, and ministers are no longer obliged to spend most of their time in purely political activities, shoring up governments that are fated to early collapse. Despite a few notorious exceptions, ministers of the Fifth Republic have much more time to run their departments and, with the help of their *cabinets*, more closely to supervise the administration. It has certainly been claimed (by Xavier Beauchamps) that the very powerful Budgetary Division of the Ministry of Finance had its power curtailed as the result of increased ministerial power. Nor has the vigilance of the pressure groups weakened under the present régime. The complex relationship between the state and the groups is dealt with in a following chapter, but it is a banality worth underlining at this point that the administration is dependent upon others to ensure the drafting, the smooth passage and the implementation of policies. The administration often needs the groups not only for their expertise but also because they help to legitimize decisions. Paradoxically, increased state interventionism makes the administration both more potentially powerful and more vulnerable to strategically placed monopolistic groups: ultimately, the danger for the French administration may spring not from its overweening power but from its exposure to powerful groups which sap its moral integrity.

The administrative state: some concluding remarks

The administration, as the principal agent of a state which has permeated most sectors of life, enjoys great *potential* power in the formulation and the implementation of social and economic policies. Unquestionably, too, certain civil servants or groups of civil servants (notably in the *corps*) occupy strategic positions and can exploit their expertise or their close political contacts to exert great influence: Feigenbaum's study of the relationship between the state and Elf, its major oil company, underlines the power of the mining engineers. Yet the power and influence of the administration are less great than the critics contend. Marie-Christine Kessler in her study of the *grands corps* argues convincingly that they are incapable of long-term strategic thinking but are well-equipped to carry out measures decided politically, and that their influence is real but sporadic. There are, in practice, real limits to administrative power. In the first place it should be remembered that the state may be ubiquitous but it is not omnipresent: France is not a totalitarian society and civil society is extensive and flourishing. Secondly, it should be noted that in some areas there has been an attempt since the mid 1960s to disengage the state: admittedly the neo-liberal programme of the Barre government was not very ambitious although it did involve the dismantling of part of the price-fixing mechanisms and also privatizing small parts of the French public sector – a policy of privatization which was denounced in the Socialist Party publication entitled, evocatively enough, *L'Agression: l'État Giscard contre le Secteur public*. But, as noted above, the Chirac government of 1986 to 1988 did carry out a significant privatization programme and it continued the policy of liberalization and deregulation pursued by its Socialist predecessor after 1984. Thirdly, there have always been areas of decision-making which the administration is unable or unwilling to penetrate. These "political no-go areas" are discussed in Chapter 11. Finally, one of the more interesting developments in recent years has been the creation by successive governments of independent and autonomous agencies to regulate or supervise particular policies or policy areas: the *Commisssion Nationale de l'Informatique et des Libertés* which expressed reservations about the government's intention of introducing a computerized identity card; the *Conseil de la Concurrence* which monitors (not always very effectively) monopolies, illicit cartels, price-fixing and other restrictive practices; the *Conseil Supérieur de l'Audiovisuel* which supervises the radio and television networks; the *Commission des Sondages* which investigates complaints about opinion polls; the *Commission des Opérations de Bourse* and the *Commission Nationale de contrôle des campagnes électorales* whose titles clearly define their role. These bodies exercise a discretionary power outside the control of the administration. Another development has been the increasing resort to committees of *sages* (wise men and women) and independent experts, especially in highly controversial and politically sensitive areas such as the reform of the nationality laws, the financing of the social security system and the freedom of the media. These two developments represent a further balkanization and autonomization of public policy-making and reduce the power of the traditional administration.

In many other areas the administration may obstruct policies, but not indefinitely, and it is rarely either able or willing to adopt an initiating or creative role: it generally reacts rather than acts, it is passive rather than active. It should also be emphasized that the administration has played no, or very little, part in the *major* decisions which have been made during the Fifth Republic: the principal diplomatic, defence, constitutional, economic and social decisions have been made by politicians not civil servants. The power of the administration is constrained not only by politicians and strategically placed interest groups (some of which colonize and dominate their sponsoring ministries, as is made clear in Chapter 11) but is also limited by its unwieldiness and its proverbial inefficiency. Its effectiveness is impaired, too, by its fragmented and divisive nature. Moreover, internal administrative controls and external political pressures circumscribe its freedom of action. Between its *potential* and *alleged* power and its *effective* power there is a gulf, and it is perhaps the realization of that gulf which explains "the crisis and the malaise of the civil service" which is so frequently referred to in France. The Fifth Republic has altered very little in its attempts to reform the administration: it is no more coherent, no more efficient, no more co-ordinated and no more subordinate to the political masters of the régime than the administration of the Fourth Republic. The intentions of the reformers have been subverted by the weight of traditional habits and prejudices. Many top civil servants continue to take refuge in a passive and prudent careerism and are characterized by unhealthy susceptibilities about personal and corporate privileges. Their subordinates cling to entrenched habits, deify precedent, resist change and obstruct the inconvenient: an epic lethargy and a legendary inefficiency mark the lower ranks of the administration. Certain officials in parts of the administration do enjoy considerable influence but they are by no means alone in the complex fabric of public decision-making, and the price of their power is dependence upon, and co-operation with, the other decision-makers.

7 The French parliament: constitutional constraints and potential power

One of the most striking characteristics of the Fifth Republic is the relatively weak position of parliament. Indeed, it is argued that from its omnipotent position during the Third and Fourth Republics parliament has now been relegated to a position of total impotence. Such a view is, however, misleading. On the one hand, the decline of the French parliament dates not from 1958 but from well before that date. On the other hand, while not denying the decline of the French parliament, its weakness should not be exaggerated. Moreover, while the body may have been very weak at the commencement of the present régime, its influence has slowly increased, and in some political circumstances it may prove to be very great.

Most French historians distinguish four phases in the evolution of parliamentary power in their country. The first period, from 1814 to 1877, from the restoration of the monarchy to the establishment of 'the republican republic', was characterized by the sporadic but apparently inexorable extension of parliamentary power: parliament asserted itself with increasing success against the executive.

During the second phase, from 1877 to 1914, parliamentary supremacy was firmly entrenched, and established as an integral and essential ingredient of the republican tradition. The government during this period was reduced to the role of a mere committee whose main task was the implementation of decisions made in parliament. Within parliament individual members exercised great power, and because of weak party discipline were able to create havoc with governmental proposals; at budget times they would badger unstable governments into concessions in favour of their constituencies. Parliamentary initiatives delayed the adoption of the budget and all too often compromised the balance between revenue and expenditure. It was small wonder that one critic (Gaston Jèze) could describe the parliamentary assemblies as 'wasteful, incompetent and irresponsible'.

The third period, 1918 to 1958, from the victorious conclusion of the First World War to the collapse of the Fourth Republic, was marked by the progressive decline of parliament. The impact of foreign and colonial wars, of military occupation, of the growing weight and technicality of legislation, and the rise of well-organized pressure groups all had their impact in reducing parliament's capacity to initiate or effectively to control legislation. After the First World War, important policies in foreign affairs, defence and economic planning often completely escaped parliamentary attention. A significant step in the demise of parliament dates from 1924, when parliament formally granted the government the right to legislate by the use of decrees. Unfortunately, while recognizing a government's right to legislate in its place, parliament nonetheless persisted in calling into question the political responsibility of the executive. Powerful and highly specialized parliamentary committees harassed hard-pressed ministers, thus earning themselves the reputation of being 'alternative' or 'counter' governments. A number of ingenious constitutional devices were introduced in 1946 to reinforce governmental authority but proved ineffective: the habits of generations proved stronger than the machinations of the well-intentioned framers of the constitution.

During this period 1918-58 parliament slowly abdicated many of its rights and was increasingly bypassed in significant policy areas. Yet parliamentary sovereignty continued to be recognized in a number of important ways: parliament had complete control of its own timetable; it decided its own rules and own agenda; it had the right to legislate in any domain it wished and that right was, in theory, exclusive to itself (although it did, in practice, often delegate its right); it enjoyed a monopoly in supplying ministerial personnel; its members enjoyed a position of power and prestige at the local level. Moreover, parliament constantly paralysed governments by frequently denying them its support: in other words, parliament was a declining yet ultimately all-powerful body, while governments could be powerful in certain circumstances but were generally short-lived. In those conditions neither parliament nor the government was really powerful. It was said that by 1958 government was being carried out not *by* parliament but essentially *through* parliament.

The fourth and final phase in the decline of parliament began in 1958 when the framers of the constitution put parliament in its largely subordinate place. That decline has been accelerated as the result of several political and personal factors. The constitution of the Fifth Republic places the French parliament in an ambivalent position, since it enunciates the principle of governmental responsibility to parliament and at the same time very seriously reduces the power of parliament. In other words, parliament is constitutionally weakened yet the government remains dependent

upon its goodwill for its survival. The weakening of the French
parliament corresponded to the Gaullists' wish to put an end to
the *régime d'assemblée* which they had so persistently criticized
during the Fourth Republic. The principal architect of the French
constitution was Michel Debré, the intransigent and inflexible
minister of justice, whose basic constitutional philosophy was
outlined in his books *Refaire la France* and *Ces Princes qui nous
gouvernent* and in his important speech to the Council of State in
August 1958. His analysis was rooted in a somewhat tendentious
reading of French history. This unrepentant Jacobin believed that
France was profoundly divided on a great number of problems
and that those divisions were reflected in an unstable multi-party
system. As a result, no government could ever rely on stable
and disciplined party support in parliament. It was essential, in
those circumstances, to create institutional mechanisms capable
of protecting the government in its relations with parliament: new
constitutional arrangements should, therefore, compensate for
the traditional absence of a parliamentary majority. Hence, the
notion of *rationalized parliamentarianism*. In place of the *régime
d'assemblée* of the Fourth Republic would be constructed a 'true'
parliamentary régime, on British lines, in which parliament could
control but not destroy or supplant executive power. As a result,
the constitution of the Fifth Republic contains several provisions
which deliberately seek to reduce the powers, the prerogatives
and the prestige of the French parliament.

The constitutional assault upon parliament: the provisions

*The framers of the constitution wished to underline the
new situation by a rigorous separation of executive and
legislative powers*

This separation was clearly inspired by General de Gaulle himself,
and included in the constitution against the advice of Michel
Debré. De Gaulle had always insisted:

> It goes without saying that executive power should not emanate
> from Parliament ... or the result will be a confusion of powers
> which will reduce the Government to a mere conglomeration of
> delegations.... The unity, cohesion and internal discipline of the
> French Government must be held sacred, if national leadership
> is not to degenerate rapidly into incompetence and impotence.
>   But how, in the long run, can this unity, this cohesion and
> this discipline be maintained if executive power is the emanation
> of the very power it ought to counter-balance...?

The separation of legislature and executive is underlined by the appointment of ministers from outside parliament, which represents a sharp break with previous Republican practice. The proportion has varied considerably, ranging from over thirty per cent in the governments of Debré (1959-62), Chirac (1974-76) and Fabius (1984-86) to less than ten per cent in the governments of Couve de Murville (1968-69), Chaban-Delmas (1969-72) and Messmer (1972-74). Moreover, Article 23 of the constitution makes membership of the government incompatible with that of parliament. If a member of parliament is appointed to a ministerial post he must relinquish his parliamentary seat to a replacement (*suppléant*) who is elected at the same time as himself. Furthermore, the minister gives up his seat for the remainder of the legislature: thus if he is appointed minister just after a general election he may have to wait another five years before entering parliament again. It was hoped that this provision would put a brake on the undignified scramble for ministerial portfolios which had characterized previous republics, for, it was argued, Deputies would think twice before sacrificing their parliamentary seats. It was also felt that temperamental ministers would hesitate before resigning (thus causing a government crisis) if they had no seat in parliament to go back to. This so-called 'incompatibility rule' was seen, therefore, as a factor which would make governments more stable. But the rule has been too much for most ministers. After officially resigning from parliament they still keep both feet firmly in their constituency which they continue to visit and assiduously to nurse. A member of their private staff is always given the task of keeping a keen eye on constituency affairs. Many ministers (and not the least, since they include such men as Chaban-Delmas and Chirac) on quitting the government have insisted that their replacements resign, which then leaves the seat empty. In the ensuing by-election the minister stands as a candidate in the hope of being re-elected. It has even been claimed that certain replacements provide their members of parliament who are possible ministers with undated letters of resignation. Those rare replacements who have obstinately refused to resign have been denounced for their treasonable behaviour. The spirit if not the letter of the constitution has been constantly violated; Article 23 has become a constitutional absurdity. The breakdown of the incompatibility rule was inevitable, since French politicians feel deprived without a local power base. It is instructive that even most ministers chosen from outside parliament strive to find a constituency in the following general election (André Malraux, minister of culture was one of the few ministers to translate his disdain for parliament into a wish never to become one of its members). They feel, not without justification, that a parliamentary seat gives them added political prestige and weight in negotiating with their ministerial colleagues and with their own ministries.

If the attempt to separate legislative and executive powers has been less than a success, the same cannot be said of the panoply of other constitutional measures which were designed to ensure the docility of parliament.

There are now severe restrictions on the time parliament is allowed to meet

Previous republican constitutions guaranteed a *minimum* period for parliamentary sessions, while that of the Fifth Republic imposes a *maximum* period. Parliament now meets only twice a year in ordinary session, for a total of not more than five and a half months a year. Special sessions are limited to a fortnight, and only on the basis of a specifically defined agenda. The purpose of these provisions was to put an end to the lengthy parliamentary sessions of the Third and Fourth Republics. But parliamentary sessions are now so short that governments often have difficulty in pushing through their own legislation, and the end of each session is characterized by an undignified scramble to complete governmental business. As a result the efficacy of parliamentary control has diminished as the disgruntlement of members of parliament has grown, and the quality of legislation has undeniably suffered. It is revealing that the Socialist governments of 1981 to 1986, which were anxious to push through a massive reform programme and which were faced with increasing obstructionism from the opposition, had to resort to convoking special sessions of parliament: seventeen such sessions compared with only four in the previous legislature. The figures are eloquent: the National Assembly sat for 1,012 hours in 1984 compared with 709 hours in 1980 and 574 hours in 1970.

Severe restrictions have been imposed on law-making by parliament

Article 34 of the constitution defines the area of law (i.e. legislation which has to be passed by parliament) in two ways:

● Parliament determines the rules on a range of specified subjects, which include fundamental liberties, civil status and civil rights, liability to taxation, conscription, penal procedures and electoral laws.

● It also lays down the general principles and the framework of laws relating to another range of subjects, comprising local government, education, property rights, trade union law, social security and finance bills. The detailed implementation of such laws is left to the government.

Any area not specified in the above two categories is left entirely to the discretion of the government. The constitutional restriction of the law-making domain represents the most important single breach of the principle of parliamentary sovereignty, and contrasts sharply with the British situation which Michel Debré was apparently trying to emulate.

The government has been given effective control of the timetable and agenda of both houses of parliament

The government can and does give priority to its own measures. The number of private members' bills (*propositions de loi*) has fallen dramatically: of the bills which were enacted nearly a third were private members' bills during the Fourth Republic, 11.7 per cent during de Gaulle's presidency, 16.5 per cent during Pompidou's period of office, 12.6 per cent during Giscard d'Estaing's, and 9.1 per cent during the first five years of Mitterrand's first presidency. The executive has not been very generous in its dealings with parliament, especially in allowing time for full-scale debates on politically important or contentious issues: between 1959 and 1974, for example, the National Assembly, which had been the major political forum of the Fourth Republic, held full-scale debates on an average of only ninety-one days a year. Again, unlike the British situation, the opposition to the government has absolutely no right at all to have time in which it can determine the nature of parliamentary business.

The committee structure of the National Assembly has been drastically altered

During the Fourth Republic there were nineteen permanent highly specialized committees, each composed of forty-four prominent members (although, in practice, they were often controlled by a much smaller group) and each zealously monitoring the activities of a particular ministry (a zeal which was often heightened by the chairman coveting the portfolio he was controlling). Ministerial bills were often savaged beyond recognition at the committee stage. These 'permanent anti-governments' of the Fourth Republic have now been replaced by six much larger committees:

Four committees of 61 members
Defence
Finance
Foreign affairs
Legal and administrative matters

Two committees of up to 121 members
Production and trade (which includes agriculture, fishing, public works and town planning)
Cultural, social and family affairs

These parliamentary committees are much less specialized and more unwieldy than the smaller committees of the previous régime, and are far less capable of detailed interference in governmental legislation. They were further weakened by another important innovation: under the Fifth Republic, parliament has to debate the text of the government's bill and not the one emanating from the appropriate committee. The present situation is recognized by many to be totally unsatisfactory. There is too much legislation for too few committees, and there have been many demands (including one from the speaker of the National Assembly) to increase their number.

The financial powers of parliament have been severely curtailed

Article 40 of the constitution and the Organic Law of 2 January 1959 stipulate that, without the consent of the government, Deputies may propose no increase in expenditure or reduction in taxation through a private member's bill. Governments under the Fifth Republic have also been given tight control over finance bills: this is to prevent the previous practice of Deputies holding up the budget in order to extract concessions from a desperate and precarious government. Parliament is now given a total of seventy days to debate and vote the budget, and after that the government has the right to impose it by ordinance. In fact, no government has invoked this provision since the foundation of the Fifth Republic, although it might prove to be a useful weapon in the future.

Parliament's power to force a government from office has been severely limited

In fact, the government has to resign in only three sets of circumstances:

● If a vote of censure is carried in the National Assembly. The means by which such a motion must be passed were clearly designed to help the government. A motion of censure has to be moved by a tenth of the members who, if the motion fails, are then precluded for the remainder of the parliamentary session from moving another motion of censure. This can be a severe restriction: from 1968 to 1973, for example, opposition Deputies represented only three-tenths of the total membership of the National Assembly. This stipulation does not apply, however, if the government makes the motion an issue of confidence. Deputies have to wait for forty-eight hours before voting on the motion: during this interval tempers may cool and the government may make promises or threats to convince the waverers. In the vote of censure, only votes in favour are counted, abstentions being considered as favourable to the government, this provision being based on the dubious yet convenient assumption that those not against the government are for it. Finally, for a motion of censure to be carried it must be voted by a majority of those present: thus absentees join the abstainers as being considered to be not against the government. The vote of censure is thus difficult to carry; since the foundation of the Fifth Republic only one, in October 1962, has been successful. In practice, a motion of censure is relatively rare: in the first seven legislatures of the Fifth Republic (1959-1986) there were only thirty one.

● The government must also resign if parliament rejects its statement of general policy, but only when it has specifically pledged its responsibility. A simple majority of the National Assembly suffices in these circumstances. The only time a prime minister is likely to pledge governmental responsibility on a statement of general policy is when he is sure of its majority or when he may wish to provoke parliament into forcing its resignation: on taking office Debré (October 1959), Pompidou (April 1962), Chirac (June 1974 and April 1986), Mauroy (June 1981) and Fabius (July 1984) pledged the responsibility of their governments, but Pompidou (April 1966), Couve de Murville (May 1968), Chaban-Delmas (June 1969) and Rocard (June 1988) refused to do so.

● Under Article 49(3) of the constitution the government may be forced from office by the rejection of any bill which it has made an issue of confidence. But once the government has made it an issue of confidence, the bill is automatically carried unless a censure motion can be prepared and carried in the circumstances outlined above. The use of this device is shown in Table 3.

Table 3   Use of Article 49(3) of the constitution

Period	Prime Minister	Number
1959–62	Debré	4
1962–68	Pompidou	6
1968–69	Couve de Murville	—
1969–72	Chaban-Delmas	—
1972–74	Messmer	—
1974–76	Chirac	—
1976–81	Barre	8
1981–84	Mauroy	7
1984–86	Fabius	4
1986–87	Chirac (year 1)	8

As can be seen, the device was frequently used during the period 1976-81 by Prime Minister Barre: when pushing through his economic policies (the so-called *Plan Barre*) in 1976, his bills on direct elections to the European Parliament in 1977 and on the financing of the social security system in 1979. In the same year he resorted to this constitutional mechanism to get the budget past an unhappy Gaullist group. His successors exploited the device either to discipline their own troops or to push through controversial legislation when pressed for time: this legislation included the wage and price freeze of June and July 1982, the Press Bill of July 1984, the Privatization Bill of July 1986 and the Bill permitting more flexible work arrangements in December 1985 and in May 1987.

The government may declare a bill to be a matter of urgency which enables it to invoke procedures to accelerate its passage through parliament

The governments under de Gaulle's presidency used this device (outlined in Article 45 of the constitution) on sixty-three occasions, those under Pompidou sixty-eight times, while the governments of Giscard d'Estaing invoked the procedure no fewer than 141 times. The Socialist governments of 1981 to 1986 frequently exploited Article 45: 27 times in 1984, 54 times in 1985 and 24 times in 1986.

Although Deputies and Senators may propose amendments to any bill the government may, at any time, insist on a single vote on its own text.

'Its own text' is the whole bill with only such amendments as the government has proposed or accepted. In other words, the government can insist on parliament making a package vote (*vote bloqué*), thus preventing parliament from destroying the coherence of a bill by amendments related to specific points. This provision, contained in Article 44(3), has been invoked regularly during the Fifth Republic: 114 times in the National Assembly and 220 times in the Senate during the de Gaulle presidency, eleven and thirty-two times respectively during the Pompidou presidency, and thirty-two and twenty-five times during that of Giscard d'Estaing. The procedure is much disliked by members of parliament, and pressure has been brought on the government to abandon this weapon. So far, the government has proved unyielding, for it is too useful a weapon, especially if members of parliament are proving to be obstreperous and obstructive. It came as no surprise that an exasperated Prime Minister Mauroy should use the procedure in February 1982 to impose the revised Nationalization Bill, after the first had been rejected by the Constitutional Council. He and Fabius were to use it on ten further occasions: eight times in the Senate and three times in the National Assembly. The Right-wing Chirac government of 1986 used Article 44(3) five times in the first six months of office, and, by so doing, was able, for instance, to prevent a National Front amendment re-establishing the death penalty.

The government has the right under Article 38 of the constitution, to ask parliament to authorize it to legislate by ordinance for a specific period on any subject normally requiring laws voted in parliament

The constitution thus formalizes the traditional practice of parliament allowing the government to legislate by way of *décrets-lois*. Between January 1958 and January 1982 this right was requested on only sixteen occasions, so its use was infrequent. Indeed, its use was often interpreted as a sign of weakness. Nevertheless, the legislation passed by such enabling acts was important and included the maintenance of public order in Algeria, the implementation of provisions of the Treaty of Rome, agricultural problems, social security, and social problems such as alcoholism and prostitution. The Socialist governments of Mauroy and Fabius resorted to Article 38 on five occasions: in January 1982, for instance, it was used to push through a package of social measures which included the lowering of the retirement age, the shortening of the official working week, and the creation of a job opportunities scheme. Article 38 was also invoked to push through the austerity measures of May 1983, the unemployment benefit reforms of December 1983, and legislation on New Caledonia (in February 1982 and again in April 1985). They were but other examples of the clash between opposition principles and governmental practice, for the Socialists had been bitter critics of the provision before May 1981. The Chirac government of 1986 did not have the same capacity to resort to Article 38, since it ran into the opposition of President Mitterrand who refused, for instance, to sign ordinances enabling the implementation of wide-ranging privatization measures and the introduction of more flexible hours and practices for French workers. The government was, therefore, forced to go back to parliament and have the bills passed by normal traditional procedures (in fact, it exploited Article 44(3) – see above – to ensure speedy parliamentary enactment).

The constitutional measures outlined above constitute a powerful combination of constraints – what has been described as a 'rigid constitutional corset' which highly restricts parliamentary initiative and control. As Professor Goguel points out, the framers of the constitution created a form of parliamentary régime without parliamentary sovereignty. But the constitutional weakness of parliament has been aggravated by other factors which will now be considered.

The decline of parliament: factors unconstitutional and extra-constitutional

The constitutional provisions outlined above have generally been interpreted in a highly restrictive manner by successive governments. The Constitutional Council, which has the task of deciding disputes between the executive and the legislature over their respective rights, has generally been as friendly towards the latter as the former. The Constitutional Council has also not been particularly ungenerous in defining the competence of parliament to make laws and in interpreting parliament's financial powers, particularly during the early years of the Fifth Republic. On occasions, however, the powers of parliament have been severely limited. For instance, in May 1960, following unrest in certain rural parts of France, a majority of the National Assembly requested a special session of parliament to debate the agricultural policy of the government. The constitution seemed clearly to indicate that the President of the Republic was obliged to convoke parliament. Yet General de Gaulle flatly refused, arguing, in essence, that the Deputies were acting out of fear and under pressure from rowdy and politically irresponsible pressure groups. The March 1960 incident was an exceptional, yet revealing incident: it demonstrated the first president's contempt for an institution to which he had never belonged and to which he attributed many of the errors of the previous regime.

A second factor which has led to a further weakening of parliament has been the attitude of certain prime ministers towards it: Michel Debré treated it with barely disguised impatience; Georges Pompidou generally affected a benign detachment; Messmer was apprehensive while Chirac was petulant and impatient and Barre was patronizing, didactic and irritable. Only Chaban-Delmas (who had been a member of parliament for many years and president of the National Assembly for ten years before his appointment to the premiership) and Mauroy (a parliamentarian of long-standing) showed any sensitivity for the feelings of the representatives of the nation, but they improved merely the form rather than the substance of the relationship between the government and parliament. All prime ministers have displayed a steady determination to maintain the subordination of parliament.

A third factor which helps to explain parliamentary weakness relates to the technical incompetence and physical incapacity of parliament to deal with present legislation. The weight of modern legislation is daunting, and given the shortness of its sessions, parliament rarely has the time to control the government's legislative programme: 878 bills were promulgated during the de Gaulle presidency, 492 during that of Pompidou, 756 during the *septennat* of Giscard d'Estaing, and over 550 during the first five years of Mitterrand's office. Important bills are given only cursory attention; an important change in the rules governing the election of the President of the Republic was debated at one meeting – during the night – in April 1976. As in other western democracies, the problem is particularly acute in the financial field. Each year a member of parliament receives from the government more than 120 separate documents representing 30,000 pages relating to the annual budget: according to one exasperated Deputy the budgetary documents of 1977 weighed more than twenty kilos. If he is conscientious he would also have to wade through the hundreds of amendments proposed by private members as well as the reports of the Finance Committee. The problem is rendered worse by the technical and intricate nature of financial legislation. The budget, with all its far-reaching and complex financial and economic consequences and implications, is increasingly based on a rationally quantifiable model (although the 'rationality' is often used to disguise some very irrational political choices), a set of forecasts (which have the genius of being invariably wrong) and a nice calculation of party and pressure group interests. The annual budget is a prodigious act of balancing, and if members of parliament upset one part of the structure the rest may collapse: in the words of Professor Lalumière, parliamentary amendments may 'disturb the internal coherence of the whole [budgetary] system'. In such circumstances,no government is likely to look kindly upon parliamentary amendments.

The fourth extra-constitutional explanation for parliamentary ineffectiveness must be sought in the acceptance, toleration or indifference shown by Deputies towards certain abuses committed by the government which have the effect of reducing parliamentary control. For instance, they have grumbled but have done little about the government sending them badly drafted bills very near the end of the parliamentary session. Nor have they taken any action against last-minute changes in the parliamentary agenda which were made to suit the government. They have also done little to insist on prompt answers to parliamentary questions. In spite of improvements since the mid-1970s delays occur all too frequently: nearly fifteen per cent of the written questions to the government between 1981 and 1986 received no reply. The situation in the early years of the Fifth Republic could border on the ludicrous: a question about the Ben-Barka affair (a leader of the Left-wing opposition of a foreign country was kidnapped in broad daylight in Paris and then 'disappeared') which was put down in November 1965 received an answer (as the government euphemistically described it) in May 1967. All too frequently Deputies have accepted, albeit with ill grace, that their questions will be treated with little respect. On 28 November 1975, for example, the junior minister for *housing* gave perfunctory replies to parliamentary questions concerning atomic energy, the French car industry, the crisis in the textile industry, and the speed limits of heavy lorries. The appropriate ministers were not in parliament, even though the rules stipulated that they should be.

It is in the all-important financial and economic domain that parliament has not asserted the rights that belong to it. It is not only that parliament's control over the numerous (over 600) public and semi-public enterprises is largely fictitious. That has always been the case. Nor is it that the government seems totally unconcerned about keeping parliament well informed about the nation's economic affairs: while parliament was piously debating the aims of the seventh economic plan in 1976 the government was simultaneously taking other measures which ensured that many of those aims would not be realized. More disturbing is what the French call the process of 'debudgetization' which has steadily increased since 1963. That ugly but useful gallicism means that the government has placed important items of public expenditure outside the official budgetary process (which is examined, however inadequately, in parliament) and has transferred the responsibility for financing such items to bodies which, in practice, completely escape parliamentary control.

The fifth major source of the extra-constitutional weakness of parliament is that body's inability or unwillingness to exploit the meagre means which remain at its disposal. Examples abound. Parliamentary questions requiring written replies are fully exploited (in 1973, for example, there were more than 6500), but the potentially more interesting question times in parliament are treated with disrespect by ministers and indifference by deputies. Parliamentary debates only rarely attract a good attendance: most debates are ill-attended and ineffective. On one afternoon during the debate on the very important regional reform of July 1972 only fourteen Deputies were in attendance, while the highly controversial issue of the financing of the social security system attracted only eighteen Deputies to the chamber when it was debated in June 1987.

Constitutional experts have pointed out that there exists a battery of devices which may seem very complex and over-ingenious but which would increase parliamentary control over financial legislation – if effectively used. Parliament has also been timid in setting up special *ad hoc* committees to examine designated public economic and financial corporations: although many such corporations badly need examination, parliament has exercised its right to do so only twice since 1959. *Ad hoc* commissions of inquiry or control are rarely established if the subject proposed is likely to prove politically embarrassing to the government. In 1975, parliament itself refused requests to investigate, among other things, the exorbitant profits of the pharmaceutical industry, the creation of nuclear energy plants, and the pollution of the mouth of the Seine.

The sixth major source of weakness of the French parliament lies in the scope of the subjects it considers. In foreign, European, colonial and defence matters, parliamentary control is derisory: in May 1977 even the very pro-governmental Deputy Le Theule was moved to protest that parliament was not even informed of vast changes in the organization of the French army. Part of the fault lies, however, with Deputies themselves, since most accept executive dominance in this area. It is instructive that of all the questions put down in the National Assembly in 1983 only 2.3 per cent related to foreign affairs. Even major domestic matters of great political sensitivity (such as the situation in Corsica, the agricultural riots in the south of France or the economic effects of the terrible drought of the summer of 1976) were not debated. The highly controversial nuclear energy programme was the subject of only one debate of a few hours (and was not followed by a vote) during the period 1959 to 1981. It is depressing, yet revealing, to consider the role of parliament during two of the great political crises of the Fifth Republic. The first was the generals' *putsch* of April 1961, when parliament was reduced to listening to a fifteen-minute message from the President of the Republic. The second was in May 1968, when members of parliament were the helpless spectators of events far beyond their control and comprehension.

Even in areas which fall within the law-making field of parliament control is often cursory. Parliament is frequently by-passed, as the government enters into direct contact with the pressure groups. Again, there is an embarrassing number of examples. One such occurred in November 1971 when the government and the main civil service trades unions agreed a salary structure for the following year. Parliament which, in principle, fixes the expenditures on civil service staff was not associated with the agreement: it merely ratified the agreement when the 1972 budget was voted. Similarly, the financial compensation given to farmers badly hit by the summer drought of 1976 was agreed between the government and the main agricultural interest groups: parliament was left with the ungrateful ritual of ratifying the *fait accompli*.

The seventh extra-constitutional reason for the ineffectiveness of parliament lies in its inability to control the implementation of even those measures which are voted in parliament. In France, most laws are, in principle, implemented by a series of decrees (*décrets d'application*). In some cases (such as the law on early retirement benefits for ex-servicemen) the decrees have been so restrictive in their interpretation that they subvert the intentions of the framers of the law. In other cases, the decrees are promulgated very late. It was reported by Prime Minister Barre that, on average, six months after the promulgation of a law half the statutory instruments had still to be issued. The law of July 1966 on sickness insurance for independent workers and the liberal professions was rushed through parliament in twenty days, but the decrees enabling implementation were promulgated only in November 1968, two and a half years later. Two years after the passage of the 1975 Handicapped Persons Act only ten of the expected forty decrees had been promulgated, and more than a year after parliament voted the Secondary Education Act of June 1975 not one decree had been issued. Many decrees are never promulgated at all: certain parts of the Higher Education Act of 1968 remained, happily, a dead letter. Even when decrees are promulgated they are frequently ignored by the people responsible for implementing them. The Savary Law on the composition of university councils was promulgated in January 1984, but by July

1987 twenty seven of the seventy four universities had not yet implemented it. The Neuwirth Contraception Bill (so called after the deputy responsible for guiding it through parliament) was passed in December 1967, but it took seven years for it to be put into effect. Certain anti-pollution measures voted in parliament in the 1960s and the 1976 law controlling the use of hormones for beef are still awaiting implementation. It has been calculated that about a third of all laws are only partially implemented and over a tenth are never implemented at all.

It is in the economic and financial field that the gap between the texts voted in parliament and the ensuing practice is most glaring. Ministries frequently change their budgets (voted in parliament) in the light of changed circumstances or new pressures, and blandly ignore the criticisms made against them by the Court of Accounts, a worthy but toothless animal. Parliament has occasionally expressed its dissatisfaction and has made an official protest about the practice. But the protest was more symbolic than real: the practice is but another example of a widely tolerated abuse.

The final and most important reason for parliamentary submissiveness towards the executive has been the lack, since 1959, of an anti-governmental majority in the National Assembly. Given the nature of the constitutional weapons at the disposal of the executive it does not require a working majority in the National Assembly. It merely has to prevent a hostile majority forming against it. Thus, the Rocard government after the June 1988 elections did not enjoy a friendly majority in the Assembly (the Socialist Party and allies were thirteen short of an absolute majority) but could survive so long as the divided opposition (which ranged from Right-wing Gaullists to Communists) did not combine to vote a motion of censure. And abstention, it must be recalled, is tantamount to backing the government. The Debré government of 1959 to 1962 also survived because the opposition parties (ranging from Communists to extreme Right-wing *Algérie Française* supporters) refused to come together and vote a motion of censure. For most of the Fifth Republic, however, the government has been able to count upon the support of a reasonably cohesive and disciplined party coalition with a majority in the National Assembly. Until the election of Giscard d'Estaing to the presidency, there was a basic identity of views between the government and the party which dominated the parliamentary coalition, since both were Gaullists. Between 1976 and 1981 the Barre government encountered some opposition from its Gaullist allies, but the prime minister had no compunction in exploiting constitutional procedures in order to bring them into line. Between 1981 and 1986 the government and assembly were once again dominated by the same coalition. The basic premiss on which the constitution was framed has proved totally unfounded: the elaborate institutional procedures devised by Michel Debré to compensate for the *lack* of a parliamentary majority, although ruthlessly exploited, have been for most of the Fifth Republic rendered superfluous. The 'constitutional corset' was placed upon a body determined to diet on the political equivalent of grapefruit and grated carrots. The government's majority in the National Assembly since 1958 has ranged from the uncomfortable (1958-62) and the precarious (1967-8, 1986-88) to the comfortable (1962-7, 1973-8, 1978-81) and the massive (1968-73, 1981-86).

The parliamentary groups within the ruling coalition are co-ordinated by a liaison committee comprising the leaders of the constituent groups. Until mid-1976 the prime minister occasionally intervened within the committee to impose presidential directives. However, between 1976 and 1981, the Gaullists, who constituted the biggest single group in the pro-governmental coalition, refused prime ministerial arbitration. The early practice seems, however, to have re-emerged under the Mauroy premiership, possibly because the prime minister was liked by all the parties of the Left.

The government has not only generally enjoyed a majority in the National Assembly but it has used its majority to colonize all the key posts in the parliamentary committees: all the chairmanships and vice chairmanships are generally in the hands of government supporters. Any attempts to give a chairmanship to an opposition party has so far failed: equity and polarized politics are difficult bedfellows.

The demise of the French parliament may be attributed to a combination of factors – the constitutional restrictions, governmental ill-will, the obstructionism of the administration, the indifference of individual members of parliament, and the domination of parliament by a disciplined pro-governmental coalition. Members of parliament are reasonably well paid, and they enjoy free travel and free postal and telephone facilities. In 1970 they were granted an allowance to employ a secretary, in 1974 they were each given an office, and in 1976 they were each awarded a grant to employ a research assistant. But the facilities, although infinitely better than those at Westminster, do not compensate for the political frustration of parliamentary life: absenteeism, which is rife, is both a consequence and a cause of the decline of parliament. In July 1971, the chairman of the six permanent committees of the National Assembly, all of whom belonged to pro-government parties, formally and publicly protested about the way the government treated parliament. And every year the presidents of the National Assembly and the Senate solemnly and ritualistically complain about the intolerable conditions of parliamentary life, but for more than twenty years the 'intolerable' has been tolerated.

A powerless parliament?

The question arises: does parliament serve any useful purpose at all? Is parliament, as many critics have claimed, merely 'a talking-shop', an elaborate and costly institution whose main function is to rubber-stamp and legitimize executive decisions? The claim needs to be modified somewhat. First, parliament, however weak, continues to define the general parameters of executive action: the president and the government are aware of what is and is not acceptable to parliament. So, too, are the leaders of the opposition. When Prime Minister Chaban-Delmas announced his famous programme for liberalizing French society, François Mitterrand, the leader of the Socialists, expressed a justifiable scepticism: for Mitterrand, it was not the will of the prime minister which was in question but the willingness of his parliamentary supporters to back him. Those supporters who had been elected in the 'elections of fear' of June 1968 were deeply conservative and fearful of many of the reforms proposed by the prime minister: they had been elected not to reform society but to protect society against subversion. The President of the Republic, Pompidou, was more in tune with the political sentiments of the National Assembly, and his opposition combined with parliamentary reticence was sufficient to prevent the realization of the prime minister's programme. It was also clear that the early reforming zeal of President Giscard d'Estaing had to be tempered by an appraisal of what an essentially conservative parliament would tolerate. By way of contrast President Mitterrand had to keep a wary eye on the much more radical National Assembly which he helped to elect in 1981; the Socialist Deputies who formed a majority in the Assembly frequently intimated their impatience with the moderation of some of the government's bills. In 1984 pressure from the more anti-clerical Socialist Deputies led to amendments to the Savary bill on private (essentially Catholic) schools – amendments which inflamed Catholic opinion and which eventually led to damaging confrontations with the Catholic school lobby, to the withdrawal of the bill by the President of the Republic, and to the resignation of the Minister of Education.

Mitterrand had also to contend with a Senate which became progressively hostile during the period 1981 to 1986. The framers of the Fifth Republic clearly assigned a subordinate role within parliament to the upper house. Elected by local *notables* for nine years (a third of the house is renewed every three years) and to a disproportionate extent from the rural areas, Senators lack the democratic legitimacy of members of the National Assembly. The Senate is a closed, autonomous, elitist body, jealous of its prerogatives and suspicious of any outside interference. It cannot be dissolved, and it enjoys certain important powers. Its president replaces on an interim basis the president of the Republic in the event of the death, resignation or incapability of the latter. The Senate also enjoys access to the Constitutional Council. According to the constitution, every law must be voted in identical terms by both houses of parliament. In the event of disagreement a commission is established comprising equal numbers of Deputies and Senators. If the disagreement persists the government has the right to give the last word to the lower house, except for organic laws affecting the Senate itself or constitutional amendments. Throughout the Fifth Republic the Senate has been influential in a non-partisan way for cleaning up highly technical bills such as those affecting company law or bills concerning individual rights (the 1966 law on adoption, the 1981 law on the rights of entry and domicile of foreigners, the 1982 housing reform) and has been especially active whenever agricultural, local interests (it played a key role in the decentralization reforms of 1979-86) or the media (particularly in 1974 and 1984) are under discussion.

Relations between the government and the Senate have varied considerably. Under the presidency of de Gaulle the Senate remained in sulky if largely ineffective opposition. It opposed the 1962 constitutional reforms [which changed the system of electing the President of the Republic] and the 1969 constitutional reforms (which included changing the nature of the upper house) of the President of the Republic whom they accused of 'anti-Republicanism'. Under Pompidou and, more particularly, under Giscard d'Estaing relations with the executive became much more harmonious. This harmony was embedded in a high degree of political agreement, since the Senate shared the moderate and conservatism of those two presidents. With the election of the Socialists in 1981, and especially after the 1983 senatorial elections which reinforced the Gaullists the upper house became an active partisan body which was determined to obstruct major government bills. It spearheaded parliamentary opposition in 1981-82 to the nationalization programme, and in 1984 to the Auroux legislation on workers' rights, the higher education reforms, the press bill and the proposals on private schools. In 1983 it even tried to obstruct the budget, for the first time since the foundation of the Fifth Republic and in July 1984 it effectively buried Mitterrand's plan to extend the use of the referendum. It never hesitated to submit a controversial bill to the Constitutional Council during this period. The Senate became, in the words of Jean-Louis Quermonne, 'the citadel of the opposition'. The Socialists had to invoke constitutional procedures to pass their legislation against the opposition of the Senate. The result was that between 1981-1986 only 75 per cent (compared with 97 per cent between 1959 and 1981) of all bills were voted in identical terms by both houses, and more than twice as many bills were passed without senatorial consent than during the previous twenty-three years: there were 38 such bills during the presidency of de Gaulle, 17 under that of Pompidou, six only under Giscard d'Estaing and 140 between 1981 and 1986. The emergence of an aggressive and politicized Senate constituted a significant change in the politics of the Fifth Republic.

There have been several cases of a president of the Republic having to drop cherished ideas because of the opposition of parliament. These include Pompidou's wish to reduce the presidential mandate from seven to five years, Giscard d'Estaing's plan to modify the 'incompatibility rule' which debars ministers from retaining their seats in parliament, and Mitterrand's planned referendum of 1984 which ran into virulent opposition in the Senate. The government has also been forced by Deputies to withdraw proposed legislation before it even reached parliament. In October 1968, for example, Prime Minister Couve de Murville had to abandon his plan to increase estate duties because of the hostility of prominent Gaullist members of parliament, and in November 1976, Prime Minister Barre withdrew a bill designed to increase the budgetary discretion of the European Assembly in Strasbourg because of Gaullist opposition.

The second way in which parliament continues to control the executive, particularly since 1974, is through parliamentary questions and through amendments to the government's bills. The number of questions has risen steadily during the Fifth Republic. The Socialist governments of 1981 to 1986 had to deal with 1,522 'questions to the government' – a system based on the British House of Commons question time – 961 oral questions without debate, and 80,898 written questions – some 15,000 to 20,000 a year (compared with 3,000 to 4,000 in the 1960s).

Amendments to government legislation have also increased throughout the period and especially after 1980. This is clear from the figures: between 1959 and 1979 an average of 2,944 amendments to government bills were proposed annually in the National Assembly, and that figure rose between 1980 and 1985 to 7,098. The corresponding figures for the Senate were 2,135 to 4,161. In the seventh legislature (1981-86) 551 laws were adopted,

38,997 amendments were registered, of which 15,711 (or 40 per cent) were adopted. The peak years for amendments were 1982 and 1984 when 10,081 and 6,180 were registered in the National Assembly and 41,752 and 8,553 respectively in the Senate. There are many instances of members of parliament forcing alterations on a reluctant government: changes which they demanded and obtained from the government relate to matters such as the independence of the Comoro Islands (May 1975), the retirement age of high-ranking civil servants and judges (June 1975), the protection of forests in the neighbourhood of big towns (April 1976), the modification of the electoral law proposed by the minister of the interior (July 1976). In June and July 1976 they rendered an already anodyne capital gains tax, inspired by the President of the Republic, even less noxious to the capital gainers, and in May 1977 they extracted from the government important concessions in the major bill relating to local finances. Most of the legislation of the 1980s on decentralisation was substantially amended as the result of parliamentary activity. The highly controversial *Sécurité et Liberté* Law of June 1980 was the object of a determined assault by members of parliament who put down 497 amendments, ninety-two of which were accepted by the government (and fifty-three of which were inspired by Socialist Deputies). Similarly, the Savary Bill on higher education in 1983 was the object of 2,204 amendments (some of which – and by no means the least significant – were adopted) while the 1984 Press Bill attracted 2,378 amendments.

Of course, many amendments were simply a means of delaying or obstructing the passage of legislation: the 1,438 amendments proposed to the nationalization legislation in October 1981 consumed 33 parliamentary sittings and 118 hours of precious parliamentary time; it took 133 hours to discuss the amendments to the Savary Bill. The 'parliamentary guerrilla' activities of the Right between 1981 and 1986 provoked the Left into similar tactics when in opposition: Socialist and Communist Deputies put down 600 amendments to the 1986 Privatization Bill, 540 to the June 1986 Press Bill and 616 to the November 1986 bill designed, among other things, to abolish the need for administrative permission to declare redundancies (the bill required 15 sittings and 54 hours of debate before being passed). The use of amendments together with procedural devices provided by the parliamentary rules could delay the passage of legislation, forcing some governments into invoking the highly unpopular *vote bloqué* procedure or, more commonly, into concessions. The Senate held up the 1979-80 decentralization reforms by seventeen months: 200 hours of debate were required to debate the 1,500 amendments proposed, many by Right-wing

Senators. In 1986 the upper house took over 180 hours to deal with the 1,844 amendments proposed to a major bill on the media. It is also the case that no budget escapes a parliamentary mauling, and several have been modified because of parliamentary opposition. In almost all cases, a government is forced to give some ground to its own hostile backbenchers, and concessions are normally negotiated before the legislation reaches parliament: this was the case in October 1986 when centrist Deputies forced the Gaullist Finance Minister to make concessions to the 1987 budget.

The third check on the executive provided by parliament is through its role as pedagogue and as the exposer of scandals. It has several means of doing this. First, on the floor of the House it may exploit all the many procedural devices available to harass the government and delay its legislation: this was notably the case with the major Decentralization and Nationalization Bills presented to parliament by the Socialist government in 1981-2. The second major or publicity-creating mechanism available to members of parliament is the committees and commissions of parliament. The permanent parliamentary committees have been responsible for sensitizing or mobilizing public opinion on issues as varied as civil service salaries, conscientious objection and conscription. The *ad hoc* parliamentary Commissions of Inquiry and Commissions of Control (there were a total of twenty-five set up by the National Assembly and seventeen by the Senate in the period 1959-86) uncovered scandals relating to illicit publicity on television, the wholesale marketing system of meat in Paris, property speculation, the lucrative but unpatriotic practices of the major petrol companies in France, the notoriously inadequate telephone network, some of the doubtful financial practices of the Dassault aircraft company, and the sinking of the *Amoco Cadiz* – the great environmental disaster off the Brittany coast in 1978. The Report of the Commission of Inquiry of September 1979 on the media was so critical of the government that the pro-governmental *rapporteur* resigned from the commission.

The fourth – and increasingly effective – means available to parliament in order to constrain the executive is through the Constitutional Council. One of President Giscard d'Estaing's early reforms was to extend to sixty Deputies or Senators the right to submit to the Constitutional Council any law they considered unconstitutional. Denounced at the time as a *réformette*, the right has been exploited increasingly by members of parliament. During the presidency of Giscard d'Estaing they seized the Council forty-seven times (forty-five times by opposition members): of the forty-seven contested measures the Council declared thirty-two to be constitutional and thirteen unconstitutional (on the remaining two occasions the Council declared the request invalid). The thirteen unconstitutional acts were by no means insignificant, for they included one destined to extend police powers to search cars (judgement of 12 January 1977), the 1980 budget (judgment of 24 December 1979), and the so-called Bonnet Law (named after the minister of the interior responsible) which was designed to tighten up controls on illegal immigration (judgment of 9 January 1980). After 1981 Right-wing opposition Deputies were clearly determined to use this weapon, and within six months of the Mitterrand election had taken the government's Nationalization Bill to the Council (the Council rejected the bill and insisted on a significant change in the compensation clauses), and a bill granting greater autonomy to Corsica (the Council backed the government on this one). Between 1981 and 1986 the Socialist governments of Mauroy and Fabius had thirty-four laws sent back for revision (they included the much contested Savary Law on Higher Education), while the Right-wing Chirac government of 1986 to 1988 had to modify parts of its legislative programme (for example, on privatization, the reform of the media and on changes in the citizenship code) after decisions from the Council. Governments of both the Left and the Right have denounced this 'government by judges' but they now know that controversial legislation will almost automatically end up in front of the Council and have begun to anticipate its reactions. Opposition Deputies have acquired, therefore, a powerful means of checking the wilder unconstitutional excesses of the executive.

There is some evidence that the docile and impotent parliament of the early years of the Fifth Republic has begun to assert itself somewhat by fully exploiting mechanisms provided by the constitution (the increasing tendency to put down amendments, the inflation in the number of written questions, by parliamentary procedure (relating to delaying tactics), and the reforms of the 1960s and 1970s (questions to the government, access to the Constitutional Council). It is certainly the case that parliament has moved more to centre stage. More significantly, the period of *cohabitation* between 1986 and 1988 clearly indicated that under the Fifth Republic the absence of a hostile majority in the National Assembly is essential for presidential primacy. During that period executive responsibility for domestic affairs was transferred from the president to a government that based its legitimacy on victory in the legislative elections and its capacity to govern with its parliamentary majority. The appointment in June 1988 of the Rocard government with its lack of a parliamentary majority opened a new phase in the parliamentary history of the Fifth Republic – one which is unlikely to be characterized by parliamentary supremacy but which will almost certainly emphasize the centrality of parliament among the political decision-making bodies of the Republic.

8 Presidential coalition-building and the transformation of the party system

A president of the Republic must build two coalitions – one to elect him and the other to sustain him for the seven years following his election. Both require the mobilization of party support. If the founder and first president of the Fifth Republic had an especially jaundiced view of the parties – the propagators and perpetrators of French divisions – the effective functioning of his régime came increasingly to depend on their co-operation, good will and organizational capacity, especially after his departure in 1969. This chapter will examine the electoral support of the presidency and will outline the factors which enabled each president to build himself a viable party coalition as the result of the transformation of the French party system during the Fifth Republic.

The electoral bases of presidentialism

The French electorate decided in the referendum of October 1962 to adopt President de Gaulle's proposal that henceforth the president of the Republic be directly elected by universal suffrage. The new system required a candidate to win more than half the votes cast at the first ballot in order to win; otherwise there is a second ballot two weeks later between the two best placed candidates of the first ballot. The conditions to be fulfilled in order to stand were surprisingly unrestrictive and in May 1974 there were no fewer than twelve candidates. Even after the conditions were tightened up somewhat (a candidate must now gather five hundred signatures from elected officials in at least thirty *départements* in metropolitan France or the overseas territories) there were still ten candidates who succeeded in standing in the April 1981 election, and nine in May 1988. However, if a candidate is to have any realistic chance of winning he must have backing, however reluctant or begrudged, from one or more of the major political parties. Candidates such as de Gaulle, Pompidou, Giscard d'Estaing and Mitterrand always entertained the fiction that their candidates were 'above' the parties, but none ever spurned their official party backing and organizational support.

In the December 1965 presidential elections General de Gaulle enjoyed the support of the Gaullist Party and of the Independent Republicans, led by Giscard d'Estaing. Georges Pompidou's election in 1969 was facilitated by the backing given him by the Gaullist Party, the Independent Republican movement and a small group of Centrists led by Jacques Duhamel who were shortly after to form a party called the *Centre Démocratie et Progrès*. His successor elected in May 1974, Giscard d'Estaing, won at the second ballot with the support of the three parties of Pompidou's coalition and also that of the *Centre National des Indépendants et Paysans*, the *Centre Démocrate* of Jean Lecanuet, the Radical Party of Jean-Jacques Servan-Schreiber and the *Mouvement Démocrate Socialiste de France* (a small group of anti-communist Right-wing socialists) – all the parties which formed the basis of his uneasy coalition.

Giscard d'Estaing was elected president of the Republic in May 1974 in the highest poll since the introduction of universal suffrage in 1848, and by only the narrowest of margins: at the second ballot he won 50.8 per cent of the votes against 49.2 per cent for Mitterrand, his Left-wing opponent. The high turn-out bore witness to the popularity of the contest and to the electorate's perception of its importance and significance. Traditional electoral geography was not upset as the result of the election: as expected, Giscard d'Estaing had his best results in the Catholic west (in the seven *départements* of that area he won more than three-fifths of the votes), in parts of the Massif Central (his native region of the Auvergne gave him a very comfortable majority), in the Catholic east (Alsace was his most single important bastion) and in the French capital where he won a majority in sixteen of the twenty *arrondissements*. His opponent carried the Mediterranean region, most of the south-west and all but one of the Pyrenean *départements* – the *Midi Rouge* lived up to its name – as well as in the densely populated 'red-belt' which almost encircles Paris, and in the arc of industrialized *départements* to the north-east of the capital. Not unexpectedly, Giscard d'Estaing won most of his support from those Right-wing electors who had previously backed Pompidou in 1969.

Compared with the electorate of Mitterrand that of Giscard d'Estaing was more feminine, older, more rural. Other polls revealed that it was better educated, wealthier and much more

religious. The social and economic boundaries of the new president's electorate were also not only smaller than those of his two
predecessors (General de Gaulle was elected with 55.2 per cent of
the votes at the second ballot and Pompidou with 58.2 per cent
also at the second ballot). It was also socially and economically
more narrowly based: while a quarter of the working class voted
for him it was a much smaller proportion than had voted for
Pompidou and especially for de Gaulle. Compared with the
population as a whole, Giscard d'Estaing enjoyed the support of
a disproportionately large number of women, of elderly, upper-
managerial, professional and commercial groups and of farmers.
The accusation of the Left that his victory was that of 'elderly,
wealthy and pious widows' was, of course, monstrously simplistic
and morally suspect (for the democrat some voters are not more
equal than others ...). But it contained a grain of comfort for a
Left which claimed the overwhelming backing of *la France jeune
et travailleuse*.

President Giscard d'Estaing was not only the leader of an
electoral coalition. He was also, in part, its prisoner. If General
de Gaulle often pointedly ignored his electorate (although his
domestic policies did little to upset it) Pompidou ensured, by
temperament and calculation, that his policies coincided with the
conservative aspirations of his electoral base. Giscard d'Estaing
was, however, faced with a dilemma. His electorate was even
more conservative than that of Pompidou, while he proclaimed the
need for creating a more socially just and more liberal society. The
nature and composition of his electorate – what the French refer
to as *les pesanteurs sociologiques* – was not conducive to reform,
especially if that reform involved any redistribution of income.
Faced with the reality of his electoral position this self-styled
'progressive conservative' became progressively conservative –
although it must be admitted that the potential reaction of his
electorate became increasingly a pretext rather than a reason for
abandoning his early reformist aspirations.

François Mitterrand was elected to the presidency at his third
attempt on 10 May 1981 – a date which will almost certainly
become an important reference point for the historically minded
French Left. He won at the second ballot, in an 85.85 per cent
turn-out, against his 1974 adversary, the sitting president, but with
a margin of victory (51.75 per cent of the voters against 48.25 per
cent for Giscard d'Estaing) which was greater than that enjoyed
by Giscard d'Estaing in 1974. His victory was the first enjoyed by
the Left during the Fifth Republic. He won a majority in sixty-five
of the ninety-six *départements*: i.e. in all types of constituency. His
most spectacular progress took place in those areas where he had

been weakest in 1974 – in the Catholic west and east where the Left had been making inroads throughout the 1970s. He strengthened the Left's hold of the industrial north, of the Paris region (although Paris remained faithful to the Right), the 'Red Midi' and the 'Republican Centre' and made great progress in parts of the Paris basin and the surrounding provinces of Burgundy, Lower Normandy and the Franche-Comté. In only four *départements* did Mitterrand win less than 40 per cent of the votes – a clear indication of the 'nationalization' of the Left-wing vote. He fared especially well among the manual workers (winning 72 per cent of their votes) and among the lower managerial classes and white collar workers (62 per cent – up 9 per cent on his 1974 performance). Studies of the transfers of votes from the first to the second ballot indicate that he retained all his first ballot support, attracted almost all the Left-wing Radical supporters of Michel Crépeau (who had stood at the first ballot with the declared intention of improving Mitterrand's chances by extending the appeal of the Left to the vital Centrist voters), and was backed by many of the first ballot extreme-Left voters (the two candidates of the extreme Left, who polled nearly a million votes, declared for Mitterrand). He also won a majority of those first ballot abstentionists and ecologists who voted at the second, 15 per cent of the first ballot Gaullist voters, and a massive 92 per cent of those who had voted for Georges Marchais, the Communist Party candidate. The latter achievement was all the more remarkable since many traditional Communist voters had already voted for him at the first ballot.

Mitterrand's re-election in April–May 1988 was a triumphal affair, especially in the light of his unpopularity only two years previously. His successful electoral strategy combined a persistent defence of acquired social and welfare rights and fundamental republican values with lofty appeals for national unity and harmony. He projected himself as the protector of the *peuple de gauche*, of the vulnerable and the underprivileged, and, at the same time, as the guardian of the cohesion of the nation and the guarantor of the continuity of the state. His programme, in marked contrast to that of 1981, contained few specific commitments. At the first ballot he came well ahead of his three Right-wing rivals, Jacques Chirac, Raymond Barre and Jean-Marie Le Pen, and trounced the Communist candidate, André Lajoinie (for details see Appendix 6). Compared with 1981 he improved his first ballot performance by nearly 6 per cent whereas Giscard d'Estaing, the only other incumbent president to stand for re-election, had lost 5 per cent between 1974 and 1981. At the second ballot he beat a resigned Jacques Chirac by a comfortable 54 to 46 per cent: an exit poll revealed that of the 54 per cent, 38 per cent placed themselves on the Left or extreme Left whilst 16 per cent classified themselves elsewhere in the political spectrum, mainly in the centre: his appeal beyond his own 'natural' constituency had clearly been successful. His second ballot performance almost equalled that of de Gaulle in 1965: indeed, he won a majority in more *départements* than his illustrious predecessor. In 1965 Mitterrand won a majority at the second ballot in only one in four *départements*, in 1974 in one in two, in 1981 in two in three and in 1988 in five in six [or 78 of the 96]. Compared with 1981 he lost some ground in parts of the south in Provence and Languedoc (the *sud laïque*), but consolidated his traditionally strong areas of the centre-west and south-west and the north-east and strengthened his position in the west, which had slowly been moving Left since the mid-1970s. He also won majorities in *départements* and towns which had never previously voted for the Left. At the second ballot he rallied all those who had voted for the extreme Left and Communist candidates at the first ballot, three quarters of those who had voted for Waechter, the environmentalist, a fifth or a quarter (depending on the exit poll) of Le Pen's voters (disproportionately from the young, the unemployed, the workers, and the irreligious) and over a tenth of those of Raymond Barre (disproportionately from the young, males and the irreligious). There were no great surprises in the socio-economic breakdown of Mitterrand's vote: he drew his support disproportionately from the unemployed, the working class, the salaried workers of the public sector, the young (especially those between 25 and 34 years old) and the irreligious. His relative weaknesses lay among the farmers, the self-employed, upper management, the elderly and practising Catholics. However, unlike 1981, he attracted a majority of the female vote (for details see Appendix 8).

Mitterrand owed his election and re-election, therefore, to a very mixed political group, comprising Socialists, Communists, Left-wing Radicals and extreme Leftists, together with a smattering of disillusioned Centrists, embittered Gaullists and hopeful yet wary environmentalists. Meeting the hopes of such a motley group is intrinsically difficult, but coalition-building for a presidential election, as in the United States, requires the merging (however fleetingly) of the most improbable elements. Nevertheless, some form of firm, durable and institutionalized party support is essential to sustain the president during his exceptionally long period of office, and for that reason no president can ignore the party bases of his power. Yet no president can simply manufacture support: he has to exploit the mechanisms at his disposal and the circumstances that are favourable.

The transformation of the party system

The Fifth Republic has seen a marked clarification of party politics, in spite of apparent complexity and confusion. New parties such as the Republican Party, the Left-wing Radicals (MRG) and the Left-wing United Socialist Party (PSU) have been founded, some, such as the MRP (an important Catholic centre party of the Fourth Republic), have disappeared or, like the CNIP (a powerful Right-wing party until the early 1960s), have virtually done so, and some – the Radical Party, for instance – have declined dramatically. The parties of the extreme Right disappeared during the 1960s and 1970s but one of them, the *Front National*, created in 1972, made a major electoral breakthrough in elections in 1984, 1986 and 1988. The four major parties of the thirty years of the Fifth Republic have all enjoyed mixed fortunes: the Communist Party, which was the biggest French party during the Fourth Republic, has suffered several severe defeats and its very survival is the object of prolonged discussion in political circles; the Socialist Party slumped dramatically in the 1960s, recovered and quickly established itself as the dominant party of France by 1981, endured reversals in 1984 and 1986 but reestablished its dominance in 1988; the Gaullist Party has lurched from dominance to anticipated destruction, only to recover but then to decline again; the UDF had an unexpectedly good start, failed to live up to its early promise but has slowly become as powerful as the Gaullists within the Right-wing coalition.

Evidence of volatility may be seen, too, by examining the electorate of each party or coalition. Examples abound: the Left received only 32.3 per cent of the votes at the first ballot of the 1965 presidential elections but 55.8 per cent fifteen years later at the first ballot of the 1981 legislative elections; the extreme Right rocketed to electoral prominence between 1983 and 1988 but lost nearly two million votes between 24 April and 5 June 1988; the Communist Party lost nearly two-thirds of its electorate between the legislative elections of 1978 and the presidential elections of 1988; the sociological and geographical bases of the Gaullist Party have changed radically throughout the period. For the student of French politics matters have not been simplified by the constant change of nomenclature (the Gaullists have changed their official party title no fewer than ten times since 1947 and five times since the beginning of the Fifth Republic), by the appearance of short-lived alliances and ephemeral coalitions and by proposed yet abortive fusions and federations, all with their own and often bewilderingly similar epithets. In the especially murky waters of Centrist politics men have swum in and out of parties with the ease of experienced dolphins (or sharks as the uncharitable might contend). Finally, political dissensions within each party and highly publicized squabbles (often of a simulated nature) between coalition partners have added to the confusion. Yet behind the apparent confusion a number of constant characteristics may be discerned. Thus, throughout the Fifth Republic, the parties of the extreme Left have remained electorally very weak (they collect 2 to 4 per cent of the votes) and the ecologists have failed to make any headway (in the presidential elections of 1974, 1981 and 1988 their candidate won 1.3 per cent, 3.9 per cent and 3.8 per cent of the votes respectively). Nationalist parties of the geographical periphery – in Corsica, the Basque country and Brittany – have also found very little electoral favour. Two major trends may also be discerned: the first was the bipolarization of the 1960s and 1970s; the second was the emergence of a new party configuration in the 1980s in which bipolarizing pressures are still apparent but in which a dominant moderate Right has come to be flanked by an extreme Right and a dominant Socialist Party by the Communist Party, its erstwhile ally.

Bipolarization 1959-1983

The process of so-called bipolarization involved initially the emergence of a reasonably coherent and disciplined party coalition of the Right (which is examined in Chapter 9) with the purpose of promoting, maintaining and defending governmental policies in the country and especially in parliament – an essential prerequisite for the smooth functioning of the political institutions of the régime. This situation contrasted sharply with that of the Fourth Republic, which was plagued by the absence of a large and disciplined Right-wing party or coalition. The parties of the Left responded – albeit slowly – by creating their own uneasy alliance, based on electoral agreements and, for a brief time, a legislative programme. Yet such a response was essential if the Left wished to win office (see Chapter 10).

The parties of the centre tried for most of the early period of the Fifth Republic to avoid being squeezed into coalition with either the Gaullists or with the Left, hoping to remain an independent and autonomous force, but they were progressively forced to make unpleasant choices. Most were gradually converted to, or well absorbed by, a presidential coalition. Political mavericks – those independents who eschewed party labels and party discipline – virtually disappeared from French politics. To save their parliamentary seats they, too, moved into the presidential orbit.

Bipolarization of French political opinion could be seen in several ways but especially at the electoral level: the parties of the Right-wing coalition presented only one candidate in most cases (in 1981 in all but eighty-six of the 474 metropolitan constituencies) as from the first ballot; after 1967 the parties of the Left negotiated a binding agreement which involved in every constituency the withdrawal before the second ballot of all but the best placed candidate of the Left at the first ballot. The number of straight fights between the presidential coalition and the Left-wing coalition at the second ballot was always very high: in the 1967 elections, of the 398 seats contested at the second ballot, 335 (or 84 per cent) were straight fights, in 1968, 269 of 316 (or 85 per cent) second ballot contests were straight fights, in 1973 there were straight fights in 84 per cent (360 of the 430) of the contested constituencies, and in 1978 in 409 of 423 (or 96 per cent). At the second ballot of the June 1981 legislative elections there were ten constituencies with only one candidate (all the others having been eliminated at the first ballot), and in 309 of the 310 metropolitan seats still at stake there was a straight fight between Right and Left.

At the local level, too, the pressures of bipolarization were felt: at the first ballot of the March 1977 local elections, for example, the presidential coalition presented a single list in 200 of the 221 biggest towns (over 30,000 inhabitants) and the Left in 204 of those towns (compared with 60 of the 159 in 1965 and 124 of the 193 in 1971). Increasingly, too, as Bruce Campbell has shown, elections were *perceived* in polarized terms by the voters, and particularly by the younger voters whose experience had been shaped exclusively by the Fifth Republic.

The second manifestation of bipolarization was at parliamentary level where, in spite of some spectacular exceptions, each coalition of the Right and of the Left acted with greater unity. Third, bipolarization could be seen at the doctrinal level: each coalition remained divided on some important questions but each, however unsuccessfully, made an attempt to elaborate a programme acceptable to all the partners. Finally, bipolarization was manifested at the executive level: governments contained members from all the component parties of the winning coalition and despite internal dissensions and sometimes public disputes solidarity was maintained (it was not until 1984 that the Communists left the government).

It should be emphasized that the process of bipolarization involved the emergence of two great party coalitions, but it did not dictate the shape, size, internal functioning or harmony of those coalitions. Bipolarization neither prevented nor encouraged the emergence of a party system which, at different stages, was dominated by one party (the Gaullists from 1962 to 1974, the Socialists after 1978) or one in which the major parties were poised in precarious equilibrium (1967-8, 1974-81). But the appearance and consolidation of two major coalitions represented a significant change in the French party system, since it involved the end to the divided and fragmented multi-party system of the Fourth Republic. The reasons for the transformation of any party system are many and complex. They are also related in a dynamic and dialectical fashion. The transformation of the French system proved to be no exception. The bipolarizing pressures which transformed the French political system may be summarized under four main headings: institutional, electoral, societal and cultural, presidential and party strategies.

Bipolarization: the institutional factor

With the emergence of the presidency as the focus of political power in France, as the major prize in the political game, it was essential that the parties organize to capture it. And since the size of the electorate required to do so (more than half the votes cast) was greater than that of any single party, alliances were imperative. Moreover, it was essential that political support be marshalled to provide the presidency with the necessary underpinning at both electoral and parliamentary level. In a modern state, parties are essential for effective and democratic government. Their task is to fulfil two ultimately irreconcilable aims: first, they must reflect, articulate, sharpen, exploit and mobilize political differences rooted in social and economic cleavages, and, second, they must also strive to transcend those political differences by aggregating political support to promote a measure of consensus, with which effective government is difficult. Parties must also provide the political elite of the nation and attempt to give some form of organized, coherent and disciplined support for their government once elected. During the early years of the Fifth Republic, President de Gaulle, who claimed to be 'above parties', excelled in disparaging remarks about them and spurned their overt support. But both he and his successors soon recognized that organized party support was vital to their own success.

The second important institutional change pushing towards bipolarization was the diminution in the prestige and power of parliament and the corresponding decline in the efficacy of its members. Voters were less concerned with the individual effectiveness of their Deputy (since his room for manoeuvre had been somewhat reduced) and were more concerned about his willingness to play a role as a defender or opponent of the government. It is instructive that Deputies who break with a party under the Fifth Republic are invariably penalized in the following election.

Bipolarization: the electoral impetus

Each election of the Fifth Republic, with the notable exception of the 1969 presidential election, became, to use Jean Charlot's expression 'a great simplifying duel' between two well-organized coalitions. The bipolarizing pressures were evident at presidential, legislative and local level. The presidential system which allows only the two best-placed candidates of the first ballot to proceed to the second had the obvious consequence of polarizing choice. The effects of the legislative electoral system, while less obvious, also provided an impetus to bipolarization. The two-ballot electoral system based on single member constituencies – the system which prevailed for all elections between 1958 and 1981 – requires a candidate to win over half the votes cast to be elected at the first ballot, but only more than any other candidate to win at the second. In most constituencies there was a second ballot: in 1978, for instance, only 68 of the 491 Deputies were elected at the first ballot and in 1981, 156 of the 491. To go forward to the second ballot a candidate had to win at least 12.5 per cent of the electorate at the first ballot – a stipulation which eliminated a great number of candidates, and automatically clarified choice at the second ballot: in 1973, when there was a 10 per cent barrier (it was raised to 12.5 per cent in 1976), 1334 of the 3092 candidates were automatically eliminated from the election, and in 1978 and in 1981 over half of the candidates were eliminated. The underlying principle of the system is that 'at the first ballot the voter chooses and at the second he eliminates': in other words, at the second ballot the electors were often being squeezed into voting for the candidate they found the least undesirable.

The system could be grossly distorting and led to some very curious results: in 1958, for example, the Communist Party with 18.9 per cent of the votes cast at the first ballot won only 2 per cent of the seats in the National Assembly while the Gaullist Party with only 1 per cent more of the votes than the Communists won 41 per cent of the seats; in 1958 the Socialists with 15.5 per cent of the votes won thirty-nine seats while, in 1962, when their share of the poll *dropped* to 12.7 per cent, they *increased* their number of seats to sixty-four; in 1967 a Gaullist Deputy was elected with an average of 27,959 votes, a Socialist Deputy with an average of 47,756, a Centrist with 74,531 and a Communist with 119,466; in 1968 the Right-wing presidential coalition won 358 seats with 46 per cent of the poll (or more than two-thirds of the seats with less than half the votes) while the parties of the Left shared only ninety-one seats in spite of polling 42 per cent of the votes. In the 1981 legislative elections the distortions of the system worked to the benefit of the Socialist Party which, with 37.4 per cent of the first ballot votes, won an absolute majority of seats (three-fifths) in the National Assembly. The Communist Party, with 16.2 per cent of the votes or slightly less than half the Socialist vote, won only forty-three seats or less than a sixth of the seats won by the Socialists. The Left won 55.8 per cent of the first ballot votes and 329 seats while the Right with 43.1 per cent of the votes found itself with only 160 seats. The distorting effects of the electoral system were due not only to the different sizes of constituencies (the biggest was nearly four times bigger than the smallest) but also to the prevailing state of party alliances and fortunes. The system not only gave a premium to a dominant party (the Gaullists in 1968, the Socialists in 1981) but also *penalized weak, isolated and unpopular parties*. At the second ballot, when most of the seats were at stake, a party needed friendly allies. This may best be illustrated by summarizing the performance of the Communist Party (see Table 4).

The electoral impetus to coalition-building was also felt at the local level. According to the rules of the electoral system, until they were changed in 1982, in the major towns (those with over 30,000 inhabitants), a successful list of candidates for the local council had to win half the votes at the first ballot or a plurality of the votes at the second. Moreover, in 1964 the law was altered to prevent *panachage*: lists could not be altered between the ballots as the result of negotiated compromises between parties. A party had thus every interest in entering into a coalition to present a single list from the first ballot. If, for example, the Socialist Party and the Communist Party each presented its own list at the first ballot, they were precluded from presenting a joint list at the second. This clearly reduced the Left's chance of winning, particularly if the Right had been united since the first ballot: it was possible for the two parties of the Left to win 66 per cent of the second ballot votes – 33 per cent each – and still lose to a single Right-wing list winning only 34 per cent of the votes. The result of the system was to accentuate the tendency towards bipolarization resultant upon the functioning of the presidential and legislative systems. As already noted, in the March 1977 local elections, the Left and the Right each presented coalition lists at the first ballot in more than 90 per cent of the major towns. Despite the 1982 change in the electoral law for towns of over 3,500 inhabitants, which introduced an element of proportionality, the Left and Right in the main

Table 4 The performance of the Communists in the general elections 1958 to 1981

Election	Votes at first ballot (per cent)	Number of seats	Comment
November 1958	19.2	10	Very isolated and very unpopular. No electoral agreement with other parties of the Left
November 1962	21.8	41	Party less isolated. Limited number of agreements with Socialists
March 1967	22.5	72	Party less unpopular and less isolated. Agreement in all constituencies with non-Communist parties of the Left
June 1968	20.0	33	Similar agreement to 1967 but party feared and unpopular as result of May 1968 'events'
March 1973	21.4	73	Similar agreement to 1967 and 1968 and party less feared and unpopular than in 1968
March 1978	20.7	86	Similar agreement to three previous elections
June 1981	16.2	44	Similar agreement but party weak and unpopular

towns presented joint lists for the 1983 local elections, in order to give the impression of political harmony in the two camps. It was clear that at both local and national level joint electoral activity had its own dynamic: it created habits and formed attitudes that were difficult to shake.

The more elections were fought by a coalition of parties the more credible that coalition became: it was clear, for example, that until the breakdown of negotiations between the parties of the Left in September 1977 first ballot Socialist voters were becoming less and less reticent about voting Communist at the second ballot, and that was not surprising, for since 1967 they had fought several election campaigns together. But as the result of the strained relations after September 1977, as many as one Socialist voter in three refused to give their second ballot vote to the Communists in the March 1978 elections. Yet the 'electoral dynamic' could still be seen in 1981. It is highly instructive that in the 1981 presidential elections traditional Communist voters gave massive support (about 95 per cent) to the Socialist Mitterrand who had been their official candidate in 1965 and 1974 – and this in spite of the Communist Party leadership's incessant campaign against him between 1977 and 1981. It is no less instructive that an estimated 71.5 per cent of first ballot Gaullist voters opted for Giscard d'Estaing at the second ballot in spite of the Gaullist Party's evident dislike of the sitting president.

Although electoral systems may be a factor which powerfully contributes to coalition-building, their effects cannot be divorced from the political context in which they function: they do not operate in a political vacuum. The presidential electoral system not only did not prevent the dislocation of the Left in June 1969 but may have exacerbated existing divisions. Nor, for example, did the legislative or local electoral systems dictate to the vacillating Socialists what kind of alliances should be contracted or prevent the Communists from attempting to undermine the Left-wing alliance after September 1977. Viable political coalitions can be rooted only in a deeper economic, social and political reality: no form of electoral system is likely to induce friendly and enduring co-operation between rural Catholic conservatives and urban atheist Communists. For a fuller appreciation of the nature of bipolarization of 1959 to 1983 it is essential, therefore, briefly to examine the changes in French society and culture.

Bipolarization: the societal and cultural factors

The existence of an unstable multi-party system during the Third and Fourth Republics was attributed to the effects of the electoral system (often some form of proportional representation which did little to discourage the proliferation and fragmentation of parties), to the workings of a parliamentary system (which gave power to individual Deputies, who could flout party discipline and even break with their party in order to obtain constituency interests in the knowledge that they would not be penalized in the following election) and, most important, to the nature of cleavages in French society. France was viewed as a fragmented and 'conflictual society', rent by bitter ideological divisions, and these many divisions were reflected in a multi-party system. Its schismatic political culture was contrasted with the integrated, homogeneous and consensual political culture of its neighbour across the Channel. The title of an influential book by Jacques Fauvet, written during the Fourth Republic, *La France déchirée*, summarized the views of most observers.

What was the nature of the basic divisions in French society? The first related to the nature of the régime itself. This was nothing new; no previous régime in French history had received anything approaching unanimous support. The Third Republic had to fight off challenges from monarchists, from imperialists, from the supporters of General Boulanger and from the followers of later fascist and other extreme Right-wing movements, as well as from the Communists. The parliamentary democracy of the Fourth Republic was also under constant challenge from the extreme Left and the extreme Right. The first organized Gaullist mass movement, the RPF (*Rassemblement du Peuple Français*), presented a serious Right-wing threat to the régime from 1947 to 1952. And from the mid 1950s the régime was again under attack – this time from the very Right-wing populist Poujadist Movement (the UDCA), which in the 1956 general elections won more than two and a half million votes and had fifty-three Deputies elected. The Movement was against the state, against Paris, parliament, big business, industrialization, French withdrawal from Algeria and (especially) taxes. By 1958 it had collapsed, victim of the incompetence of its leaders and the incoherence of its programme. The Fourth Republic, while contending with these challenges from the Right, had also to combat an equally serious threat from the Left. The French Communist Party, after its withdrawal from government in 1947, never ceased to be perceived as a threat to the stability and indeed the survival of the régime. Well organized and well supported (it always captured about a quarter of the votes in general elections), its tactics (at that time mostly dictated from Moscow) towards the Republic ranged from violent and bloody opposition (in the great political strikes of the winter of 1947-8) to a resentful truce.

French political society was, therefore, divided between the opponents and supporters of the parliamentary democracy of the Fourth Republic. But there were other important divisions in French politics. First, there was the clerical/anti-clerical dispute, a dispute which had overshadowed all others during the early years of the Third Republic and which continued to complicate and embitter the politics of the Fourth. The issue of state aid to church schools crystallized deep-seated and ancient antagonisms, and rendered difficult co-operation between political parties which might have reached compromises on other issues. Many Socialists and Radicals, guardians of a long secular tradition, still viewed any agreement with the church as incompatible with the republican ideal, and it is instructive that when the Socialist Prime Minister Guy Mollet entered into preliminary negotiations with the Vatican he had to do so by employing secret intermediaries. The liberal and often Leftish Catholic MRP leadership was obliged on many issues to follow its less tolerant, less compromising and less Leftish electorate.

The class conflict was as present in France as in other countries, but it was argued that it was particularly acute in France, where trades unions were weak, bitterly divided and politically motivated (this was certainly true of the Communist-dominated CGT) and where there was a long tradition of anarcho-syndicalism. The absence of highly representative, well organized, united and disciplined trades unions deprived France of institutional channels which have the general effect of moderating the debate (by canalizing specific and conflicting demands into generalized and negotiable packages), and thus led to a more acrimonious dialogue between workers and employers. Moreover, the class war in France spilled over, in certain instances, into the specifically political domain, and deserted the safer territory of negotiable issues such as wages, working-conditions and holidays. In short, it frequently seemed that the working class was not only interested in its share of the national cake but was also keen to determine its ingredients, control its cooking and supervise its eating. Complicating the class equation was the presence in France of a large agricultural community: although rapidly decreasing in numbers, it still represented by 1958 nearly one in every eight Frenchmen. There were in France major differences of outlook and interests between industry and agriculture, between town and country, between producers and consumers.

To these divisions must be added a legacy of bitter strife: it is revealing that the dates which figured (and continue to figure) most prominently in the French historical consciousness – 1789, 1793, 1830, 1848, 1871, 1936, 1940 and 1944 – were all periods when Frenchmen were at their most bitterly divided. When a British politician invokes history it is normally to buttress an unconvincing appeal to national unity, whereas a French politician normally cites historical examples to illustrate the perfidy of his adversaries. And no dispute in French politics is complete without constant recourse to history. The political battles of the Fourth Republic were infused with a peculiar venom, as each released the accumulated rancours of generations. The great political battles of the Fourth Republic – over, for instance, the European Defence Community, over Indo-China and Algeria or over state aid to church schools – were all rendered more intractable by constant and emotional appeals to history.

Finally, it was argued (not without some justification) that compromise in French political society was rendered difficult to attain by three other factors. The first was the tendency of the French to intellectualize problems: concrete problems were generally raised to the level of abstract and universal principles which much reduced the possible area of bartering: after all, the Pope is, or is not, infallible. The second factor lay in the nature of French political language which was so excessive and so emotionally explosive: no British politician since the war had even approached the level of personal vilification used by Pierre Poujade and some of his supporters against Pierre Mendès-France, or the intense vituperation employed by *L'Humanité*, the Communist Party newspaper, against anybody or anything not conforming to the orthodox Stalinist line, or the sheer nastiness of Michel Debré in his fulminations against any 'capitulation' in Algeria (that he was prime minister when that country was granted its independence was but another touch of the tragic irony so characteristic of the Algerian affair). The third factor was the fossilization of political attitudes because of the closed and immobile nature of political society. Old divisive attitudes persisted because of entrenched and unchanging educational and family socialization patterns.

What emerges from this short outline of the nature of French political society during the Fourth Republic was that the country was heterogeneous, fragmented and divided. These characteristics were reflected in the number of parties and the nature of the relationship which existed between them. Some parties (the extremist anti-régime parties) were totally excluded or excluded themselves from dialogue with the others, while between the pro-régime parties there existed deep and, on some issues, unbridgeable cleavages. Moreover, political parties in order to retain their electors felt obliged to emphasize their distinctiveness and declare their resolution to have no dealings with the others. But many of the parties, from the moderate Right to the moderate Left, whatever their differences, were forced into wary intercourse, in order to defend the Republic itself against its enemies. Unfortunately, the gulf between the lofty ideals proclaimed and the baser compromises negotiated served merely to reinforce the contempt felt by many towards the politicians and the régime.

France was pictured, therefore, as a country divided into warring and irreconcilable political camps, each camp forming its own party. Hence, big, durable and stable coalitions were impossible. But it was clear that such a picture was simplistic even during the Fourth Republic and that it had become grotesquely so under the Fifth Republic. It could be argued that even during the Fourth Republic some of the social cleavages (notably the religious ones) were no longer intensely felt and for the electorate were decreasingly salient. Political parties were giving expression to, and helping to perpetuate, outmoded cleavages. Paul Warwick, writing about the Popular Front government, refers to 'the structural incongruence of French party politics' in the late 1930s: the same description seems equally fitting for the years of the Fourth Republic. It should also be noted that many of the bitter disputes between the parties were frequently more rhetorical than real: ideological slanging matches in public did not prevent peaceful accommodation in parliament.

Moreover, the salience of traditional cleavages was weakened by changes in post-war France. French society since the 1950s has rapidly undergone a transformation under the impact of the traumas of military defeat and occupation, of a rapid population increase, of massive industrialization and urbanization with their consequences for population mobility and the occupational structure of the country, of the communications revolution, of the explosion of educational opportunities, and of widespread and increasing economic prosperity. Some of the changes have been quite dramatic: the decimation of the number of farmers; the increase in the numbers of white-collar workers and managerial staff; the vast influx of women into the labour market; the extraordinary degree of mobility (in 1975 one Frenchman in two did not live in the same house as in 1968, one in three lived in a different commune and one in ten lived in a different region). Accompanying, and partly resultant upon, these changes was the breakdown of traditional patterns of authority due to the diffusion of permissive ideals, the collapse of established family norms and the weakening of religious practice: the number of practising Catholics in France dropped dramatically: a *Sofres* poll taken just before the 1981 presidential elections showed that two-thirds of the French considered themselves as non-practising Catholics

(48.9 per cent) or 'without religion' (11.4 per cent) or belonging to another religion (4.7 percent).

Finally, it was at least arguable that there was a growing consensus on certain key issues during the 1960s and 1970s – a point stressed by President Giscard d'Estaing in his *Démocratie française*, published in 1976: for the president many of the divisions of the French were artificial, more apparent than real, expressed by the political parties rather than felt by the electors. And there was opinion poll evidence to support the view. What is clear is that after 1962 the poisonous and divisive problem of decolonization was largely over, and the thaw in the Cold War in the 1960s rendered the 'East-West' conflict in French politics less acute. The régime/anti-régime cleavage also virtually disappeared. A small group of Right-wing fanatics of *Algérie française* from 1960 to 1962 made, and certain extreme Left-wing *groupuscules* continued to make, the régime itself one of the objects of their hate, but all the major political parties were happy to function peacefully within the régime, even though some were bitterly critical of some of its aspects. Opinion polls were unanimous in indicating widespread satisfaction with the Fifth Republic – a striking contrast with the situation under the Fourth Republic. This did not mean that France was not plagued with economic and social problems: increasingly, marginal groups such as farmers and shopkeepers were treated insensitively; the country's new wealth was unevenly distributed between regions and social groups; social services were inadequately provided for; universities were ill equipped to meet the massive intake of students. The explosion of May 1968 represented a concatenation of many and often violently conflicting protests, frustrations, yearnings, ideals and aims, economic, educational and political. However they were rarely related to the divisive issues of the Fourth Republic.

The evidence of the polls and of the elections in the 1960s already suggested that political opinion in France was not lined up into warring camps each impregnated with a hatred of the others. It indicated rather *considerable fluidity in electoral choice.* Even the Communist Party, traditionally the most stable of French parties, was affected: in 1958 it lost more than a fifth of its supporters to the Gaullists and suffered particularly in its working-class bastions, and a quarter of the Communist Party voters of 1962 voted for other parties in the following election of 1967. Such fluidity of electoral behaviour may be attributed to many factors, including the relative weakness of family and environmental political socialization in a country in the throes of great economic, demographic and social change and where groups affiliated to political parties were weak and therefore unable to reinforce innate political sentiments. Moreover, the parties seemed to encourage political fluidity by their attitudes and recommendations. The Socialists, for example, asked their first ballot supporters to vote at the second ballot for the Gaullists in 1958 and for the Communists in 1962. They saved their towns in the 1959 and the 1965 local elections with anti-Communist support but their parliamentary seats with Communist support in the 1962, 1967 and 1968 legislative elections. Linked with great fluidity of electoral behaviour was the *low degree of party identification* which characterized French party politics. Professors Dupeux and Converse, writing at the beginning of the Fifth Republic, showed that in France there was no widespread or intense psychological attachment to particular parties. Fluidity of electoral behaviour weakened party identification, and weak party identification facilitated great fluidity of electoral behaviour. The circle was closed. But both the fluidity of behaviour and the weakness of party identification were essential ingredients in the political realignments of the Fifth Republic.

Of course, resistance to realignment was still powerful: loyalties were fixed by sub-cultures, by family, religion, class, region, trade union affiliation, and by lethargy as well as by the action of the parties themselves (since they both help to create the political culture and reflect its influence). Nevertheless, during the early years of the Fifth Republic the conditions were propitious for a major restructuring of the French party system: the traditional cleavages of French society had never been as sharp or as salient as the party system implied and were becoming less intense and less salient as the result of changes in French society; the presidency provided an institutional focus for a new party or new coalition or both; the presidential, legislative and local electoral systems placed a premium upon coalition-building; the electorate was susceptible to realignment as the result of weak party identification. But it required the will, leadership and ability of successive presidents of the Republic to exploit this situation and to mobilize electoral support behind them in new political form. This was achieved, with differing degrees of success, by each President of the Republic.

Bipolarization: presidential and party strategies

Institutional changes do not impose bipolarization but simply create a new environment in which party organizations, strategies and even tactics have to adapt. Similarly, as Frank Wilson has also reminded us in some recent admirable work, socio-economic changes merely provide a 'favourable milieu that might support party transformation'. They are perhaps vital in appreciating long-term changes in the party system or the fortunes of a particular party, but they rarely give a clue to understanding specific events or particular elections. It was widely held in France in the 1970s that the country was becoming 'sociologically more Left-wing', that the industrialization, urbanization, and secularization of French society (in which traditional, hierarchical patterns of behaviour were disappearing) were combining to produce an inevitable Left-wing victory. The Right-wing victories of 1974 and 1978 were written off as some form of aberration: François Mitterrand subscribed to this thinking, and was to describe his 1981 victory as 'the meeting of sociological and political' France. Such sociological determinism seems somewhat perverse: a much more industrialized, urbanized and secularized country such as Britain was to elect Mrs Thatcher only two years before France elected Mitterrand.

Increasingly, French psephologists, after years of obsession with crude correlations between socio-economic variables and voting behaviour, are turning their attention to refining those variables. Of course, the traditional *pesanteurs* – (the 'weighty' socio-economic variables) continued (and continue) to shape electoral behaviour: religion, class and age; practising Catholics vote far more than the irreligious for the traditional Right; the manual working class is much more inclined to vote Left than Right; the elderly are more disposed than the young to favour the Right. Yet these key variables are under increasing question: for example, what is the electorally significant dimension of age? the number of years of an elector? the period in which he or she was born and the political and party configuration of the time? the generation to which he or she belongs? Furthermore, differential mortality rates change the gender and social composition of ageing groups, making it difficult to distinguish the impact of age (however defined). Recent work has also shown that the impact of religion on voting has been analysed far too simplistically: establishing correlations between religious practice (which covers a variety of motives) and voting behaviour may be somewhat misleading: the religious dimension of voting must be rooted in an understanding of the wider social and cultural context. Religious practice may be an indicator of religious belief, but it may also be a tribal badge (as in Northern Ireland) and more probably an indication of adherence to a wide range of social, cultural and moral values. It is equally apparent that there is nothing immutable about the relationship between certain variables and voting behaviour: gender was always presented as a 'weighty', 'durable' factor influencing voting. But the drift of women in France towards the Left (under the impact of entry into the labour market, unionization, increasing education, secularization and feminist propaganda) since the 1970s has been such that the variable has come under scrutiny: clearly it might not be the quality of being feminine that provides the clue to voting behaviour.

Psephologists are also looking at the 'supply' side of the electoral equation: what the parties propose and what image they project. It is clear, for example, that Left-wing voters are disproportionately sensitive to issues of social security, those of the Right to national security, and those of the extreme Right to personal security. It is equally clear that some voters are influenced not only by issues but also by the political stakes involved in an election: can they, for example, afford to make a protest vote without dire political consequences (as in the elections to the European Parliament). In other words, there may be a voter 'rationality' however imperfect, partial and distorted. And it is shaped not only by socio-economic factors and sub-cultural affiliations but also by self-perceptions and the images and the programmes of the political parties and party coalitions.

The size, shape and fortunes of party coalitions during the Fifth Republic have been determined, therefore, not only by the pressures of socio-economic change, or changes in the institutional and electoral system. To reiterate a point, they have also depended on the action of party politicians with often conflicting perceptions of what constituted a credible, a winning or even a morally tenable coalition, and those perceptions have been formed by both rational and calculated assessment and by unconscious fears and prejudices. Between 1959 and 1981 successive presidents, for example, always deliberately polarized opinion at election times, thus attempting to transcend existing cleavages. This polarization of opinion into two great coalitions implied a division over one basic issue: de Gaulle presented it as a choice between himself and his régime on the one hand and 'chaos' on the other; under Pompidou the electors were asked to chose between 'peaceful change' and 'revolutionary adventurism'; in no less Manichean fashion, Giscard d'Estaing confronted the electorate with a choice between his pluralistic, liberal, democratic, socially just and quietly reformist régime and the revolutionary, collec-tivist, bureaucratic, illiberal and undemocratic régime associated with the Left; President Mitterrand was no less culpable, and at elections divided France between the friends and enemies of reform. Successive presidents also kept a wary eye on their own coalitions: de Gaulle indirectly; Pompidou much more openly; Giscard d'Estaing rather clumsily; Mitterrand almost obsessively. And it is difficult to understand the nature of the party system between 1958 and 1981 without taking into account the strategy and tactics of each president: de Gaulle's and Pompidou's as-siduous protection of the Gaullist Party; Giscard d'Estaing's tortuous relationship with his UDF, founded in February 1978 to compete with the Gaullists whom he was willing to wound but not to destroy; Mitterrand's tenacity in pursuing a strategy of Left-wing unity with the Communist Party in spite of the latter's open hostility and of the growing criticism within his own Socialist Party.

The impact of events and how they were perceived and exploited should not be underestimated: the Algerian war, the 'events' of May 1968, the referendum of 1969, the death of Pompidou in 1974, the very poor economic performance of the country in the year leading up to the presidential election of 1981 – all were to leave their mark on the party system. Each presidential election was also the occasion for realignments: the opening to the centre by Pompidou in 1969 and a further push to the centre by Giscard d'Estaing in 1974 are notable examples. Finally, mention should be made of specific sectoral discontent in influencing the size and shape of party coalitions: among the factors which led to the defeat of the Right in 1981 was the desertion of discontented groups such as the Jews (who criticized Giscard d'Estaing's policy in the Middle East) and the ecologists (who were adamantly opposed to the president's nuclear energy policy).

In conclusion, the transformation of the French party system during the first thirty years of the Fifth Republic was the result of a series of complex, interrelated factors: the declining intensity and salience of traditional cleavages and conflicts; the emergence of new divisions; the structural changes in the political system which like presidentialism placed a premium on coalition-building, or like the various electoral systems discouraged party isolation; the emulatory factor – if one side (as was the case) successfully exploited the new conditions the other side would follow suit; the emergence of new social aspirations as the result of socio-economic changes and changes in the political culture; the strategy of the parties and of their leaders and their skill, tenacity and courage in exploiting new circumstances.

The changing party system of the mid-1980s

The bipolarization of the French party system into the two major *blocs* which dominated the electorate, the legislature and the executive reached its high point in 1981. Thereafter, various factors have intervened to counteract, if not destroy, the impact of bipolarization. The precipitous rise of the extreme Right after 1983 and the no less precipitous demise of the Communists from 1981 together with their self-imposed marginalization, the increasing strains within the Right-wing coalition, the consolidation of the hegemony of the Socialists on the Left and their transformation into a governmental party – all of which are described in the two following chapters – have combined to change the shape and nature of the party system. By the end of 1988, an increasingly fragile Right-wing coalition was being challenged by an aggressive extreme-Right whose leader had just won 14.4 per cent of the votes in the presidential elections and whose party, the *Front National*, had gained 9.7 per cent of the votes in the legislative elections, and on whose support the Right relied to control five regional councils. On the Left, the Socialists formed the biggest party in the country, and their effective (if not nominal) head was at the Élysée, one of their leaders in the Matignon, and several others in the government. But their alliance with the Communists – the basis of their political and electoral strategy in the 1970s – was essentially defunct. By mid-1988 there were thus still two major *blocs* dominating French politics – a shaky moderate Right *bloc* of Gaullists and Centrists and a Socialist one – but each was now flanked by an unwelcome and hostile neighbour.

The impact of the years of bipolarization has not, of course, been entirely eradicated: it may be seen at the level of the electorate, and at the level of party strategies and practices. The Right, for example, fought the 1984 European elections on a joint list even though the electoral system was one of proportional representation, and, with very few exceptions, was represented by a single candidate in the legislative elections of 1986. The enduring pressures may be seen in the presidential elections of 1988 when Chirac received the great bulk of his support from the Right while Mitterrand derived his from the Left. More than four fifths of Raymond Barre's voters in the first ballot voted for Chirac in the second, and almost all first ballot Communist voters favoured Mitterrand at the second ballot. Even at the legislative elections of June 1988, and despite the atmosphere of *ouverture*, the Right (from the first ballot) and the Left (at the second) struck up electoral agreements: the second ballot saw a straight fight in 425 of the 453 seats at stake (122 Deputies were elected at the first ballot) between candidates of the Right and the Left. In parliament, too, the Left and the Right sustain their polarized attitudes, despite querulousness in the ranks of the Right and bitter divisions within the Left, particularly when the Communists quit the Left-wing government in July 1984. Finally, bipolarization is still evident at the local level: in the regional, departmental and town councils, united and generally harmonious Left-wing and

Right-wing teams confront each other. However, by 1988, there were unmistakable signs of a loosening up of the pre-1981 highly polarized party system, with some Socialists and Centrists openly flirting with one another.

In analysing the reasons for the change it is important to recall what has not changed. First, the presidency remains the focus of major political ambitions, and the method of electing to the office has remained unchanged. Second, although the electoral system for legislative elections was altered by the law of 10 July 1985 to one based on modified proportional representation, with party lists (electors could not change the order on the list or vote for candidates on two or more lists) for enlarged constituencies based on the *départements*, it was used only once – for the elections of March 1986 – and it was abolished by the law of 11 July 1986 which re-established the previous system. The system used in 1986 had undeniable short-term effects, since it reduced the majority the Right would have enjoyed under the previous system, helped to bolster the parliamentary representation of the Socialist Party, and enabled the National Front to enter the National Assembly. But it did not appear to have any enduring impact on the bipolarizing tendencies of the régime.

Any explanation of the changes must be sought not in institutional arrangements or electoral mechanics but in a combination of socio-economic changes, cultural factors, new political divisions, evolving political events, party strategies and personal rivalries, all of which constantly interact in unpredictable and unmeasurable fashion. These factors are touched upon in the following two chapters, but it is perhaps worth illustrating each of these transformative factors. Socio-economic change would include the full impact of the post-1979 second oil crisis which brought inflation and rising unemployment (especially among the young), the rapidly changing nature of the labour market and the collapse of 'smoke stack industries' (which had consequences for the unions and for working-class solidarity and for the Communist Party). Cultural factors would include the accelerating destruction of certain sub-cultures (for example Catholic and Communist) which had fixed loyalties and inhibited certain patterns of behaviour and also the increasing impact of better education which, it is contended, is creating a significant group of electors who are sensitive to issues and the political stakes involved in each election. Among important political events which have shaped party and electoral behaviour – both directly and indirectly – have been the rapid absorption of France into Europe, raising fears among nationalists and threatened groups, the social democratization of the Socialist Party (which make it less unattractive to some Centrists), and the policy changes of the Gaullist party which disappointed its more populist and anti-European supporters.

New divisions have appeared, as immigration and law and order have been placed firmly on the political agenda by an extreme Right which succeeded in exploiting the diffused fears and real apprehension of part of the electorate, but whose very success is contributing to a realignment of political forces on the traditional Right. Causes and consequences are, as with all factors, difficult to disentangle. Thus the demise of the Communist Party and the rise of the extreme Right are the result of a variety of social, cultural and political factors, but they also contribute to social, cultural and political change. Finally, the personal rivalries between Giscard d'Estaing, Chirac and Barre have clearly helped to destabilize a fragile Right-wing coalition.

By mid-1988, therefore, the French party system was undergoing a process of slow realignment. It was still unclear, however, what the nature of the realignment would be. It may revert to the traditional two coalition system; it may be internally reshaped, with the Centrists rallying to the Socialists and the Right embracing parts of the extreme Right; it may disintegrate into a three or four party system, depending on the fate of the *Front National* and the Communist Party. The only safe generalisation is that the 1980s have introduced elements of unpredictability into the French party system.

9 The Right: the politics of co-operation and conflict

The history of the French Right during the Fifth Republic falls into four main periods:

- *1958-1962*, a period of bitter division over the creation and consolidation of the new regime, and over de Gaulle's policies, especially those concerning the Algerian war.
- *1962-1973*, the years of the foundation and strengthening of the Right-wing coalition.
- *1973-1988*, the years of cooperation and conflict.
- *post-1988*, which is characterized by great uncertainty and possible schism, with the Centrists of the coalition clearly indicating their desire for greater autonomy.

This chapter will concentrate on the period since 1962, since it was not until that year that the distinguishing characteristics of the present coalition began to be defined.

From 1962, after the legislative elections of that year, until 1981, with the election of François Mitterrand to the presidency of the Republic, the politics of the Fifth Republic was dominated by the Right which controlled the presidency, the government and the National Assembly. Even the Senate, which in the early years displayed occasional opposition to President de Gaulle, was eventually to align itself to the *majorité* – the name given in France to the ruling coalition: ironically, it was the Senate that alone survived the Left-wing holocaust of May to June 1981.

The emergence and consolidation of the Right-wing coalition centred upon the presidency of the Republic: it was essentially a means of electing a president and then providing him with the necessary backing in the exercise of his office. The process was by no means smooth, and relations between the constituent elements were not always harmonious. Yet, for almost a generation the coalition held together, thus ensuring the dominance of the Right, facilitating the strengthening of the presidency and enabling the new Republic to acquire age, stability and even legitimacy.

The growth of the Right-wing coalition involved the periodic absorption into the governmental camp of the so-called parties of the centre. This absorption took place by distinct stages, with elections playing a catalytic role. These stages can be seen in Table 5.

Very briefly, the 1962 elections forged an alliance between the Gaullists and the Independent Republicans led by Giscard d'Estaing, the 1969 presidential elections enabled Georges Pompidou to consolidate the alliance and widen it by attracting the support of some Centrists belonging to the *Centre Démocratie et Progrès* of Jacques Duhamel, the second ballot of the 1974 presidential elections gave Giscard d'Estaing the opportunity of extending the alliance even further by embracing those Centrists who had remained in opposition, and the 1978 elections were the moment at which the president created the *Union pour la Démocratie Française* or UDF (which grouped his Giscardians and the various pro-Giscardian Centrists) to improve the electoral chances of his coalition and to strengthen his own supporters within that coalition. By 1981, therefore, the Right-wing comprised two distinct elements: the Gaullists of the RPR led by Jacques Chirac and the Giscardians of the UDF led (in practice, if not officially) by Valéry Giscard d'Estaing. The smooth functioning of the institutions of the Fifth Republic during the presidencies of General de Gaulle and Pompidou rested on the harmonious relationship which existed between themselves and their governments on the one hand and, on the other, a party coalition which enjoyed a majority in the National Assembly and which was dominated by a Gaullist Party totally subservient to presidential directives. No motion of censure was passed against the government after October 1962, and only between 1967 and 1968 (when the government's majority in the National Assembly virtually disappeared) was the unquestioned dominance of the Gaullist-dominated coalition briefly disturbed. From 1968 to 1974 de Gaulle and then Pompidou were backed by a comfortable majority in the National Assembly, with their own party, the Gaullists, holding a hegemonic position within the coalition.

Relations between the Gaullists and the Giscardians were, on the whole, very good during the de Gaulle period, although from 1966 to 1969 Giscard d'Estaing himself was occasionally to provoke the anger of the Gaullists by his barbed remarks about General de Gaulle's authoritarianism and some of his policies: he was even to oppose the Gaullists at the 1969 referendum which led to de Gaulle's resignation. During Pompidou's presidency relations between the Gaullists and the Giscardians remained very good. Giscard d'Estaing himself kept a discreet silence as the finance minister (a post he held throughout the

Table 5 The growth of the Right-wing ruling coalition 1958–81

Legislative elections 1958	Gaullists (UNR)
Legislative elections 1962	Gaullists (UNR-UDT) + Independent Republicans (RI)
Presidential elections 1969	Gaullists (UDR) + Independent Republicans (RI) + *Centre Démocratie et Progrès* (CDP)
Presidential elections 1974	Gaullists (UDR) + Independent Republicans (RI) + CDP + *Centre Démocratie* (CD) + Radicals + *Centre National des Indépendants et Paysans* (CNIP) + *Mouvement Démocrate Socialiste de France* (MDSF)
Legislative elections 1978	Gaullists (PRR) + *Union pour la Démocratie Française* (UDF) + Republican Party (ex-Independent Republicans) + Radical Party + *Centre des Démocrates Sociaux* (or CDS, fusion of CDP and CD) + *Mouvement Démocrate Socialiste* + *Clubs Perspectives et Réalités* + Young Giscardians + CNIP

presidency), and only Michel Poniatowski, his faithful friend and political henchman, made the occasional pointed criticism of the Gaullists.

The 1974 presidential elections proved a testing time for the alliance, since the official Gaullist candidate, Jacques Chaban-Delmas, was opposed by Giscard d'Estaing. The equation was complicated by the rallying to the Giscard camp of a number of Gaullist Deputies led by Jacques Chirac and a number of Centrists who had remained out of the alliance previously because of their anti-Gaullism. Giscard d'Estaing beat Chaban-Delmas easily at the first ballot and went on to win the presidency at the second. But the new president's position was not comfortable: he was elected with a small majority, he inherited a National Assembly dominated by the Gaullists who were very wary of him, and his coalition was further divided by the inclusion of virulently anti-Gaullist elements. The appointment of Jacques Chirac to the premiership did little to mollify the Gaullists and nothing to dampen the anti-Gaullism of some of the Centrists, notably that of Jean-Jacques Servan-Schreiber, leader of the Radical Party which had rallied to Giscard d'Estaing at the time of the 1974 presidential election. Servan-Schreiber's dislike of the Gaullists was as profound as it was durable: when President de Gaulle resigned after his defeat in the April 1969 referendum Servan-Schreiber publicly declared that it was 'the happiest day of my life'. After May 1974, but especially after Chirac's dramatic resignation as prime minister in August 1976, the harmony which had characterized presidential-*majorité* relations no longer prevailed. President Giscard d'Estaing was faced with four distinct problems:

- *The increasing electoral vulnerability of the ruling coalition* Elections to the departmental councils in March 1976 and to the local councils in March 1977, successive by-elections and all the opinion polls revealed the extent of the decline and augured badly for the March 1978 elections to the National Assembly. But the divisions and the stupidity of the Left and the widespread and tenacious fear of the Communists saved the Right from defeat. Yet the Right felt that it had won a breathing space only, that it had only temporarily stemmed the inexorable rise of the Left: the results of the 1978 elections constituted not a well-earned victory but a 'divine surprise'.
- *The imbalance within the president's coalition* The Gaullist Party, the least sympathetic towards him, continued to dominate the coalition in the National Assembly, even

after 1978. In the National Assembly it formed the biggest and most coherent group of the coalition; it had, unlike the other parties of the coalition, a mass membership; in contrast with those other parties, it had a centralized, disciplined, efficient and well-financed electoral machine; finally, in Jacques Chirac it had a dynamic, audacious, autocratic and effective national leader.

- *The organizational weakness and internal divisions of the Giscardians* (see below).
- *The constant tension within the coalition* This was the inevitable result of the struggle between the component elements for preponderance and even predominance. That tension was maintained by fractious and sensitive party leaders and also by memories of past battles between the coalition partners. Dissension within the coalition raised real problems of co-ordination at parliamentary and electoral level. President Giscard d'Estaing described the basis of his party coalition as one of 'tolerant and organized pluralism', although the coalition frequently presented the spectacle of intolerant and disorganized anarchy. Chirac when prime minister was unable effectively to co-ordinate a coalition which he likened to 'a basket of frogs all jumping in different directions', and Prime Minister Barre proved even more ineffective: Chirac was constantly defied by the Centrists and Barre had little control over the Gaullists, who constantly harried his government with guerrilla tactics in the National Assembly.

It was not only the Gaullists within the presidential coalition who displayed limited enthusiasm for the early timorous reforms of the president. In the vote on the Abortion Bill in November 1974 only fifty-five (or 32 per cent) of the 173 Gaullist Deputies, seventeen (or 26 per cent) of the sixty-five Independent Republican Deputies and twenty-seven (or 52 per cent) of the fifty-two of the Centrist Deputies voted in favour, and the bill was carried only because of the support of the Socialists and the Communists. When the Abortion Law was renewed in 1979 (it had been introduced for an experimental five-year period) it again needed the votes of the Left to carry it: only twenty-four Gaullists and forty-five Giscardians voted in favour. The June 1975 bill liberalizing the grounds for divorce was also given a very lukewarm reception (many pro-government Deputies voted against or abstained). In June 1976 during the passage of the bill introducing a timid capital gains tax the government's nominal supporters were diluting the impact of the proposed measures so much that

François Mitterrand, the Left-wing leader, could quip that if they continued in the same way the bill would ultimately cost the state a great deal of money! Yet the three bills on abortion, divorce and capital gains tax were all known to enjoy presidential blessings. There was clearly a gulf between a president who, at least in the early years of his presidency, proclaimed the need for a tolerant liberalism and for greater social justice and equity, and most of his parliamentary supporters who, pushed by their conservative electorate, pined for the traditional values of social responsibility, family, order, work and religion.

The Right-wing coalition during the period 1974-81, however divided, and however much parts of it were less than enthusiastic about presidential policies, remained intact if not united. It was a shaky political edifice, but the cracks were filled by the cement of fear and hatred of the Left (particularly of the Communists), of electoral self-interest and the 'poisons and delights' of office – a powerful if unattractive combination. The shakiness of the edifice was to be revealed during the presidential campaign of 1981. But the campaign equally revealed, though less spectacularly, the adhesive quality of the cement. No fewer than three Gaullist candidates stood against Giscard d'Estaing; the official Gaullist candidate, Jacques Chirac, and two dissidents, Michel Debré (the first prime minister of the Fifth Republic, and more Gaullist than de Gaulle) and Marie-France Garaud (once an influential member of Pompidou's private staff and ex-adviser of Chirac). All three were highly critical of Giscard d'Estaing during the campaign, and by their incessant demand for 'a change of course' helped to legitimize Mitterrand's claim that an alternative strategy to that of the president was possible. Their joint campaign was to contribute to the 'destabilization' of the incumbent president and to feed the anti-Giscard sentiments of the Gaullist activists. At the first ballot of the elections the four candidates of the Right (Giscard d'Estaing, Chirac, Debré and Garaud) totalled 49.3 per cent of the votes: the Right maintained its performance of 1978 and 1979 (legislative and European elections) but was ominously down on its 1974 presidential election performance when it won 52.6 per cent of the first ballot votes. Thus, the first ballot exposed both the decline and the divisions of the Right. Between the two ballots Jacques Chirac and Michel Debré declared for Giscard d'Estaing – although in very lukewarm fashion – while Madame Garaud announced her intention of spoiling her second ballot vote. The defeat of Giscard d'Estaing in May 1981 constituted the first electoral defeat of the Right during the Fifth Republic, but, revealingly, it was greeted with ill-concealed pleasure by many Gaullist leaders and activists. Giscard d'Estaing had few illusions, and in a burst of intemperate candour accused Chirac of 'premeditated treachery'.

The Right entered the campaign for the legislative elections of June 1981 in a state of division, disarray and demoralization. With only 43.1 per cent of the votes in metropolitan France the Right suffered a crushing defeat: in the 1973 legislative elections it had won 53.3 per cent, in the 1974 presidential elections 52.6 per cent, in the 1978 legislative elections 47.9 per cent, and at the first ballot of 1981 presidential elections 49.3 per cent. In 1973 the Right won a majority in seventeen of the twenty-two regions, in 1978 in seven and in 1981 in only three (Alsace, Lower Normandy and the Pays de la Loire). Brittany voted for the Left for the first time since universal manhood suffrage was decreed in 1848. The extent of the defeat may also be seen at the level of the *départements*: in 1973 the Right enjoyed an absolute majority in sixty-seven of the ninety-six metropolitan *départements*, in 1978 in forty and in 1981 in only seventeen. In the National Assembly the Right lost 132 of its 287 seats (eighty-three Gaullists instead of 153, sixty-six Giscardians in place of 125 and six others instead of nine). The defeat led to a renewed bout of mutual recrimination between the Gaullists and the Giscardians: never had their relations been so embittered.

If the presidential and legislative elections were fully to reveal and exacerbate the divisions of the Right and accentuate its electoral decline they were also, paradoxically, to underline its basic unity even in the most difficult of circumstances. This unity was manifested at two levels: at the level of the electorate and the party leadership level. The electoral unity of the Right may be seen in the fact that more than seven-tenths of the first ballot Gaullists in the presidential election voted for Giscard d'Estaing at the second. Unity at the level of the party leaders was amply demonstrated during the legislative election campaign. In spite of the anger and bitterness which followed the defeat of Giscard d'Estaing (the defeated president made a vitriolic speech against Chirac the day after his defeat) the leaders of the Right, intent on saving something from the *débâcle*, realized that unity against the Left was essential. Together they hastily concluded an electoral agreement which involved the creation of the Union for the New Majority (*Union pour la Nouvelle Majorité* or UNM), and, in 385 of the 487 constituencies they fielded a single candidate. However, the elections resulted in the 'historic victory' of the Left, with the Socialist Party winning an absolute majority in the new legislature.

By June 1981 the Right had, therefore, lost the presidency, control of the government and its majority in the National Assembly. It had also paraded its internal differences in unprecedented fashion. Yet it did not fall apart despite the traumas of defeat and the loss of office.

During the following seven years – the first *septennat* of François Mitterrand – three major changes on the Right may be discerned: a return to electoral favour; the loss of Gaullist electoral and parliamentary domination within the Right; a radicalization of parts of the Right and increasing conflicts between the parties and within each of them. The return to electoral favour was a clear reflection of the slump in the fortunes of the Left after the initial honeymoon period. Opinion polls, local elections of 1983 (which led to victory in many of the big towns) and the European elections of 1984 (in which the common list of Simone Veil won 42.8 per cent of the votes and a majority of the French seats) and the elections to the departmental councils in 1985 revealed the electoral lead of the Right over the Left. In the 1986 legislative elections – the only legislative elections of the Fifth Republic to be based on a limited form of proportional representation – the parties of the Right united around a common programme. Together they won a disappointing 42.1 per cent of the votes but were able to form a small majority in the National Assembly with the help of a small group of independent Right-wingers.

During the early period of *co-habitation* after March 1986 opinion polls continued to suggest a victory of a Right-wing candidate in the April–May 1988 presidential elections. However, those elections saw a complete rout of the candidates of the moderate parties of the Right. At the first ballot Jacques Chirac won only 19.9 per cent of the votes compared with 18 per cent in 1981. However, in 1981 two other Gaullist candidates together won 3 per cent of the vote, thus giving a total Gaullist vote of 21 per cent. Compared with the overall Gaullist performance of 1981 Chirac made gains in 23 *départements* of metropolitan France but lost in the remaining 73. Raymond Barre, the candidate of the UDF, with only 16.5 per cent of the votes fared worse than Giscard d'Estaing in 1981 in every French *département*. With a total of only 36.6 per cent of the votes cast the performance of the moderate Right was the worst of the Fifth Republic. At the second ballot, Chirac with 46.0 per cent of the votes fared less well than Giscard d'Estaing in 1981 and 1974, Pompidou in 1969 and de Gaulle in 1965. In the legislative elections which followed the dissolution of the Chamber by Mitterrand, the dispirited Gaullists and the UDF cobbled together an electoral alliance under the unhappy acronym of URC (*Union de Rassemblement et du Centre*). The alliance fielded a single candidate in 536 of the 554 constituencies of metropolitan France. Unlike 1981, the Right suffered limited electoral damage but it lost its majority in the National Assembly. In mid-1987 it had fully expected to be, a year later, in charge of the presidency, the government and parliament. In the event it was denied all three. It was scarcely surprising that coalition unity should be sorely tested and that differences which had been simmering for years should resurface with greater acrimony.

The loss of Gaullist domination within the Right-wing coalition may be seen at both electoral and more particularly at parliamentary level: by 1981 there were 83 RPR Deputies and 61 of the UDF; in 1986 the figures were 145 and 129 respectively; in June 1988 there were 130 members of the RPR group, 90 of the UDF and 41 of the newly formed Centrist group, the UDC. For the first time the Gaullists formed a minority within the Right in the National Assembly, and this was also true in the Senate.

Throughout the 1980s several forces were at work which contributed to a loosening of the Right-wing alliance: the decline of the Communist Party and the collapse of Left-wing unity; the transformation of the Socialist Party into 'a party of government'; the rise of the extreme Right in the shape of the National Front; the radicalization of parts of the Right in a neo-liberal direction; the loss of office and patronage in 1981 and again in 1988. Leaders of the Centrists were freed of their fear of the Communists, reassured by the moderation of the Socialists, dismayed by the anti-statist liberalism of some of their colleagues, alarmed by the rise of a xenophobic and racist Right, and resentful of the loss of office. They were, therefore, extremely susceptible to the appeals of Mitterrand and Rocard during the two election campaigns of 1988. The creation of an autonomous Centrist group in the National Assembly (see below) in June 1988, the acceptance of governmental posts by a small number of prominent *Giscardians*, and the manoeuvring behind the scenes of other disgruntled Centrists may presage a reshaping of the landscape of the Right.

The Gaullists

Since the beginning of the Fifth Republic the Gaullists have changed their official party title no fewer than five times: *Union pour la Nouvelle République* (UNR) in October 1958; UNR-UDT

(*Union Démocrate du Travail*) in December 1962; *Union des Démocrates pour la Ve République* (UDVe) in November 1967; *Union pour la Défense de la République* (UDR) in 1971; finally, *Rassemblement pour la République* (RPR) in December 1976. For the sake of convenience the party will be referred to throughout the chapter as the Gaullist Party – even though at no stage does there appear in its official name the word 'party' – a dirty word in the Gaullist vocabulary.

It is one of the many ironies of the Fifth Republic that its founder, General de Gaulle, who disliked and despised the parties, should endow France with its first great organized, well structured, cohesive and disciplined party of the Right. The Gaullist Party has confounded the fears of its founders and defied the hopes of its adversaries by proving to be no transient phenomenon: it survived the resignation of de Gaulle (June 1969) and his death (November 1970), the death of Pompidou (April 1974), and the elections of non-Gaullists to the presidency in 1974, 1981 and 1988.

There have been six distinct phases in the history of the Gaullist Party under the Fifth Republic.

1958-62: the search for identity

It was during this period that the party acquired a centralized organization, internal discipline and cohesiveness, especially after the purge of pro-*Algérie française* elements, and a privileged relationship with the President of the Republic by being the subservient instrument of his policies.

1962-72: growth, consolidation and hegemony

This is the period of the so-called *Gaullist phenomenon* which involved the following:

The propagation of a set of doctrines based on:

- the primacy of national unity and a denial of the Marxist notion of class war;
- the need for order and authority in all branches of public and private life;
- the defence of a powerful state and strong executive authority as expressed in the new constitution;
- the creation of a modern industrial economy;

● the assertion of national independence in foreign and European affairs.

The consolidation of a powerfully organized party with the task of defending presidential policies in parliament and in the country, especially at election times Much of the power of the Gaullist Party resided in its symbiotic relationship with the President of the Republic. It was the principal buttress and guardian of the presidency, the dispenser of unconditional and even obsequious support; its subservience was total and was demonstrated in 1971 when President Pompidou refused to allow it to elect its own leader. It was rewarded with the lion's share of *investitures* at elections: it was given the sole right to represent the presidential coalition in a number of constituencies, which opinion polls suggested was disproportionate to its real strength in the country. Thus, in 1973, in the 403 constituencies in which there was only one pro-Governmental candidate presented at the first ballot the Gaullists were present in 281 (or 70 per cent), even though the opinion polls gave them only the same number of votes as their coalition partners. During the period until 1972 the Gaullist Party grew in importance and in influence. Its electoral growth was spectacular (see Table 6).

The rise of the Gaullist Party was such that Professor Jean Charlot, the leading expert on Gaullism, could contend that it had altered the régime in a *qualitative* or *structural* manner: the multi-party system which had predominated in France since the beginning of the Third Republic had been transformed into a 'dominant-party system', with the Gaullists as the dominant party. That dominance was especially marked in parliament: in the 1968 elections, the party won a majority of seats (296 of the 487) in the National Assembly – the first occasion since 1870 that any party had achieved such a feat – and was no longer even dependent on the support of its allies. The nature of Gaullist support was likened by André Malraux to 'the rush-hour crowd in the underground', in that it represented a cross-section of the French population in general. That claim was never quite true, since the party always enjoyed the disproportionate support of the elderly, of women, of the higher income groups and of practising Catholics.

The domination of an electoral and parliamentary alliance first with the Independent Republicans of Valéry Giscard d'Estaing and then, after 1969, with the Independent

Republicans and the *Centre Démocratie et Progrès*, a Centrist group led by Jacques Duhamel.

The penetration of the state apparatus Key posts in the administration, the nationalized industries and the para–public corporations, the radio and television network were given to political sympathizers. The extensive network of political patronage bordered on the scandalous, and it was this unsavoury aspect of the régime which led to Michel Poniatowski's wounding denunciation of *les copains et les coquins* who sullied the reputation of the régime.

By 1972 the Gaullist Party provided France with a vague yet pervasive set of doctrines, its president, its prime minister, a majority of its ministers, and it dominated parliament (and all the parliamentary commissions) and the presidential coalition, and its sympathizers were well placed in key sectors of public activity. Its dominance was such that Jean-Jacques Servan-Schreiber could refer to the *État-UDR* – the Gaullist state. Some observers argued that the Gaullist Party had become progressively 'radicalized'; that it had come to resemble the Radical Party of the Third Republic in a number of important respects: it had become the major force in parliament; it provided most ministers; it was a clientele party, distributing patronage to gain or consolidate political support; it was slowly putting down local roots; it was gaining seats in the traditional Radical areas south of the river Loire; it was divided into many and often conflicting currents of thought. There were, however, important differences between the two parties: unlike the Gaullist Party, the Radical Party had an almost obsessional suspicion of strong leaders, even

Table 6   The rise of the Gaullists in parliament 1958–68

Election	Votes	Votes cast (per cent)
November 1958	4,165,505	20.3
November 1962	6,507,828	35.5
March 1967	8,448,982	37.7
June 1968	9,667,532	44.5

those from its own ranks; decision-making in the Gaullist
Party was (and remains) centralized and hierarchical whereas
in the Radical Party it was diffused among a large number of
independent-minded provincial and parliamentary *notables*; the
Gaullist Party was (and is) a disciplined organization which never
hesitated to expel recalcitrant Deputies, while the Radical Party
was always plagued by the endemic indiscipline of its leaders;
ideologically, the two parties differed considerably – for example,
whereas the anti-clericalism of the Radicals found no echo in
the doctrines of the Gaullists, the chauvinistic posturings of
the Gaullists in foreign policy were largely absent in that of
the Radicals.

1972-6: decline and disarray

There were clear signs in the early 1970s that the Gaullist
Party was in decline. In the 1973 elections it suffered a severe
electoral setback: compared with 1968 it lost 2,300,000 votes
and polled only 25.5 per cent of the votes, and it also lost seats
and was deprived of its majority in the National Assembly. It
was deprived of its crushing predominance in the presidential
coalition (in 1968 82 per cent of the presidential coalition
Deputies were Gaullists and in 1973 this proportion dropped
to 61 per cent). Moreover, the opinion polls indicated that
the Gaullists enjoyed no greater support in the country than
their coalition partners. In other words, the real extent of the
Gaullist decline was effectively masked in the elections by their
having been granted the lion's share of the *investitures* for the
presidential ruling coalition. It was the death of Pompidou and
the subsequent presidential election which were fully to expose
the extent of the decline.

The electoral base of Gaullism was not only becoming smaller,
it was also becoming socially more conservative: it was older,
more rural, more female and more Catholic.

The death of President Pompidou in April 1974 dealt a severe
blow to the Gaullists, since it left leaderless a party already
reeling under the impact of its recent electoral setback and a
series of property and tax scandals. The party's candidate in the
May 1974 presidential elections, Chaban-Delmas, won only 15
per cent of the votes at the first ballot. The party was also badly
split by the election, since an important minority, led by Jacques
Chirac, refused to back Chaban-Delmas and favoured Giscard
d'Estaing, and a small Left-wing element of the party supported
Mitterrand at the second ballot. The election of Giscard d'Estaing

to the presidency also spelled trouble for the Gaullists, since the new president was determined to dismantle the 'Gaullist state'. He chose Chirac – 'the traitor' – as prime minister, drastically reduced the number of Gaullist ministers, appointed notorious anti-Gaullists to key ministerial posts, and purged key parts of the administration of Gaullist sympathizers. The party was also weakened by the departure of some Left-wing leaders and by the schism of a small group led by Michel Jobert (Pompidou's foreign minister) who formed his *Mouvement des Démocrates* in March 1975, for he could not stomach the party's subservience to the overtly European and Atlanticist Giscard d'Estaing. Equally alarming to the Gaullists were the opinion polls which suggested the collapse of their support in the country. The Gaullists who lost the presidency in May 1974 suffered another blow when they lost the premiership after the resignation of Chirac in August 1976. The structural bases of the Fifth Republic which had been based on the close and symbiotic relationship which bound the president, the prime minister and the dominant party of the National Assembly were thus undermined.

1976-81: organizational renovation, electoral decline and the quest for independence

The period after the resignation of Jacques Chirac from the premiership was characterized by a not unsuccessful attempt to breathe new life into the declining party and also to assert its independence *vis-à-vis* the President of the Republic. On 5 December 1976 the party changed its name to the *Rassemblement pour la République* (RPR) and altered its statutes in a way designed considerably to strengthen the leader of the party. Chirac, effective leader since December 1974, was elected to the presidency of the party with Soviet-like ease (96.5 per cent of the delegates voted for him). The party organization was strengthened: by January 1979 the RPR was claiming over 750,000 members compared with the 285,000 of the UDR, with active federations in each of the ninety-six *départements* and even 200 factory groups. While the figures and the claims must be treated with some scepticism, the party had undoubtedly received a new lease of life. However, organizational renovation was accompanied by electoral decline: in the March 1978 election the RPR won only 22.6 per cent of the votes cast (admittedly better than Chaban-Delmas's disastrous performance in 1974, but worse than in 1973 and much worse than in 1968), and in the following year, in the elections to the European Parliament, the

Gaullist list won only 16.2 per cent of the votes and was well behind the Giscardian list headed by Simone Veil (which won 27.5 per cent). It was during this period that the Gaullist Party became increasingly critical of President Giscard d'Estaing.

1981-1988, from one presidential campaign to the next: the defeat of Chirac, the victory of Chiraquisme and the defeat of Chirac

In the 1981 presidential elections Jacques Chirac won 18 per cent of the votes cast, running well behind Giscard d'Estaing and François Mitterrand. It was a disappointing performance compared with the heady expectations of his many zealous activists, and it was poorer than that of the Gaullist Party in 1978. Yet Chirac was well satisfied: there were two other dissident Gaullists who together collected nearly three per cent of the votes; he was standing against an incumbent president who attracted the so-called 'legitimist' vote and who was openly supported by many prominent Gaullists who were holding ministerial office; he fared better than Chaban-Delmas in 1974 and better than the Gaullist list in the European elections of 1979; he did far better than the early polls had predicted. His personal position and prestige were undoubtedly enhanced by his dynamic campaign, and that and his good result combined to establish his credentials as the leader of the Right – especially in the light of Giscard d'Estaing's failure. They certainly confirmed his hold over the Gaullist Party.

In the legislative elections of June 1981 the Gaullist Party of Chirac won 20.9 per cent of the votes (compared with 22.6 per cent in 1978) – a small drop in the percentage of votes which was nevertheless translated into a dramatic loss of seats (it lost seventy of its 153 seats). Yet the party was still the biggest party of the Right and its leader had strengthened his position within that Right. With his solid local base in the Limousin (he is the political boss of the *département* of the Corrèze) and in Paris (where he has been a very successful mayor since 1977), his safe seat in the National Assembly, his unassailable position in the Gaullist Party which remained the biggest, best organized and most disciplined of the Right, and an enhanced prestige because of his presidential campaign performance, Chirac staked out a strong claim for the leadership of the Right-wing. This did not mean that he and his party were without problems: they had to work out a satisfactory alliance with the wounded and resentful Giscardians; they had to widen their electoral appeal (the socio-economic base of their electorate was very narrow); they had to keep a fine balance between attacking Mitterrand, the party leader, and Mitterrand, the President of the Republic; they had to strive to keep the various strands of Gaullism woven into a cohesive whole.

During the first *septennat* of Mitterrand, Chirac tightened his grip on the Gaullist Party (in May 1987 he was re-elected to the presidency by 70,123 votes of the 71,118 cast!) and made it the principal instrument of his presidential ambitions. With his optimism, his dynamism and immense energy, his capacity to elicit great loyalty, his series of clientelistic networks and his mastery of the best-organized party of the coalition, Chirac quickly reinforced his position as the leader of the Right after the 1981 elections. He was clearly perceived as such when the Right won the legislative elections of 1986 and he was called to form a government. He was to be prime minister for two years, and during this period his government carried out a major privatization programme, dismantled various state controls of the economy, abolished the wealth tax which had been introduced by the Left, took a tougher stance on public order issues and promised major changes in the legislation on citizenship. In short, Chirac and his government carried out resolutely Right-wing policies. But this did little to disarm the criticisms of the extreme Right with which the Gaullists had a troubled and ambivalent relationship. In opinion polls on the presidential elections he initially trailed Raymond Barre, but by the start of the official campaign he had overhauled his Right-wing adversary.

Chirac's disappointing performance at the first ballot of the elections (he won only 19.9 per cent of the votes) his resounding defeat at the second and the defeat of the Right in the June legislative elections raised serious questions in the ranks of the Gaullist Party: had the party not become too bourgeois and too Right-wing? had the electorate of the party not become that of a traditional conservative party? had the party not strayed too far from its historic Gaullist legacy on the Atlantic alliance, on Europe and on economic matters? had the party not sacrificed itself on the altar of one person's presidential ambitions? had the party not compromised its integrity by its ambivalent attitude towards the extreme Right? was the party capable of reversing the slow erosion of its electoral base? A group of *rénovateurs*, led by the Left-wing Gaullist Philippe Séguin, a minister in the Chirac government of 1986-88, openly criticized the functioning, the policies and the general strategy of the party. When Séguin stood for the leadership of the Gaullist parliamentary group in

June 1988 he was beaten by only one vote. Discontent was widespread within the party, and it was voiced to Alain Juppé, the newly elected general secretary of the RPR, when he visited provincial cadres.

The Gaullists were badly shaken and divided by the 1988 elections, and the position and policies of their leader questioned by sections of the party. However, despite clear signs of the electoral weakness of the Gaullists and despite their relegation from the position as the dominant party of the Republic to one of equal partner within a shaky Right-wing coalition, the importance of the RPR within the French party system should not be underestimated. Even after the 1988 defeats the party had 127 Deputies, 77 Senators, 373 regional councillors (of whom 6 presided over a regional assembly), 730 departmental councillors (including 24 presidents), 5,429 mayors (47 of whom were running towns of over 30,000 inhabitants), and twenty members of the European Parliament. And its organizational efficiency and activist base (it claims to have some 850,000 members) are the envy of all other parties.

Within the party there are several distinct – almost chrono-logical – strata; the *Gaullisme gaullien* of the historical Gaullists who are bound by idealism, patriotism and fidelity to the memory of General de Gaulle, 'the man of 18 June 1940'; the *Gaullisme droitière* which first appeared at the time of the RPF Gaullist Party of the Fourth Republic and which is fired by a virulent anti-communism; the managerial Gaullism of many leaders who are reformist, modernizing and politically pragmatic and who accept the Gaullists because they gave France much-needed political stability; the *Gaullisme opportuniste* of those for whom the party means patronage and place and potential office; the *Gaullisme présidentiel* – that of the so-called 'legitimists' who backed Giscard d'Estaing because he was President of the Repub-lic, *de facto* leader of the Right-wing coalition and upholder of the institutions of the Fifth Republic; *Gaullisme Chiraquien* – that of the RPR which revelled in the aggressive, muscular, populist, nationalist and voluntaristic utterances of Chirac between 1976 and 1986; *Gaullisme de gouvernement* after 1986 which, under the influence of some of Chirac's lieutenants, became more conservative in social policies, more liberal in economic matters, and more Atlanticist and pro-European in foreign policy.

There is no real unity within the party over some basic policies: the party harbours economic liberals and economic *dirigistes*, social liberals and social conservatives, protagonists and adversaries of military conscription, pro- and anti-Europeans. Furthermore, there have always been opportunists in the Gaullist

Party ready to sacrifice their principles for the greater good of their own ambitions: in May 1952 an important group of Gaullists Deputies defied orders from the leadership and voted for the investiture of Prime Minister Pinay (the spiritual father of Giscard d'Estaing), and in the May 1974 presidential elections Chirac led a group of forty-three Gaullist members of parliament in refusing to support the party's official candidate. During the period 1976-81 when relations between the Gaullist Party and President Giscard d'Estaing were full of tension and friction there was always a small, but influential, group of Gaullist ministers and Deputies who were highly critical of Chirac for his anti-presidential posturing. There are clearly, too, divergences in political temperament between the leadership, the big local bosses and the party activists. Yet in spite of the various currents of thought, ideological tendencies and different degrees of party loyalty the Gaullist Party under the leadership of Jacques Chirac is likely to hold together and act in a united way, focusing its short and medium-term energies into establishing for itself a powerful local and parliamentary base with a view to facilitating its long-term objective – the election of one of its leaders to the presidency of the Republic.

The non-Gaullist moderate Right

In February 1978 – only a month before the legislative elections of that year – the non-Gaullist parties of the ruling coalition formed an alliance, the *Union pour la Démocratie Française* (UDF). They were inspired by an awareness that their divisions would be electorally penalized, and they were motivated by a desire to break the dominance of the Gaullist Party within the ruling coalition. Their purpose was to strengthen those elements in the coalition which were favourably disposed towards President Giscard d'Estaing: their colours were revealed by their name, since *Démocratie Française* had been the title of the President's recent book. The UDF brought together the Republican Party and the *Clubs Perspectives et Réalités*, the *Centre des Démocrates Sociaux* (CDS), the Radical Party and a number of small groups and parties such as the *Mouvement des Démocrates Socialistes* (MDS). Several attempts had already been made or projected to weld some or all of them into a united and effective force. However, the Reformist Movement of November 1971, the still-born 'great federation of the Centrists' envisaged by Poniatowski in August 1971, the Movement of the Reformist Left founded in January 1975 and the projected 'great liberal party' had all quickly collapsed even when they managed to struggle into life. But the election to the presidency of the Republic of Giscard d'Estaing who had always claimed that France wanted to be 'governed from the centre' placed a premium on the organization, co-ordination, strengthening and disciplining of a Centrist movement or party. The increasingly hostile attitude of the Gaullists and the odour of impending electoral disaster in 1978 merely accelerated the realization of a long-standing presidential desire. It was not surprising that the major party of the UDF should be the president's own party, the Republican Party.

The Republican Party was founded in May 1977 as the direct heir to the Independent Republican movement, itself founded after 1962 by Valéry Giscard d'Estaing when he and several other members of parliament broke away from the conservative CNIP (*Centre National des Indépendants et Paysans*) in protest against that party's growing anti-Gaullism. The CNIP was destroyed as a viable national political force in 1962, although it still limps along on the local level as a home for conservative councillors with an aversion to both party labels and rigid principles. It is a party with few leaders and fewer troops, no organization, no defined policies and no illusions. It was replaced by the Independent Republicans who became, in Malcolm Anderson's words, 'a focus for conservatives who wished to rally to the new régime and to gain access to political power'. But they were never more than a *centre d'accueil* (the description of Poniatowski, one of its leaders) for conservatives who were prepared to back the government but who had no wish to join the Gaullist Party. The Independent Republican movement (the FNRI) was dominated by a small group of parliamentary *notables*, never built a mass following and was organizationally weak (it was estimated that at the time of the 1973 elections it had only eleven to twelve thousand members). Even in the period following the election of their leader, Giscard d'Estaing, to the presidency of the Republic the FNRI failed to grow or to organize itself. It was clearly an inadequate political instrument for the president, particularly as the Gaullists were being given a new lease of life under the leadership of Chirac. Indeed, it was the creation of the Gaullist RPR in December 1976 and the victory of Chirac in the Paris elections of March 1977 (he beat the president's personal candidate) which finally galvanized the Giscardians into action, with the creation in May 1977 of the Republican Party. Its first leader was Jean-Pierre Soisson (now a Minister in the Rocard government of 1988!) who was a close political ally and friend of the President of the Republic. Soisson expressed the hope of transforming the party into a movement with mass electoral support and a heavy contingent of activists.

In his attempt to emulate the Gaullists, Soisson wished to forge 'an effective instrument of political action' at the disposal of the president of the Republic. He failed to do so and, in 1978, was replaced, as secretary general, by Jacques Blanc, a young deputy. The party did begin to increase its membership quite sharply: from 95,000 in April 1978 to 190,000 by the mid 1980s. The self-proclaimed '*parti du Président*' had links with other Giscardian organizations: the *Mouvement des Jeunes Giscardiens*, a group of well-bred and generally well-dressed youths (including the son of the president, Henri Giscard d'Estaing), the *Collectif des Étudiants Libéraux de France* (CELF which had some success in student elections and benefited greatly from ministerial largesse), and the political clubs. Linked with the Republican Party are two pro-Giscardian movements – the *Mouvement Génération Sociale et Libérale*, a movement founded in September 1974 and claiming an implausible membership of 35,000, and the political *Clubs Perspectives et Réalités*, founded in 1965 by Giscard d'Estaing and claiming to have 20,000 members in 1985. These movements spawned ideas and suggestions for a party leadership which solemnly shelved them.

The second party to join the Giscardian UDF was the *Centre des Démocrates Sociaux* (CDS) founded in May 1976 and presided over by Jean Lecanuet until 1982, when he was replaced by Pierre Méhaignerie. It was created by the merger of the *Centre Démocrate* (CD) of Jean Lecanuet and the *Centre Démocratie et Progrès* (CDP) of Jacques Duhamel which had split away from the *Centre Démocrate* in 1969. The latter was founded in October 1966 following Lecanuet's relatively successful candidacy in the December 1965 presidential elections, but it never achieved the electoral success anticipated by its leaders, and it was also seriously weakened by the departure of the *Duhamelistes* in 1969. The *Lecanuetistes* and the *Duhamelistes* came together again at the second ballot of the 1974 presidential elections when they both supported Giscard d'Estaing, and shortly after they joined forces to create the CDS. The CDS was the direct descendant of the now defunct Catholic centre party, the MRP, which in 1946, with 28 per cent of the votes, was the biggest party in France. And it is the spiritual heir to a long social Catholic tradition which had sought to reconcile French Catholics to the ungodly Republic. In 1986 it claimed a membership of 49,000.

The third party to join the UDF was the Radical Party, which, from being the most important party of the Third Republic and one of the influential pivotal parties of the Fourth, had been reduced to a marginal and insignificant force during the Fifth. It had been seriously weakened by the departure of its opportunists to the Gaullist Party and of its Left-wingers who, in 1972, had created a separate party which entered into alliance with the other opposition parties of the Left (see Chapter 10). After October 1969 it was dominated by its leader, Jean-Jacques Servan-Schreiber. JJSS, as he was familiarly known, was a man of unquestionable courage and ferocious intellect but of highly questionable political judgement: he was a politician who was totally unaware of the virtues of occasional silence and temporization. In spite of his undeniable energy (often expressed in unseemly tantrums), his genius for self-publicity and his gift to the party of a far-sighted manifesto (it was read with apprehensive consternation by some of the party's leaders and with bland disapproval by others), he was unable to instil any real life into the largely moribund carcass of the Radical Party. The Radical Party rallied to the presidential camp in May 1974 when it backed Giscard d'Estaing at the second ballot of the presidential elections. It remains a marginal force within the UDF: in 1985 it claimed 20,000 members.

Several other very small groups or parties joined or were to join the UDF: the *Mouvement Démocrate Socialiste* (ex-*Mouvement des Démocrates Socialistes de France*) founded in 1979 (a motley collection of anti-communists who had abandoned the Socialist Party of François Mitterrand) and which claimed 4500 members in that year, and the *Carrefour social démocrate* which was created in July 1977 by a group of socially minded Centrists with the intention of giving the UDF a centre-Left orientation.

The UDF started well: the amalgamation of the weak, the unimportant and the plainly derisory produced something more than the insignificant. It won 21 per cent of the votes in the March 1978 elections and formed a separate group of 123 deputies in the National Assembly. In the June 1979 European elections the UDF list, headed by Simone Veil, won 27.5 per cent of the votes, beating the Socialist, Gaullist, and Communist lists. By the time of the 1981 presidential elections, the UDF was gathering a mass membership (by French standards at least), claiming 300,000 (about 70,000 of whom were reported as 'direct' – people who had joined the UDF directly and not indirectly through one of the constituent parties), it had a group of 123 in the National Assembly and 109 in the Senate, and at local level it controlled forty-one of the biggest towns of France (those with 30,000 or more inhabitants), while eight of the twenty-two regional councils and thirty-two of the ninety-six departmental councils were presided over by its members. It had a leader, the President of the Republic, who placed many UDF sympathizers in key positions in the state apparatus, hefty financial backing, and a vague set of guiding principles culled from the writings of Giscard d'Estaing. It also had a basic aim: to provide political backing for Giscard d'Estaing and to work for his re-election in May 1981.

The 1981 presidential election was to prove traumatic for the UDF. In the first place, Giscard d'Estaing did not use the UDF as his principal campaign organization: he relied essentially upon his own personal campaign headquarters and on the Élysée staff at national level and groups of 'apolitical' *notables* at local level. So unlike the Communist, Socialist and Gaullist parties the UDF as a movement was scarcely mobilized, being reduced to a secondary role. The result was not a little resentment and frustration. Second, Giscard d'Estaing was unexpectedly beaten, and the result was not only to deprive the alliance of the presidential office and the patronage that accompanied it, but also a leader, since Giscard d'Estaing, after a petulant and impetuous attack on Jacques Chirac, initially withdrew into wounded and haughty silence. The Giscardians who went into the June 1981 legislative elections in a state of disarray, swallowed pride and principle and concluded an electoral alliance with the Gaullists. In the event, they fared quite well, since their share of the vote fell from 20.6 per cent in 1978 to 19.2 per cent. However, the number of their Deputies dropped to only sixty-six, a loss of fifty-nine.

The UDF emerged not only leaderless and weakened from the two elections of 1981, but also very divided. The divisions which had always been there were intensified and articulated in defeat and in the political post-mortem which followed. The failure of Giscard d'Estaing opened up new divisions within the UDF, since some within the Republican Party remained faithful to the ex-president, while some others wished to take a prudent distance.

Between 1981 and 1988 the presidential contest within the UDF was resolved in favour of Raymond Barre, although neither the choice nor the subsequent support was overwhelmingly enthusiastic. The ex-premier, a courteous man in private, could appear condescending in public. His cautious, pragmatic and moderate approach, his *Gaullien* dislike of party politics, his refusal to court the activists of the UDF, his barbed remarks about the policies of the Chirac government (which contained UDF ministers) combined to ensure only a lukewarm reaction to his candidacy from many in the UDF. His defeat in the elections provoked neither surprise nor tears.

If the UDF was unlucky in the choice of its presidential candidate it was, as noted above, more successful in combating the dominance of the Gaullists within the coalition: its own candidate, Simone Veil, headed the joint Right-wing list in the 1984 European elections; it negotiated a fair share of *investitures* for its own candidates in the 1986 and 1988 elections, and it was well represented in the Chirac government of 1986-88. More significantly, at the 1988 legislative elections more UDF than Gaullist Deputies were elected. The UDF has also retained an influential place within the political system, especially at local level: even after the 1988 elections it had ninety Deputies, (and there were a further 41 in the UDC Centrist group), 144 Senators, 14 presidents of regional councils, 42 presidents of departmental councils and 38 mayors of towns with more than 30,000 inhabitants. But the parties of the UDF live in a constant state of tension. At present, they are divided over personalities and principles, for each party represents a distinct current of thought which has been nourished by a distinctive historical tradition: the CDS has a social Catholic past while the Radicals are the historical champions of the anti-clerical secular republic: the Republican Party has a moderate opportunist conservative heritage whereas the *Mouvement Démocrate Socialiste*, as the name indicates, is wedded to the concepts of social democracy. The centre Right of the UDF was nervous of Giscard d'Estaing's early reformist utterances while the centre Left was critical of his failure to translate those utterances into policies. On issues such as abortion, divorce, sex equality, nuclear energy, regionalization and the role of the state and of the public sector within the economy there have been quite sharp differences both among the UDF members of parliament and among the activists. The UDF is also divided in its attitude towards the Gaullists, some leaders urging confrontation, others advocating conciliation and even unity, and there are differences of opinion on how to deal with the Socialists, since some are already co-operating with them (in government), some are seeking future collaboration and some wish resolutely to remain in Right-wing opposition. Finally, to these various divisions are added the differences of opinion over the very nature of the UDF, since an influential group favours the merger of the constituent parties, while the leaders of those parties generally resist such a policy. The UDF resembles, therefore, an 'unstable chemical body which could either dissolve or stabilize' (Jean-Christian Petitfils); it is finding its way, torn between the centrifugal force of the 'party patriotism' of its constituent elements and their ideological diversity and the centripetal force of electoral survival.

The divided Right

Each of the two basic components of the Right-wing coalition – the Gaullists and the UDF – are internally divided. But the divisions are less than those which separate them. Since the summer of 1976 (when Chirac resigned as prime minister) many of the latent conflicts between the Gaullists and the UDF have surfaced.

At the level of personalities

Since 1976 there has been a highly personalized '*querelle des chefs*' between Jacques Chirac, Valéry Giscard d'Estaing and Raymond Barre, all of whom have had presidential ambitions. The rivalry between Chirac and Giscard d'Estaing between 1976 and the mid-1980s was replaced by that between Chirac and Barre after 1986. It was revealing that between August 1976 and May 1981 Giscard d'Estaing met his ex-prime minister on only six occasions – and each was purely formal and demanded by protocol. The Gaullist leader's decision to reject the president's nominee for the position of Mayor of Paris in the elections of March 1977 and his defiant gesture in presenting himself as a candidate for the post was only the most spectacular manifestation of the discord which reigned between Chirac and the then President of the Republic.

The battle between the two men at the time of the 1981 presidential election made matters worse: the mutual recriminations during the first-ballot campaign had a decidedly personalized edge to them, and the apparent unwillingness of Chirac fully to mobilize the Gaullist vote behind Giscard d'Estaing at the second ballot merely confirmed the belief in the mind of the latter that the former was guilty of 'premeditated treachery'. The Gaullists had always been wary of Giscard d'Estaing whose attitude towards General de Gaulle had been ambiguous and exploitative: he derived many benefits from a presidency towards which he was careful to mark his distance. His *oui-mais* speech of 10 January 1967 in which he indicated his reservations about some of de Gaulle's policies, his *exercise solitaire du pouvoir* speech of 17 August 1967 in which he attacked, albeit guardedly, de Gaulle's quixotic and arbitrary way of governing, his ambiguous attitude during the turbulence of May 1968, his hostile stance during the December 1968 budgetary debates, his ultimate apostasy at the time of the April 1969 referendum when he openly expressed his opposition to de Gaulle's proposals – all combined to render him suspect in the eyes of the increasingly sensitive Gaullists. During the Pompidou presidency he retained the key post of finance minister, yet this did not prevent him from strongly intimating his dislike of some Gaullist practices and personalities. After his election to the presidency in 1974 (during which he beat the Gaullist candidate and managed to divide the Gaullist leaders) he dramatically reduced the number of Gaullist ministers and began to oust Gaullists from key posts in the administration and the state-run media. Chirac's highly personalized campaign against Giscard d'Estaing touched, therefore, a responsive chord in the Gaullist Party.

The defeat of the Right in the 1981 presidential elections was followed by a period of disarray and demoralization, and by bouts of bickering among the chieftains, and this intensified as each asserted his claim to represent the Right at the presidential elections. By the mid-1980s four major candidates emerged: Chirac, Giscard d'Estaing, ex-Premier Raymond Barre and François Léotard, the Minister for Culture and leader of the Republican Party. Giscard d'Estaing eventually withdrew from the presidential scramble into a feigned statesmanlike aloofness, while Léotard was quickly perceived as lacking serious presidential qualities and he, too, withdrew.

The Barre–Chirac rivalry was clearly fired by past enmity. The tensions between the two men which began during Barre's premiership of 1976-1981 were heightened during Chirac's second premiership of 1986-1988. Barre's outspoken denunciation of *cohabitation*, his constant sniping at government policies, his barely veiled criticisms of Gaullist hegemonic pretensions, his allusions to the lack of presidential calibre of Chirac excited the intense dislike of the RPR, and particularly its activists.

At the level of policies

During the Giscard d'Estaing presidency, in economic matters the Gaullists opposed a new system of local taxation proposed by the government, they severely mauled the government's bill on capital gains, they opposed the Barre budget in 1980, they demanded a more expansionary economic strategy to combat rising unemployment, and they were severely critical of some of the neo-liberal doctrines of the last years of the Giscard d'Estaing presidency. In international and European affairs, the Gaullists opposed the extension of the budgetary powers of the European Assembly at Strasbourg and expressed serious reservations about the election of the European Parliament by universal suffrage. They also criticized the proposed ratification of the new statutes of the International Monetary Fund agreed at the January 1976 meeting in Jamaica and which envisaged a reduction in the role of gold and increased French participation in the fund. They were especially critical of Giscard d'Estaing's attitude during the Soviet invasion of Afghanistan, accusing the president of timidity and procrastination. In the area of defence policy they demanded an increase in the defence budget, a diversification of the strategic nuclear deterrent and a restructuring of military service. They feared, too, a deep-seated Giscardian plot to Europeanize French defence, particularly after Poniatowski, who was known to be a very close friend of the president, advocated a European nuclear deterrent in June 1980.

After 1981 and especially during the 1986-88 Chirac government, policy differences at party level were evident over, for example, the means of financing the social security system, the reform of the nationality laws (the divisions were openly admitted by the Justice Minister), the censorship measures decreed by the Interior Minister in March 1987, the treatment of drug offenders, and the student disturbances of November–December 1986. Foreign policy differences were clear over the responses to the siting of Pershing missiles in Europe and to Gorbachev's disarmament proposals. The privatization programme of the Chirac government, which involved industry, banking, the media and parts of the prison service, tapped all the tensions of the Right-wing coalition. So, too, did the appointment of ministers in April 1986, the nominations to key posts in the administration and the nationalized industries, and the redrawing of constituency boundaries for the legislative elections. In all these latter cases the UDF was convinced that the Gaullists were attempting to reassert their hegemony within the Right.

At the level of political strategy

Between 1974 and 1976 Chirac, as prime minister, wanted a more combative attitude towards the Left and in 1976 asked for an early election – which President Giscard d'Estaing refused. The Gaullists also wanted the president to take a more resolute part in the 1978 election campaign as the effective head of his coalition and insisted that as such he should resign from the presidency if he was beaten – a proposal categorically rejected by the president. They also requested that he show less soft-heartedness in denouncing the Left and its policies. At bottom, many Gaullists suspected that the president harboured secret sympathies for the Socialists and that he would like to make a deal with them at their expense. After 1981, differences of strategy focused on three essential issues, all of which were increasingly important after 1986: the attitude to adopt towards the rise of the extreme Right of Jean-Marie Le Pen; whether or not to unite to form a single Right-wing party; how to react to the Socialist policy of political *ouverture*. Increasingly, some Centrists of the UDF were tempted by the siren calls of the moderate Socialists, since they were no longer inhibited by the fear of communism (following the decline of the Communist Party and the collapse of the Left-wing alliance) no longer repelled by a Socialist Party which had been deradicalized, and increasingly worried about the extreme Right towards which certain Gaullists had adopted too placatory an attitude. After Mitterrand's triumphant re-election in May 1988, prominent UDF members spoke openly of the need for some form of co-operation with the Socialists, and in June two prominent Centrists joined the Rocard government. In the same month CDS Deputies, led by their president Pierre Méhaignerie, created a separate parliamentary group (the *Union du Centre*) in the National Assembly. By mid-1988, therefore, there were clear indications of the extreme fragility of the Right-wing coalition.

The Gaullists and the UDF have different leaders, somewhat different policies, strikingly different styles, very different organizational structures, and rather different electorates, although the polls provide somewhat conflicting evidence on this last issue. The electorate of the moderate Right parties has become generally more bourgeois, more wealthy, less popular, more conservative (although UDF voters place themselves less on the Right than do those of the Gaullist Party). More farmers and more old people vote Gaullist than Centrist, more managers vote Centrist than Gaullist. On economic values there appears to have been convergence between the views of the two electorates, but on social issues the Centrists tend to be more traditional and conservative, and on political matters they are generally critical of the Gaullist tendency to claim the lion's share of any available posts. However, at the second ballot of successive elections the electorate of the Right has demonstrated its loyalty and discipline.

The parties of the Right are also locked into a battle for supremacy within the coalition. Tension between them is, therefore, inevitable. Those of historical inclination might trace the source of that tension to the distinct and, in some respects, antagonistic political traditions of the Gaullists and the parties of the Right: the former are heirs to a long Bonapartist, populist and nationalistic tradition while the latter trace their ancestors to the liberal, parliamentary, elitist and moderate conservatives who served any régime which served them. Others relate the tension to different ideological perspectives (over France's place in the world, over the role of the state, over the place of private enterprise in the economy, over the capacity of a government to bring about change). Whatever the source of the tension, it undeniably exists, and it will continue to bedevil relations between the two great families of the Right. Nevertheless the gap between the two should not be exaggerated. In the first place, at the level of the two elites there exists a certain political fluidity: there has always been a pro-UDF group among the Gaullists and a pro-Gaullist group among the UDF – groups which, through personal opportunism or political conviction or both, always rallied to the winning side. Second, the electorate of the Right is relatively homogeneous, and is certainly much more united on basic values than that of the Left: on most fundamental points the electorates (whatever the quarrels at the top or among the activists) are in remarkable agreement and perceive themselves in very similar terms. Indeed, it has been argued that the real cleavage at electoral level exists not between the Gaullists and the UDF but *within* each camp. This relative homogeneity of the electorate of the two principal movements of the Right may do little to defuse the conflict-ridden situation at the level of the leaders, but it greatly facilitates Right-wing electoral discipline. Furthermore, the fluidity at elite level ensures that any Right-wing president or prime minister can build a relatively stable coalition. It is too easily forgotten that in spite of persistent tension and sporadic conflict the Gaullists and the Centrists ruled France for more than twenty years in harness if not in harmony. Without the powerful cement of office and patronage it has proved to be more difficult to hold the coalition together, yet the prospects of both, the internal logic of the presidential and legislative electoral systems and their common dislike of the Left remain powerful incentives to unity. It must be recalled that in 1981, 1986 and 1988 the Right confronted the elections with a common platform and, in the vast majority of constituencies, a single candidate. It should also be emphasized that in the regional, departmental and local councils Right-wing coalitions have been completely unaffected by the squabbles of the national leadership.

The power of the Right

Even when out of office the Right is not deprived of influence:

● In the first place, it always remains powerful at parliamentary level, and particularly in the Senate where it enjoys a majority.
● At the local level it controls a majority of the twenty-two regional councils, a clear majority of the ninety-six departmental councils and some of the major cities of France, including Paris, Lyons and Bordeaux.
● Its ideas are propagated by some of the most influential pressure groups in the country: the CNPF which represents the business community, the FNSEA which is the main farmers' union, the Unapel which protects Catholic private schools and the Peep (*Parents d'élèves de l'enseignement public*)

which defends a Rightist viewpoint in the organization of the state schools.

● As the result of successive reforms it has been deprived of its privileged and much abused position in the state media but the Right still enjoys access thereto and exploits it to very good effect. Furthermore, the Paris press is largely (though not exclusively) in the hands of the Right.

● The Right has many sympathizers in the administration and, as a consequence of *pantouflage*, in key positions in private and public sector industries.

● The Right enjoys an intellectual vogue in certain circles: the neo-liberal Right has organized several campaigns, has the support of sympathetic newspapers such as *Figaro-Magazine* and has the backing of a network of clubs.

● Finally, the Right exerts a constant electoral pressure on the Left. Every electoral victory it enjoys in by-elections or local elections is a reminder to the Left of the narrowness of the parameters of decision-making and of the vulnerability of its power base.

The rise of the Extreme Right

One of the most surprising and, to many, most alarming features of the 1980s has been the re-emergence of the extreme Right as a major political force. With rising prosperity, the healing of the wounds of Vichy and the colonial wars, and the growing legitimacy of the regime, it was felt that the extreme Right was destined to extinction. In the 1965 presidential elections, the candidate of the extreme Right Tixier-Vignancour, gained 5.3 per cent of the votes, but thereafter the extreme Right went into rapid decline, and was also torn by bitter rivalries. There was no extreme Right-wing candidate in the 1969 presidential elections, and in the 1974 presidential elections Le Pen, leader of the recently (October 1972) formed *Front National*, won only 0.7 per cent of the votes. By the early 1980s it was a broken force, lacking effective leadership, elites or followers: its electoral performance was lamentable. In the 1981 presidential election Le Pen, one of its leaders, could not even scrape together the five hundred signatures necessary to stand, and in the 1981 legislative elections candidates of the extreme Right won only 0.3 per cent of the votes. Seven years later, however, Le Pen was to delight his supporters and shock the rest of France by winning 14.4 per cent of the poll at the first ballot of the presidential elections: he was just behind Raymond Barre and well ahead of André Lajoinie, the Communist candidate (in 34 of the 53 towns of over 30,000 inhabitants under

Communist Party control Le Pen won more votes than Lajoinie). And if his party, the *Front National*, was to lose some ground in the June 1988 legislative elections – it won only 9.7 per cent of the votes – the combined results of the presidential and legislative elections were to convince observers that the extreme Right was likely to become a durable feature of French politics, particularly as exit polls of 1988 confirmed that it was acquiring a stable and faithful electorate.

The electoral rise of the National Front dates from the victory of the Left in May–June 1981 and the economic difficulties of the Left-wing government after 1982: in the 1983 municipal elections it enjoyed limited successes in a number of towns (notably Paris); in the local and legislative by-elections in 1983 (especially at Dreux where it won 16.7 per cent of the votes) and 1984 it made major breakthroughs; in the European elections of 1984 it won 11 per cent of the votes and ten seats in the European Parliament; in the March 1985 departmental elections it won 8.8 per cent of the national vote, but in the *cantons* in which it was represented its average rose to 10.5 per cent; in the March 1986 legislative elections it won 9.7 per cent of the votes, and performed especially well in areas with high densities of immigrant populations. But the major triumph came in the 1988 presidential elections when Le Pen not only gained 14.4 per cent of the vote but succeeded in 'nationalizing' the vote of the extreme Right. He won more than 20 per cent of the votes in eight of the 96 metropolitan French *départements*, and in nine *départements* was the best placed Right-wing candidate. His major successes were in Alsace (on the German border) and in the South-East *départements* of the Mediterranean coast with heavy concentrations of immigrants. In major towns such as Marseilles, Nice, Antibes, Toulon and Avignon Le Pen scored heavily, thus putting down markers for the 1989 local elections.

The leader of the party, Le Pen, is an energetic, articulate and intellectually able person who projects the attractive side of his personality with great force, conviction and professionalism. His speeches are direct, truculent, simplistic and plausible, spiced with home-spun aphorisms and not a little humour. He is expert in exploiting fear and bigotry, and in a period of doubt and uncertainty, his dreadfully simple solutions, proclaimed with authority and certainty, have their attraction. His major themes on law and order, on the degeneration of France, on immigrants, are hammered home with eloquent consistency.

The leadership of the party reflects a merging of several elements: monarchists who are still fighting the war against 1789; war-time collaborators and ex-supporters of Petain; anti-semites;

sympathisers of *Algérie française* and even of the OAS (the quasi-military terrorist arm of the movement); Catholic fundamentalists; opportunist Right-wing *notables* who had been marginalized by the other parties of the Right. There is a reasonably respectable visible elite and a murky and far from respectable hidden group within the leadership core. It has its 'moderates' (some of whom resigned in September 1987 after Le Pen's reference to the gas chambers of the Second World War as a 'historical detail') and its hard-liners, and harbours those who seek collaboration with the other parties of the Right and those who eschew all co-operation.

The electorate of Le Pen and the *Front National* in the presidential and legislative elections is disproportionately masculine and non-practising Catholic, and attracts support from all age groups (though relatively well among the 18 to 24 years old) and all social classes (but especially among small shop-keepers and artisans, upper management and the young unemployed). It is worth noting that as many workers voted for Le Pen as they did for Lajoinie, the Communist candidate. The groups which are most resistant to the appeal of the party are the elderly, women, trade-unionists, the irreligious and the well-educated (especially teachers), and practising Catholics. An exit poll taken after the first-ballot voting indicated that Le Pen attracted three distinct electorates: radicalized Right-wingers (49 per cent), 'new voters' – those who were too young or who abstained in 1981 (32 per cent), and ex-Left-wingers (19 per cent). Of the 'new voters' 49 per cent had voted for the moderate Right in 1986. In the legislative elections of June 1988, the *Front National* lost ground, compared with its leader in the previous April, among farmers and traditional conservatives (who reverted to their normal voting behaviour) and among the workers and the 25 to 34 year olds (who reverted to their traditional Left-wing voting).

The policy priorities of extreme Right-wing voters tend to be somewhat different from those of other parties' voters: much greater weight is attached to the problems of immigration and law and order. They dislike abortion, and strikers, and generally favour the police and tough methods (including the death penalty) for dealing with criminals. There is some evidence to suggest that those who voted for Le Pen for the first time in 1988 were slightly more concerned than the faithful (those who had voted in 1986 for the *Front National*) about unemployment than immigration. Interestingly, Le Pen attracted voters from the Left, many of whom (an estimated one million) were to vote for Mitterrand at the second ballot of the presidential elections, and to desert the *Front National* in the legislative elections.

Several explanations have been put forward to explain the re-emergence of the extreme Right. Some observers attribute it to fundamental *social* changes: the 'decomposition of the social tissue of France' with industrialization, urbanization and secularization; the 'diffused anxiety' of a population which is afraid of the unknown and the foreign during a period of rapid social transformation; the collapse of the Catholic sub-culture which integrated foreigners and inhibited xenophobia within the sub-cultural community; the loss of 'national identity' as the country is slowly sucked into Europe. Other specialists see the *economic* crisis, which intensified after 1979, as the major source of National Front strength: rapidly rising unemployment and the failure of both Left and Right-wing governments to deal with it provided fertile ground for extremists who pointed out, with implacably faulty logic, that with two million unemployed and two million immigrants the solution to the problem was obvious. There are, finally, a series of *political* factors which have been put forward to explain the success of the *Front National*: the dynamic leadership of Le Pen who dared to proclaim in public what the electors whispered in private; the change in the electoral system in 1985 to some form of proportional representation (which in 1986, gave the party 35 seats in the National Assembly and a new political propaganda arena); the disappearance of the Communist sub-culture and the dramatic weakening of the Communist Party and the CGT, the Communist-dominated trade-union confederation; the traditional weakness of partisan identification and socialization in France; the radicalization of parts of the Right-wing electorate following the Left-wing victories of 1981; the growing disillusionment with the four major parties – the 'gang of four'; the policy changes in the Gaullist party which became less populist, less nationalistic, more bourgeois, more European (in the 1984 European elections, the Gaullists joined the list headed by Simone Veil who is Jewish, liberal and as Minister of Education, had pushed through the abortion laws, thus earning for herself in extreme Right-wing circles the title of the *'tricoteuse sanglante'*); the failure of the Right-wing government of Chirac to carry out resolutely Right-wing policies, especially over immigration and the promised reform of the nationality laws; the ambiguity of the moderate Right which rejects any national alliance with the National Front, but which has collaborated with it in certain localities and in certain regions; the intellectual respectability afforded certain theories of the extreme Right by parts of the Parisian press.

In fact, any explanation of the rise of the National Front must be rooted in a combination of factors: historical traditions which remain dormant, ready to be activated; new socio-economic cleavages and the decline in the salience of traditional ones; the prevailing political and economic circumstances; the capacity to catalyse, to channel and to extend disgruntlement and protest.

The party is against Jews (though generally not openly so) immigrants (especially from North Africa), homosexuals, intellectuals, bureaucrats, penal reformers, drug addicts, social 'do-gooders', liberal Catholics, trade unionists, Communists: its litany of dislikes and hatreds is truly impressive. It supports traditional family and Catholic morality, a reduction in the role of the state, strong-arm tactics for criminals (it backs, of course, bringing back capital punishment), and a policy of sending back immigrants to their homelands. '*Les Français d'abord*' '*Les Français à l'Élysée*' are among its major battle cries. Immigrants are the major scapegoats, responsible for the rise of both crime and unemployment: the offended against becomes the offender in the tortured logic of the extreme Right.

For the optimists, the *Front National* is a mere flash-party, similar to the Poujadist movement of the 1950s which disappeared as spectacularly as it emerged. They point to the relative failure of the June 1988 legislative elections, when the party lost many of the Le Pen voters: it lost almost everywhere, and in only thirty constituencies did it win more than 12.5 per cent of the electorate. In only nine constituencies was it the best-placed party of the Right, and eight of the nine were in one *département* (Bouches-du-Rhône), and it elected only one deputy who subsequently resigned from the party after another anti-semitic outburst from Le Pen. Yet, there is evidence of the party putting down firm roots: it is backed by a network of clubs and circles (notably the Republican Action Committees of Bruno Megret and the GRECE, a group convinced of the biological superiority of the Aryan race and led by Alain de Benoist); it is clearly not short of financial resources; it has ten members in the European Parliament (the biggest component of the Parliament's extreme-Right-wing group); it has 137 regional councillors and holds the balance of power in five of the twenty-two regions; it has a membership estimated at between 35,000 and 60,000; it enjoys some support in the national press. The evidence suggests that the nature of the *Front National*'s electorate changed somewhat between 1984 and 1986 (for example, about a third of the *Front*'s voters of 1984 voted for other parties or abstained in 1986), and again between 1986 and 1988, since Le Pen attracted some traditional Right-wing voters who were disappointed with the performance of the Chirac government. It would now appear, however, that the extreme Right is acquiring a stable core of faithful electors (some ninety per cent of the *Front National* voters of 1986 voted for Le

Pen in 1988). It is unlikely ever to win the presidency, or even to enter government, but it has real influence in squeezing the other parties of the Right into dealing with policies they would prefer not to have on the political agenda. Its very existence has divided the traditional Right and may contribute to a reshaping of the French party system.

10 The Left: the troubled alliance

The bipolarizing pressures of the Fifth Republic, which squeezed the parties of the Right and Centre into coalition, also made themselves felt on the Left. The two major parties of the Left – Socialists and Communists – were forced to respond to the success of the Right-wing alliance, and each did so by concerting tactics with the other while jealously guarding its own autonomy. Unlike the parties of the Right, they responded only very slowly to the challenges of the new regime, believing (and hoping) that Gaullism and presidentialism were but transient phenomena.

During the first years of the Fifth Republic the Left was profoundly divided and hence very weak: President de Gaulle could well have reversed the famous aphorism and proclaimed that with enemies like that who needed friends? The first stage of Left-wing unity took place in October 1962, when Socialists and Communists came to a limited number of second ballot electoral agreements. Three years later, in December 1965, both supported François Mitterrand in the presidential elections, even though he belonged to neither party, and in the March 1967, June 1968 and March 1973 legislative elections they concluded a nationally binding second ballot electoral agreement. Those agreements were cemented by a "common platform" in February 1968 and by the Joint Programme of Government which was signed in June 1972. But the path to unity during the Fifth Republic was far from smooth: from 1958 to September 1962, from June 1968 to the end of 1969, from October 1974 to January 1976 relations between the two *partis-frères* were strained and occasionally embittered. After September 1977, the two parties were once again locked in angry confrontation after the failure of negotiations designed to update the Joint Programme of Government. Their relations were not as violently antagonistic as during the period following the foundation of the Communist Party in December 1920, from 1928 to 1934 when the same party was wedded to a strategy of "class versus class", or from 1947 to 1953 at the height of the Cold War. Nevertheless, the intensely and intrinsically conflicting nature of the relationship constantly surfaced. The Left went into the 1978 elections without a Joint Programme and even without the customary second ballot agreement (this was cobbled together after the first ballot). The

215

unexpected defeat of the Left poisoned relations between the Socialists and the Communists still further, and at the twenty-third PCF congress in 1979 unity with the Socialists was buried amid a torrent of critical remarks. But the mutual vilification was to reach its height later, fed by the Communists Party's reactions to events such as the Soviet invasion of Afghanistan (which it justified) and the military crack-down in Warsaw (which it forgave). Yet the *esprit unitaire*, the yearning for Left-wing unity was not dead, and it was to resurface during the 1981 presidential elections.

François Mitterrand was elected President of the Republic in May 1981 with the votes of a very diverse coalition, but within that coalition two elements dominated – the Socialist and the Communist. He was not, as he had been in 1965 and 1974, the *candidat unique de la gauche* – the sole candidate of the big and organized parties of the Left: he was first and foremost the candidate of the Socialist Party, the party he had helped to found in 1971 and had powerfully contributed to shape throughout the 1970s. In the 1981 elections he was opposed by a Left-wing Radical Michel Crépeau, the leader of the party, and by a Communist, Georges Marchais, the secretary general of the party. Yet Crépeau's declared intention was to help Mitterrand: he felt a Left-wing Radical would more easily attract the vital centre vote at the first ballot, loosening it from its traditional fear of the Left, making it more ready to vote for the Left at the second. The moment the results of the first ballot were announced Crépeau declared for Mitterrand.

The case of the Communist Party was a little more complex. During the campaign it intensified the attacks it had been making against Mitterrand since September 1977 and refused to be bound by any agreement with him. There was widespread suspicion that Marchais and most of the remaining Communist leadership viewed the prospects of a Mitterrand victory with alarm and consternation. But the Communist base thought otherwise. For Communist voters Mitterrand remained the man who incarnated Left-wing unity, who understood their aspirations, who personified the struggle against twenty years of Right-wing government. His programme was immensely popular with them and his sensitive references to *le peuple communiste* endeared him to them. During the campaign pro-Mitterrand sentiment hardened among Communist voters (this may be seen in the increasing number who proposed to vote for him at the second ballot). At the first ballot Mitterrand already captured many Communist voters, and the feelings of the others were so manifest that a chastened Communist Party leadership was forced officially to support him at the second ballot. The result was a massive rallying of Communist support to the Mitterrand camp. However divided, therefore, the parties of the Left emerged from the presidential elections with at least the appearance of unity. And in spite of his difficult and strained relationship with the Communist Party, Mitterrand was perceived by its followers as the natural leader of the Left.

In the legislative elections of June 1981 which followed the presidential elections, the two parties again came to a second ballot agreement, and immediately after the Left-wing victory, four leading members of the Communist Party joined the Mauroy government: for the first time since 1947 there were Communist ministers, and a facade of Left-wing unity was maintained. Yet the seeds of future discord were already sown during the presidential and legislative elections of 1981, since they accentuated the growing electoral gap between the increasingly popular Socialists and the increasingly unpopular Communists (see below). After an initial honeymoon period which lasted about a year, relations between the two parties became increasingly tense: there were *duels de petites phrases*, as successive deflationary and industrial restructuring programmes in steel ('a tragic mistake', according to the Communists), textiles, shipbuilding and engineering rapidly pushed up unemployment, especially in the heartlands of urban communism. The PCF was also angered by the increase in social security charges and the easing of business costs (a 'present to the bosses'). But there were other divisive issues: the Communist Party criticised the French interventions in Chad and the Lebanon, Mitterrand's pro-American stand on the installation of Pershing missiles in western Europe, the concessions made in Brussels on agricultural policy, and the withdrawal of the controversial Savary Bill which had envisaged the closer integration of private (mainly Catholic) schools into the state system. The Socialists attacked the Communists for their attitude towards the war in Afghanistan and the "normalization" process in Poland. While Communist ministers remained ostensibly (and in the case of two of them genuinely) loyal to the government, and Deputies voted motions of confidence in the government (in June 1982, April 1983 and April 1984), Communist leaders, especially those linked with the CGT, were increasingly critical. This conflicting message irritated the Socialists – and disoriented some of the PCF's own followers. The appointment of Fabius to the premiership in July 1984 was the pretext for the Communists to leave the government. Thereafter, relations deteriorated sharply, with the Communists denouncing the Socialists as Right-wingers who had sold out to the big business lobby: in July 1984, the Communists abstained on the declaration of general policy of Fabius and in December 1984 voted against the budget. The twenty-fifth PCF congress officially buried Left-wing unity. In the European elections of 1984 and the 1986 legislative and regional elections, which were based on a single ballot proportional representation list system, the parties of the Left presented separate lists. However, in the elections for the town councils in 1983 and in those for the departmental councils in 1982, 1984 and 1986, second ballot agreements were struck. There was thus a growing gulf between national and local strategies: the national leaderships venomously denounced each other while the local parties' elites worked in quiet harmony.

The April–May 1988 presidential elections were, in some respects, a rerun of those of 1981: Mitterrand attracted many Communist voters at the first ballot and the remainder unanimously rallied at the second. In the June 1988 parliamentary elections, fought on the two ballot majoritarian system which had prevailed between 1958 and 1986, the two parties were squeezed into second ballot agreements. The Left-wing voted with remarkable discipline, thus demonstrating that the *esprit unitaire* – the spirit of unity – had not entirely evaporated. The Communists did not join the Rocard government in June 1988, but indicated that they would not join the Right in voting a motion of no confidence. By late 1988, therefore, the situation on the Left was rather curious. Unity at the base – among the local elites in regional, departmental and town councils – was intact, and the electorate demonstrated "republican discipline" by backing the best placed candidate of the Left in second ballot battles with the Right. Yet at national leadership level all contacts had ceased: the friendly co-existence of the early 1970s had given way to cold war. Before examining more closely the changing nature of the relationship between the parties of the Left it is important to look at each one of them.

The fragmented Left

For the sake of convenience, the Left may be divided into four main categories: the extreme and revolutionary Left; the centre Left; the Socialists; the Communists.

The extreme and revolutionary Left

The extreme Left in France is characteristically splintered into many warring factions, clans and *groupuscules*, and it is perpetually torn between its centrifugal aspirations and its centripetal practices: unity is proclaimed as vital yet eschewed as opportunist.

The major element is the PSU (*Parti Socialiste Unifié*), which, since its foundation in 1960, has been the object of constant

schisms. It was seriously weakened in October 1974 with the departure of many of its leaders (including Michel Rocard) and members
who joined the new Socialist Party of François Mitterrand. It
claims 7000 members, an optimistic claim that is taken seriously
by no one. Among the other movements of the extreme Left
are the Trotskyist groups – the *Organisation Communiste des
Travailleurs* (OCT), the *Parti Communiste Internationaliste* (PCI),
most of whose members joined the *Mouvement pour un parti
des travailleurs* [MPPT] formed at the end of 1985, the *Alliance
Marxiste Révolutionnaire*, the *Ligue Communiste Révolutionnaire*
(which had changed its name several times) led by Alain Krivine,
a well-bred and well-spoken intellectual who perturbs rival revo-
lutionaries by his ideas and his tie-wearing (he is nicknamed
Krivine-la-Cravate), and, finally, *Lutte Ouvrière* (headed by the
intelligent and articulate Arlette Laguiller, whose proletarian credentials are impeccable). There are several anarchist groups (the
*Fédération anarchiste, the Organisation Révolutionnaire anarchiste,
the Jeunesse anarchiste communiste*) and as many Maoist groups
(the *Gauche prolétarienne* and the *Front Uni* are the main ones).
These movements are electorally weak: in the 1981 presidential
elections Laguiller won 2.3 per cent of the votes (almost the same
as in 1974 and somewhat more than in 1988), while Bouchardeau,
the leader of the PSU, won only 1.1 per cent; in the 1984 European
elections, based on proportional representation, three extreme
Left-wing lists collected a combined 3.7 per cent of the votes; and
in the 1988 presidential elections candidates of the extreme Left
(including Pierre Juquin, a dissident Communist) attracted 4.5 per
cent of the votes. In the legislative elections of June 1988, most
extreme Left-wing parties did not even present candidates. Each
of these parties is internally divided (the initiated may discern at
least four rival currents in the *Ligue Communiste Révolutionnaire*,
while the shifting currents of the PSU defy analysis) and hold one
another in mutual lack of esteem. They are united in their support
of the social revolution and their hatred of the traditional parties,
but on most concrete issues they are bitterly divided.

The parties of the extreme Left are characterized by a surfeit
of ideas and a paucity of followers, and embarrassed by the lack
of a coherent or popular strategy. They frequently resemble an
army with very few troops and led by resentful and rebellious
lance-corporals. But they are not without influence. They have an
audience in certain academic circles, are active in certain factories,
particularly among the immigrant workers, and in the slum areas
of the big towns, and they support four newspapers (all of which
are carefully dissected by the police) which have unearthed some
of the seamier aspects of the regime. If they no longer enjoy the

mobilizing capacity of the heady days of May 1968, they have successfully organized campaigns over Vietnam, over the soldiers who
were accused of "subversive" activities (they were complaining
of their living conditions) in November to December 1975, over
abortion, over prison reform, over the plight of immigrant workers
and the eviction of tenants by property speculators – all subjects
which bored or embarrassed the "establishment" Left. They have
also been very active in the environmental protest movement and
especially in the growing opposition to nuclear power stations.
And they were prominent and enthusiastic participants in the
student protest of December 1986. If they dislike one another,
they dislike even more the "reformist" and "revisionist" (two of
the milder adjectives frequently employed) Left, which seems only
too ready to work within the existing system.

The Centre Left

Within this category may be placed the Left-wing Gaullists and the
Left-wing Radicals. The Left-wing Gaullists are themselves divided into several groups, the main three being the *Fédération des
Républicains de Progrès, the Initiative Républicaine et Socialiste*,
and *the Union des Gaullistes de Progrès*. Many of the leaders
of the Left-wing Gaullists previously belonged to the progressive
wing of the Gaullist Party; they were opposed to the conservatism
of Pompidou and even more so to the pro-Europeanism and
pro-Americanism of Giscard d'Estaing whom they disliked for
his anti-de Gaulle declarations in the 1960s. Electorally they are
weak and politically they have very little weight, but their support
is welcomed by the rest of the Left, since many elections have
been decided by such narrow margins. Brief mention should be
made, too, of the *Mouvement des Démocrates*, a tiny party headed
by Michel Jobert, ex-Foreign Minister of President Pompidou,
who rallied to the Mitterrand camp during the 1981 presidential
campaign and who was later rewarded with ministerial office.

Of greater importance are the Left-wing Radicals who compose
the *Mouvement des Radicaux de Gauche (MRG)*. The MRG was
created in 1972 as a break-away group from the Radical Party
headed by Jean-Jacques Servan-Schreiber. In July of that year
it signed the Joint Programme which had just been negotiated
between the Socialists and the Communists, and it also entered
into a first ballot electoral agreement with the Socialist Party
with which it continues to be closely associated. The party has
no autonomous group in the National Assembly and lacks a
charismatic leader (its leaders tend to be provincial mayors who

look and act like provincial mayors). It is a loosely structured party which is dominated by a few provincial members of parliament, and it is electorally weak (in the 1981 presidential elections Michel Crépeau, its leader, won only 2.2 per cent of the votes). Its electoral survival depends essentially on the goodwill of its Socialist allies (in the 1984 European elections when it separated from the Socialists and presented an independent list with some ecologists and dissident centrists it won 3.3 per cent of the votes, and in the 1986 parliamentary elections which were also fought on a proportional representation system its lists won a derisory 0.25 per cent of the national vote). The party is also badly divided over personality issues and over the strategy to adopt towards the Socialist "big brother". But with its small cohort of Senators and Deputies, 200 departmental councillors, over 3000 town councillors and 25,000 members it is a useful addition to the Left, especially since its moderate policies and image reassure those electors who are suspicious of the Socialists and afraid of the Communists.

The Left-wing Radicals are the rightful heirs to those Radicals who founded the one, indivisible and secular Third Republic and who provided the Fourth Republic with so many of its leaders. Economically conservative, financially orthodox and socially progressive, they traditionally backed the Left at election times (in the name of "republican discipline") and the Right between elections. The more cynical observer might unkindly point out that most of the party's present Deputies owe their parliamentary seats (which are concentrated in the south-west) to the good will of the other parties of the Left.

The Socialists

One of the most important political changes of the Fifth Republic had been the renewal and transformation of the French Socialist Party (*Parti Socialiste*, or PS). For the first ten years of the Fifth Republic, the then socialist party (the SFIO) seemed incapable of arresting its apparently inexorable decline. Its leadership was ageing and politically insensitive, its image was tarnished (it was too closely linked with the crises, the compromises and chaos of the Fourth Republic), its membership was in decline (from the 1946 peak of 335,000 to a generously estimated 70,000 in 1969), its press had virtually disappeared, and its electorate was sharply decreasing (in 1946 it received 23.4 per cent of the votes and by November 1962 only 12.6 per cent of the votes). In the 1967 and 1968 legislative elections, the decline of the party as a member of the Federation of the Left continued and in the June 1969 presidential elections its candidate, Gaston Defferre, won a humiliating 5 per cent of the votes. Furthermore, the party was deprived of office during the early years of the Fifth Republic, and during the Fourth Republic office had compensated for its decline and sclerosis.

After the disastrous legislative elections of June 1968 and the *débâcle* of the presidential elections of June 1969, the French Socialist Party, the party of Jaurès and Blum and the main party of government from 1936 to 1938, 1944 to 1951 and from 1956 to 1958, was reduced to a marginal and badly divided political force. But the trauma of 1968 and 1969 proved salutary, and after 1969 the fortunes of the party so dramatically changed that within ten years it had become the largest single party in France. After the presidential and legislative elections of 1981 it enjoyed a dominant position within the political system, with its members occupying the presidency, the premiership, a majority in the Council of Ministers and in the National Assembly, and key posts in the public and semi-public sector. The first four years of Socialist government were disastrous for the electoral fortunes of the party: in the 1983 local elections it lost many of the towns it had gained in 1977 and in the 1984 elections to the European Parliament it slumped to only 20.8 per cent of the votes. Thereafter, the party improved its position. Although it lost office as the result of the 1986 elections it established itself, with 32 per cent of the votes, as the biggest party in the country – a position it consolidated in May and June 1988 when its candidate, Mitterrand, won a resounding victory for the presidency, and when it won 34.8 per cent of the votes (and its allies a further 2.8 per cent) and almost an absolute majority in the National Assembly. As in 1981 the party had become the dominant party in the country.

The new Socialist Party dates essentially from the Epinay Congress of June 1971 ("year one of the renaissance of democratic socialism in France" according to Paul Quilès, one of the PS leaders), although much of the groundwork had been prepared at the Congress of Issy-lès-Moulineaux in July 1969 when Alain Savary took over the leadership of the Socialists. At successive party congresses (they are held every two years) the new party was forged and enlarged. When the party was founded at Epinay in 1971 there were six main factions within the party – and they are still in evidence today despite all the shifts that have taken place:

● *Members of the now defunct SFIO* led by Mauroy (Mayor of Lille). This faction has always played a pivotal role in the party although it has generally sided with the faction close to Mitterrand. In May 1988 Mauroy, prime minister from 1981 to 1984, became first secretary of the party.

● *Members of the CERES led by* Jean-Pierre Chevènement, a Left-wing ginger group which had previously belonged to the SFIO and which forms a powerful independent force within the present party. In April 1986 the CERES was renamed *Socialisme et République*. It has become less Marxist and more pragmatic and "Republican".

● *Members of a group of political clubs* – the *Convention des Institutions Républicaines* (CIR) – closely associated with François Mitterrand. This faction expanded during the 1970s to become the dominant force within a party which was increasingly geared to the election of Mitterrand to the presidency. However, in the construction of a "presidential party" it was always dependent on other factions to attain a majority.

● *Members of the Left-wing clubs* associated with Alain Savary or Jean Poperen. This group has always remained a relatively small minority.

● *Ex-PSU members* who entered in several waves and whose leader is Michel Rocard: they are known as *Rocardiens* and have always been perceived as a moderate faction devoted to the presidential ambitions of their leader.

● *The previously unattached* – a motley collection composed of those who are completely new to party politics (and many of whom were "politicized" during the events of May 1968), some disabused ex-Gaullists, some idealistic Left-wing Catholics and the inevitable cohort of unprincipled opportunists and ambitious political adventurers.

The Socialist Party since its inception has been a battleground for the various factions. At many party congresses (which occur every two years) delegates vote by tendency, on texts presented by each one of them. This enables each faction to take stock of its position. Moreover, such factionalism is encouraged by the process by which key posts are distributed according to the strength of each faction. These *courants* are sociologically and ideologically heterogeneous, and differ in their views over the role of the state, over class analyses, over party alliances, and over internal party organisation. They differ, too, over specific policies such as defence, Europe and macro-economic policy. They may also be distinguished by their historical and ideological reference points. Grouped around powerful party figures who harbour presidential ambitions – the so-called "elephants" of the party – they interact in subtle and even devious ways in order to further the interests of their own faction or, more generally, to veto the interests of rival factions. The result is a certain fluidity in internal party alliances.

Many of the factions' leaders joined the Left-wing government formed in 1981 and played out their differences within it. Although the experience of government between 1981 and 1986 taught them the limits to political power and pushed all the factions into reluctant revisions of their positions political and personal divisions persist and render the party difficult to lead. Furthermore, since François Mitterrand has been distancing himself from the party the dominant *courant* has become increasingly fragmented, thus rendering the balance of power even more unpredictable.

Since the early 1970s the Socialist Party has transformed its situation in several respects:

It has a leader of unquestioned ability and great popularity. Between June 1971, when he took over the leadership from Alain Savary, and May 1981 when he won the presidential elections, Mitterrand established himself as the undisputed master of his party and of the Left-wing opposition in general. Indeed, a great part of the Socialists' success is due to Mitterrand's brilliant leadership which was asserted during the presidential campaign of May 1974, when he came within an ace of winning, and which was reaffirmed by his standing in the polls. Helped by his "court" (composed of close friends), he dominated his party to such an extent that he earned for himself the nickname of "the Prince" and "the Pope". Mitterrand was an indefatigable organizer, a shrewd and tough negotiator and an ambitious politician. He managed to out-manoeuvre all his party opponents first to grasp and then to retain his leadership of the party.

After the 1981 campaign and his election to the presidency Mitterrand withdrew as first secretary of the PS, and since then has held no official position within the party. But he continues to dominate it, for he has placed his friends in all the key positions: for example, from 1981 to 1988 he was replaced as first secretary by Lionel Jospin, a highly talented organizer whose fidelity to Mitterrand never wavered. There were differences between the party and Mitterrand during his first *septennat:* for instance, in 1982 the party clearly disliked the decision to restore the career rights of any officers involved in dissident activities during the Algerian War; in 1983-84 it was uneasy about the deflationary economic policy of the president; in 1984 it was unhappy about the withdrawal of the Savary Bill designed to integrate the private schools more closely into the state system; and in 1986 it demonstrated its qualms about the continued nuclear explosions in the South Pacific. Yet at no stage did the party organize a revolt against the president – even when his poll ratings were disastrously low. Furthermore, when he declared himself a candidate for his own succession as president the entire party immediately rallied around him and became the principal instrument of his campaign.

The party has enlarged and completely renewed its elite. A new younger, more educated and more enterprising generation of Socialists now controls most of the directive organs of the party. Already under Savary's leadership (1969-71), 70 per cent of the secretaries of the local federations had been replaced and the average age of the holders of those key posts fell by twenty years. A study of the 687 delegates at the Nantes party congress in June 1977 showed that more than half (54 per cent) were under 40 years old, that only a quarter (26 per cent) had belonged to the Socialist Party before 1969, and that more than half (51 per cent) had university degrees or the equivalent. The renewal of the party elite can also be seen in the National Assembly, where half the Socialist Deputies elected in 1978 and 1981 were total newcomers to parliament, and also in the departmental and local councils.

The party has increased its membership. By 1969, the membership of the Socialist Party had fallen to a mere 70,000 and in certain parts of France (notably in Alsace, Lorraine and Brittany) organized party activity had virtually ceased. The early recruitment drive was considered disappointing by many party leaders, but with 170,000 members in 1978 it had more than doubled in eight years, and most of the new members were much more dynamic than those of the SFIO. It was clear that previously moribund local federations were totally rejuvenated. The post-1978 recruitment drive proved no less disappointing (the party claimed 188,000 members at the end of 1978) and there was evidence of growing discouragement among the activists after the traumatic election defeat of that year. However, figures and spirits were restored before and during the 1981 presidential campaign: the PS was said to have 200,000 members after the 1981 presidential elections. Thereafter, membership figures stabilized: in 1986 the party claimed 196,000 members.

The PS has increased its electoral appeal. In the March 1973 legislative elections, the Socialists for the first time during the Fifth Republic not only arrested their electoral decline but actually reversed it. It formed a first-ballot alliance – the *Union de la Gauche Socialiste et Démocrate (UGSD)*, with the Left-wing Radicals, which it dominated and which won 20.6 per cent of the votes, bettering the performance of the Federation of the Left (FGDS) – its previous electoral alliance – in 1967 (18.9 per cent of the votes) and in 1968 (16.5 per cent of the votes). In many respects, the 1973 electoral achievement of the party was its best since the Liberation, since not only did it increase its share of the poll but it also put down roots in Catholic areas such as Alsace, Lorraine, Brittany and Savoy where it had previously been weak or even non-existent. The increased integration of the Catholics into French political life, the waning of passions in the church–state dispute, the pronounced Left-wing sentiments of many younger members of the clergy, the political neutrality of most, and the sympathy of some, of the church hierarchy, the increasingly important role played by young Catholic trades unionists within the party, all combined to attract some Catholics to a party which had traditionally been one of the bulwarks of anti-clericalism. This phenomenon should not, however, be exaggerated: the big majority of practising Catholics continued (and continue) to vote for the Right: the evidence suggests that the party has made its gains in "Catholic France" among the increasing number of non-practising Catholics who live there. The party also improved its position in 1973 in the growing urban areas of France and among working-class voters. In the 1978 elections the party increased its share of the poll by 4 per cent, consolidating and improving the gains of 1973, and supplanted the Communists as the biggest party of the French Left – a position it had not enjoyed since 1936.

The excellent performance of its leader in the May 1974 presidential elections, its progress in successive by-elections, its success in local elections in 1973, 1976 and 1977 and in the general election of 1978 all demonstrated the electoral strength of the party. Its showing in the departmental elections was also indicative of its growing success (in 1970 the party won 14.8 per cent of the votes, in 1973 21.9 per cent and in 1976 26.5 per cent). By the end of the 1970s the Socialist Party had become, according to the opinion polls, the most popular party in France (far more popular, incidentally,than Mitterrand, its leader) and its electorate most closely corresponded to a cross-section of the French population: it was a party *à l'image du pays*.

The great electoral breakthrough took place in June 1981 in the wake of Mitterrand's presidential victory: the symbiotic relationship between leader and party was sealed in mutual triumph, for if the party's popularity had contributed to Mitterrand's victory, his popularity (running at a record level after his election) certainly helped the party. In a landslide victory, the PS took 37.8 per cent of the first ballot votes, becoming the biggest party of France, establishing itself as the biggest in every one of the twenty-two regions except Corsica and in seventy-nine of the ninety-six *départements*. In only four *départements* did its vote fall under 30 per cent. It made gains in all social and economic groups and in all age categories: it made spectacular progress among the working class (44 per cent), white-collar workers and middle management (45 per cent), upper management (38 per cent), and among the young (45 per cent of the under-35s). It bettered the previous performance of any Socialist Party in France and significantly improved on Mitterrand's first ballot showing. It also won a majority of seats in the National Assembly and, like the Gaullists from 1968 to 1973, was able to provide a majority without depending on allies. It was a truly remarkable achievement.

The Socialists fared disastrously in the European elections of 1984 when they won only 20.8 per cent of the votes, but far better in the legislative elections of 1986. Although they lost the election, they were able to "celebrate their defeat", since their share of the vote – 30.6 (31.8 per cent with allies) – meant that they remained the biggest party in France and in the National Assembly. After the victory of their candidate François Mitterrand, in the April–May 1988 presidential elections, they again performed impressively in the legislative elections which followed in June. Although deprived of an overall majority in the National Assembly, the Socialists enjoyed their second best electoral performance of the Fifth Republic: they won 34.8 per cent of the votes at the second ballot and their close allies a further 2.8 per cent. They reinforced their position in their traditional bastions – in the south west for example, and consolidated their vote in their more recent strongholds of the north Paris basin and parts of the west. On the other hand, they lost ground in some areas such as the Côte d'Azur and parts of the Languedoc which had previously been among their bastions. On the whole, the 1988 elections represented a further stage in the "nationalization" of the electorate of the PS.

The Socialist Party has undergone an "ideological renaissance". After 1969 the party indulged in an orgy of doctrinal debate: study groups on every conceivable subject pullulated like weeds in a wet, warm spring. Under the impact of its more radical, more Left-wing and more intellectually aggressive elements, and unbridled by the tiresome responsibilities of office, the party programme became more radical, more aggressive, more Left-wing and more irresponsible. At the National Convention of the party at Suresnes in March 1972 it adopted a new programme – *Changer la vie* – a title which revealed both its ambition and its naïveté. Marxism, or rather Marxist terminology, was rediscovered and often gave intra-party debates an esoteric and antediluvian flavour. Elements of Marxism were amalgamated with the newer concepts of *autogestion* (workers' control), decentralization and citizen participation. Moreover, the party had to make concessions to the Communist Party when it signed the Joint Programme of Government in June 1972, a programme to which it remained committed even after the breakdown of negotiations to update it in September 1977. The result was that the party appeared committed to a vague and not always intellectually consistent set of doctrines.

At the Metz Congress of 1979 an equally radical, "break-with-capitalism" type programme was adopted by the party activists. However, it was very instructive that the wily Mitterrand, who accepted the programme as first secretary of the PS, rejected it as candidate for the presidency of the Republic. He went into the election with a much less radical set of proposals and came out of it unsaddled by the revolutionary commitments of the official Socialist programme. It is also clear that the sobering reality of power after 1981 tempered the wilder ideological excesses of the party. Initially, disenchantment was widespread and profound among the party faithful who, unlike most members of the ex-SFIO or of the old British Labour Party and the present German Social Democratic Party, had not learnt to distinguish between policies and rhetoric. However, from the mid 1980s the party appears to have undergone a genuine conversion. Freed from pressure from a declining Communist Party and from a weakened CGT, the Communist-dominated trades union confederation, influenced by the technocrats who have always been numerous in the party, and increasingly sensitive to the exigencies of the market and to the limits to the capacity of the state (both domestically and internationally) the party has embraced the politics of modernisation, moderation and gradualism. Marxism has been eschewed in favour of a pragmatic advocacy of the welfare state, the mixed economy and political pluralism. This shift in the values, beliefs and objectives of the party affects all the major *courants* of the party, but with varying degrees of intensity. The congress at Toulouse in October 1985 clearly indicated that the party had become reformist, governmental and even social democratic, even if the congress at Lille two years later (when the party was in opposition) revealed the reluctance and the reticence about its transformation. There is no doubt, however, that the ideological axis of the party has moved to the right and that the party is more .ideologically united than it was during the 1970s. This does not, of course, prevent differences from surfacing with monontonous regularity: for instance, immediately after the June 1988 elections the party was divided over the entry of the Centrists into the Left-wing government of Michel Rocard and over the rate of the newly proposed wealth tax. But these differences are over strategy and specific policies and not over fundamental values or ultimate ends.

The party, from a position of relative strength, has renewed its alliances with other parties of the Left. During the 1960s the Socialists were bitterly divided over their choice of allies. One group, comprising mainly SFIO *notables* (and including the mayors of several important towns), advocated the kind of "Third Force" type alliance which had operated during periods of the Fourth Republic: this involved a wide-ranging alliance with most of the parties of the centre to the total exclusion of both the Gaullists and the Communists. A second faction of the party, led by Gaston Defferre, favoured a federation of centre parties which could count on the support, however reluctant, of the Communists at the second ballot of elections. Defferre attempted to create such a federation in 1964-5 to further his candidacy for the 1965 presidential elections by trying to forge a *Grande Fédération* composed of the Socialists, the Catholic MRP and a number of Left-wing clubs. But the venture failed and Defferre withdrew from the presidential race. A third element of the party emerged after the electoral catastrophes of 1968 and 1969; the new party leader, Alain Savary, backed by a majority of the party, preached the need for a firm and speedy alliance with the Communists. The fourth faction within the party was led by Mitterrand who argued that its first priority should be to strengthen the non-Communist Left, which from a position of strength would negotiate a formal electoral agreement with the Communists on the basis of a compromise programme. Essential to Mitterrand's thinking was the need to *rééquilibrer la gauche* – to redress the balance of Left-wing forces in favour of the non-communist Left. Mitterrand's strategy had prevailed between 1965 and 1968 when he formed the *Fédération de la Gauche Démocrate et Socialiste* (the FGDS, not to be confused with the UGSD formed in 1973) comprising the SFIO, the Radicals and various Left-wing clubs and which had negotiated a second-ballot agreement with the Communists. The federation collapsed in late 1968 under the strains imposed by the "events" of May of that year and contacts between Socialists and Communists were broken off. Mitterrand's strategy prevailed again after 1971, especially after he had strengthened his own party, its machine and organization and his position within it. The problem of negotiating an agreement with the other non-Communist Left-wing parties was facilitated after 1972 when the Radical Party split, the pro-Socialists leaving to form the Movement of Left-wing Radicals (MRG). The Socialists forged a close (if not frictionless) alliance with the MRG and in the 1978, 1981 and 1988 legislative elections they fought a common campaign as from the first ballot. With the Communists things were not so easy (see below), although they started very well. By the summer of 1972 the two major parties of the Left had signed (27 June 1972) a Joint Programme of Government (a programme which bound the two parties for the period of a legislature) and they had concluded a second-ballot electoral agreement. The high point of the alliance came in the legislative elections of March 1973 and more particularly in May 1974 when Mitterrand carried the banner of the united Left into the presidential elections. However, from the autumn 1974 by-elections in which the Socialists fared well and the Communists badly, relations between the two parties soured, and after the 1977 local elections (which they fought together) they were to become positively poisonous. The 1978 legislative and 1981 presidential campaigns furnished occasions for the intensification of the acrimony which by now generally characterized their relations. Yet Mitterrand's stunning and· unexpected victory in May 1981 (achieved with the help of Communist voters) forced a previously reluctant Communist Party into alliance. In June 1981 Mitterrand rewarded them, by giving them four ministerial posts. As noted above, relations with the Communists were increasingly uneasy and tense until July 1984 when the PCF decided not to join the newly formed government of Laurent Fabius. Thereafter, they became openly acrimonious, as the Communists castigated the Socialists as "class traitors" and Right-·wingers. In the European elections of 1984 and the legislative elections of 1986 the *partis-frères* presented separate lists: the proportional representation system which operated for both elections did nothing to encourage co-operation. However, in all the local elections and in the presidential and legislative elections of 1988 "republican discipline" was re-established, and second ballot agreements negotiated. The alliance with the PCF functions, therefore, at local level in the councils of the regions, *départements* and towns, and at national level for electoral purposes. Its fragile and tension-ridden nature is analysed later in this chapter.

The Socialist Party is undoubtedly in a very strong position: it dominates the executive and legislative branches of government; it enjoys a high level of electoral support; it has an enthusiastic and active membership; it has brought forward a highly talented elite; it is powerfully entrenched at the local level; it enjoys a hegemonic position with the Left. The party has moved into new and better-equipped headquarters at the Place Palais-Bourbon (which is next door to parliament) and enjoys greater financial security than the old SFIO.

But the party also faces problems. The first main problem facing the PS is that of its weak links with civil society: it has no roots in the trade union movement (though many trade unionists are activists and voters) or institutional bases in the youth movement (the *Fédération Léo-Lagrange* is connected only tenuously with the party). Its relations with movements such as feminists and ecologists are distant and suspicious. Consequently, the party has no strong infrastructural underpinning and lacks sub-cultural supports. Second, there is still the problem of party unity. Despite the ideological *rapprochement* of the 1980s the party remains plagued by the skirmishes of feuding clans which were fully apparent, for example, in the battle for the sucession of Jospin as first secretary in 1988 and which ended in a vistory for Pierre Mauroy, Prime Minister from 1981 to 1984, over his younger rival, Laurent Fabius, Prime Minister from 1984 to 1986. Although the PS is forging a party loyalty it remains a brittle alliance. It is, in Mitterrand's own phrase, 'a crossroads of contradictions' and is divided over a large range of subjects which include the European Common Market, state aid to church schools, the Middle East conflict, the French nuclear deterrent, the nature of the alliance with the Communists, the extent of the state sector and the role of the market in socialist France. The battle for supremacy within the party is permanent and often bitter, and the presidential ambitions of some of the party leaders merely add urgency to the battle. The party now is held together by a brilliant (if distant) leader, by its electoral success and by the patronage that goes with office. The test of its viability will come when it loses all three.

The third major problem confronting the party – and it is linked with the first – is that of harmonizing and co-ordinating the activities of the various layers of the party: the governmental, the parliamentary, the activists and the electors. The years of Mitterrand's first term of office as president were marked by several conflicts between and within these elements: over the pace of implementing the social reforms; over the austerity programmes; over the wealth tax; over the expulsion of immigrants who had entered the country illegally; over the new labour code (the so-called Auroux Act); over nuclear energy policy; over the financing of the social security system. Furthermore, restoring harmony is not helped by the internal decision-making mechanism which, based on proportional representation, encourages fragmentation and factionalism.

The fourth major problem of the party is maintaining its electoral momentum. Given the increasing volatility of the electorate, support can evaporate quickly – as it did between 1981 and 1984. Finally, there is the continuing problem of the party's alliances. The relationship with the Communists is far from satisfactory but is defended by some who view with great suspicion the policy of *ouverture* – the opening to the centre – which is being pursued by the Rocard government. Alliances, however, are shaped not by just one partner – real or potential – and the party has only limited control over this crucial question.

The French Communist Party (PCF)

Several facts strike the political observer about the French Communist Party under the Fifth Republic:

- The party appears reluctant to integrate itself fully into French political life.
- It has liberalized some of its doctrines but none of its basic methods of internal decision-making.
- It seems reluctant to cut its umbilical cord with the Soviet Union, even though it has taken its distance on certain issues.
- It has difficulty in renewing or strengthening its organizational base.
- It is beset with problems of an apparently intractable nature.
- It appears to be caught in a process of accelerating decline.

The integration of the PCF into French political life

The political isolation of the PCF in the very early years of the Fifth Republic was complete: its position recalled those earlier periods when the party was in a ghetto – the years following the Congress of Tours of December 1920 when the party was founded, the period of the "phoney war" from September 1939 to May 1940 after the signing of the Molotov–Ribbentrop pact, and the height of the Cold War from 1947 to 1953. The isolation of the party at the beginning of the Fifth Republic was due to a number of factors: the bitter and recent memories of the Cold War; the party's slavishly pro-Moscow line which led it to support the Russian intervention in Hungary in 1956; its equally unpopular opposition to the Anglo-French fiasco in Egypt (opposed by the British Labour Party but inspired by the French socialist premier, Guy Mollet); its ambiguous position over the Algerian War (which was intensified after 1956 by Premier Mollet); its opposition to the popular return of de Gaulle in May 1958 and to the new constitution which was approved by four-fifths of the French electorate in the September 1958 referendum. During the Fifth Republic the process of integration has been enthusiastically pursued at times (1962-74), and reluctantly at others. And there have been times (between 1978 and 1981 and post-1984) when the party seemed intent on returning to the ghetto of the early Fifth Republic. The appointment of Communist ministers – the ultimate act of political integration – was welcomed by the party leadership, but only as a means of saving something from the electoral *débâcle* of April and June 1981. After 1977, the party appeared to be undergoing a process (not unknown in its history) of withdrawal and introspection: it was searching for its own soul rather than for its place in French society. The electoral jolt of 1981 reminded it that there was no salvation outside that society. However, after leaving government in 1984 it once again turned in on itself: the strategy of the "fortress party", safe behind self-constructed barriers, is once again being pursued. Nevertheless, at local level PCF elites co-operate with other Left-wingers in managing, in harmonious fashion, the affairs of the councils they control.

In its sporadic attempts to assimilate itself into French political life the PCF has been helped by the changing international situation (the thaw in the Cold War and the policy of *détente* as well as the Gaullist policy of *rapprochement* with the USSR all combined to make the party's pro-Moscow stances less "treasonable" and less objectionable), by the changing tactics of the Socialists (who after apparently irreconcilable opposition sought some form of alliance) and by the party's own periodic efforts in liberalizing its policies and image. But there have always been limits to the PCF's integration into the French body politic: it is clear that there is still widespread opposition to the idea of Communists acquiring the key ministries of the Interior, of Foreign Affairs and of Defence. And opposition to the appointment of a Communist prime minister or the election of a Communist president of the Republic is very marked – even among Socialist voters. There is always an important segment of the Socialist Party voters which refuses to vote Communist at the second ballot (even when there is no other Left-wing candidate standing). Anti-communism was a powerful propaganda tool which was ruthlessly manipulated by successive Right-wing governments in the elections of the 1960s and 1970s.

The liberalization of the party's doctrines

The liberalization of the PCF which took place during the 1960s and 1970s was often described, somewhat misleadingly, as its Italianization. The Italianization of the party involved the acceptance of a democratic, parliamentary and governmental vocation and the modification of many of its cherished dogmas: it has rejected the notion of the *parti unique* – the single revolutionary vanguard party during the transitional phase to socialism – in favour of multi-partism; it has accepted the ballot box as a sole source of democratic legitimacy; it has adopted the principle of alternate government (a Left-wing government beaten at the polls must withdraw from office); it now resolutely defends the freedom of association of the press, of opposition groups and parties, free-doms which were previously dismissed as "bourgeois", formal and meaningless; at the XXII Party Congress of February 1976 it official-ly sacrificed the doctrine of the dictatorship of the proletariat as "out-moded" for France. Other parts of the traditional covenant to be dis-carded include dialectical materialism: a good Communist can now move from party cell to church confessional with easy conscience.

The leader of the PCF, Georges Marchais, has constantly reaffirmed his party's attachment to democratic ends and means. Finally, greater discussion within the party has been encouraged (token dissidents are even allowed to speak at party congresses) and the party has been less neurotically secretive in its relations with the outer world (it has even allowed television cameras into its bullet-proof headquarters at the Place Colonel Fabien).

The liberalization of the party was encouraged by the accession of Waldeck Rochet – "the Pope John of the PCF" – to the party leader-ship in 1964 after the death of Maurice Thorez, whose thirty-four years of autocratic and illiberal rule more readily recalled that of Pius XII. Liberalization was also encouraged by the gradual promo-tion to key party posts of a new generation of Communists – *les nouveaux communistes* – who were less marked than their elders by the passionate and angry battles and memories of the past, and who were anxious to play an active role in the government of the country.

Liberalization of doctrines has not, however, always been matched by liberalization of methods. Decision-making is still based on the Stalinist practice of democratic centralism, with the base sometimes merely informed of changes of policy: the party's apparently dramatic switches, in 1977, over the French nuclear deterrent (which overnight became acceptable), over direct elec-tions to the European Parliament (previously denounced by Mar-chais as a "crime against France" but adopted with some reserva-tions by the party barely a year later), and its dramatically changing relations with the PS are but three of the more striking examples. The brutality and ruthlessness of the party's campaigns against its Socialist ally between September 1977 and May 1981 and again after July 1984 awakened disquieting memories of its Stalinist past, and provoked unprecedented unrest in the ranks of the faithful who were disoriented by the party's constant shifts of policy and alliance strategy. The party's response to the critics is characteristic: it marginalizes them, isolates them, evicts then from posts of respon-sibility, or pressurizes then into resigning from such posts (the cases of Marcel Rigout and Claude Poperen who quit the Central Committee in 1987) and, in some cases, expels them.

Some *rénovateurs* or *reconstructeurs* as they describe them-selves (they are referred to as *liquidateurs* by the party bosses) have tried to remain within the party in order to "renovate" it from within. In May 1988 they publicized the programme of the recently created *Initiative pour la reconstruction communiste (IRC)* which attracted 1,800 signatures, including those of more than a hundred Communist mayors. There is some discreet backing for the *rénovateurs* among key figures in the Communist-dominated CGT (it is rumoured that they include Krasucki, the leader) and among the powerful group of Communist mayors. However, the history of the PCF suggest that internal dissidence has little chance of success. Other dissidents, disgusted by the party's strategies and tactics have simply withdrawn, most quietly, some less so. Pierre Juquin, a party hatchet-man of long standing (he was the party's official spokesman from 1976 to 1985) who became increasingly disenchanted with the party's policies, resigned in June 1987 and stood in the 1988 presidential elections as a dissident communist. His amiable and articulate campaign attracted the support of *The Ligue Communiste* of Alain Krivine and the backing of feminists, peaceniks and ecologists (he was "the red who turned green" it was alleged), but won only 2 per cent of the votes.

The limited de-Sovietization of the PCF

The so-called de-Sovietization of the PCF has been a slow and painful process for the most pro-Stalinist Communist Party in Western Europe. Its reaction to Khrushchev's denunciation of Stalin in 1956 was one of stunned disbelief, and it was not until 1966 that it was prepared to take an open stand against the USSR when *L'Humanité*, the party's newspaper, published an attack on the Daniel and Siniavski trial. Since then there have been many occasions when the PCF has ostentatiously taken its distance from the Soviet Union: in August 1968, Waldeck Rochet, then the leader of the party, condemned the Soviet Union's invasion of Czechoslovakia; in December 1970, the PCF critized the Soviet repression following the workers' insurrection in the Baltic ports; in early 1971 it publicly appealed for justice for Soviet Jews; in October 1975 it intervened successfully in favour of Leonid Plyusch, the dissident Soviet mathematician; in the following month it made a pointed attack on labour camps in the USSR; in October 1976, Pierre Juquin, one of the party's liberals, attended a public meeting which had been organized to demand the release of political prisoners in Latin America, in Czechoslovakia and in the USSR – Pinochet's Chile and Brezhnev's Soviet Union ('the motherland of socialism') were thus bracketed together. The party constantly reminds the Soviets – and the French electorate

– that its policy is determined in Paris and not in Moscow, and that it is resolved to take "the French road to socialism". Even since 1977, when the party has been striking a more sympathetic stance towards the Soviet Union, it has *generally* remained critical of violations of human rights in the Soviet bloc, and on several occasions has insisted that the Soviet experience is not a model to be emulated. This de-Sovietization of the PCF was greatly facilitated by the evolution of the international situation: the thawing of the Cold War following the death of Stalin; the process of de-Stalinization of the USSR; the break-up of communist international solidarity especially following the Sino-Soviet split; the development of the doctrine of polycentrism inspired by the Italian communist leadership.

But the process of the de-Sovietization of the PCF is far from complete. The party's instinctive reactions are pro-Soviet: when another political party attacks the Soviet Union it is denounced by the PCF as a bourgeois protagonist of the Cold War. The PCF is also a very firm supporter of Soviet foreign policy: its foreign policy differences with the Soviets are minimal and minor. It could justify the Soviet invasion of Afghanistan, and to underline its support sent its secretary general to Moscow during the 1980 Olympic Games where he made a grotesque and ostentatious display of himself. It also made clear its opposition to the deployment of American Pershing missiles in Western Europe even though President Mitterrand had expressed his approval. It could also, in spite of growing disquiet in party ranks, justify the military *coup* in Warsaw against the Solidarity Union movement and the "normalization" process which followed the *coup*. Finally, the party has asserted that the balance sheet of the Soviet bloc is *globalement positif* ("on the whole good") – an astonishing verdict which upsets its Socialist allies and some of its own members but one which continues to be a defining characteristic of the PCF.

The difficult reconstruction of the party base

The PCF has never enjoyed the mass membership of the British Labour Party, the German Social Democratic Party or the Italian Communist Party, and even at its peak, at the time of the Liberation, membership never reached a million. During the Fourth Republic the party lost two-thirds of its membership, which by 1958 had dwindled to about a quarter of a million. Membership oscillated between 225,000 and 275,000 throughout the 1960s, but during the 1970s the party leadership made a successful effort to increase it: figures released by the party at the beginning of 1979 indicated that the party had passed the 700,000 mark, which meant more realistically, however, a figure of about 500,000. The 1980s have seen a steady reduction in membership – a reflection of the general decline of the party. In January 1987 the party claimed 604,000 members, but more realistic figures suggest about 350,000 at most.

The enlarging of the party base does not automatically mean its strengthening. Indeed, there was abundant evidence that in the years leading up to the 1981 presidential campaign the activists of the party although more numerous were less assiduous, less enthusiastic and less docile to party directives than the party leadership desired. There is, moreover, a conflict between carrying out the party's self-declared role of vanguard – a role which assumes the presence of a disciplined, cohesive, well-trained and politically-conscious minority–and pursuing a policy of building up a mass membership, many of whom pass through the party like water through a sieve.

The problems of the PCF

The PCF faces a number of problems apart from its electoral decline (see below) and the widespread suspicion about its motives and intentions: it is sensitive to the danger of being outflanked on the Left, as in May 1968; its *rapports* with the CGT, described neatly by George Ross as ones of "strategic complementarity", are much less smooth than are generally supposed, since the CGT is frequently more syndicalist than Communist; it has always been plagued by the soul-searching of its own increasingly restless intellectuals (although this problem is resolving itself with the disappearance of the intellectuals in the party); its membership is declining in numbers and it is neither as subservient nor as militant as the leaders would wish; many of its policies (over Poland, over immigrant workers, over Afghanistan) are unpopular with the faithful; it is increasingly unable to mobilize and to discipline its traditional voters (the European elections of 1979 and the presidential elections of 1981 and 1988 bear eloquent testimony to this fact); the party press, like the rest of the French press, is in a parlous state (in 1946 there were seventeen Communist newspapers, thirty years later there were only four with dismally low circulation figures and a readership composed exclusively of the party faithful); many of its satellite organisations have disappeared, while others such as the *Union des Femmes Françaises* and the *Mouvement de la Jeunesse Communiste* are decreasingly effective; its leadership is increasingly divided (even the four Communist ministers disagreed in July 1984 on the issue of whether the party should withdraw from government).

There are even more fundamental problems confronting the PCF:

- The party has the difficult task of balancing the demands of its highly disparate electorate, and all too frequently it resembles less the vanguard of the proletariat than the broker of the conflicting demands of its discontented (and sometimes reactionary) constituent elements.
- The party has yet successfully to tackle the vexed problem of internal party democracy: in spite of increasing intra-party debate, the Leninist principle – or rather the Stalinist practice – of democratic centralism still holds good. Decisions are frequently *diktats*, imposed from above on a bewildered membership.
- In spite of reiterated declarations that the party is taking "the French path to socialism" and in spite of increasing criticism of the USSR, the PCF refuses to sever its umbilical link with the "motherland of socialism". The party now argues that socialism and democracy are inseparable, but while admonishing the Soviet Union and the East European regimes for lack of democracy it refuses to castigate them as being unsocialist. The illogicality was pointed out by Pierre Daix (who was expelled from the party for his audacity – one should never be right too early in the PCF) and constantly highlighted by Jean Elleinstein, the ex-Communist Party historian and *enfant terrible* of the party.
- The next fundamental problem of the party is related to the previous two: the three ends of the party's apparent strategy (de-Sovietization, liberalization, national integration) are not only inconsistently and merely partially pursued (the point just made), sporadic in implementation and often begrudged in motivation, but they have also been somewhat incoherently applied. There has been no gradual unfolding of a coherent strategy but, to all appearances, a series of disjointed tactical responses to the immediate and the urgent–responses of an uneasy and contradictory nature. The party leaders never fully appreciated that all three strategic ends were inextricably linked, that each impinged upon the other and that each was pregnant with consequences for many aspects of party life. Old problems were simply replaced by new dilemmas. Moreover, on all three prongs of the strategy the party projects the opposite impression – that of being pro-Soviet, illiberal and a party of the ghetto.

● Relations with the Socialists provide the PCF with another fundamental problem. The Communists rightly suspect the Socialists of hegemonic designs but they rely on their support to re-elect their declining numbers of mayors and Deputies. The party cannot make up its mind whether it is a "governmental party" or merely a party ready on occasions to participate in government. The distinction may seem theological, but it is vital because it helps to define the nature of the party and its long-term vocation. More urgently, the party must decide on its tactics if in government and faced with policies of which it disapproves. Before 1981 it had always proclaimed its intention never to "manage the crisis of capitalism", but four of its members became ministers in the Mauroy government which did precisely that. While in government those ministers were models of discretion and on occasions supported policies which were denounced by the party in parliament and more especially by the CGT.

● The party is faced with the seemingly irresolvable dilemma which arises out of its pursuit of revolutionary ends by reformist means. Ronald Tiersky, in his excellent study of the PCF, defined the four basic roles of the party as those of:
A *revolutionary vanguard party* – the self-styled exclusive repository and propagator of Marxist truth.
A *counter-community*, or what Annie Kriegel calls a "microcosmic anti-society', and which generates its own organizations, rites, norms and language.
A *tribune or organ of the protest* and frustrations of the underprivileged.
A *governmental party* with a managerial vocation.

According to Tiersky, the four basic roles develop simultaneously, "partially in harmony and partially in contradiction", one or another being emphasized, depending on the prevailing circumstances. Now it is clear that in fulfilling these four roles, the party helps to stabilize the French political system: as a revolutionary vanguard party and the bearer of a chiliastic message it gives hope to the discontented of the advent of the new millennium; as a counter-community it provides a focus for the loyalty and potentially disruptive energy of its followers; as a tribune party it articulates grievances and diverts them into institutional channels, thus preventing them from finding expression in anti-system violence; as a managerial party its members have permeated innumerable commissions, committees and councils of both an appointed and elected nature, and often as a result they are more managerial than militant, becoming the "objective collaborators" (one of their own favourite phrases) of the system. The cumulative effect is that the PCF, which has the avowed intention, however ultimate, of destroying the existing system, has become one of its principal props: far from undermining the system, it underpins it and even, to some extent, legitimizes it. Thus, to use Annie Kriegel's expression, the party has become "one of the agents of the pluralistic cohesiveness of established society". The extreme Left, totally disabused by the timorousness of the PCF during the events of May 1968 and disillusioned by its subsequent moderation, vilifies it for its lack of revolutionary zeal. The Right, however, denounces it for its revolutionary ambition, arguing that it is merely more skilfully disguised than in the past.

The final major problem confronting the PCF is its dramatic electoral decline – a decline so precipitous that the party's very survival appears to be at stake. This decline is the subject of the following section.

The electoral decline of the PCF

During the Fifth Republic the size of the Communist electorate first declined, then stagnated, then fell sharply. Table 7 indicates the nature and extent of the decline.

Table 7   The electoral performance of the PCF 1936–88 (percentage of voters at first ballot)

	Year	Voters %		Year	Voters %
Legislative elections	1936	15.4	Presidential elections	1969	21.5
Constit. elections	1945	26.1	Legislative elections	1973	21.3
Constit. elections	1946	25.7	Legislative elections	1978	20.6
Legislative elections	1946	28.6	European elections	1979	20.6
Legislative elections	1951	26.4	Presidential elections	1981	15.5
Legislative elections	1956	25.6	Legislative elections	1981	16.1
Legislative elections	1958	18.9	European elections	1984	11.2
Legislative elections	1962	21.8	Legislative elections	1986	9.8
Legislative elections	1967	22.5	Presidential elections	1988	6.8
Legislative elections	1968	20.3	Legislative elections	1988	11.3

Table 7 clearly shows the two "black" periods for the PCF: 1958 and post-1980.

In the November 1958 elections, the first of the Fifth Republic, the party won only 3,870,000 votes (compared with 5,503,000 less than two years previously), and its representation in the National Assembly was decimated, falling from 146 in 1956 to only ten in 1958. In the following election the party regained some but not all of the ground lost, and in the 1960s and 1970s its share of the vote hovered around the 20 per cent mark. By 1978, the PCF, once the biggest party in France, was no longer even the bigger party of the Left. Moreover, its best performance of the Fifth Republic was worse than its worst during the Fourth Republic. But there was worse to come.

The elections of 1981 were disastrous for the party – the worst since 1936 (when the party actually gained votes): in the May presidential elections Georges Marchais, the Communist leader, gained only 15.5 per cent of the votes – and was clearly outdistanced by his Socialist rival. The June 1981 legislative elections were quite as bad as the presidential elections: indeed, although its share of the vote increased slightly the party lost a further 400,000 in a smaller turn-out: thus its share of the electorate dropped from 12.4 to 11.3 per cent. Both elections took place in normal political circumstances: there was no constitutional upheaval as in 1958 or no "events" as in 1968 to excuse the poor performance. And there was an economic recession unparalleled in recent French history – which should have favoured the electoral chances of the party. Compared with 1978 the party lost ground in all types of constituencies, even in its traditional bastions. It did so largely, but not exclusively, to the Socialist Party. It remained an electoral force in the north of the Paris basin and in the Paris suburbs, as well as in the northern Mediterranean regions of the south. But it virtually disappeared in some regions: in five of the twenty-two regions it received less than 10 per cent of the votes in the legislative elections (these included Brittany with 9.7 per cent, Lower Normandy with 6.6 per cent and Alsace with only 3.12 per cent). It received less than 10 per cent of the vote in 169 (of the 491) constituencies, compared with sixty-four in 1978 and fifty-six in 1973. It even lost its privileged position among working-class voters: in 1978 37 per cent voted Communist and 26 per cent Socialist, whereas in the 1981 legislative elections only 24 per cent voted Communist and 44 per cent voted Socialist.

The European elections of 1984, at which the party presented its own list, saw its vote drop further to 11.2 per cent. The 1986 legislative elections were based on a system of proportional representation and the party again presented its own lists. The results showed a further decline to 9.8 per cent: in metropolitan France it received fewer votes than the *Front National*.

The party's weakness is amply demonstrated in Table 8.

Table 8   Electoral performance of the PCF in the 96 départements of Metropolitan France 1978–1986

Voters	Legislative 1978	European 1979	Legislat. 1981	European 1984	Legislat. 1986
Less than 10%	9	6	30	45	58
From 10 to 15%	15	19	24	31	27
From 15 to 20%	27	29	17	15	8
From 20 to 25%	22	22	13	5	3
More than 25%	23	20	12	0	0
Total *départements* in Metropolitan France	96	96	96	96	96

In 1986, in only three *départements* did the party receive more than twenty per cent of the votes (in its three rural strongholds of the Allier, the Cher and the Haute-Vienne) whereas in 1978 it had done so in 45 *départements*. The 1986 electoral collapse was followed two years later by the unmitigated disaster of the 1988 presidential elections, when André Lajoinie, the party's candidate. received only 6.8 per cent of the votes - the worst performance in the history of the party. Lajoinie received fewer than half the votes won by Marchais in 1981, and compared with the party's poor vote in 1986 he lost ground in 92 of the 96 *départements* of metropolitan France. In only one *département* – the Allier, which is his home ground – did he win more than 15 per cent of the votes; in 14 he won between 10 and 15 per cent, in 51 between 5 and 10 per cent and in 28 he won fewer than 5 per cent. In Paris, once a relative stronghold of communism, he received only 4 per cent of the votes. He was beaten by Le Pen, the leader of the extreme Right, in most *départements* and even by Waechter, the humble ecologist, in sixteen *départements*. Only in parts of the industrial north, of the Paris region, and of the centre west and Mediterranean area were there any signs of survival. Of the 151 biggest towns with Communist mayors, Lajoinie was beaten by Mitterrand in 145 and by Le Pen in 79 of them. Among the youngest voters (18 to 24 years old) he won only 6 per cent (in 1978 the party had won 28 per cent) and he collected only 15 per cent of the working-class vote (in 1981 Marchais had won 30 per cent) compared with 40 per cent for Mitterrand and 21 per cent for Le Pen. Even *L'Humanité*, the party newspaper, could find nothing to salvage from the wreck.

The party improved its performance in the June 1988 legislative elections – the party gained 700,000 votes more than Lajoinie and 11.3 per cent of the votes compared with the 6.8 per cent of Lajoinie. But this improvement took place in a context in which there was no dissident Communist competition, in which there were very few extreme left-wing candidates, in which there was no Mitterrand to divide the loyalties of Communist voters and in which the Socialist Party was openly flirting with the Centrists (thus irritating some of its Left-wing supporters). Furthermore, its parliamentary representation was reduced from 35 to 27 (below the number required to form a parliamentary group) and many of its major figures were defeated. It is also highly instructive that the party survived best where it presented local *notables*: of the twenty-four Deputies elected in Metropolitan France twelve had never before been in parliament, and of those twelve ten were mayors and one a departmental councillor. This reliance on powerful mayors runs counter to the traditions of a party which has always been suspicious of local party bosses (since the late 1970s they have harboured a disproportionate number of critics of the party's attitude towards the Socialists).

Compared with its disastrous performance in 1986 it gained only 12,000 votes. Furthermore, while the party won more than ten per cent of the electorate in 48 *départements* in 1981, and in 21 in 1986, it did so in only 15 in 1988. Compared with 1986 it improved its situation or remained stable in 40 *départements* (normally in its crumbling urban bastions) but lost ground in 56 (especially in those rural areas which had previously been the firmest basis of Communist support). And in no *département* did the Communists outdistance the Socialists. It retains a significant presence in parts of the Paris region, the Limousin and the industrial north, but in many areas of France it has virtually disappeared. It won 12.5 per cent of the electorate (the electoral eliminatory threshold) at the first ballot in only 72 of the 577 constituencies, and in all but 25 of those it had to stand down before the second ballot in favour of a better placed Socialist candidate. In the legislative elections of 1988 the party won 2,053,000 votes and this was hailed by relieved party spokesmen as a relative success. Only ten years previously it had won 5,828,000 votes and this result was greeted with some disappointment. The measure of the Party's decline is evident in this comparison.

The electoral demise of the PCF has been attributed to a combination of factors: some structural, long-term and social in character, others spring from the political environment and party actions. They may be summarized as follows:

- *the transformation of French society* from one based on solidaristic sub-cultures to one characterized by permissive individualism.
- *the changing nature of the working class* on which it bases so much of its strategy. Indeed, the PCF's proudest claim is to be *the* party of the working class, even though it has deserted the party in vast numbers. Moreover, as elsewhere in Western Europe, the working class is not only a minority but a declining one – particularly that part of it in the big factory-based and geographically concentrated smoke-stack industries. The working class (or at least that part of it in work) is increasingly affluent, increasingly fragmented and hetero-geneous, and increasingly mobile. The great working-class communities of yesteryear are slowly disintegrating, and with them is slowly dissolving that class consciousness (attested to by opinion polls) which was one of the bonds of the party. This "deproletarianization" of the working class has taken place while the party has clung to its *ouvriériste* ideology, language and image.
- *the decline in the infrastructural underpinning of the party.* Its satellite organizations have been weakened. This is notably the case with the CGT – a trade union confederation which has declined disproportionately within a declining trade union movement.
- *the collapse of the Soviet model* as a positive reference point, and to which the PCF leadership remains emotionally at-tached. The fading of the memories of the role played by the USSR during the Second World War combined with the widespread unpopularity of its policies in Poland and Afghanistan (the so-called "Kaboul effect" on the PCF) has helped debase the image of the Soviet Union.
- *the transformation in the nature of political activity.* Success based on the zeal of local activists (where the party is traditionally strong) has been replaced by one based on the exploitation of national media such as television (where the party has always been weak).
- *the impact of presidentialism and electoral alliances.* Many Communist voters, realizing that their candidate has no chance of winning the presidency, have learnt to vote "usefully" from the first ballot. In 1965 and 1974 there was not even a Com-munist candidate, and in 1981 and 1988 the party chose the unappealing Georges Marchais and the sacrificial Lajoinie respectively. Furthermore, Communists have been enjoined by the party leadership in successive elections (1965, 1974, 1981 and 1988) to vote for François Mitterrand at the second

ballot. Equally, in the name of "republican discipline", they have been asked by their leaders to vote for the best placed candidate of the Left at the second ballot of parliamentary and local elections – and in an increasing number of constituencies this means voting for the Socialists. Consequently, Communist voters have learnt to be more Left-wing and less specifically Communist: they have lost their partisan identity and gained a Left-wing alliance one.

- *the rise of the Socialist Party*. During the 1950s and 1960s the Socialists were weak, divided and politically compromised. The renaissance of the French Socialist Party – based on presidentialism and capturing the imaginations and votes of widely conflicting forces – presented a challenge to a party which was incapable of responding because of its intellectual sclerosis.
- *the party's strategic errors*. Thus, between 1981 and 1984 it remained in a Left-wing government during a period of extreme unpopularity (and was thus associated with it) but left when the government began to regain popularity (and was thus not associated with it).
- *the archaic language of ageing party bosses*. Unlike the Socialist Party which completely renewed its leading cadres in the 1970s, the PCF has been heavily reliant on a self-perpetuating system of careful selection which weeds out those not created in the orthodox image. The governing clique couches its messages in an arcane and archaic language which identifies the party with the past, and is impervious to new ideas which are potentially destabilising. *Rénovateurs* are to be kept at bay: *perestroika* is not for domestic use. It is no surprise that its few intellectuals have fled in despair. It has been suggested that the absence of intellectuals in the party may be part of the crisis of Marxism which is apparent throughout Western Europe. Whatever the reason – and it is linked to its "Stalinist culture" (to borrow a phrase from Tony Judt) – the party has been unable to formulate policies more appropriate to rapidly changing social conditions: its instinctive *ouvriérisme* prevents it from being sensitive to new social movements such as feminism and environmentalism.
- *the incoherence and inconsistency of its policies*. The ideological and political "zigzags" of the PCF – presented as a series of volte-face – have disoriented and demoralized the party faithful: it has oscillated between virulent denunciations of the Socialists and intimate collaboration with them; it proclaims that its policies are not dictated in Moscow (which is now probably true) but it defends the indefensible in Afghanistan and Poland; it proclaims its attachment to

democratic pluralism but stills any dissent in its own ranks; its wishes to be both a party of management and a party of class struggle.

Many of these factors are mutually reinforcing: fewer voters means fewer Deputies and mayors, which signifies fewer resources, which leads to a diminished electoral capacity. It may well be that the party has now fallen below a critical level which enables it to sustain its own sub-cultural underpinning, and the absence of such underpinning removes one of the brakes on the decline of the party.

Whatever the reasons for the electoral decline of the PCF, it is having a profound impact on the French party system, since it has altered the terms of party competition. For instance, it almost certainly contributed to the Socialist victories of 1981, for a seriously weakened Communist Party no longer provided the Right with one of its most powerful electoral weapons – the fear of communism: neither Mitterrand nor his party could plausibly be portrayed as "prisoners" of the PCF – one of the favourite, and effective accusations of the Right. The further weakening of electoral communism relaxed the Left-wing pressure on the Socialists who felt much freer to move to the Right – thus rendering them more attractive to the Centrists. Even in its decline the party continues to structure French politics: no wonder it continues to provoke such irritated fascination.

The Left under the Fifth Republic: the troubled alliance

The electoral performance of the Left during the Fifth Republic has been a mixed one. This is made clear in Table 9.

As Table 9 indicates the Left has won a majority of the votes in only one parliamentary election – that of 1981. Even in 1988 the Right won a slight majority of the votes. In only two elections have the parties of the Left won a majority in the National Assembly: in 1981 and 1988 (see Table 10). The electoral low points were clearly 1968 – the *élections de la peur* – when a France, shaken by the events of May, took refuge in the Right, and 1986 when the Communist vote collapsed. The entire period of the Left-wing government of 1981 to 1986 was electorally disastrous for the Left. It not only lost its massive majority in the National Assembly in 1986, but fared badly in the elections to the departmental councils (by 1986, 69 of the 96 were in the hands of the Right), and performed poorly in the 1983 town elections

Table 9 The electoral performance of the Left in parliamentary elections 1946–88 (per cent of votes cast at the first ballot)

Election	PCF	Non-communist Left	Total
November 1946	28.6	30.3	58.9
June 1951	26.4	24.3	50.7
January 1956	25.6	30.1	55.7
November 1958	18.9	24.0	42.9
November 1962	21.8	20.4	42.2
March 1967	22.5	21.1	43.6
June 1968	20.3	20.4	40.7
March 1973	21.3	25.0	46.3
March 1978	20.6	28.9	49.5
June 1981	16.1	39.7	55.8
March 1986	9.8	31.8	41.6
June 1988	11.3	37.9	49.2

Table 10 Representation of the Left in the National Assembly 1958–88

Election	PCF	Socialists and Allies	Other Left	Total Left Deputies	Total Deputies
November 1958	10	77	–	87	552
November 1962	41	104	2	147	482
March 1967	73	118	4	195	467
June 1968	34	57	–	91	483
March 1973	73	101	1	175	490
March 1978	86	114	1	201	491
June 1981	44	283	6	333	491
March 1986	35	214	–	249	577
June 1988	27	276	–	303	577

(when it lost 35 of its 155 towns of over 30,000 inhabitants to the Right). In the 1986 regional elections (held at the same time as the legislative elections) the Left managed to win control of only two of the twenty-two councils.

In presidential elections the fortunes of the Left have varied. In December 1965, François Mitterrand, the only candidate of the Left, won 31.7 per cent of the votes at the first ballot and a respectable 44.8 per cent at the second against de Gaulle. In the June 1969 elections, which saw the victory of Georges Pompidou, there were no fewer than four Left-wing candidates (Defferre the Socialist, Duclos the Communist, Rocard the leader of the PSU and the Trotskyist Krivine), who together mustered only 30.9 per cent of the votes. Because the best placed Left-wing candidate, Duclos, ran third, the Left was eliminated from the election and was unrepresented at the second ballot. Five years later, in May 1974, the Left came within an ace of winning the presidency when François Mitterrand, again the candidate of the Socialists and the Communists, won 43.2 per cent of the votes at the first ballot and 49.2 per cent at the second. At his third attempt at the presidency, Mitterrand triumphed: he won 25.8 per cent of the first ballot votes (the Communist Georges Marchais 15.3 per cent, the Left-wing Radical Crépeau 2.2 per cent and the two candidates of the extreme Left together polled 3.4 per cent) and went on at the second ballot to beat Giscard d'Estaing, the sitting president, by collecting 51.8 per cent of the votes. Mitterrand was thus to give the lie to the claim that he was an "eternal loser" and another unkindly claim (made by Jacques Chirac, the Gaullist leader) that "the Left wins the opinion polls but never the elections".

Mitterrand's re-election in 1988 was even more convincing than his election in 1981. At the first ballot he won 34.1 per cent of the votes while other Left-wing candidates trailed far behind: Lajoinie, the Communist with 6.8 per cent; Laguiller the Trotskyist candidate with 2 per cent; Juquin, the dissident Communist with 2 per cent; Boussel, the candidate of the Trotskyist *Mouvement pour un Parti des Travailleurs* (MPPT) with 0.4 per cent. At the second ballot he won 54 per cent of the votes by rallying all left-wing voters, a small minority of Raymond Barre's first ballot electorate, and 20 to 25 per cent of those who had voted for Jean-Marie Le Pen, the candidate of the extreme Right. It was a brilliant achievement for a person who had only two years previously been the most unpopular president of the Fifth Republic.

By June 1981 the two major parties of the Left were united in running the government, in monopolizing all the key posts in the National Assembly, and in governing many of the regions and *départements* and most of the big towns. The coalition which embraced the Socialists and the Communists had, in some respects, been welded together a little more firmly than in previous years, both ideologically (because of the radicalization of the Socialists and the liberalization of the Communists) and also over specific policies (such as Europe and the French nuclear deterrent) where there was a closer identity of views. It had also fought several election campaigns together – notably those of 1965, 1973 and 1974 which were to create "a unitary spirit" particularly among Communist voters – a spirit which was greatly to profit Mitterrand in 1981 and 1988. The coalition was also for a time (June 1972-September 1977) bound together by a Joint Programme of Government which committed both parties for the period of a legislature. But the coalition remained very fragile. Even the Joint Programme (the interpretation of which divided the signatories) was elaborated in part because neither partner basically trusted the other. Each party accepted the alliance as a means of strengthening itself and furthering its own ends, and each party was determined to retain its separate identity. Tension between the partners was inherent in the alliance, for each viewed it not only as a means of beating the Right but also as an instrument for establishing its own hegemony. Tension heightened when one partner seemed to be profiting more than the other: when, for instance, the Socialists fared very well and the Communists rather badly in successive by-elections after 1974, relations between the two were soured and strained to breaking point. Furthermore, each party suspected the motives and intentions of the other: many Communists chastised the Socialists for being essentially electoralist and reformist, while many Socialists feared the fundamentally revolutionary, undemocratic and anti-parliamentary intentions of the PCF (fears which seemed to be confirmed by the PCF's support for the Stalinist Cunhal in Portugal in 1975). The PCF also disliked the electoral growth of the PS, while the PS was suspicious of the organizational strength of the PCF.

Between the two partners there also remained wide differences over policies: over the deployment of the French nuclear deterrent which, after a remarkable volte-face in May 1977, the Communists came to defend as indispensable (it had previously been perni-cious); over the extent of nationalization and over the means of compensating those whose property had been expropriated; over the Middle East (the PCF was critical of Mitterrand's policy in Lebanon); over the nature of workers' control, which the PCF suspected as a means of furthering and legitimizing class collaboration and as a manifestation of that "spontaneity" which they abhor. Policy differences were exacerbated by ideological disagreements related to issues such as intra-party democracy, the role of the party (the PCF still views itself as the sole repository of scientific Marxism), the Communist Party's claim to be *the* party of the working class, the nature of the transitional phase to socialism, and the PCF's relations with Moscow. As the breakdown in the negotiations between the parties in September 1977 clearly revealed, there was even fundamental disagreement over the nature, the interpretation and the function of the Joint Programme of Government: for the Communist Party leadership it was but a starting point and a mechanism for triggering off the activity of the masses as well as a means of "irrevocably" transforming the French economy. For some Socialists, notably Michel Rocard, it was merely a compromise between two distinctive Left-wing cultures and traditions. For other Socialists, mainly those associated with the CERES group of the party, it was an *instrument de dépassement* – a part of a dialectical process which would help to transform both parties in a way which would facilitate ultimate unity. The coalition was not only uneasy, it was also increasingly unbalanced, with the Socialists, once a junior partner, emerging as the unquestioned master. This may be seen in the small number of ministries that Mitterrand granted (it was not negotiated beforehand) to the grateful Communists in 1981 and in the subsequent share-out of key public sector posts. The imbalance was particularly evident in the National Assembly (283 Socialist-MRG Deputies and only forty-four Communists) and at the electoral level. In June 1981 the Socialists won twice as many votes as the Communists, led the Communists in ninety-four of the ninety-six metropolitan *départements* (compared with seventy-one in 1978 and fifty-three in 1973). In 1978 the Socialists won 51 per cent of the Left-wing vote, and in 1981 68 per cent. At constituency level the figures were no less striking: in 1967 the Communist Party led the Socialists in 258 of the 470 metropolitan constituencies, 253 of the 470 in 1968, 197 of the 473 in 1973, 153 of the 474 in 1978 and only forty-five of the 474 in 1981.

It was this growing imbalance which was to bring the divided coalition to breaking point. After 1981 the precipitous decline of the PCF and the consolidation of the PS as the dominant party of the country firmly entrenched the hegemony of the Socialists within the Left. By 1988 the Socialists led the Communists in every one of the ninety-six metropolitan *départements* and in all but twenty-seven of the 577 parliamentary constituencies. The Socialists also openly boasted of their *vocation majoritaire* – their ambition to win an electoral majority and thus eradicate their dependence on allies. The 1980s introduced two further elements of destabilization for the shaky alliance. The first was the social democratization of the PS, which was freed from the pressure of a weakened PCF and constrained by the exigencies of office. The second was the change taking place in the Right-wing coalition under the impact of the move to the Right of the Gaullists and the emergence of the extreme Right. Centrists, uneasy on both scores, began to look at the increasingly moderate Socialists as potential allies. By 1988, therefore, all the signs of party *dealignment* were present. However, the reticence of some Socialists, the enduring and harmonious Left-wing alliance at local level, the unitary behaviour of the Left's electorate remain powerful obstacles to *realignment*.

The uneasy Left-wing alliance must be considered as a tactical response to the challenges of the regime: the most powerful cement of Left-wing unity of action was Right-wing unity of action. The PS and the PCF were condemned to live together, but they remained distinct entities in terms of their electoral audience, their membership, their policies, their basic ideology, and even in their language, folklore and loyalties. Their relationship was inherently ambiguous: the self-interest of each dictated both complicity and competition with the other. The real test of the alliance came when it was confronted with the unpopular choices of office, and it failed that test. The Popular Front experiment from 1936 to 1938 ended in ignominy, and the period of Left-wing governmental collaboration from 1944 to 1947 was brought to an end in acrimony. The unhappy experience of 1981 to 1984 had, therefore, revealing precedents. Without a radical transformation of either the Communists or the Socialists or both, the Left is inevitably locked into mutual suspicion and hostility. Neither the historical auguries nor present party trends are encouraging.

The bases of the Left's power

It is frequently asserted that the Left has been "out of power" for most of the Fifth Republic. But such as assertion is too simplistic, for it confuses "office" with "power". And even if the official organs of legislative and executive authority are seen as the unique repositories of power, the assertion would still rest on a highly restrictive interpretation of power, which is an ubiquitous commodity and a nebulous concept. It could be argued that in certain policy areas President de Gaulle (in foreign affairs) and Giscard d'Estaing (in social matters) held "Left-wing" views. Certain ministers belonging to the Right-wing governments could also be described, with some justification, as Left-wing: Gaullist ex-ministers such as Buron and Pisani were to join the Socialist

Party after 1971, while others – Jobert and Hamon – were to enter into alliance with the Left after 1981. Prime Minister Chaban-Delmas fell foul of the very conservative private staff of President Pompidou because, as Chaban-Delmas was later to recount in his memoirs, he was considered to be doing the work of the Socialists. It is also clear that Left-wingers were influential in certain private staffs – those of Chaban-Delmas between 1969 and 1972 and of President Giscard d'Estaing after 1974 are good examples – and in certain parts of the administration. The Left is certainly powerfully entrenched in the lower echelons of the civil service where decisions are often made and unmade.

The power of the Left may be discerned in other ways. First, the parties of the Left might be deprived of national office but they have always been solidly ensconced at local level. Certain areas such as the great industrial ghettos of the Paris red-belt or parts of the *Midi-rouge* where the Socialists and Communists win more than 90 per cent of the votes are veritable rotten boroughs of the Left. At the time of the 1981 presidential election the Left which had not held national office for over twenty years dominated the councils of eleven of the twenty-two regions and it also enjoyed a majority in the councils of forty-four of the ninety-six French *départements*, while the communal elections of March 1977 reaffirmed the supremacy of the two major parties of the Left, especially in the big towns. Even after the electoral set-backs of the early 1980s the Left continued to be dominant in the major towns (Table 11).

Table 11 Big Towns (over 30,000 inhabitants) controlled by the Left after the local elections of 1971, 1977 and 1983

Party in control	1971	1977	1983
Total number of towns	221	221	220
PCF	5	71	57
PS	45	82	61
Left Radicals	3	2	2
	53	155	120

The second main area of Left-wing power is in the numerous organizations which are either satellites or merely sympathetic: youth clubs, women's organizations, secular sports clubs and intellectual groups. The Left also has a complex and troubled but privileged relationship with the major trades unions, most of whose members are Left-wing party activists, and through the Communist-dominated CGT exercises some influence in certain nationalized industries such as electricity and railways.

Thirdly, the Left exercises an intellectual hegemony which amounts, according to the critics, to a "pervasive terrorism" in certain circles which are not organically linked with it: the dominant ethos of the economic planning agencies, the educational establishment, influential sections of the press, the environmental groups, the consumers' associations, the social security system and many Catholic lay organizations are progressive, egalitarian and Leftist. Certain policy communities such as health and housing function on Leftish assumptions and premises. *Nos idées sont au pouvoir* is a traditional cry of the Left which derives some compensation when denied the psychic gratification associated with national office.

Finally, the power of the Left when out of office may be seen in the constant electoral pressure it exerts on the Right: this has often been described as "the intimidatory power" of the Left. At each election the Right-wing presidential coalition is prodded or frightened into advocating reforms which are part of the Left-wing programme. It is perhaps worth concluding that France, which before 1981 had only very rare and very short-lived bouts of Left wing government, had none the less embraced many (if not all) of the basic economic and social principles of social democracy.

These various power bases will remain intact whatever the electoral performance of the Left at national level: they are its fortresses and refuges, and, in or out of office, they will always be there.

11 The state and the pressure groups

The first prime minister of the Fifth Republic, Michel Debré, proclaimed his intention in August 1959 of destroying 'the feudal forces' which were dismembering the French state: by 'feudal forces' he meant the powerful pressure groups. During the Fourth Republic, in his *Ces princes qui nous gouvernent*, he wrote that it was vital to make war upon those vested interests which 'divide the State and leech upon it with scarcely a thought for the nation or the citizens'. President de Gaulle also refused to see the state as a mere 'juxtaposition of particular interests, capable only of feeble compromises' and claimed that it was 'an instrument of decision, action, ambition, expressing and serving only the national interest'. Yet his view of the groups was less jaundiced than that of the prime minister, for numerous incidents showed that he was not against the groups as such: they could and should be consulted. Indeed, his April 1969 referendum, which sought to bring them into an enlarged and somewhat modified upper chamber, provoked widespread criticisms of neo-corporatism. But President de Gaulle, while accepting their role in policy-making, refused to tolerate their direct interference in politics. It was a fine yet vital distinction. Hence he accepted the right of student leaders to discuss their working conditions but contemptuously dismissed their protests about the size of the educational budget and denied their right to criticize his Algerian policy. In March 1960, in a reply to the president of the National Assembly about the farmers' main pressure groups, he noted that 'however representative this group may be in regard to the particular interests it defends, it is nevertheless, from the legal point of view, bereft of authority and political responsibility'. While Debré hinted at an authoritarian and hostile approach to the 'intermediate bodies' in the name of state purity, General de Gaulle appeared to accept that they had a legitimate but subordinate place in policy-making. Whatever the differences, the views of both men involved an onslaught on the *régime des intérêts* (another fashionable and misleading description of the Fourth Republic), and a radical change in the relationship between the state and the groups. It is the nature of that relationship during the Fifth Republic that serves as the framework of the following discussion.

Models of state–pressure group relations

Analysing the relationship (or rather relationships) between the state and the pressure groups is fraught with difficulty. Problems abound. There is, first of all, the usual problem of certain political parties (such as the Left-wing Unified Socialist Party) being essentially intellectual pressure groups, and certain pressure groups (such as the ecologists or the Corsican nationalist *Union du Peuple Corse*) acting occasionally like political parties by fighting elections and winning seats in local councils.

Second, there is the problem of deciding whether, for instance, an individual firm should be counted as a pressure group, particularly if it employs thousands and is in direct and frequent contact with the state over matters such as labour practices and disputes, loans, subsidies, orders, anti-pollution measures. Some powerful major firms are as important as the government in structuring the activities of many other smaller ones: for instance, Régie Renault, the public sector car group, determines the fate of some 1,200 small firms which depends on its orders. Such firms – public or private – exercise enormous influence within the state machine through their 'monopoly of legitimate expertise'.

Thirdly, the interpenetration of the state and the private sector poses particular problems: for example, the employers' peak organisation represents both public and private sector firms, and major public firms have private shareholders and *vice versa*. Thus, Paribas, the vast banking and financial empire with an extremely diversified holding policy was, before its nationalization by the Socialist government in 1981, already partially owned by the state banks (which sometimes acted in close collaboration with the private banks). Similarly, when the *Crédit Commercial de France*, a major private bank, was in anguished consultation with the Socialist government over its nationalization plans it emerged that one of the principal share-holders was a state holding company.

The fourth major problem in analysing state–pressure group relations follows on from the third: parts of the state machine might be considered as pressure groups defending their own corporate interests in competition, or even in rivalry, with other parts. The French nuclear energy programme of the 1970s was pushed through by the joint effort of groups which included the nationalized electricity industry (EDF), the *Commissariat à l'Énergie Atomique*, the then privately-owned Creusot-Loire company and the Communist-dominated trade union, the CGT. These groups were opposed by the ecologists, the socialist-leaning trade unions, the CFDT, and to some extent also by the nationalized coal mining industry (which was starved of resources) and the newly created state agency responsible for solar energy. The public sector banks and petroleum companies are also, in practice, powerful actors enjoying great autonomy – they represent but another example of the so-called 'states within a state', groups that pressure the state they are supposed to serve. To return to a point made in a previous chapter, the more diversified the activities of the state the more conflicts, often of a corporate nature, are likely to take place within the machinery of the state.

The fifth problem in studying state–pressure group relations concerns the Europeanization and internationalization of the French banking, industrial and agricultural sectors: relations are distorted by the fact that in some decisions neither the French state nor the pressure groups may be the ultimate arbiter. Agricultural policies are fixed in Brussels and the employment prospects of a town may be decided by the foreign headquarters of a multi-national firm. A complex triangular relationship replaces, therefore, the traditional dual one. In this relationship the state is both a pressure group and a pressured group.

The final two problems relate to the methodological approach to be adopted. In the first place, given the enormous variety of policy areas in which the numerous and very diverse groups come into contact with the ubiquitous and fragmented state, is it wise to study state–pressure group relations as though they were meaningful conceptual entities? For this reason recent authors have suggested the need to study 'policy communities' or 'policy networks' (in, for example, industry, agriculture, finance, social policy). Second, there is the problem of the general approach to the subject. In France, several approaches are discernible. There is, for example, an important Marxist school which has rooted its empirical research in a number of areas: the internationalization of the French industrial and financial markets and the process of urbanization in the major towns have been given special attention. Put very crudely, the Marxist critique argues that in a capitalist system the state is, by its very nature, sensitive to the interests of the dominant class and big capital, although it is sometimes conceded that the worst social effects of capitalism may be attenuated by the state influenced by other groups: on the whole political actors have a limited role, and their actions serve merely to reinforce the existing *status quo*, or to ensure the social conditions that are optimal for the development of capitalism. The empirical work of some of the Marxist scholars has been immensely useful and has provided documented insights into the role and influence of certain (often little studied) groups such as the banks and property companies. But the theoretical underpinning of the work has sometimes been tendentious, implausible and methodologically simplistic (a fact admitted by the better Marxist scholars), since it has been inspired by a theological rather than an intellectually agnostic approach to the problem.

A very different general approach is the functionalist one, in which state–pressure group relations are seen in different terms: the actions of the state and its agents are interpreted as a series of responses to needs – generally the needs to balance and to integrate divergent interests in the name of social harmony or consensus. The problem with the functionalist approach is that it is at best very general, rather unspecific, and at worst extremely banal. Like most over-arching theories it succeeds only in over-arching and theorizing: it gives little clue to the awesome complexity of many political situations.

Cutting across such general approaches are a number of analyses which suggest patterns or models of state–pressure group relations. In the literature on pressure groups during the Fifth Republic – and it is, unfortunately, somewhat sparse (although the recent work of American scholars such as Wilson, Keeler and Ambler has filled some of the gaps) – it is possible to discern four such models: for the sake of convenience they may be called the domination-crisis model, the endemic conflict model, the concerted policies model and the pluralistic model. Each has its supporters who root their analysis in the nature of French political society. But while each model has some justification, all are inadequate and somewhat simplistic in their explanations. Yet by using their analyses it is possible to portray some of the complex reality and answer some of the problems raised above.

The domination-crisis model

This model is largely associated with Michel Crozier and Stanley Hoffmann, who together, although from somewhat different viewpoints, reformulated in more systematic fashion the views and prejudices of a long line of observers. Those views are anchored in an analysis of French attitudes towards authority and change, and may be briefly summarized as follows:

● The French fear face-to-face relations, and they very readily have recourse to impersonal, highly formalized, distant and hierarchical rules imposed from above to govern social intercourse; only such rules are likely to prevent arbitrariness. Hence a powerful and centralized bureaucracy exists to impose the rules.

● French political culture is characterized by both 'limited authoritarianism' and 'potential insurrection against authority', and the French oscillate between a normal servility towards authority and sporadic rebellions against it. Closely associated with this idea is the fashionable view expressed by Michel Poniatowski (who echoed Tocqueville) that 'France is a profoundly conservative country which dreams of revolution but rejects reform'.

● In a highly individualistic, atomized and anomic society, associational life is weak, for a Frenchman fears the loss of his liberty and individuality which results from belonging to groups. Those groups that do exist are highly fragmented, badly divided, thoroughly egotistical and generally anomic, and all reject the principle of fruitful interdependence. There is an absence of genuine bartering, of dialogue, of compromising between the groups. Each group ferociously defends its rights against other groups, and resists any attempts by the state to impose change which might be prejudicial to its acquired interests.

● Since the groups defend the *status quo*, change within society must be imposed by the bureaucracy: there is thus a gulf between a modernizing administration and its highly conservative *administrés*.

● The state is viewed with mistrust by the ill-organized groups, since it threatens to impinge upon entrenched rights. Authority must, therefore, be resisted. This 'perpetual resistance' to authority found its early philosophical justification in the writings of *Alain* – the pseudonym of Émile Chartier – who told his countrymen to build themselves 'barricades' against the encroachment of the state: the first rule in the handbook of government, he contended, was 'heroic idleness'. The result of this unremitting and obscurantist resistance is stalemate – *la société bloquée*.

● The state authorities view the groups as 'delinquent communities' (Jesse Pitts), as 'subservient clients' (Jack Hayward), which may be treated with authoritarianism (because of their normal servility) and with contempt (because of their obscurantism). Yet their traditional rights must be respected, because of their predilection for revolt.

In this political culture dominated by fear and suspicion and by a 'perpetual resistance to the ruling elites', change can be brought about to break the stalemate not by peaceful means but only by sporadic upheavals, by violent social spasms. But these 'functionally innovative crises' which introduce reforms are then followed by long periods in which the traditional rules of the game reassert themselves. In the domination-conflict model, the state dominates the groups and imposes its directives upon them in authoritarian fashion. But, fearful of insurrection, it is unable to impose radical reforms which can be effected only during a crisis.

There is some evidence to support the points outlined above: groups in France are very fragmented and badly divided; the bureaucracy does play an important role in the life of the nation; parts of that bureaucracy have proved themselves modernizing as the economic reconstruction of the country bears witness; governments and the administration have certainly acted with extraordinary authoritarianism on occasions (the way in which Prime Minister Barre formulated and implemented his 1976 anti-inflation plan was but another example of the iron fist in the mailed glove); the obscurantist and remorseless resistance of pressure groups may be seen in the activities, described below, of the small shopkeepers and certain farming groups; the absence of dialogue and compromise is evident in the relations between the employers' organizations and certain trades unions; May 1968 may be considered as yet another 'functionally innovative crisis' which was followed by stifling and routine-ridden conservatism, since the important rights wrested by the trades unions were whittled away, and the impetus towards important educational reform was skilfully broken by the traditional academic establishment. Yet some of the points raise legitimate objections: certain parts of the administration may be modernizing in outlook but others have been obdurate defenders of the *status quo*, especially if its disturbance entails a possible diminution in their own power; the state may be authoritarian on occasions but it has also proved itself permanently sensitive to the demands of certain groups; the bloody-minded conservatism of some groups has been matched by the forward-looking dynamism of others such as the Young Farmers Association; constant compromise is evident in the behaviour of many groups, but it is by nature less spectacular and less obvious than its absence; if May 1968 and, more arguably, May 1958 constitute 'functionally innovative crises' it is also true that the Fifth Republic and its predecessor have shaken up large sectors of French society in a persistent and pragmatic way, unswayed by the pressures of immediate crisis. The social and political reforms introduced by President Giscard d'Estaing which profoundly affected both the individual and the family were not introduced in a revolutionary spasm but under the normal and healthy impact of electoral fear. Similarly, the Socialist reform programme, introduced after May 1981, was occasioned by a presidential election – a perfectly normal political event, not 'a functionally innovative crisis'. Furthermore, the *'société bloquée'* thesis, so cherished by certain intellectuals, seems difficult to sustain, given the immense changes, peacefully elaborated and equally peacefully implemented, which have taken place in France since the end of the Second World War.

The domination-crisis model of state–group relations provides useful insights but not a convincing total explanation. Like most models, it raises more questions than it answers, and it is too neat and too selective in its choice of facts to convey the full complexity of the situation.

The endemic and open conflict model

This model is linked with, but is distinct from, the previous school of thought. It shares certain assumptions about the authoritarian nature of the state, the fragmented nature of the groups and the impact of revolutionary crisis as a creative and reforming force. But it differs from the domination-crisis model in an important respect: its assumptions rest less on a view of the innate character-istics of French society than on an argument about the functioning of the political institutions of the Fifth Republic. It is maintained that with the decline of parliament, the natural safety-valve of the Third and Fourth Republics, and the growth of a disciplined pro-governmental party coalition, the political leverage of the groups has been severely limited. Decreasing influence has led to increasing frustration. And frustration has led to mounting pressure of an extra-institutional and often violent nature. Jean Meynaud, writing in 1962, pessimistically observed that:

> In spite of the end of the Algerian war and the political liquidation of the OAS [the secret army organization fighting for *Algérie française*] and the Poujadists, the political régime of the Fifth Republic will continue to live in the midst of protest movements, sometimes of a brutal nature.... This is not so much the result of the increasing difficulties of neo-capitalism; rather it is the quasi-automatic consequence of the functioning of the new institutions.

Extra-institutional pressure has become endemic and has taken the form of open conflict, and this pressure has been instrumental in wresting concessions from governments. According to this school, the groups in their relations with the state are less quiescent clients than belligerent defenders of their interests.

Extra-institutional pressure has taken several forms throughout the Fifth Republic: strikes, demonstrations, illegal obstruction and violent confrontation. Strikes are more numerous in France than in Great Britain, but because of lack of militancy or lack of trades unions, or both, they rarely last as long. For instance, in 1983 only six per cent of industrial strikes lasted longer than fourteen days and only two per cent more than a month. French workers normally resort to one-day stoppages or 'lightning' strikes (which may last only two hours), which are politically affective rather than economically effective. This is equally true of those rare (there was none between 1980 and 1985) 'action days' (*journées d'action*), when all the unions call for a one-day general strike. French strikes rarely receive unanimous support: for instance, the national strike of 7 October 1976 against the government's anti-inflation plan, which was considered by union leaders to be one of the most successful of the Fifth Republic, involved four-fifths of the country's teachers and miners, but only two-fifths of the postmen and a third of the railwaymen, and in the private sector only a third of the workers joined the strike. Moreover, since the late 1970s working-class militancy as expressed in strike action has clearly been on the wane (see Table 12).

Table 12   Number of working days lost in France 1974–1987

1974	3,380,000	1979	3,656,000	1984	1,350,000
1975	3,869,000	1980	1,674,000	1985	885,000
1976	5,011,000	1981	1,496,000	1986	1,042,000
1977	3,660,000	1982	2,327,000	1987	950,000

The figures for 1985, 1986 and 1987 were the lowest since 1946: rising unemployment clearly helped to demobilize the working class. It is not only the working class which has gone on strike. Middle-class university students and grammar school pupils, doctors, lawyers and architects have all employed this eminently proletarian weapon (often because they are appalled at the prospect of being proletarianized...).

Illegal activity has taken various forms. Steel workers have disrupted the Tour de France cycle race, burnt down public buildings and held managers hostage, lorry drivers have blocked motorways, and the more irate farmers have tipped their unsold artichokes, tomatoes, peaches and apples onto the streets – tactics designed to disrupt traffic and to slow down even French drivers.

The ecologically minded also have blocked the sites of proposed motorways, closed down ports to protest against oil pollution and, in Brittany, have invaded proposed atomic energy stations. A favourite target of direct action groups is the local prefecture or sub-prefecture, the physical representation of state authority in the provinces.

Mass demonstrations and processions have always been a traditional French means of expressing support or protest, and the Fifth Republic has had its fair share. In 1975, not a particularly troubled year, there were 612 demonstrations in Paris, of which 312 necessitated the mobilization of the police. The events in Algeria triggered off massive demonstrations in favour of peace, some of which degenerated into terrible bloodbaths. During May 1968 Paris, Bordeaux, Nantes, Strasbourg and other big university towns experienced massive processions, mixtures of the rally and the circus, both moving and cathartic. Demonstrations by French students are no new factor in French history; the events of Algeria, of May 1968, and the protests against certain unpopular measures such as the Debré Law of 1973 (which had the impertinence to treat middle-class students like all other Frenchmen by tightening up the law on national service deferment) and the proposed education reforms of Fontanet in 1973, and of Haby in 1975 surprised observers only by the numbers involved. The outbreak of massive student protest in December 1986 against certain stipulations of the Devaquet Education Bill escalated into bloody confrontations with the police, led to one death and wide-scale destruction of property. The protest widened to encompass other unpopular measures such as a proposed illiberal reform of the nationality laws. The Right-wing government of Jacques Chirac, haunted by fears of 1968 and wracked by internal dissension, withdrew the Devaquet Bill. The student protest also contributed to the withdrawal of the government's nationality reforms.

The Left-wing government of 1981 to 1984 had to contend with waves of demonstrations from doctors, civil servants, miners, primary school teachers, customs officers, steel-workers, lorry drivers, businessmen (some 25,000 demonstrated at Villepinte in December 1982). The FNSEA, the major farmers' union, mobilised 120,000 farmers who marched in the streets of Paris in March 1982. But the biggest demonstrations (over one million people in one of them) were those organized by the Catholic school lobby in 1983 and 1984 which pushed the government into a humiliating climb-down.

Violence has been a frequent feature of the politics of the Fifth Republic, and it has been used by many groups. According to the official statistics there were about a hundred *attentats* a year in the

1960s and early 1970s, rising to 480 in 1976, 555 in 1977 and over 600 in 1978. Some of these attacks on persons and property were foreign-inspired (notably by the/ Armenians and the Palestinians) and must be excluded from this analysis of state–pressure groups relations. Nevertheless, violence has been resorted to by many French groups intent on bringing pressure on the government. This violence has had three main, interrelated sources: political, nationalistic and sectoral.

Among the politically violent groups on the extreme Left must be counted *Action directe* which is largely anarchist in sympathy and which derives part of its inspiration from Third World struggles. *Action directe* carried out several armed attacks against state buildings and officials in the late 1970s and 1980s. It was officially dissolved in 1982 but it continued to wreak havoc: in 1986 it perpetrated several particularly bloody *attentats* before its leaders were rounded up and imprisoned. After 1970 the Maoists of the *Gauche Prolétarienne* were tempted by violent illegality when they created the *Nouvelle Résistance Populaire*, but the movement soon collapsed. On the extreme Right there have been several terrorist groups, starting with the OAS, the paramilitary arm of the supporters of a French Algeria, which committed many violent acts in 1961 and 1962 (including an almost successful attempt on the life of President de Gaulle). Later groups on the extreme Right (such as SOS-France) have been responsible for attacks on the homes of Left-wingers and on Jewish offices and synagogues: the bombing of the Jewish restaurant Goldenberg in Paris in August 1982 which left six people dead and twenty-two injured was perhaps the most spectacular act of mindless bloodshed. There have also been several political groups whose political sympathies have been obscure but whose acts have been all too evident: in November 1976, for example, a uranium mine was blown up in the Haute-Vienne (a *département* in central France) by a COPEAU (the graphically named *Commando d'Opposition par l'Explosif à l'Autodestruction de l'Univers*).

Violence of a nationalistic nature has taken place in the Savoy and 'in the Basque Country (the Basque separatist group Iparretarak carried out sixty or so *attentats* between 1973 and 1986 before it was officially dissolved), but more especially in Brittany and Corsica. In both these places, moderate autonomous groups are flanked by more revolutionary and more unruly paramilitary factions. In Brittany the FLB-ARB (*Front de Libération Bretonne – Armée Républicaine Bretonne*) and the *Résistance Nationale Bretonne* (founded in September 1977) specialize in the destruction of television masts, although their other less laudable and more spectacular operations have included the blowing up of an aircraft at Quimper airport in August 1974. Between June 1976 and August 1977, the FLB-ARB carried out no fewer than fifty armed attacks on state property, and claimed responsibility for blowing up part of the museum of the Palace of Versailles in the summer of 1978. There is also an important legal organization, the *Union Démocratique Bretonne*, founded in 1964, which defends Breton rights through the ballot box: it has won seats on several local councils in Brittany, normally by allying itself with the parties of the Left. In Corsica, there are four legal movements for autonomy and as many illegal ones. The principal legally recognized bodies are the *Union du Peuple Corse* (UPC), which fought the 1982 Corsican assembly elections, and the *Association des Patriotes Corses* (APC), which replaced the now banned *Action pour la Renaissance de la Corse* (ARC). The APC, like the UPC, is essentially moderate (by Corsican standards) and demands not independence but a greater degree of autonomy for the island. The four banned and clandestine movements, the two most active being the *Front de Libération Nationale Corse* (FLNC), founded in May 1976 and banned in January 1983, and the *Action Révolutionnaire Corse*, created in 1966, all demand the independence of the island. They have been responsible for some very spectacular actions which have included the destruction of wine cellars belonging to the *pieds noirs* (the French who left north Africa and who are wrongly accused of taking over the best land) and the blowing up of a Caravelle at Bastia airport in March 1974 and a Boeing 707 in September 1976 at Ajaccio airport. In 1975 and 1976 there were more than 200 officially recorded *attentats* against life or property on the island and in 1978, 1979 and 1980 more than 350. After a brief pause during and after the 1981 presidential election campaign violence broke out again in 1982 when there were no fewer than 800 *attentats*: it was the Corsican nationalists' response to the Socialist government's measures to increase Corsican autonomy – measures which they considered totally inadequate. Throughout the 1980s *attentats* in Corsica have averaged over 300 a year.

Sectoral discontent has taken a violent turn on many occasions during the Fifth Republic. And many groups, including peasants, industrial workers, students and small shopkeepers have resorted to violent means.

Extremists in the ranks of the normally mild-mannered environmental groups have been tempted into violence: in May 1975 they blew up part of a nuclear power station at Fessenheim in Alsace; in July 1976 the offices of the main building of the atomic energy authority at Tours were blown up; the confrontation with the police at the proposed nuclear power station at Creys-Malville in the Rhône valley in August 1977 ended in tragic deaths; the site of Larzac which the army was gradually taking over to turn into a vast military camp and of Plogoff in Brittany which the government was proposing to transform into a nuclear power station provided the two great (and often violent) rallying points of the ecologists in the 1970s. Not unnaturally, the most violent groups have been those whose very existence appeared menaced. These marginal groups include the unemployed in certain areas of France, small shopkeepers, the wine-growers of the south, and, to a lesser extent, the industrial workers of the depressed regions of the north and east of France. When cultural or national vulnerability is combined with economic or political deprivation, however relative, the danger of violence increases, as the activities of the marginal farmers of Brittany, Corsica and Languedoc amply demonstrate. Many poor peasants have developed a siege mentality, which is scarcely surprising, for nearly half the farm population has been forced from the land since 1954 and many of those who remain are heavily in debt (loans from the *Crédit Agricole* multiplied by eight between 1960 and 1974); most earn less than the minimum industrial wage. The peasants' response has been a series of violent outbursts in 1961, 1963, 1967, 1970, 1971 and almost every year since 1974: those of the winter of 1981-82, termed '*la révolte des paysans*', were the worst since 1961. At one stage, in Normandy, the Minister of Agriculture had to flee an angry mob of incensed peasants.

Many of the threatened groups of the Fifth Republic have both their moderate spokesmen who try to negotiate peacefully with the authorities and also their *enragés* who are frequently grouped in paramilitary organizations. The small shopkeepers are represented by the CID-UNATI (which claims about 150,000 members), which organizes discussions with the government as well as running clandestine 'self-defence groups' created in 1976 and direct heirs to the *brigades anti-fisc* (a programme in a name!) founded in 1973. These self-defence groups or commandos comprise ten to fifteen members, are organized on a local basis, and their task is 'to oppose by any means the "abuses" of the tax inspectors' (which simply means the auditing of accounts and the collection of taxes). The 'any means' have included armed attacks on tax offices, the theft of tax files and the threatening and manhandling of tax collectors. Many of the wine-growers of the south are represented in the official *Fédération Nationale des Syndicats d'Exploitants Agricoles*, the biggest farmers' union, and the local Agricultural Chambers. But in the 1960s and 1970s, they also formed unofficial departmental action committees, veritable commando groups which have caused considerable damage. In

1975, for example, they overturned 112 lorries (and set light to another four) which were carrying cheap imported Italian wine, pillaged the wine cellars of a prominent Toulouse wine merchant, ripped up railway lines and blocked the port of Sète (where Italian wine arrived). In March 1976, during a *journée d'action* in the *département* of the Aude, the local action committee clashed violently with the police, injured an unsympathetic journalist, pillaged or burnt down six tax offices, attacked a branch of the *Crédit Agricole*, interrupted rail traffic, damaged toll-booths on the A9 motorway, blew up a television mast and blocked several roads. In 1979, 1980, 1981, 1982 and 1984 they seized several loads of Italian wine and poured oil into it, thus rendering it as undrinkable as the local wine they were hoping to protect.

Grumbling resentment punctuated by occasional violence can suddenly erupt into bloody confrontation. There have been several incidents which have highlighted the importance of violence as an ingredient of French political life: the events of March 1976 at Montredon in Languedoc, when 3000 peasants gave battle to contingents from the police, ended with the deaths of one policeman and one peasant; the August 1977 confrontation between police and ecologists ended in tragedy; in Corsica violence and terrorism led to deaths in August 1975, January 1980 and February 1982; the violent protests of the unemployed workers of Longwy, Valenciennes and Denain in the spring of 1979 and again in 1982 and 1984 involved the destruction of property and violent clashes between the workers and the police.

The history of the Fifth Republic appears to prove that extra-institutional methods frequently pay. There are numerous examples of a previously insensitive government meeting demands in the face of conflict, muted or violent. The strikes of the miners in 1963, of the wholesale vegetable and fruit merchants of 1973, of the doctors in 1983 and of the train drivers in 1986-1987, forced an apparently resolute government to make major concessions. The small shopkeepers were rewarded for their turbulence with the Royer Act of December 1973 which gives them an important say in deciding whether supermarkets may be opened in their *département*: it is rather like placing the decision of the opening of new pubs in the hands of the Plymouth Brethren. Concessions have also been made to the wine-growers of the south; worried French governments have constantly violated the rules of the Common Market and placed a temporary ban on Italian wine imports (and at the same time crowing about the anti-European attitudes of the British ...), and have announced 'costly programmes for the restructuring of the wine-growing areas of the Midi'. The bloody events in Corsica extracted from the government in February 1977 a massive long-term aid programme, and the violence of the steel workers in the north and the east of France in the early spring of 1979 compelled the government to yield on several points to the unions.

The endemic and open conflict model, while usefully under-lining an important aspect of state–group relations, suffers on a number of accounts:

● It fails to note that extra-institutional means have frequently been totally ineffective in forcing concessions: the violence of the OAS in 1961 and 1962 was even exploited by the government and merely accelerated Algerian independence. Certain groups, through extra-institutional means, have been able to slow down policies, but they have rarely been able permanently to defy the weight of public opinion or the pressures of the market: the determination of the well-backed wheat-growers and of the bakers' lobbies has been unable to prevent the French from eating less bread and more meat and fruit; the antics of Gérard Nicoud, the militant leader of the small shopkeepers, did not slow down the rush to the supermarkets; the rage of the southern wine-growers has not altered the French desire for better wine. Facts have a habit of taking their revenge.

● The second defect of the model is that many of its assumptions about the Fifth Republic are no less valid for previous régimes. Extra-institutional activity by the groups – even violence – is a congenital characteristic of French political society and not an acquired defect of its latest political offspring. Even in the last two generations, 1934, 1936, 1944, 1947 and 1953 stand out as conflict-ridden and violent years. And such bucolic pursuits as the tarring and feathering of tax-collectors who had the effrontery to demand tax payment stopped, not started, with the Fifth Republic. This is not to deny that the Fifth Republic has not been spared or has not prevented bloody violence – the campaign of the OAS in 1961 and 1962 and the events of May 1968 and November–December 1986 are eloquent affir-mations to the contrary – it is merely to place the problem in a wider historical perspective. Furthermore, it must be recalled that France has no equivalent of the Italian Red Brigades, of the West German Red Army Faction, of the Spanish ETA or the British IRA. Violence is generally directed against property and not persons. Only very rarely, too, does it spill over into areas not directly affected (the Breton nationalist attacks against the Palace of Versailles in 1978 and the Corsican nation-alist outrages in Paris in 1979 were exceptions to the rule).

- The third major defect of the endemic and open conflict model is that, like the previous model, it seriously underestimates the degree of genuine, peaceful and fruitful dialogue between the groups and the state.
- Finally, the model often misinterprets the real nature of conflict and violent confrontation, for they are not always motivated by mindless, purposeless and uncontrollable frustration. Violence is often orchestrated in careful and ritualistic fashion, and has always been an intrinsic element in the French bartering process. The deliberate dramatization of a negotiation may enable a group not only to extract concessions from the sponsor ministry but it may also be exploited by both the group and the ministry in bringing pressure to bear on the government as a whole. Occasionally such dramatization may help the government to persuade tax-payers that concessions are vital or, in the case of the farmers and wine-growers, to convince its Common Market partners that without concessions revolution would be imminent.

The corporatist and concerted politics models

If the two previous models of state–group relations lay stress upon the conflictual nature of those relations and emphasize the generally authoritarian and insensitive nature of the organs of the state, the corporatist and concerted political model describes the relationship as one of partnership; constant, permanent and mutually beneficial. Concerted politics, writes Jack Hayward, 'stresses the interdependence of the government and the interest groups, and the interpenetration of "public" and "private" decision-making characteristics of a mixed economy in which an increasing measure of state intervention has to be reconciled with an increasing measure of interest group intervention in all spheres of social activity'. It is clear that the concerted politics model is both descriptive and prescriptive: it sees the state–group partnership as both desirable and inevitable. Indeed, for many proponents of the concerted politics model, relations between the state and the groups were to take place 'within the framework of social justice', provided by the planning of the French economy. Concerted politics was very fashionable in the 1950s and 1960s.

Underlying the attempt to direct state–group intercourse into institutional channels was the search for consensus and for 'rational' decision-making. But the search proved illusory, for it was based on the myth that such a consensus existed, that it was possible, by the alchemy of concertation, to reach decisions acceptable to all interests. Concerted politics implicitly denied the primacy and inevitability of politics, and rejected the intrinsically conflicting nature of decision-making; one protagonist of concerted politics could even proclaim the need 'to depoliticise the major policy options of the nation'. In a country so ideologically divided this was a pious and foolish aspiration. The organs of concertation may have provided useful forums for airing grievances and occasionally played a useful educative role: but they were less the instruments of concertation than the institutionalized agents of muted conflict. This was gradually recognized, even by the economic planners: one of the later planning commissioners, Jean Ripert, discreetly abandoned the concept of *concertation* in favour of *consultation*.

If concerted politics was the fashion in some circles in the 1950s and early 1960s, corporatist politics became the academic mode of the 1970s and early 1980s. The two models are, in fact, closely linked, since both emphasize the non-neutral nature of the state and the closeness and durability of the links between the state and the groups, and both insist upon the importance of consensus building and conflict management as integral elements of the relationship. Finally, both point to the institutionalization of the state–group dialogue. But there are differences between the two models; the corporatist model introduces notions such as hierarchy, integration, discrimination and privilege which are absent from the concerted politics model.

Philippe Schmitter has defined corporatism as 'a system of interest intermediation in which the constituent units are organized into a limited number of singular, compulsory, non-competitive, hierarchically ordered and functionally differentiated categories, recognized or licensed (if not created) by the state and granted a deliberate representational monopoly within their respective categories in exchange for observing certain controls on their selection of leaders and articulation of demands and supports'. Very briefly, the corporatist model envisages the incorporation by the state of certain powerful monopolistic groups (normally peak organisations) into permanent institutionalized arrangements. The group follows the directives of the state, coerces and disciplines its members, and in return, receives certain privileges which thus strengthen it even further. Rival groups may even be discriminated against, thus weakening them and rendering them less attractive – which is a source of further weakness. The example which is most quoted to illustrate the corporatist case is that of the biggest farmers' union, the FNSEA, to which about half the farmers belong. It comprises 30,000 local farming organizations with 700,000 members and runs its own influential network of banks, schools and co-operatives. There are basically three constituent elements: thirty-six produce organizations (cereals, meat, milk, wine, tobacco, etc.) of a specialized nature; ninety-three departmental chambers of agriculture, which are 'horizontal' organizations; affiliated bodies such as the CNJA (*Centre National des Jeunes Agriculteurs*). The FNSEA, which was founded in 1946 and is at present led by Raymond Lacombe (its previous leader, François Guillaume, became Minister of Agriculture in the Right-wing government of 1986-1988), is flanked (and often outflanked) by several hostile rival organizations. Before the arrival of the Left-wing government in 1981 it was argued that the state used and abused the FNSEA to push through its modernization of French agriculture. In return, the FNSEA was granted privileged access to the state machine (to the point of almost colonizing parts of it), was given financial concessions and subsidies, was allowed to regulate parts of the industry, and accorded a role in implementing the policies finally decided. There thus existed a close, symbiotic, corporatist-type relationship.

But such a relationship is very much the exception in France. This is not to argue that close, almost intimate relations, do not exist between the state and certain groups (they are described below). Furthermore, since the Second World War several attempts have been made to institutionalize the dialogue between the state and the groups: both are represented in the various organs of the five year National plan; in the Economic and Social Council, a body composed essentially of representatives of employers', workers' and farmers' organizations which serves as 'a barometer of social and economic group opinion' (Jack Hayward); in the regional economic and social committees; and in the consultative and advisory committees which have proliferated in recent years. Some governments of the Fifth Republic have attempted to devise other mechanisms and means further to facilitate and consolidate the dialogue between the state and the groups: these have ranged from the aborted attempt by General de Gaulle in the 1969 referendum to give the groups a bigger say at regional and national level (in the Senate), to the policy of Prime Minister Chaban-Delmas who for three years after 1969 negotiated with the CNPF, the employers' peak organisation, the issues of employment security, maternity pay, union representation and technical training and who introduced a limited form of incomes policy by way of 'contracts' in which workers, employers and the state were involved. The Socialist government's repeated meetings with the so-called '*partenaires sociaux*' in 1982 provides another example. Finally, the state has discriminated against certain groups and favoured others in order to pursue and implement its policies (see below).

Yet, apart from the case of the FNSEA before May 1981, the corporatist case lacks any real empirical backing. France is not Sweden, Austria or West Germany. Its groups are always fragmented, divided, often unrepresentative, and generally autonomous: for all those reasons they are unsuitable partners in a corporatist schema. Even the FNSEA by 1988 (at its forty-second congress) was faced with the risk of implosion as the result of increasingly acrimonious internecine struggles. Moreover, most major groups are traditionally apprehensive about co-operation with the state and resist any attempt to incorporate them into collusive decision-making. Finally, the state itself has generally avoided being enmeshed in the thicket of corporatism: it negotiates specific deals with big firms rather than general policies with the employers' peak organisation and it often favours politically sympathetic or compliant groups which are not necessarily representative or influential. Finally, corporatism rests on some form of consensus about long-term macro-economic goals – and such a consensus has rarely if ever existed in France. The role of the state is such that collaboration is necessary and even desirable, but collaboration does not necessarily imply permanent collusion or involve acquiescence. The corporatist model fails to take account of the very real lessons of the previous two models and the following one.

The pluralist model

The pluralist model argues that a government, whatever it may proclaim, seeks less to implement the general interest than continually to bring about adjustments between the particular interests which are in constant and inevitable conflict. A neutral state provides an institutional framework for the struggle; far from dominating the groups, it seeks, by a policy of accommodation and incrementalism, to facilitate dialogue between them. It further argues that France has undergone a revolution in the last generation, and that the cultural stereotypes propagated by Michel Crozier are less and less convincing. Associational life may have been weak in the past (but even that proposition is highly questionable) but it certainly is not so today. France, it is contended, positively pullulates with pressure groups, ranging from the major economic groups to the ARAP, an association dedicated to the protection of foxes and other vermin. No level of life is without its groups: even the spiritual life is catered for by a wide range of groups which encompass the church (itself at the centre of a vast range of organizations, associations and groups) at the one extreme and the *Union des Athées* at the other. The consumer lobby, while weak, is growing in size and influence and is represented by the *Institut National de la Consommation* (INC) founded in 1968 by the Economics Ministry (and for that reason somewhat suspect) and by the *Union Fédérale des Consommateurs* (UFC), founded in 1951, which has 35,000 members organized in 140 local unions and a monthly review *Que Choisir* which has over 200,000 subscribers. It was calculated that by 1976 there were nearly 200,000 associations in France dealing with social questions such as consumer protection, housing, the aged and the mentally handicapped. And in July 1977 the Environment Minister estimated that there were more than 6000 environmental groups comprising 300,000 members in the country, and that they were increasing at the rate of a hundred new groups a month.

In the pluralist model, power is not concentrated but diffused: there is a proliferation of decision centres, sometimes informal, often anti-hierarchical in structure, frequently transient, generally ever-shifting. The government is essentially a broker which, in its search for social consensus, is obliged to modify its policies and to bring about concessions in the light of evolving circumstances. Decision-making is seldom 'heroic', and only rarely results from the imposition of rationally calculated policies, but involves rather the negotiation of marginal adjustments to the *status quo*. It necessarily precludes major shifts in policy which would be offensive to certain groups which could jeopardize the harmony of social institutions. In short, governments buy peace in the search for social harmony. Political elites are mediators or arbitrators in a vast and endless bargaining process in which coalition-building has to take place between groups with incomplete and overlapping memberships.

The pluralistic model has been empirically substantiated by a long list of 'concessions' or 'incremental adjustments' brought about in non-crisis situations by the normal, legitimate and peaceful bartering process: the Education Ministers' unsuccessful attempts to cut school holidays in 1959 and 1969 as the result of resistance from the teachers' unions (who were, of course, motivated by a touching concern for the children); Edgar Faure's decision not to introduce selection at entrance to university in 1968; the withdrawal of the 1973 law on architecture which was adopted by the Senate but never reached the National Assembly; the presidential decision, in September 1976, to scrap the plan to charge motorists in eastern Paris who use the A4 motorway; the burying of the Deniau recommendation for the restructuring of French agriculture in 1976; the decision to prevent the price-cutting activities of a hypermarket chain in 1976 following protests from petrol station managers (yet another breach of the principle of competition which the then Right-wing régime proclaimed as sacrosanct); the withdrawal from parliament in December 1979 of a bill to change the method of electing university presidents because of determined pressure from academics and students; the modification of the 1980 bill on workers' participation in industry after the government bowed to pressure from the employers; the concession made by the Socialist government in 1981 to the employers who argued that social charges were a hindrance to investment. Several studies (Jacques Fommerand on the 1968 reform of higher education and Aline Coutrot on the 1959 secondary schools reform, among others) have pinpointed the pluralistic nature of decision-making.

The list of pluralistic decisions could be extended without difficulty. Yet even a complete list of measures directly influenced by the groups would give only a partial picture of their real and discreet power. First, it is almost impossible accurately to define the *self-imposed parameters of governmental action* – the area in which a government *feels* free or able to act. The political and psychological limitations imposed upon governmental activity are often more easily discerned than defined, but they are none the less real. Any government knows that there are political no-go areas; limits that cannot be transgressed, conventions that cannot be violated, or rights that cannot be trampled upon, and those limits, conventions and rights are established and protected, often unconsciously, by the groups. Indeed, it has been argued that the power of the groups in some areas (health and education, for instance) is such that for a determined government to impose its will it must, first of all, 'destructure' the existing group network, by changing the rules of the game by weakening the entrenched and the resistant and strengthening the sympathetic.

Second, the extent of group influence even before the formal introduction of proposals in confidential and informal discussions in ministerial corridors cannot be accurately assessed: the introduction of the anti-trusts bill in 1976 was preceded, according to the government, by eighteen months of 'intensive negotiations', but it was never made clear with whom or what concessions were made. Finally, the power of certain groups may be manifested in their steady and successful resistance to legislation even after it has been passed. The 'treasures of imagination' released in the academic community during the heady days of May 1968 (*l'imagination au pouvoir* was a description as well as an exhortation) has been skilfully used to undermine some of the more important reforms of Edgar Faure's Higher Education Act: the 'mandarins', imaginative and otherwise, are back in firm control of their university departments.

However plausible as a general explanatory model, the pluralistic model suffers on a number of counts: it presents the state as neutral when in many policy areas it clearly is not; it assumes that interests are generally organized when often they are not or only (as in the case of consumer groups) very badly; it underestimates the extent and significance of extra-institutional activity and even violence; it pôsits the free interplay of groups, when relations are in fact distorted by the presence of certain very powerful groups enjoying hegemonic or monopolistic positions; it underplays the extent to which the state can direct the activity by groups or even impose its will upon them by exploiting their divisions; it ignores the fact that there is frequently no interplay at all between groups and between the groups and the state even in the same policy area.

The untidy reality

The Fifth Republic has been described as crisis-ridden (because it too readily ignores the groups), as neo-corporatist (because it has attempted to insert them and subvert them in a proliferation of functionally organized institutions) and as 'an interest-dominated régime' (in a solemn protest of the chairmen of the parliamentary committees in July 1971, it was claimed that a régime dominated by the parties – the Fourth Republic – was being little by little replaced by a régime dominated by pressure groups). The reality is, of course, infinitely more complex. There is too ready a tendency in discussing state–group relations to think in terms of the confrontation of monolithic blocks, when, in reality, both are highly fragmented and highly divided. It has been shown in earlier chapters that both governmental and administrative institutions are riddled with functional, ideological and personal divisions, and as Ezra Suleiman has aptly noted, 'centralisation mainly concentrates jurisdictions. It does not necessarily concentrate effective power'. Equally, the term 'pressure groups' hides an infinite variety of situations, for they differ in size, structure, strategy, tactics, aims and power.

All the major economic and social interests of France are characterized by extreme fragmentation. The industrial workers who belong to trades unions – and they are a small minority – are distributed in five main peak organizations which, it should be noted, also represent other categories of workers (white collar and managers).

● The CGT (*Confédération Générale du Travail*) is the oldest (it was formed in 1895), best organized and most powerful of the workers' unions. It comprises no fewer than 19,000 separate unions organized in forty-four federations, 910 local unions, ninety-five departmental federations and twenty-two regional federations. It is especially powerful in the steel, building and chemical industries, in the mines, the ports and docks, and the nationalized EDF and GDF (electricity and gas industries) and SNCF (railways). The power of the CGT lies in its size, its professionalism, the work and mobilizing capacity of its activists, its centralized organization. It has a close, complex and often troubled relationship with the Communist Party. Its leadership is dominated by Communists: its general secretary, Henri Krasucki who was 'elected' in 1982, is, like his predecessor, Georges Séguy (1967-82), a prominent member of the PCF hierarchy (despite his rumoured differences with the party). Krasucki is to retire in 1989 and his replacement will be someone who is acceptable to the PCF leadership (the favoured son is the Communist hard-liner Louis Viannet). On all major issues (over Poland, Afghanistan, the presidential elections, to mention three striking examples) the CGT follows the Communist line.

- The second biggest workers' peak organization is the CFDT (*Confédération Française Démocratique du Travail*) the heir to a long Catholic social tradition, though since 1964 it has been officially secular. It has been committed to socialism and to workers' control (*autogestion*) since 1970: although not officially linked with the Socialist Party many of its activists belong to the party. Since 1971 it has been headed by Edmond Maire, a talented if mercurial character. He is scheduled to hand over to Jean Kaspar in 1989. The CFDT is well entrenched in the oil industry, in the textile and electrical construction industry and in the banking and insurance sectors, and its geographical bastions are in the west.

- The third largest workers' peak organization is the CGT-FO (generally referred to as the FO or *Force Ouvrière*) which was founded in 1948 as a breakaway minority from the militantly-communist CGT. It is slightly smaller than the CFDT but is very powerful in the civil service, the banking and insurance sectors. Since 1963 its general secretary has been André Bergeron, tough, avuncular, anti-communist, who believes in constant negotiation with any government, is ready to compromise more readily than the leaders of the other unions and more reluctant to use the strike weapon. Though an active member of the Socialist Party he is a strong believer in keeping political and union activities distinct, and is deeply critical of the CGT for failing to do so.

Bergeron, like the leaders of the two previous bodies, is due to retire in 1989.

- The fourth workers' peak organization is the CFTC (*Confédération Française des Travailleurs Chrétiens*) formed in 1964 as a breakaway minority group from the CFDT, because it disagreed with the latter's policy of secularization. As its name suggests, it retains a strong affective link with the Catholic Church, drawing much of its inspiration from the social doctrines and teaching of the church.
- Finally, there is the CFT (*Confédération Française du Travail*) which totally rejects the use of the strike, denies the concept of class war and sturdily defends the existing capitalist state. Its size is debatable and its political docility when the Right is in office is legendary.

Despite its decline since the mid-1970s, the CGT remains the most representative of the industrial workers' peak organisations: this was made clear even in the 1987 elections to the councils of *Prud'hommes* which regulate industrial and labour disputes (Table 13).

Table 13   Elections to the councils of Prud'hommes 1979, 1982, 1987 (percentage of votes cast)

Peak organization	1979	1982	1987
CGT	42.4	36.8	36.3
FO	17.4	17.7	20.4
CFDT	23.1	23.5	23.1
CFTC	6.9	8.4	8.3
CGC	5.1	9.6	7.4
Others	4.6	3.7	4.3

Among the industrial workers the CGT enjoyed a clear lead: in the twenty-two regions where elections took place, it led in eighteen. Between the various workers' unions there is a long legacy of bitter conflict: the *Force Ouvrière*, because of its readiness to negotiate with the employers, is viewed by its rivals as a tool of the Right; the CGT is feared for its connections with the Communist Party and accused of sclerosis and authoritarianism; the CFDT is criticized for irresponsibility and 'puerile *gauchisme*'. The CFT elicits the ill-disguised contempt and dislike of all other unions. There have been sporadic displays of workers' unity of action, but they are never followed by any long-term strategy: in their reactions to most major issues such as industrial restructuring or flexibility they have demonstrated their profound dissensions.

The fragmentation of the industrial working class is matched by that of other socio-economic groups. The business community is divided between big business which dominates the *Conseil National du Patronat Français* (CNPF) and the owners of the smaller and medium-sized firms whose main spokesman is the *Confédération Générale des Petites et Moyennes Entreprises* (CGPME) which is affiliated to the CNPF. Relations between the two have not always been harmonious. It should be noted, too, that within the CNPF both public and private major firms are represented, and their interests have often diverged. Representatives of the big firms try to co-ordinate some of their actions through the *Association des Grandes Entreprises Françaises faisant appel à l'épargne* (AGREF). The CGPME – the representative of the smaller firms – came increasingly to be challenged by the *Syndicat National des Petites et Moyennes Industries* (SNPMI), led by the fire-brand figure of Gérard Deuil who denounced other industrialists' organizations for their emollient attitude towards the government.

The professional middle classes are no less divided than the workers and businessmen, and all attempts to forge a minimum of united action have failed. Bodies such as the *Comité National de Liaison d'Action des Classes Moyennes* created in 1947, the *Syndicat National des Classes Moyennes*, founded in December 1975, or the *Groupes Initiative et Responsabilité*, formed in March 1977, are very weak because their potential constituents are themselves so badly divided. The doctors are a good example: most belong to the *Confédération des Syndicats Médicaux Français* (which is itself divided between an apolitical majority and a socialist minority), although a few wealthy consultants who initially refused to enter the social security system are members of the *Fédération des Médecins de France*, and a small number of Left-wing general practitioners have joined the *Syndicat de la Médecine Générale*. Even their professional organization, the *Ordre National des Médecins*, a highly conservative and self-perpetuating Paris-dominated elite, is being called into question by a militant Left-wing minority.

The managerial and executive classes are equally divided. Their largest single peak organization is the CFE-CGC (*Confédération Française de l'Encadrement-Confédération Générale des Cadres*), founded in 1944 but renamed in April 1979, and at present headed by the capable and conciliatory Paul Marchelli. In successive elections to the councils of the *Prud'hommes* it has won over a third of the votes of the *cadres*, compared with less than a fifth won by the CFDT (represented by the *Union Confédérale des Ingénieurs et Cadres*), the CGT (represented by the *Union des Cadres et Techniciens*, and the *Force Ouvrière*.

The school teaching profession is particularly well organised by the FEN currently headed by Jacques Pommatau. The FEN (*Fédération de l'Éducation Nationale*), which was founded in 1947-8 (as the successor to the *Fédération Générale de l'Enseignement* which was created in 1928), has a membership of about 500,000, grouped in forty-nine separate unions, which comprise over four-fifths of the teaching and administrative staff in French schools. The FEN provides a wide array of services for its membership, has been accorded wide delegated administrative powers, and enjoys excellent access to decision-makers (especially when the Left is in power). The FEN's biggest component (three-fifths of the total membership) is the SNI (*Syndicat National des Instituteurs*) which derives a great deal of its considerable influence from its ability to speak for nine-tenths of primary school teachers. The SNI organizes its own insurance policy, own para-medical service, its own co-operative system, own banking system and even its own printing house: most of these services are run by primary school teachers on secondment.

The biggest farmers' union is the powerful FNSEA (the *Fédération Nationale des Syndicats d'Exploitants Agricoles*) to which more than half the farmers of France belong. It competes with the FFA (the *Fédération Française de l'Agriculture*, a Right-wing farmers' organization which resulted from a schism within the FNSEA in December 1969) and which claims a very unlikely 60,000 members, and with three Left-wing farmers' unions: the MODEF (*Mouvement pour la Co-ordination et la Défense de l'Exploitation Familiale*) founded in 1959 to resist the threat posed by the capitalist transformation of agriculture in the post-war period (it claims 100,000 members, largely among the small farmers of southern France and many of its leaders are Communist Party members or sympathisers); the CNSTP (*Confédération Nationale des Syndicats des Travailleurs Paysans*), created in June 1981 but which merely brought together existing *Paysans-Travailleurs* groups which used to specialize in commando-type operations and which wins most of its support in the west; and the MONATAR (*Mouvement National des Travailleurs Agricoles et Ruraux*) founded in February 1975 and close to the Socialist Party.

The history of the farmers' unions of the non-communist Left after 1981 has been one of merger and schism: the latest move took place in April 1988 with the creation of the *Confédération Paysanne* which brought together the CNSTP and the *Fédération Nationale des Syndicats Paysans*. Together they had won nearly thirteen per cent of the votes in the elections to the Agricultural Chambers.

What is true of the economic and social groups is equally true of those of a regional or nationalistic nature: as already noted, all these groups are very divided.

The first consequence of the fragmentation of most groups is to prevent them from aggregating group demands: they reflect and also perpetuate the lack of social cohesion and instability. Second, fragmentation weakens the groups in their relations with the government. A determined and clever minister may exploit divisions so as more easily to impose his policy: for instance, important reforms in medical training and teaching and in hospital structures were introduced in the 1970s when the Health Minister succeeded in breaking up a previously united doctors' front. Finally, fragmentation leads to increased verbal militancy, since certain groups are competing for the same clientele. There is a wide gulf between the expectations they raise and the goods they deliver, and the result is disillusion and a further weakening of the groups. The vicious circle closes.

The *intérêts* are not only fragmented. They also differ considerably in their power, influence or what Rod Rhodes has described as 'discretion' (the room for decisional manoeuvre). But that power, influence or discretion is not immutable: it is ever-changing, shifting according to new circumstances. Before returning to the question of state-group relations it is worth considering the resources which contribute to a group's power.

Access to decision-makers

This can be considered as both a consequence and a cause of a group's power. During the Fifth Republic the groups tend to focus much more attention than under the previous régime on the executive with its increased political power and on the administration with its wide regulatory powers: favourite targets are the private staffs of the ministers and the highly compartmentalized and vertically organized divisions of the central administration. The clientelistic and collusive relationship between the FNSEA and the Ministry of Agriculture (studied by John Keeler) between the fishing industry and its monitoring administration (analysed by Michael Shackleton), and between the notarial profession (organized by the wealthy *Conseil Supérieur du Notariat*) and the Ministry of Justice (examined by Ezra Suleiman) provide very good examples. Other major pressure groups, such as the CNPF, are in constant consultation with the executive. However, links with parliament and the parties are maintained: the CGT, for example, has a permanent link with parliament through Communist Deputies and Senators, while the employers finance and inform a *groupe d'études parlementaire* which, in 1979, embraced eighty-six Senators and Deputies of the sympathetic Right. The farmers, the small shopkeepers and ex-servicemen's organizations all have their parliamentary supporters: the farming lobby is well organized at parliamentary level by the *Amicale Parlementaire Agricole et Rurale* which includes members of all parties. Other groups, such as the well-financed *Union Nationale de la Propriété Foncière* (representing the building industry) has many connections with the parties of the Right, and it certainly brought considerable pressure to bear on them during the debates on the Land Tax Act of autumn 1975. The Aranda scandal which broke in 1972-3 also revealed a network of contacts between certain groups, the private offices of certain ministers and Gaullist Deputies.

The strategic importance of the group in the social and economic life of the nation

This is an obvious point: as elsewhere, air traffic controllers, water plant workers, doctors (who indulge in 'shroud-waving' whenever their privileges are threatened) and dockers have greater influence than the generally defenceless university teachers. Yet for a group to optimize its position it is essential for it fully to perceive and exploit its strategic position (which is not always the case) – a position which must also be recognized by the state. This was certainly the case with the steel employers of the *Chambre Syndicale de la Sidérurgie Française* (CSSF) headed by Jacques Ferry during the 1960s and early 1970s: in an expanding market and at a time when it was a government axiom that 'France needs a steel industry' they were able to extract concessions and public finance from the state on a colossal – and scandalous – scale. The whole, sad story is recounted by Jean Padioleau in his well documented account, *Quand la France s'enferre* published in 1981. However, the mounting losses of the industry pushed the state into action: the powerful steel masters of the early 1970s were marginalized by the government in the late 1970s: after 1978 the steel industry was effectively brought under state control.

Its electoral importance

Many groups, such as old-age pensioners, have only one weapon – the vote – at their disposal. However, it can be a potent weapon, and in the feverish electoral atmosphere of the Fifth Republic such groups must be heard and heeded: between 1958 and 1988 France experienced five presidential elections, nine general elections, two European elections, and six referenda (all of which were viewed as votes of confidence in the government of the day), as well as several politically important local elections. The closer the election results (and some have been desperately close) the more sensitive the government is likely to be: even the stern and apparently unbending de Gaulle allowed major tax concessions to the shopkeepers, self-employed craftsmen, farmers and small businessmen (the bulwark of his electoral support) during the 1965 presidential campaign. Social and economic changes which appear adversely to affect the influence of a group may be offset by electoral considerations. Thus, the farmers have dramatically declined in numbers during the Fifth Republic but their votes were increasingly important in keeping the ruling Right-wing coalition in power. In 1962, Pisani, a determined Minister of Agriculture, could push through, with some concessions, an important agricultural bill, but by the mid 1970s the situation had altered: successive laws for the restructuring of French agriculture have been ostentatiously scrapped. This need to reassure groups which, although diminishing in numbers, were vital to the survival of the Right-wing *majorité* helps to explain the passage of the Royer Act of December 1973 which gave shopkeepers an important say in whether supermarkets could be built in their *département*. It was extremely revealing that during the 1981 and 1988 presidential elections all the major candidates made direct and open appeals to specific groups: heady speeches about the national interest were combined with more pedestrian meetings with pressure group representatives.

The backing of public opinion

Although not essential, public support may be useful. The widespread popular support enjoyed by the miners during their strike in 1963 led to a slump in the government's standing (President de Gaulle's popularity ratings in the opinion polls reached their lowest point during his ten years of office) and contributed to the government's humiliating climb-down. Equally, the public support which the students elicited in December 1986 when they were rampaging through the streets of Paris in protest against certain provisions of a Higher Education Bill contributed to the government's withdrawal of the offending proposals. All groups tend to marshall public support by presenting their sectional interests in terms of a wider national interest. In a study of the reform of French secondary education Donegani and Sadoun show that all the interests involved in the process tried to legitimize their corporate egoism by reference to ends such as 'democracy', 'pedagogical efficiency' or the economic exigencies of society. Businessmen who were in favour of raising the school-leaving age (because a better educated school force was more likely to adapt rapidly to changing techniques) presented their arguments in the name of increasing equality of opportunity (an end which mysteriously disappears in their arguments about income distribution). Virtue was once again mobilized in support of utility. The government and the administration are no less reticent in their recourse to higher abstract principles to buttress essentially selfish ends. That conveniently nebulous concept of 'the national interest' is frequently wielded against 'the particularist and egotistical interests', especially when civil servants are quite nakedly defending a departmental prejudice.

The social and political circumstances

There is nothing immutable about the relations between governments and a particular group. A change in the social and political climate may radically affect the standing of certain groups. The decline in anti-clerical sentiments partially undermined the strength of the secular school lobby, and the mounting desire for peace in Algeria from 1959 to 1962 weakened the previously influential North Africa lobby. The growing influence of the environment groups in the 1970s reflected a widespread urge to put an end to the process of making parts of France resemble an industrial suburb of Tokyo. The impact of the prevailing political climate on the fortunes of a group is also illustrated by the case of the *Mouvement de la Paix*, once merely a relay for the policies of the Communist Party during the Cold War. This peace movement went into sharp decline in the 1960s and 1970s, but was given a new lease of life at the beginning of the 1980s during the campaign against the neutron bomb and the installation of American missiles in Europe. The decline in trade union influence after 1981 has not been the result of anti-union legislation (unlike the Thatcher government in the United Kingdom, governments in France have generally left unions alone). It has been, to some extent, self-inflicted as the result of the unions' unpopular politicized strategies of the 1970s, their growing divisions both at national and at plant level, their archaic organisational structures, and their inability and even unwillingness to adapt to changing industrial and technological environments (a fact now recognised by union leaders). But the decline was also a consequence of the economic crisis and rising unemployment which decimated already weak union membership (and hence resources), and made it difficult to mobilize those who remained in employment. It is also attributable to long-term trends in the labour market (more part-time and more temporary non-unionized workers) and to growing management militancy and to new management techniques (often imported from Japan) which involve unions being by-passed at plant level. Moreover declining industrial sectors (like mining) had traditions of collective action while the growing sectors (services, administration, high technology) have not.

Political change or crisis may also affect the influence of certain groups. The change of régime in 1958 led to the decline of the influence of groups such as the ex-servicemen's association and the notorious alcohol lobby (which during the Third and Fourth Republics had successfully defended the inalienable right of every Frenchman to drink himself to an early death), whose main leverage had been in parliament and among the undisciplined but strategically placed Deputies of the Right and centre. The events of May 1968 convinced the government that major concessions, even to the working class, were infinitely preferable to the prevailing chaos: the result was the 'Grenelle agreements' which gave the unions 'a charter of rights' and their members unprecedented wage increases. The election of a Socialist president and the appointment of a Left-wing government in May 1981 changed the status of certain groups: for example, the privileged status of the CNPF, the employers' major body, was weakened by the official recognition of rival associations (such as the SNPMI) as legitimate representatives of the business community. The trade unions (notably the CFDT, the CGT and the FEN) saw their position strengthened, while the Catholic schools lobby which had extracted major financial concessions from Right-wing governments in 1959 (the Debré Law) and 1977 (the Guermeur Law) had to go on to the defensive. Similarly, the Left-wing groups in agriculture (such as the communist-led MODEF and the recently formed *Confédération Nationale des Syndicats-des Travailleurs-Paysans* (CNSTP) – a merging of pro-socialist movements) and in the universities were treated with greater respect. Yet there were limits to the change after 1981: the Left-wing government did not hesitate to impose an austerity programme, a wages freeze and an unpopular industrial restructuring programme on a hostile trades union movement and refused the pleas of the FEN to expand the number of teachers. It also soon recognized that the privileged position of the FNSEA – the Rightist main farmer's union – would have to be maintained, that friendly contact with the CNPF was useful, and that any change in the status of church schools (a veritable hornets' nest) would require delicate and prolonged negotiations with the church lobby. The failure to treat the problem with sufficient delicacy was to mobilize the Catholics whose massive mobilisation was to destroy any attempt to change the *status quo* (see below).

Policy changes decided by the government

A change of governmental policy may suddenly alter the position of certain groups. After the failure of the electricians' strike in 1969, which caused such damage and such bitterness, the Chaban-Delmas government (inspired by Jacques Delors, the social councillor of the prime minister's private office) decided to introduce *une politique contractuelle* – a policy of negotiating contracts to put industrial relations on a more coherent and peaceful footing, based on negotiated and binding agreements for a specified period. To sugar the pill, the *politique contractuelle* was underpinned by a promise to guarantee an automatic 2 per cent annual increase in the standard of living. This introduction of collective bargaining inevitably involved close links with the unions, and if the CGT refused such close collaboration in principle (in later practice it was as supple as a medieval Pope) and if the CFDT was characteristically ambivalent in its attitudes, other unions were less reluctant to play the government's game. Similarly, the influence of the CGPME (the small- and middle-sized business organization) was enhanced in 1976 when the government decided to switch its industrial strategy from one based on the creation of massive industrial complexes by encouraging mergers and take-overs (the Japanese recipe for growth) to one resting on the strength of smaller businesses (the German model). Yet, once again, caution is required: Giscard d'Estaing was known to be favourable to the business community (which supported him in the 1974 elections) but he pushed through several early measures which it found repugnant, and even his neo-liberal prime minister, Barre, who was dedicated to 'improving the position of the firm' and who maintained close touch with François Ceyrac, head of the CNPF, increased the social charges of firms.

The attitude of individual ministers

Jacques Fommerand has shown how a politically sensitive minister such as Edgar Faure, aware of the need to legitimize his controversial reform of higher education in 1968, multiplied his contacts with various university groups. The reformist Edgard Pisani as Minister of Agriculture assiduously courted the modernizing young farmers of the CNJA in order to push through his restructuring of French agriculture in the early 1960s. The minister responsible for higher education during Giscard d'Estaing's presidency, Alice Saunier-Seïté, a person of legendary bad temper , pushed through several reforms of the universities by mobilizing the help of the (largely unrepresentative) Right-wing *Union Nationale inter-Universitaire* and the *Fédération Nationale des Syndicats Autonomes*. Her Socialist successor, Alain Savary, on the other hand, mobilized the support of the Left-wing *Syndicat National de l'Enseignement Supérieur* (known as the SNE-Sup) and the *Syndicat Général de l'Éducation Nationale* (SGEN) in his quest to undo the damage of his predecessor.

The power of countervailing forces

These forces almost always exist: indeed, without them there would be no conflicts and no politics. Employers conflict with employees, farmers with industrialists, environmentalists with the protagonists of growth, the small shopkeepers of the CID-UNATI with the much more discreet but no less effective *Fédération Nationale des Entreprises à Commerces Multiples*, which looks after the interests of the supermarkets, the Catholic *Union Nationale des Associations des Parents d'Élèves de l'Enseignement Libre* (UNAPEL), the vigilant defender of Catholic private schools, with the *Comité National d'Action Laïque* and the *Ligue Française de l'Enseignement*, which are sturdy guardians of the secular state. The conflict between the Catholic and the secular school champions was highlighted between 1982 and 1984 when the Catholics organized massive demonstrations in favour of private education and the secular lobby responded with no less impressive (but less effective) *fêtes de laïcité*.

The degree of representativeness enjoyed by a group

The FNSEA, the farmers' main peak organization which enjoys the support of half the French farmers is in a weaker position than its British counterpart, the National Farmers' Union, to which nine out of ten British farmers belong. But it is in a far stronger position (as the Socialist government of 1981 was quickly to discover) than the French trades union movement which is weakened not only by its ideological fragmentation and its internal political dissensions but also by its total lack of representativity: it has been calculated that less than 15 per cent of the French work-force belong to a trades union (a much lower union density than for most of France's European neighbours), and that in certain industries trades union activity is non-existent. In 1986 the biggest union, the CGT, claimed 1,600,000 members (it had dropped from 6,000,000 in 1946), the CFDT 800,000, the CFTC 400,000, the *Force Ouvrière* 750,000, and the CGC 350,000. However, more realistic assessments put the figures at less than a million for the CGT, 500,000 for the CFDT, 400,000 for the FO, 150,000 for the CFTC and 200,000 for the CGC.

Certain groups such as the FEN (school-teachers union) and the FNSEA (the main farmers' union) enjoy hegemonic or monopolistic situations which strengthen their bargaining positions with the state. Also among the monopolistic groups are the powerful professional orders. Thus, the infamously antediluvian and reactionary *Ordre des Médecins*, created in October 1940 under the Vichy regime and given a monopoly in September 1945 by de Gaulle, may be under increasing pressure from a discontented base (there exists a nationally organized campaign for its dissolution), but it continues rigorously to apply the law by insisting on membership before allowing the practice of the profession; doctors who have refused to pay their annual subscription have been taken to court. Mitterrand's pledge to reform the body came to little. Similarly, no one works in the French docks or on the production side of the Paris press if he is not a member of a union which is affiliated to the Communist-dominated CGT. When the *Parisien Libéré*, a Right-wing newspaper, decided to break the monopoly enjoyed by the *Ouvriers Parisiens du Livre* and transferred its printing presses to outside Paris, the workers responded by occupying the existing building and by occasionally stopping the publication of other Paris newspapers (seven times in 1975, six times in 1976 and twice in 1977). The closed-shop middle-class professions of architects, auctioneers, notaries (the subject of a characteristically perceptive study by Ezra Suleiman) and pharmacists have always been able to defend the indefensible. Yet a monopolistic or hegemonic position does not ensure constant success: the FNSEA has not halted the rapid decline in the agricultural population, and it was unsuccessful in its attempt to block the entry of Spain, Portugal and Greece into the European Community; the violent opposition of the FEN and the SNI did not prevent state subsidies to church schools; the well-organized resistance of the *Ordre des Médecins* (backed by the *Confédération des Syndicats Médicaux*) did nothing to restrain doctors from joining the state-run health service (by 1978 98 per cent of all doctors belonged to it) and it had to make unwelcome concessions on the setting of fees after 1981; the CNPF, which represents almost all French employers, could not stop the nationalization programme of the Socialist government in 1981; the notaries resisted the reforms of the Left after 1981 but eventually had to accept a compromise in 1986.

The group's internal cohesion

The workers' peak organizations are divided not only between themselves but within each other. All are organized on a functional and a geographical basis (the CGT comprises 19,000 separate unions, the CFDT 3,500, the FO 8–9,000 and the CFTC 1,500), and all contain militant minorities politically opposed to the leadership. The CGT is dominated by the Communist Party, but like the party is increasingly divided (some major figures are *rénovateurs* and backed Juquin and not Lajoinie, the official PCF candidate, in the 1988 presidential elections, and some of them have advocated a loosening of the links with the party). The CGT also harbours an active and recalcitrant socialist minority. The *Force Ouvrière* has many Socialist Party sympathizers but, proof of its political pluralism, also includes a small but influential Trotskyist element. The CFDT is particularly badly divided: there are debates of peculiarly theological intensity between the supporters of the Socialist Party, those of the more Left-wing PSU and those of *Ligue Communiste Révolutionnaire* and *Lutte Ouvrière* (both Trotskyist organizations). There are disputes between the national leadership and many of the local organizations, who demand disciplined action but crave autonomy, and there is a permanent battle between those who see the union as a political force espousing and propagating a global view of society and those who claim the union is an economic movement dedicated exclusively to the material well-being of its members. Like the CGT and the FO, the CFDT tries, generally unsuccessfully, to resolve the conflicts between its distinctive and conflicting ideological traditions: reformism, Marxism, anarcho-syndicalism and Christian socialism. Within the FEN, there are conflicts of interest and politics between the SNI (which is close to the Socialists) and the important union of secondary school teachers of the SNES (which is close to the Communists). The FEN has also to contend with the rivalry of teachers from the private schools and rival unions which are significant in secondary and higher education. These conflicts and rivalries impair the effectiveness of the FEN. John Ambler has argued that its influence may be used to delay rather than shape legislation: it is reactive rather than active in educational policy-making.

The CFE-CGC also suffers from its lack of cohesiveness. It is dominated by 'powerful barons' who represent the different elements of the white-collar and managerial classes. The battles in the CGC, as it was then known, in 1978 were such that they almost destroyed the confederation.

Most businessmen are grouped in the peak organization CNPF (*Conseil National du Patronat Français*), but it, too, is badly divided, since it embraces highly disparate groups. It tends to be dominated by the very big industries organized in the so-called AGREF (or *Association des grandes entreprises françaises faisant appel à l'épargne*) even though the nationalization measures of 1981-2 weakened their position. But with its 800 separate unions, organized both horizontally (on a professional basis) and vertically (on a geographical basis), its present leader, François Périgot (who was elected in 1986), has difficulty in holding its divergent interests together. The CNPF élite is divided into 'clans' whose bitter rivalries surfaced in the battles for the leadership in 1981 and 1986. Differences centre on personalities, on the relationship to be constructed with the government of the day, and on the general political and economic strategy to be pursued: within the CNPF there are 'statists', neo-liberals and paternalistic social Catholics. Among its affiliated members is the CGPME (*Confédération Générale des Petites et Moyennes Entreprises*) which was founded in 1936 to protect the interests of the small businessman and which champions the small man against big business, against multi-national companies, money-grabbing governments and the technocrats of Paris. Its long-standing leader (he was president from November 1944 to October 1978) Léon Gingembre, was a flamboyant figure with a gift for colourful threats uttered in even more colourful language. He was replaced in October 1978 by the more discreet René Bernasconi. The CGPME has been affiliated to the CNPF since 1954. At the other extreme is the CJP (*Centre des Jeunes Patrons*), which has strong Catholic sympathies and which has become the spokesman of the young, more dynamic and more progressive business elements.

The main peak organization of the farmers – the FNSEA – has been described as 'a battleground of feudal warlords', and it has certainly had problems in keeping together the wealthy farmers of the north and the marginal farmers of the centre and the south, the various specialist produce groups, the reactionary elements and the more enlightened young farmers belonging to the affiliated CNJA: by the late 1980s there was a serious risk of implosion, such were the internal tensions.

The group's financial resources and technical expertise

Money is vital to employ an efficient full-time staff and organize adequate research facilities. Business, banking and insurance groups score heavily in this respect. Part of the weakness of the French trades unions may be attributed to their weak financial position (there are twice as many full-time trades union officials in Denmark even though the work-force is ten times smaller). According to a study of the *Centre d'observation sociale*, members provide only about ten per cent of the unions' finances, and all are heavily dependent on public subsidies. Their inadequate finances also mean that the CGT has no strike fund at all while those of the FO and CFDT are very small. Expertise and specialized knowledge are useful bartering counters, for politicians and officials need both: the success of the highly expert and specialized farmers' groups and the pharmaceutical lobby rests on the permanent dialogue that they enjoy with the government and specialized sponsor divisions in the ministries which require their expertise. Yet financial and technical resources, although useful, constitute no guarantee of success. The UIMM (*Union des Industries Métallurgiques et Minières*), which employs 1000 people (200 at management level) and enjoys great financial backing was helpless to prevent a *de facto* nationalization of the steel industry by the Right-wing Barre government, and its official nationalization by the Left-wing Mauroy government in 1981. Similarly, the immensely wealthy *Union Nationale de la Propriété Immobilière* and *Fédération Nationale des Agents Immobiliers* representing the building industry and house agents, had to accept a new Tenants Rights Act in 1982 which they viewed as 'an intolerable revolution'.

Its ability to mobilize its members and its general level of combativity

The CNPF, the employers' peak organization, claims to represent 800,000 firms, but its control over these firms is largely fictional. At the other extreme, the *comité d'action viticole* of the Aude can quickly mobilize 1000 men and count on the unflinching support of all the wine-growers of the area. Other effective groups in this respect include the primary school teachers' union (the SNI), and the Communist-dominated dockers' union and typographical union, which are affiliated to the CGT and which enjoy the privilege of a closed shop, and the FNSEA whose disgruntled farmers need little prodding. Some apparently docile and ill-organized groups may be mobilized to combat a specific policy the Catholic school lobby in 1982-4 furnishes a particularly good example. Incensed by proposed legislation aimed at integrating the private (mainly Catholic) schools more closely into the state system, it organized a series of massive protest demonstrations, culminating in one in Paris which assembled over a million people. The government was forced to withdraw the offending bill.

The state and the pressure groups: some concluding remarks

The basic *leitmotiv* which runs through the preceding analysis is that it is misleading to speak of state–group relations and more accurate to think in terms of relations between a particular public decision-maker and a specific group. There is, in truth, an infinite and bewildering variety of situations. The influential Rueff-Armand Report made clear that some groups had been totally 'domesticated' and were essentially agents of the administration. Others, such as the FNSEA (the farmers' union), totally colonize and dominate their sponsor ministry or division within the ministry: some organs of state have been transformed into 'institutionalized pressure groups' (Henry Ehrmann). This so-called clientele relationship is most likely to be found in highly specialized and vertically organized divisions of the central bureaucracies. The practice is not necessarily corrupt: France is not a 'banana republic'. Money rarely exchanges hands and its defenders claim that such practices greatly facilitated industrial concentration – one of the Fifth Republic's early and obsessive priorities. Between complete domination and total subservience there is a wide variety of other situations. The appropriate organs of state may adopt other attitudes.

Entering into collusion with certain groups This appears to be the case in the building industry, where certain powerfully entrenched groups which form privileged clubs benefit from a disproportionate share of state contracts, even though free competition is proclaimed as a cardinal virtue of the régime. In some cases, collusion has even been institutionalized: in the *Association Professionnelle des Banques* representatives of the state banks, which dominated the market, co-existed with those of the private banks and credit houses, and on occasions came to collective decisions. Such collusion, as Ezra Suleiman rightly argued, was unfair (because it affected the privileged few) and was dangerous because it blurred the vital distinction between public and private interest and could lead to 'the imperceptible dilution of the public interest'. The nationalization of the private banks in 1981 put an end to the practice.

Genuinely collaborating to form a symbiotic relationship Both sides retain their autonomy, independence and even aggressiveness: the cases of the agricultural, fishing and certain professional sectors have been noted above.

Ezra Suleiman underlines three reasons for the administration's willingness to collaborate with the groups:

● It facilitates the formulation and implementation of policies.
● It provides a government with information.
● It enables a government to explain its decisions and to foresee opposition.

A good example of a group displaying public disgruntlement and private collusion is provided by the *Syndicat National de l'Enseignement Secondaire*: between the top levels of the union and the minister there is virtually no contact, but a network of committees links the administrations of both. Perhaps the best example of this sort of relationship is that which exists between certain divisions of the Education Ministry and the SNI, the primary school teachers' union. Founded in 1920, the SNI has managed to create a powerful organization at national, departmental and local level which embraces nine out of every ten primary school teachers. It clearly articulates the aspirations and disgruntlement of the basc, and a strike call will always mobilize at least 70 per cent of the members: in the May 1977 general strike 82.5 per cent of the primary school teachers went on strike. The SNI is in permanent negotiation with its sponsor ministry and has managed to wrest concessions concerning the size of classes, sabbatical leave, the length of school holidays and the reduction in working hours. It has frequently been accused of practising 'corridor politics' and of unholy connivance with officialdom.

Discriminating for political reasons, in favour of some groups and against others Successive governments have used their resources of access and subsidies to accomplish this. The Gaullists tried unsuccessfully to replace the powerful but hostile Association of French Mayors by an organization of their own creation. During the 1960s and 1970s the CFT was frequently given as much weight and as many subsidies as the CGT, which was twenty times bigger. But the CFT, unlike the CGT, was against strikes, a sturdy defender of the existing economic order, and abhorred class war. The subsidies given to the students' unions bore little relationship to their strength but rather to their political docility. The Socialists after 1981 tried, for political reasons, to restructure the relationship between the state and certain groups but was not particularly successful in doing so (see above). However, it was more successful in channeling public subsidies to politically sympathetic trade union and farmers groups. A group may initially be treated with hostility, but if it is persistent and seems to be mobilizing public support an attempt may be made to absorb it into an institutional framework with the aim of more readily controlling it. This was clearly the case with the CELIB, a Breton regionalist group which made itself an active nuisance in the 1960s.

Viewing the groups as bodies simply to be resisted Until recently, for example, governments of the Fifth Republic viewed the small and middle businessmen's organizations, the CGPME, in the same way as John Stuart Mill considered the House of Lords: 'an irritating type of minor nuisance'. Its demands were invariably considered unreasonable and reactionary and it was generally pacified by fiscal advantages of an obscure and complicated nature. Consultation was largely perfunctory. Similarly, Prime Minister Barre entertained a hostile view of many groups which he treated with ill-disguised contempt, since they had the temerity to question his handling of the economy.

Refusing all collaboration with certain groups This is invariably true with the illegal terrorist groups but also with the more moderate nationalist groups in Brittany and Corsica. But other groups have also been frozen out. The unruly students' union UNEF was deprived of all contact with government departments from 1960 to 1963 by short-sighted and vindictive governments. Annoyed by the students' noisy opposition to the war in Algeria, the Government stopped all subsidies, refused to meet its delegations and even helped to establish and then subsidize a rival union--the *Fédération Nationale des Étudiants de France* (FNEF). Later, between 1976 and 1981, the students' union UNEF (ex-Renouveau), which was dominated by the Communists, never once met the minister, who preferred the infinitely more pliable *Collective des Étudiants Libéraux de France* (CELF) which was of Giscardian persuasion. Before 1981 the Ministry of Agriculture met representatives of the FNSEA (the farmers' main peak organization) every week, but it always refused to recognize agricultural unions such as MODEF, *Paysans-Travailleurs* and the *Mouvement des Travailleurs Agricoles* which are of Communist or Socialist persuasion. This situation was changed in 1981 with the appointment of a Left-wing minister.

Adopting an attitude of apprehensive and embarrassed tolera- tion or appeasement The tax evasion of certain groups such as small businessmen, shopkeepers, hotel-owners and farmers is denounced every year by the Minister of Finance but tolerated by successive governments who have a wary eye on the electoral consequences of over-zealous tax-collecting. In the wine-growing areas of the south where there was a growing tide of violence in 1975 and 1976, the government was unprepared to act against the action committees for fear of inflaming passions even further. Angry farmers who indulge in illegal violence are rarely brought to justice. It took the government more than two years to put an end to the flagrant illegality of the typographers of the *Parisien Libéré* who were occupying the newspaper's Paris offices, and it finally did so by financing the climb-down of the newspaper's owners.

It should be noted that there are groups which eschew all contact with the organs of state and which exploit the latter's tolerance, laxity or ignorance. The massive property speculation in Paris and on the Côte d'Azur was accomplished by both rule-bending and, in some cases, rule-breaking. Other groups profit from the inefficiency of the state machine in the control of their activities: widespread price-fixing, recognized in the official reports of the economic and financial studies service of the Finance Ministry, goes largely unchecked. And the strengthening (in 1976) of the *Commission de la Concurrence* (and later of its successor, the *Conseil de la Concurrence*) which is supposed to look into abusive monopolies, was testimony to the inadequacy of the previous control. Finally, there are groups which exploit the divisions of the state apparatus: Cohen and Bauer, in their analysis of the relationship between the state and the major firms, have shown how the latter, with their multiple points of access, their expertise and their stable management, are able skilfully to exploit those divisions.

In conclusion, the relationship between the different organs of official decision-making and the various groups, when they exist (and they may not, out of choice or incapacity), ranges from domination to subservience, from collusion and complicity to baleful and begrudged recognition and even outright hostility. The agents of the state and the groups have resources at their disposal, but how those resources are employed and how effective they are depends on a variety of factors which have been explored in this chapter. To appreciate fully the complex and shifting nature of the relationship between the state and the groups requires an intellectual eclecticism and tolerance: all the various models outlined at the beginning of this chapter contribute to our understanding, and it is clear that no general theory suffices. Perhaps the only statement that can safely be made is that the relationship between the fragmented state and the no less fragmented groups during the Fifth Republic is like the rest of government – infinitely complex, intrinsically untidy and constantly changing.

12 Provincial pressures in a Jacobin state

Economically, intellectually and culturally France is dominated by its capital. The Paris region, which covers only 2 per cent of the national territory, houses 20 per cent of the nation's population, 35 per cent of its business headquarters, 60 per cent of its research scientists, and almost all its actors and its few decent musicians. It is also frequently contended that Paris completely dominates the political life of the country, crushing the provinces under the weight of its *diktats* and whims. Traditionally, the capital was depicted as the malevolent centre of revolution which, in 1789, 1814-15, 1830, 1848 and 1871, disturbed the contented and peace-loving provincials. It was also portrayed as the diabolic purveyor of those modish doctrines and those timeless temptations which were designed to undermine the austere virtues of provincial life, and as a harlot whose mindless frivolity had brought the country at least once (in 1870) to the brink of humiliating disaster: the church of the Sacré-Coeur in Paris was the provincials' act of repentance (though some claim vengeance) for the impiety of the capital. Paris was, in short, a politically turbulent Babylon.

But the Jacobins who fashioned the First Republic and who bequeathed later régimes with most of their institutions and many of their attitudes did not see the capital in such a light. They saw it as an island of culture, a city of enlightenment, a torch bearer of progress assailed by oafish – and reactionary – rural clods, the ignorant troops of the church and the château. Like the monarchs of the *ancien régime* they imposed centralization as their means of strengthening the régime against internal opponents, but also against external enemies. Napoleon perfected and future régimes consolidated the centralizing work of the Jacobins. Each was uneasily aware not only of its own fragility but also of the very precariousness of the French national fabric. France is a country of great geographical and cultural diversity and was created by bringing together (with the persuasion of the axe and the sword) peoples as distinct as the Basques and the Bretons, the Béarnais and the Burgundians, the Alsatians and the Auvergnats, the Normans and the Provençals. Parts of France such as Nice and Savoy are recent acquisitions (they were annexed in 1860), and Alsace has twice this century (1918 and 1945) been taken back from the Germans. Autonomous sentiments have always been regarded with obsessive suspicion and crass insensitivity because it was felt that they could lead to the temptation of secession if allowed to flourish. Centralization was also the instinctive reaction of governments to successive wars, invasion and occupation when national boundaries were violated: 1814-15, 1870-1, 1914-18 and 1940-45.

Centralization tendencies have been accentuated during the twentieth century. For latter-day Jacobins such as Michel Debré, the first prime minister of the Fifth Republic, centralized state authority was essential to combat not only the potential dissidence in the provinces but also powerful "professional feudalities", those major groups who threatened the interest of the state in their pursuit of selfish particularist interests. Centralization was also the inevitable result of the need to impose minimum standards in electorally sensitive areas such as education, housing and health: in other words, it was a response to the egalitarian aspirations of the French. Finally, centralization of a political and administrative nature was both a cause and a consequence of the modernization of industrial and financial structures and the revolution in communications and the media.

As the result of historical, cultural, social and economic pressures, decision-making became increasingly concentrated in Paris, and strong, unified and centralized authority became the basis of "the one and indivisible republic". It was argued in the 1960s and 1970s, especially in opposition circles, that France had become excessively centralized: Paris, it was contended, decided everything and imposed a rigid uniformity upon the unhappy and the unwilling provinces. It was, therefore, scarcely surprising that among the top priorities of the Socialists (who were well entrenched at local level but rarely in office at national level), when they came to power in 1981, was to implement a radical programme of decentralization; indeed, the programme was described as the *"affaire du septennat"*.

The Socialist Reform Programme 1981–1986

With the blessing of President Mitterrand and the backing of Prime Minister Mauroy, the Minister of the Interior, Gaston Defferre, embarked upon a decentralization process which was designed to reverse the centuries-old process of centralization, instil new life into the French provinces and help to forge the "new citizenship" which was referred to in the Socialist prime minister's first speech to the National Assembly. The first major step in the process was the March 1982 Act which affected all levels of local government and most of the actors involved. Between 1982 and 1986 (when the Left lost office) 48 laws were passed, 269 decrees adopted, and innumerable circulars distributed in the push to implement the decentralization programme.

Several major strands may be discerned in this programme. First, the government increased the political power of local elected officials by transferring executive responsibility to them in the regions and the *départements*. This involved a demotion of the prefects who also saw their administrative and financial supervisory powers weakened. Second, new powers were granted to the local authorities: the communes received increased powers in urban planning (in towns of over 10,000 inhabitants mayors were authorized to issue building permits); the powers of the *département* were enhanced in areas such as health, social welfare, education, road maintenance and school bus transport; the regions were given new powers in planning, land-use planning, economic intervention (helping firms in difficulty) and professional training. The big towns and *départements* were disproportionately favoured by the reforms, while the small communes received essentially nothing. The third major strand was a strengthening of the elective principle. Not only was the power of elected officials increased, but the regional councils were henceforth to be elected by the people. Fourth, there was a reinforcement of the democratic principle as a result of the change in the electoral system for the main towns. Prior to the law of 19 November 1982, in the towns of over 30,000 inhabitants winning lists took all the seats in the council. The new law ensured that in towns of over 3,500 inhabitants the majoritarian principle would be preserved but that minority lists would win some representation. At the first ballot, if a list wins more than half the votes it receives half the seats on the council, and the remainder are distributed proportionately among those lists (including the winning one) which win more than five per cent of the votes. If no list wins half the votes there is a second ballot, but lists which win fewer than 10 per cent of the first ballot votes are automatically eliminated. At the second ballot the list with the most votes is accorded half the seats, and the remainder are distributed on a proportional basis to the lists which have stood (including the winning list). This system ensures the emergence of a majority for the winning list and representation for the minority lists. Fifth, local finances were somewhat rationalized, some specific grants were transformed into block grants, and new financial resources were made available to the localities. Sixth, the law of 24 January 1984 constituted a local public civil service. And, finally, certain tasks previously carried out in Paris were transferred to the local field services of the state. It will be several years before the final shape of centre–local relations is discernible, and it is, therefore, premature to draw up a balance sheet of the achievements (or damage) of the Socialist government. Yet a number of preliminary remarks should be made:

● The Socialists showed great determination and not a little courage in their decentralization programme which was pursued despite pressing priorities elsewhere, a busy parliamentary agenda and, more especially, Right-wing victories at local level throughout the period: the Right made sweeping gains in town elections in 1983, and tightened their grip on the departmental councils in the elections of 1983 and 1985 (after which they took control of 69 of 96 *départements*). In the short run at least, the Left was handing over increased power to the Right.

● The Socialists' programme, though radical, was in some respects the culminating point of a long, piecemeal and often begrudged process of reform undertaken by their Right-wing predecessors, and in other respects, it represents the legalization of practices merely tolerated previously.

● The transfer of powers, personnel and archives to local authorities took place with surprising ease, and by 1988 the new services were installed (often in costly new buildings).

● Some of the basic elements (such as financial and technical resources) which determine the relationship between Paris and the periphery and the actors involved in that relationship remain unaffected by changes in the law.

● Some major problems were not tackled. These include the problem of policy co-ordination and simplification. No attempt was made to apportion the powers of the various local authorities in any overall or rational way: the existing powers of each were left intact and new ones were simply added: duplication and overlapping competences will continue to bedevil local government. Nor was there any restructuring of local government boundaries. France will continue to live with its 36,000 communes, 96 *départements* and 22 regions – one of the most fragmented systems of local government in western Europe. The government refused, too, to reform the internal decision-making structures of the local authorities: the power of local potentates – "local presidentialism" – remains intact.

● It is not possible that all the aims of the reform programme can be met, since some are inherently contradictory.

● Centralizing pressures will remain and perhaps may even increase if the economic recession which the Socialists inherited persists.

The long-term implications of the programme are difficult to predict. There is some evidence to suggest that the decentralization measures have created their own dynamic: if centralization provoked further centralization, decentralization may trigger off demands for increased decentralization. Before illustrating or elaborating upon these points it is worth taking a brief look at the principal institutions and the actors at local level.

The institutions and the actors

Local government in France is organized at three levels: regional, departmental and communal. In metropolitan France there are twenty-two regions, ninety-six *départements* (divided into 320 *arrondissements* and 3530 *cantons*) and 36,034 communes. The regions are a creation of the Fifth Republic (they were envisaged by an *ordonnance* of January 1959, created in June 1960 and given their present shape in March 1964, July 1972 and March 1982), while the *départements* were created in December 1789. The communes date from 1789 but are based on the parishes of the *ancien régime*. The size of the various territorial units varies widely: in 1985 a fifth (8,900,000) of the French population lived in the 36 towns with over 100,000 inhabitants and a half (27,800,000) in the 801 communes with more than 10,000 inhabitants, while 25 per cent lived in the 32,000 with fewer than 2,000 inhabitants. In 1988, 22 *départements* had a larger population than the Limousin region while 14 regions had a smaller population than the *département* of the Nord. Inevitably, there is a wide diversity of resources between the types of territorial unit and within each type. Thus, in 1984 Paris had a budget of 15 billion francs and employed over 40,000 agents while the vast majority of communes had derisory budgets and employed a part-time secretary. The budgets of the regions and *départements* vary enormously. The impact of any decentralization measures must, therefore, be assessed in the light of the ability of the territorial unit fully to exploit them. Yet, despite this enormous diversity, each type of territorial unit – region, *département* and commune – has the same internal structure and, from a juridical point of view, enjoys the same powers. The uniform structures and juridical powers are imposed upon widely divergent agents.

In principle, the relationship between the three types of local authorities is not a hierarchical one: it is supposed to be based on complementarity. In practice, however, as the result of overlapping jurisdictions (inevitable in all policy-making), there is some duplication, competition and even rivalry. The departmental and communal councils are deeply suspicious of any attempt on the part of the regions to co-ordinate their activities (the case too, in Italy and Spain). The departmental councils are very protective about their influence in the rural areas and the important mayors highly defensive about their power within their own towns.

Of the three types of local authority, the most dominant in decision-making terms is the commune and the weakest is the region. Of the 1,100,000 local agents in 1985, 765,000 were employed by the communes. A breakdown of the overall local budget is revealing (see Table 14).

Table 14   Local budgets 1984 (in billion francs)

Resources	Communes	*Départements*	Regions	Total
Taxes	102.7	50.6	8.5	161.8
Grants	101.2	49.4	2.8	153.4
Loans	39.7	11.6	3.2	54.5
Other	42.8	5.4	0.7	48.9
Total	286.4	117	15.2	418.6
Expenses				
Current	181.1	86.3	5.5	272.9
Investment	100.4	28.2	9.7	138.3
(including interest on loans)	(15.5)	(4.7)	(0.4)	(20.6)
Total	281.5	114.5	15.2	411.2

It is worth pointing out, however, that regional budgets since 1981 have been rising more sharply than those of the *départements* and communes: between 1980 and 1984 they rose by a startling 157 per cent – a situation which was denounced by Jacobins in Paris and tax-payers in the regions themselves.

Decision-making takes place at all three levels, and the local decision-makers belong essentially to four categories of institution: the representative assemblies; the prefectoral administration; the provincial field services of the Paris ministries; and the professional associations and the local pressure groups.

The representative assemblies

At all three levels of local government may be found representative assemblies. At the regional level there are two assemblies; the regional council which ranges in size from 41 to 197 and which, since 1986, has been directly elected (on a departmental list and modified proportional representation system), and the economic and social committee, which is indirectly elected by representatives of the various professional associations and pressure groups within the region. The powers of both assemblies are defined in the 1972 and 1982 Acts and the implementing decrees which followed. At the departmental level there is the departmental council (*conseil général*) composed of members who each represent a canton. The departmental councils range in size from seventeen (Lozère) to 109 (Paris). Like members of the regional councils, departmental councillors are directly elected, with elections taking place every three years when half the councillors are elected: a councillor's term of office is thus six years. The powers of the departmental councils are outlined in the 1884 Act and were extended by the Defferre Act of March 1982. Finally, at the level of the commune is the town or village council (*conseil municipal*), which is directly elected every six years, which elects a mayor, and which exercises the powers defined in the 1871, 1884 and 1982 Acts.

Until March 1982 (or more precisely until March 1986 when they were directly elected and thus rendered operative the 1982 Act) the twenty-two regions were merely organs "for the concerted action of the constituent *départements*" (President Pompidou) with the task of contributing to regional development through studies, proposals or financial participation in state public investment projects, or even, to a limited extent, by carrying out their own projects. The executive officer of the region was the regional prefect who was assisted by two assemblies: the regional council and the economic and social committee. The region did not enjoy the same legal status as the *département* or the commune. The task of the regional council was to vote the budget of the region, and it could vote resolutions within its decision-making competence which were enforceable *per se* by the regional prefect. It also debated and was consulted about the regional options of the national five year plan and about the allocation of state grants for public investment of a local nature. The role of the economic and social committee was largely consultative. As a result of the 1982 Act the powers of the region were enhanced. Not only is the regional council now directly elected (thus endowing it with a new sense of legitimacy), but its legal status is now the same as the other two levels of local government; its chairperson has replaced the state-appointed regional prefect as the chief executive officer of the region and has at his or her disposal a number of services (previously directed by the prefect). The economic and financial powers of the region have also been extended. The economic and social committee remains indirectly elected, although it has been democratized somewhat by the inclusion of more workers' representatives. Its role remains consultative.

The departmental council meets for a maximum of only six weeks a year, although it has a small permanent standing committee called the departmental commission. Until March 1982 its executive head was the departmental prefect who prepared its agenda, its timetable and its budget. It met twice a year to discuss and vote the departmental budget, which it did, often after ritualistic grumbling and symbolic resistance. The council was essentially a servicing agency for the state (for matters such as roads, schools, and certain welfare services), and it also enjoyed a limited initiative and discretion in areas not specifically precluded by the law. At this level, too, the Socialists introduced fairly radical reforms: prefectoral *a priori* supervision (*tutelle*) was abolished and replaced by a rather elaborate system of *a posteriori* control (see below); the chairperson of the departmental council (who is elected by the councillors from their midst) has replaced the prefect as the chief executive officer of the *département*, and it is the chairperson who now has the control of departmental personnel involved in implementing the decisions of the departmental council (they have been transferred from the state); the competence of the departmental council has been extended in the economic and financial domain. Together with the big towns, the *département* was the principal beneficiary of the Defferre reforms.

In each of the 36,000 French communes there is a local council which has two basic tasks that were unaffected by the Defferre Act of 1982. The first is to implement the duties assigned to it by the state: it is a servicing agency incurring obligatory expenses. Its second task is to exercise its competence in areas which are not specifically forbidden by law. It is obliged to present a balanced budget. The 1982 Act officially abolished prefectoral *tutelle* (i.e. an *a priori* supervision and control) and replaced it by a system of *a posteriori* control: the prefect has the right to contest an illegal act or an unbalanced budget before bodies which have been specially created for that purpose. The economic role of the communes has been extended, although conditions governing the nature of such economic interventionism are laid down in the 1982 Act. In most cases the local council merely gives its official blessing to decisions made by the mayor it has elected. Indeed, it is no great exaggeration to claim that the task of the 465,000 local councillors of France is to elect the 36,000 mayors. Unlike his British counterpart, the French mayor is an important and influential personality. Almost all mayors remain in office for at least six years, and the great majority are re-elected after their first term of office. The mayor has two main official roles. First, he is the *representative of the state in the commune*; as such he promulgates and ensures the implementation of laws, regulations, circulars and instructions emanating from Paris. He is also the official registrar of births, deaths and marriages, and he is responsible for drawing up the electoral list and for compiling official statistics (such as the census figures) for the state. Second, he is the *executive officer of the local council*; in that capacity he represents the commune in judicial proceedings, is the head of all communal staff, implements the decisions of the council, supervises its accounting and manages its revenues. He is officially responsible for the order, safety, security and sanitation of the commune. In the big towns, the mayor has a third role: that of entrepreneur. He attempts to attract industry, services and tourists to his town and spends a great deal of his time in Paris in the corridors of the ministries in an attempt to extract subsidies to improve the town's infrastructure. In practice, the mayor is the gentle autocrat of the commune, its principal arbitration officer, its father confessor and the guardian of its interests. Endowed with undeniable prestige, *Monsieur le maire* readily feigns a plausible political agnosticism, and in his quest for communal consensus constantly invokes the "general interest" of the commune. He is judged largely by his ability to keep peace in the commune, ensuring that the norms that govern communal behaviour are not transgressed, and also by his capacity to intervene for his citizens with the prefectoral authorities, or the state's local field services.

The prefectoral authorities

The prefectoral corps is composed of regional prefects, departmental prefects and sub-prefects (one in each *arrondissement*). The initial intention of the Socialist reformers was to keep the prefectoral corps as a professional association but to change the nomenclature at local level to *Commissaire de la Republique* (which had a revolutionary ring to the historically minded Left). However, this provision of the 1982 Act was abolished by the Right in 1986: to everyone's relief, *Monsieur le préfet* is once again *Monsieur le préfet*.

The regional prefect

The regional prefect is a recent creation, dating only from 1959. His headquarters is in the principal town of the main *département* of the region, and in spite of his heavy responsibilities he also remains the prefect of that *département*. His powers were defined in measures enacted in June 1960, March 1964, July 1972 and March 1982. His basic task is to impart stricter unity and greater cohesion to administrative activity, particularly in the area of economic planning. To that end, he must, in practice, co-ordinate and direct the work of the departmental prefects in regional development planning. He is helped by a regional mission (*mission régionale*), a kind of brains trust of young civil servants which advises him and executes his decisions, and a regional administrative conference (known as the CAR) which brings together every two or three months the departmental prefects of the region, members of the mission, the regional representative of the Ministry of Finance and appropriate members of the field services of the Paris ministries. Although he has lost his role as the chief executive officer of the region he may, with the agreement of the chairman of the regional council or at the request of the prime minister, address the regional council.

In principle, the regional prefect (together with elected officials) has to guide and direct local investment policies in a co-ordinated and rational regional manner. In practice, he has to become one of the main agents for articulating departmental grievances and for transmitting to Paris an economic package which bears all the marks of traditional incrementalism. The position and authority of the regional prefects were much contested in the early years but they have now fully established their place in the local decision-making structure.

The departmental prefect

In each of the ninety-six *départements* of France there is a prefect who is helped by a small number of sub-prefects (one in each *arrondissement*). The prefect is an essentially Napoleonic creation (but he can trace his ancestry to the *intendant* of the *ancien régime*) and his official roles have not changed since then.

He is the representative of the state in the département. He is the personification of state authority, the living embodiment of the one and indivisible Republic. He has an official uniform, an official residence in the main town of the *département*, the *Hôtel de la préfecture*, normally the best *hôtel* in the *département* and certainly the most sumptuous, an official car and sometimes princely living expenses. He receives all visiting dignitaries and presides over all important ceremonies, and represents the state in its dealings with the local authorities.

He is the representative of the government in the département, with the task of supervising and co-ordinating the work of the field services of the Paris ministries (with the exception of some parts of the work of Defence, Justice, Education and Labour, which escape his official jurisdiction) and he ensures that laws and governmental directives are implemented. His powers as the "departmental overlord" were considerably augmented by reforms announced in March 1964, and in March 1982.

The prefect is the main agent of the Ministry of the Interior in the département, and, as such, is responsible for taking action against local authorities guilty of illegality or financial abuses. As the agent of the Ministry of the Interior he directly supervises all the field services of the ministry responsible for the maintenance of law and order. He has the right to ban a film, a demonstration or a procession if he feels it is likely to be prejudicial to public order. Finally, the prefect organizes local elections, and is still considered to be the main electoral agent of the Minister of the Interior, although there is no doubt that this aspect of his work has steadily declined. He still gives advice, information and warnings to pro-governmental candidates but he rarely intervenes overtly in election campaigns. He realizes the inefficacy of such intervention, accepts that after the election he will have to live with politicians from all the parties, and is aware that if the opposition wins the elections his chances of survival are negligible.

Until March 1982 the prefect was the chief officer of the departmental council: he prepared the timetable, the agenda and the budget of the *département*, and implemented the measures decided by the council. Although he has now lost this role to the chairman of the council he retains the right (with the latter's permission or at the request of the prime minister) to address the council. Furthermore, his co-operation is essential if the departmental chairperson is to carry out his new role efficiently. It is also highly revealing that several local authorities have recruited ex-prefects to head their administrative services.

The local field services

Although the March 1982 Act involved the transfer of some state officials to the regional and departmental level most retained their links with state-organized professional associations or unions (one of the major tasks of the reformers will, incidentally, be fully to "localize" officials who previously belonged to the central state machinery). Moreover, the central state remains powerfully organized at local level. Each ministry retains its representatives in the provinces. The Ministry of Defence is represented by a general in each region and *département* (and is responsible for the local *gendarmerie* among other things), the Ministry of Education by a rector, the Ministry of Justice by a procurator. But the five most powerful officials in any region or *département* are the Treasurer and Paymaster General (TPG, who is the main agent of the Ministry of Finance), the Director of Infrastructure (*directeur de l'Équipement*), the Director of Agriculture. Each of these officials heads an army of lesser state officials, and his task is to implement decisions coming from Paris and also to supervise the work of the local authorities. Some of these men, especially those belonging to highly prestigious technical corps which have their own national networks of influence, are very powerful figures.

The regional courts of accounts

The regional courts of accounts (*Chambres Régionales des Comptes*) are a creation of the Defferre Act of March 1982. A court has been established in each region composed of magistrates (and as such are irremovable), some of whom may be directly recruited from the highly prestigious national Court of Accounts situated in Paris: the president of a regional court has to be a seconded member of the national court. The role of the regional court is constantly to assess the accounts of all the local authorities (or dependent bodies) within its area of jurisdiction, and it plays a crucial part in the *a posteriori* financial control exercised by the prefects over the local authorities. It may even comment on the way a local council runs its finances.

Other local bodies

Among the other influential local decision-makers must be counted the para-public bodies which have grown considerably since the war: these have been particularly active in the economic domain (*sociétés d'économie mixte*), in urban planning and in housing. In some towns a major decision-maker is often an individual firm or a particular industry because its investment and employment policies may be crucial to the financial and economic health of the community. Mention should also be made of the various chambers (*chambres*), the most influential of which are the *Chambres de Commerce et d'Industrie*, the *Chambres des Métiers*, the *Chambres de l'Agriculture*, which are composed of representatives of the main economic groups and which are present in all the regions, *départements* and main towns. Most of the major national pressure groups have local branches, although some pressure groups, notably in the cultural field, are exclusively local in character. Information on the power of these groups is scant, but there is some evidence to suggest that they are occasionally very influential. Studies of Bordeaux and Abbeville have shown that the chambers of commerce enjoy close and fruitful relations with the mayors. Other studies have revealed that the building of the great petrochemical complex at Fos in the south of France was organized largely in co-operation with the local chamber of commerce, and that the Chamber of Commerce of Rennes inspired and facilitated the building of the giant Citroën car plant in the town. It is also clear that in many rural *départements* the agricultural groups enjoy easy access to, and influence with, local officials. Many prefectoral decisions are made on the advice of committees on which these interest groups are represented.

The bases of central power

After that brief description of the principal institutions and decision-makers at local level it is possible to return to the central problem of the nature of the relationship between Paris and the provinces. In spite of successive waves of decentralizing measures since the 1960s and even those of the Socialists, the position of the centre remains very powerful. There are several sources of central power:

- The statutory weakness of the local authorities and the obsessive control exercised by Paris and its provincial agents, the prefects and the technical field services.
- The archaic nature of the present structures which renders local government especially ineffective, and vulnerable to central pressure.
- The unrepresentative nature of local elites which deprives them of legitimacy in their dealings with state officials.
- The financial dependence of the local authorities on Paris, which is almost complete.
- The centralization of most political, economic and financial sectors.

The statutory weakness of the local authorities and the obsessive control exercised by Paris and its provincial agents

Traditionally, there were three types of central control over the local authorities: judicial, technical and financial. This was especially true at regional and departmental level, where the prefects prepared the timetable, the agenda and the budgets of assemblies which did not have their own administrations to enable them to control or to propose counter-measures to prefectoral plans. If any local authority wished to beg or borrow, add a new tax or change the basis of an existing one, build a new school or even name a street after someone, Paris could, and often did, intervene. Professor Legendre in his book on the history of the French administration quotes the case of the decree, signed by the President of the Republic, which regulated the cost of the dog licence at Saint-Jean-des-Vignes (a tiny village) in 1898. Furthermore, by their laws, decrees, circulars, recommendations, instructions and warnings Paris and its provincial agents exercised a constant control of local decision-makers. The so-called "reglementary ardour" (an obsessive insistence on abiding by the rules) of the state administration involved imposing uniform rules on such important matters as the height of coat-rails in schools, the size and position of windows in restored houses, the colour of paint to be used on outside walls. And it must be conceded that obsessive uniformity in a country as diverse as France could lead to some very strange results. Such control of a judicial or technical nature was further reinforced by that of the financial inspectorate and the Court of Accounts (which examine the accounts of the local authorities) and the administrative tribunals and the Council of State (which judge any complaints against the local authorities). Paris control was thus of a technical, financial and judicial nature, and it was all the more effective since its agents were omnipresent in the provinces: it must be emphasized that many of the tasks carried out by local government staff in Britain were executed by state-paid officials in France.

Heading the vast army of state civil servants were the prefects, described by the more charitable as "colonial governors", "miniature emperors", and "provincial potentates". Indeed, two prominent Socialist leaders, Defferre (the Mayor of Marseilles) and Mauroy (the Mayor of Lille) referred to the Fifth Republic as the *"régime des préfets"*, and they were only two of many provincial *notables* who were critical of the powers of the prefects, whose supervision of the regional and departmental assemblies was apparently so overwhelming. Certainly, the texts endowed the prefects with considerable powers over the local assemblies. To the general supervision of the prefect had to be added the financial and the technical control of other field services. As already noted, the traditional judicial and financial *a priori* control exercised by the prefects over the acts of a local authority has been replaced by an *a posteriori* control and audit, involving appeals to a local administrative court (*tribunal administratif*) in the case of suspected illegality or to a court of accounts (*chambre régionale*

des comptes) in the case of financial irregularity. The Defferre Act
also contains general measures designed to weaken the technical
supervision of the local authorities.

Yet the total impact of the abolition or reduction of supervision
and control is unlikely to be very great. Most observers agree that
traditional judicial control of the local authorities had virtually
disappeared before 1982: the Defferre Act merely formalized the
existing situation. They also agree that the centre will continue
to impose its norms in most key areas, and that it will be able
to do so because it has many financial weapons at its disposal.
Moreover, it matters little who has the *formal* control over the
agents implementing decisions at local level: what matters is who
trains them and protects them. Thus, transferring agents of the
state to local level control means little if those agents persist
in perceiving themselves as belonging to a centrally organized
network. Finally, most local authorities will continue to encourage
the technical control of their plans by inviting the field services to
draw them up: they do so because they lack qualified staff, because
they recognize the need to send well-presented plans to Paris to get
permission to finance and to implement them, and because they
wish to exploit the wide network of relations enjoyed by many of
the local technical services. The Defferre Act may help the *big*
towns (which have qualified personnel) to assert their autonomy,
but it is unlikely to impinge upon the attitudes of the vast number
of small communes.

The archaic nature of the present structures renders local government especially ineffective

Local government structures date from a period when France
was almost entirely rural and when social and economic expectations were non-existent. The population explosion and the
rapid industrialization and urbanization of the country, growing demands for better social services and minimum standards
throughout the country have combined to render totally inadequate the old uniform structures. That inadequacy has been
demonstrated by the emergence of absurd anomalies: for example,
the 1977 Peyrefitte Report on violence and crime in France
revealed that the town of Vitry in the Paris region, which had a
population of over 100,000 and an alarming crime rate, had no
police station merely because it was not the main town of a canton
(which was a criterion defined in 1871). The inadequacy of the
traditional system was amply shown in the 1950s and 1960s by the
economic planners who found that the *départements* were far too
small to be viable planning units. But the most glaring inadequacy

concerns the vast majority of small communes which are clearly incapable of meeting the demands placed upon them.

France, with 36,034 communes, has more units of local government than the rest of her Common Market partners put together. All but two per cent of these communes have fewer than 10,000 inhabitants, whilst 32,405 (or 90 per cent) have fewer than 2000 inhabitants; two-thirds have fewer than 700 inhabitants and nearly 30 per cent have fewer than 200 inhabitants. There are some four thousand communes with fewer than 100 inhabitants and there are even about 100 communes with no population at all! This vast mosaic of small communes no longer reflects the demographic, occupational and economic reality of the country. Small communes do not have the financial resources to build or maintain the basic social facilities now widely demanded, and are, therefore, totally dependent upon the financial and technical services of the state. Thus the transfer of new powers to the communes by the decentralization programme of 1982-86 was rendered meaningless for the vast majority of French communes by the continuing dependence on the centre for such services. Several attempts were made to reduce the number of communes through a process of merger. But in spite of pretectoral pressure, ministerial exhortation and financial inducements the number of mergers remains obstinately small: between 1959 and 1970 only 746 communes agreed to merge into 350. The July 1971 Act was designed to speed up the process, but local resistance proved too effective: in the year following the 1971 Act only 300 communes had agreed to some form of merger, and by the beginning of 1975 only 779 mergers had taken place involving the disappearance of 1130 (or less than 3 per cent of the total) communes.

In December 1972 the government created nine new towns in the rapidly developing Paris region. This involved the disappearance of only sixty-four communes. It seems likely that France will live with her vast mosaic of communes for many years hence. The recommendations for local government reform, contained in the Guichard Report of October 1976, envisaged the creation of 750 urban communities and 3600 communal communities (in rural areas) which would have had jurisdiction over the main tasks of planning, transport, housing, education and health. The existing 36,000 communes would remain and their mayors would carry out minor administrative tasks. Guichard recommended that the *first* stage of the changes be completed by 1985 – an indication of the foolhardy alacrity with which local government is reformed in the Paris-dominated Republic! And even that distant date seemed widely optimistic, for the serried ranks of rural mayors made clear their opposition to a reform which would have relegated them to the role of second-class officials. The Guichard proposals were never implemented, and the Bonnet Reforms of 1980-1 and the Defferre Reforms of the 1980s in no way touched upon the highly fragmented nature of local government units.

Successive governments have been more successful in attempting to ensure collaboration or co-operation between the communes. These attempts have taken four forms:

- Single purpose syndicates (*syndicats à vocation unique*) which involve a voluntary grouping of communes for only one specific and defined purpose. There are just over 10,000 such syndicates.
- Multi-purpose syndicates (*syndicats à vocation multiple*). Since the January 1959 *ordonnance* communes have been allowed to cooperate on a voluntary basis to carry out any number of tasks which they themselves specify, and a law passed in January 1988 made the arrangements even more flexible: a commune may join a multi-purpose syndicate for specific functions only and does not have to co-operate in all the functions carried out by the syndicate. The system has become, therefore, *à la carte*. By mid 1985 there were 19,157 multi-purpose syndicates grouping nearly twenty thousand communes with a population of over twenty million.
- Districts are the heirs to the urban districts (also created by the January 1959 *ordonnance*) and are designed to induce co-operation between communes in the same conurbation. In 1985 there were 153 districts (which grouped 1284 communes and 5,445,000 inhabitants or over 10 per cent of the French population). They are obliged to carry out certain services such as housing and fire-fighting, and they also have competence over any other areas defined by the constituent communes. The districts have greater financial control than the multi-purpose syndicates over the constituent communes.
- Urban communities (*communautés urbaines*). The law of December 1966 created the four urban areas of Strasbourg, Lyons, Lille and Bordeaux which involved the grouping of 199 communes. Since then five new urban communities have been voluntarily formed in the conurbations of Cherbourg, Le Mans, Dunkirk, Le Creusot and Brest. The nine urban communities group 252 communes with a total population of over four million inhabitants, or nearly 8 per cent of the French population. The creation of an urban community involves the obligatory transfer from the constituent communes to the community of services such as housing, fire-fighting, the construction and equipment of primary and secondary schools, water, rubbish disposal and cemeteries,

public transport, town planning and public works. The council of the urban community is composed of representatives of the councils of the constituent communes.

The profoundly unrepresentative nature of the local elites deprives them of legitimacy in their dealings with state officials

The unrepresentative nature of the local elites is geographical and social. The size of local constituencies varies widely, particularly in the departmental councils, and the enormous disparities were not ironed out by the Defferre reforms. Within the same *département*, there are very wide disparities: in the Bouches-du-Rhône the smallest canton has fewer than 2,000 inhabitants, the biggest 65,000; in the Bas-Rhin in Alsace the figures are respectively 3,000 and 45,000. In the Seine-Maritime in Normandy the size of the cantons ranges from 3000 to 20,000, and as a result, the 75 per cent of the population who live in the towns are represented by only 36 of the 70 departmental councillors. In all the departmental councils rural areas are given undue weight, and the big urban and growing suburban areas are penalized. This produces a politically conservative bias in the departmental councils. The socially unrepresentative nature of local councils is notorious. This may be seen by looking at the professions of the departmental councillors elected in 1982 and 1985 and of the mayors (see Table 15).

Table 15 Occupation of departmental councillors elected in 1982 and 1985 and of mayors elected in 1987

Occupation	Of 3694 elected in 1982 (%)	Of 3810 elected in 1985 (%)	Of 36,000 Mayors (%) 1987
Liberal professions	24.0	24.0	5.4
Teaching	18.1	16.4	7.8
Salaried private sector	14.8	13.4	14.1
Industry and Commerce	12.2	12.4	11.8
Agriculture and Fishing	10.8	10.1	36.7
Civil Service	6.6	6.8	3.4
Salaried public sector	2.1	1.4	1.4
Retired and no profession	7.7	10.3	19.3
Others	3.6	5.2	0.1

Only 2 per cent of the councillors were women, who represent over half the population of France, while the workers, who represent almost a third of the population, provided less than 2 per cent of the departmental councillors.

Two in every five mayors came from the farming world whereas only two in every hundred were manual workers. Only 2.8 per cent of the mayors after 1977 were women: as a result of the 1983 elections this figure rose to 4 per cent. Mayors and departmental councillors tend also to be elected from among the ageing and the aged: a third of both groups are over 60 years old and four-fifths of both groups are over 50 years old. Only 4.3 per cent of the departmental councillors elected in 1982 and 1985 were under 35 years old. The not totally inaccurate portrait of the average mayor or departmental councillor projects him as an ageing male representative of a traditional social elite from a rural area. He is seen as cautious and conservative, totally unsympathetic to the moods and needs of *la nouvelle France* and technically ill-equipped to meet its challenges.

It was hoped that the composition of the regional councils would become more socially representative as the result of the introduction of direct suffrage. But the first elections – those of 1986 – saw the return of the traditional elites: over nine-tenths (92 per cent) were men, over two-thirds were over 50 years old, nearly a half (47 per cent) belonged to upper management or the liberal professions, over a half (53 per cent) were university educated – and three quarters already had another local mandate.

The financial dependence of the local authorities is virtually complete

For the critics, what autonomy is left to the local authorities is rendered illusory by financial restrictions. Almost all French communes are heavily in debt: it was estimated that between 1964 and 1974 the debts of the communes tripled, and that an increasing proportion of new loans were contracted to repay old debts. Local authorities complain that governments create public services but then leave the whole or part of their financing to the local authorities – which they then accuse of profligacy: for British observers it all has a familiar ring.

The independent resources of the local authorities are totally inadequate to meet their needs, and it has been calculated that about half their income comes from central government. This financial weakness is particularly marked at regional level: the overall budget of the twenty regions more than tripled between 1981 and 1986 (from 6.6 billion to 24.3 billion francs) but it still represented only a small per cent of the overall local budget. Furthermore, whereas 90 per cent of the regions' overall budget was spent on investment projects this figure had dropped to 60 per cent by 1986. The lack of real financial autonomy at communal and departmental level is apparent, since well over ninety per cent of an average annual budget is committed. Nor has the much-discussed financial crisis of local government been solved by rapidly rising local taxes (between 1976 and 1984 by an annual average of 16.5 per cent), or by the slow and limited process of transferring to the general state budget of items previously on local budgets. The reform of the block grant system (it is based on a transfer of a proportion of the value added tax) was only a partial palliative, not a remedy.

The subject of local government finance has always been politically explosive, and governments have always moved with the utmost circumspection in tampering with the basic structures. In spite of countless governmental and parliamentary reports between 1917 and 1970 it was not until the 1970s that limited reforms were introduced. It was highly instructive that Defferre left himself plenty of time to tackle the subject, since it was the most complex and delicate of all the aspects of local government reform. Five years after the Socialists came to power the localities were still awaiting the much promised improvement in their financial position.

There are four basic ways of raising revenue at local level: self-financing through local taxes; loans on the private market which are very expensive; charges on services rendered by local authorities; state loans and subsidies. As noted above, French local authorities raised 162 billion francs from local taxes, 153 billion from transfers (grants from the state), 55 billion from loans and 49 billion from other sources. State assistance is vital, and provides the state with considerable leverage over the activities of the local authorities. It has been argued that the state has exploited this financial leverage in four ways:

● As an instrument of macro and micro economic policy by regulating local investment levels.
● As a method of directing the individual choice of local authorities.
● As a means of encouraging the reorganization of local government (by providing incentives, for example, to induce inter-communal co-operation).
● As a procedure for buttressing the electoral chances of the politically sympathetic.

The system of allocating state loans and subsidies resembles a vast and immensely complex maze: a senatorial report of 1973 enumerated no fewer than 150 kinds of subsidy available to the local authorities, channelled through seventeen different agencies such as the FIAT (*Fonds d'Intervention pour l'Aménagement du Territoire*) or the FNAFU (*Fonds National de l'Aménagement foncier et de l'Urbanisme*). Four bodies at local level play a key role in allocating state loans; the *Caisse des Dépôts et des Consignations* which handles infrastructure loans, the *Crédit Foncier* which looks after loans for land requisition and housing, the *Crédit Agricole* which is involved in loans for rural improvement projects, and the CAECL (*Caisse d'aide à l'équipement des collectivités locales*). From the late 1970s some attempt was made to simplify the procedures for allocating state subsidies and loans, yet they remain numerous and complex: in 1979 there were still fifty separate types of specific grants operated by ten ministries. The situation did not improve in the 1980s despite further attempts at simplification: the 1988 annual report of the Court of Accounts noted that state financial assistance to the local authorities was massive (about 15 per cent of the state budget), highly complex, not very coherent, distributed according to unclear criteria and inadequately monitored.

State aids may be of a global or "block grant" nature or may be very specific. They may be intended to cover operating costs or to help finance investment projects. Of the 142 billion francs of total state grants to local authorities in 1988, 103 were for operating costs, 22 for investment purposes and 17 for the cost of transferring certain powers from the centre to the localities. During the 1970s a new form of state aid emerged in the form of contracts with particular areas (Corsica, the Massif Central, Brittany, the south west) or medium-sized towns (between 1974 and 1981 there were seventy such contracts) or even *pays* (small towns and their surrounding communes – there were 240 contracts between 1974 and 1981). Some contracts were agreed with particular towns for a specific purpose (Lille and Marseilles to deal with the problem of immigrants, Strasburg because it was a "European capital"). The best known of these contracts were the *contrats de plan*, the planning contracts which authorized the subsidizing of integrated proposals for urban development in the bigger cities. Finally, mention should be made of the state resources channelled to the provinces to meet a particular purpose: the special industrial-restructuring fund of 1978 to help the crisis-ridden regions of Lorraine and the Nord; the rural fund of 1979 which was meant to help no fewer than thirty-three *départements*; the funds to encourage tourism, to improve forests, to foster culture.

In all these arrangements state officials negotiated with the localities and were able to impose certain conditions, norms and standards. Subsidy, it is argued, involved subordination. And since the state provides, through loans or subsidies, about two-thirds of the finance for local capital investment projects and over half of local authority current operating costs, the subordination is marked – and keenly felt.

Local taxes account for just over a third (in 1980 35.4 per cent) of local revenues – a proportion which has risen since the early 1970s when it was under thirty per cent. Rising local taxes coupled with the transfer of fiscal resources to the local authorities have enhanced their financial autonomy. Yet it is questionable whether there will ever be a radical increase in the financial autonomy of the local authorities. In a prolonged period of recession characterized by high inflation no government – whatever its political complexion – is likely to want to lose its already precarious control of overall public expenditure levels. Already by the mid-1980s there were plans for a *pause fiscale*, for a halt in escalating local taxes.

The centralization of most political, economic and financial actors

In spite of all the decentralization reforms, France will remain a profoundly centralized country: the principal means of communication are focused on Paris; the media, especially television, are national in character (even though local stations have proliferated in the 1980s); the banks and financial institutions are all situated in or controlled from Paris; the major industrial groups are increasingly centralized; the policy networks of teachers, planners, architects, doctors, and other professions are all forged in a common national mould. Politically, too, France has all the hallmarks of a centralized country: the seat of the executive, legislative and administrative authority is in Paris; the political parties and most major pressure groups are national, and elections – even local – are conducted as national competitions. Finally, the political culture of France has been deeply influenced by Jacobinism: a "central value system", to use Shils's term, is all-pervasive, structuring both mentalities, expectations and actions. It is within this highly centralized framework that the relations between the state and local authorities are determined. It is no accident that major local politicians spend most of their time in the capital.

In conclusion, whatever the intentions and impact of the Defferre Act of March 1982, the local authorities continue to have their autonomy circumscribed by the supervisory activities of the prefects and the state field services, by the intrinsic weakness and archaism of their structures, by the inadequacy of local officials, by their financial vulnerability and by the centralized framework of public and private policy-making. The picture appears, therefore, a sombre one, with the innocent and virginal provinces assailed and violated by a brutal and insensitive capital. In truth, however, the situation is much less melodramatic and infinitely more complex.

Local influences in the one and indivisible republic

One cannot understand the political and governmental system of the Fifth Republic without taking into account the influence of local forces. The rigours of centralization are tempered by various factors which ensure that local decision-makers are not the inactive spectators of their own collective fate. Those factors may be summarized as follows:

- The state depends on the localities in certain respects.
- Provincial elites are able to exploit differences of opinion and outlook in Paris.
- State officials are often sensitive to local requirements.
- The position of locally elected *notables* is much more powerful than the texts suggest.
- The power of the prefects has always been exaggerated and its nature misunderstood.
- The financial dependence of the local authorities, though real, should not be overestimated.
- There has been an increase in the number, the size and the autonomy of big towns.

The state depends on the localities in certain repects

The local authorities employ over a million people (800,000 full-time), raise nearly a fifth of overall tax revenue, account for nearly three quarters of non-military public investment projects, spend about half of the total state budget, act as a vital servicing agency for the centre, and play a direct and initiatory role in areas such as primary schools, crèches, housing, transport, culture, urban planning, local roads, traffic control, sanitation, and sports facilities. As noted above, the Defferre Reforms gave the local authorities increased powers in nine policy areas, including urban policy (mayors now have the right to issue construction permits and approve local plans), housing, transport, education (their powers now extend to the construction and running of secondary as well as primary schools), social security (welfare assistance), regional planning, culture and the environment, and police. These increased powers have been allocated in the main to the *départements* and the regions. Also, the transfer of the executive from the prefects to elected officials at regional and departmental level has been accompanied by a transfer of state personnel to the local level.

The investment and employment policies of the local authorities can make an enormous impact on the financial and economic policies of the central government and their non-cooperation can be a source of considerable embarrassment. The collaboration of the periphery in all spheres of decision-making is essential. In the 1950s and 1960s an effort was made to integrate the local system into a framework of national economic imperatives. The problems of economic growth, regional imbalances and urban planning led rationally minded state technocrats and bureaucrats into an assault on the "irrational" incrementalism of the existing system. The prefects and the technical field services were to be the transmission belts of Paris orders to the localities. The planners soon acknowledged that local consultation and co-operation were vital to legitimize decisions and also to acquire vital information. They also discovered that tawdry electoral considerations had also to be taken into account: the DATAR carried out its work of industrial decentralization with one eye on economic imperatives and the other on the polling booths. Moreover, it soon became apparent that local state officials, far from being the agents of enlightened national economic rationalism, readily remained the spokesmen for local interests and the instruments of self-interested incrementalism.

Provincial elites are able to exploit differences in Paris

Paris in its relations with the provinces is far from being a homogeneous entity. It is not "Paris" or the "state" which has relations with the periphery: both are convenient shorthand terms (even if the French do invest them with some quasi-mystical quality) embracing a vast variety of political, administrative, public and semi-public agents. Jacques Antoine, in his book *Le Pouvoir et l'opinion* (1970), reveals that the administrative group established to study concrete proposals for regionalization in the 1969 referendum had great difficulty in pinpointing all the various Paris bodies concerned with local affairs. The labyrinthine state system (if "system" is the appropriate word) for allocating subsidies has already been referred to above. Further evidence may be gleaned from the group reporting on local finance for the sixth five-year plan (1971-5), which noted that an application for a loan or subsidy normally involved no fewer than sixty procedures in nine ministries, while the Bouvard Senatorial Report of 1976 indicated that before the March 1964 reforms a local application for a loan to build a secondary school required the intervention of at least seven Paris administrations. Even after the 1964 reforms the building of a university hospital involved fifty decision-makers in a hundred-stage process. In spite of the reforms of the 1970s and early 1980s which both decentralized (to locally elected officials) and deconcentrated (to state officials in the provinces) powers to local level, in spite of all the measures designed to rationalize and simplify procedures the number of administrative decision-makers in Paris involved in local affairs remains high. And between these decision-makers conflict is endemic and sometimes bitter. All is not always sweetness and light between, for example, the Ministries of the Interior and Finance, between the Ministry of Infrastructure and the DATAR, between the Ministry of Finance and the *Caisse des Dépôts*. These disputes and dissensions can – and frequently are – exploited by informed, astute and unscrupulous local *notables*. Finally, as Sidney Tarrow has rightly insisted, the effectiveness of the Paris bureaucracy has declined as its size and scope for intervention have increased. As already noted in other spheres the administration is overwhelmed by the weight of its tasks and responsibilities.

Locally elected officials can also exploit the rivalries which exist at local level between the various field services. These rivalries are such that in order to avoid too open conflict the various field services frequently practise "*évitement réciproque*" or mutual avoidance, and they compound the problem of co-ordination by rejecting prefectoral co-ordination and arbitration. This situation enables elected officials to play off some parts of the local administration against others. Finally, locally elected officials can take advantage of the differences which exist between the central administration and its local officials: Jean-Claude Thoenig has shown that between these two there has developed "an elaborate game of hide and seek", and the necessary link between them is sometimes provided by a powerful local political figure. In other words, elected officials at local level can exploit the lack of any effective horizontal co-ordination in, and the defective vertical integration of, the French state administration.

State officials are often sensitive to local requirements

Some Paris-based bureaucrats hold local office. Unlike their British counterparts, top civil servants in France are allowed to stand for local office, and they do so frequently on highly partisan lists or under well-defined political labels. It has been argued that such men are merely "technocrats in search of a spurious legitimacy", but the truth is much simpler:. many Paris officials have firm family roots in the provinces and wish to retain and even to strengthen them by serving their local community. The result is that no departmental council is complete without at least one top civil servant based in Paris, and that among the French mayors may be found members of the Paris administrations, of the private staffs of ministers (the *cabinets*) and of the *grands corps*. For a commune it is immensely useful to have a top civil servant as mayor, for he can speak on equal terms with the prefect, bring pressure to bear upon him through Paris or even bypass him completely. Such officials seek patronage for their own communes or cantons and generally sensitize the administration to local needs and problems.

At the local level, too, state officials are far from impervious to local influences. The field services are given a certain discretion in interpreting directives from Paris, and often display great inventiveness in ignoring, modifying or even violating them: as noted above, one of the main problems for Paris bureaucrats is to make their provincial subordinates obey them. Local field services are frequently manned by officials who remain a long time in the same area and who are gradually sucked into the whirlpool of local pressures. There is another pressure which renders the local field services sensitive to local pressures: money. Three-fifths of the work of the state field services is for the local authorities which request and pay for their help in the initial preparation of a project and later in its implementation. Since they are also often involved in verifying its legality and its compliance to technical norms this places them in a dubious moral position. But any moral qualms have long ago disappeared under the deadening weight of established practice and the anaesthetizing effect of the percentage they are paid for their work. The practice underlines the mutual dependence of elected and non-elected officials: the technical dependence of the elected official creates and then sustains the financial dependence of the non-elected.

The position of the locally elected notables is much more powerful than the texts suggest

This observation, according to historians, was true as early as the July Monarchy (1830-48). The position of local *notables* is reinforced by their justifiable claim that unlike the prefects and most other officials, their roots are firmly planted in the locality: Marchand noted that in 1958 and 1964 fewer than 3 per cent of the departmental councillors lived outside the *département*, and that almost nine-tenths lived in the cantons they represented. Second, most elected *notables* hold office for a considerable length of time. Howard Machin has pointed out that during de Gaulle's presidency (1959-69) thirty-five of the eighty-seven departmental councils outside the Paris region voted no change in their chairmanship while another forty saw only one change. A study of the *département* of the Ardennes in 1973 showed that since 1945 only one departmental councillor had not been re-elected after his first six years of office, and that six of the thirty-one members of the departmental council had represented their canton, without interruption, since the end of the Second World War, a period of twenty-eight years. There are even more astonishing cases of elective longevity: the indestructible Antoine Pinay, prime minister during the Fourth Republic and Finance Minister during the Fifth, was departmental councillor of Saint Chamond for more than half a century.

Stability of office is also the case in the communes. A study of the mayors of the rural *département* of the Calvados in Normandy in December 1976 revealed that more than a third had headed their commune for at least a quarter of a century. Some of the main towns of France have elected the same mayor since the war: Chaban-Delmas in Bordeaux, Defferre in Marseilles and Pflimlin in Strasburg are among the better known examples. Local office is often handed on among the family heirlooms. When Médecin, the Mayor of Nice since 1928, died in 1965 he was immediately replaced by his son, who is still mayor of the town. Jeanne Becquart-Leclerq in her study of four northern *départements* showed that half the mayors were the sons of mayors or town councillors. Some rural areas are dominated by the same family for generations: the Basque canton of Saint-Étienne-de-Baïgorry has been represented in the departmental council by a member of the Harispe family since the 1830s. The position of the elected *notable* is undoubtedly strengthened by his claim that he knows the people and the problems of the area far better than the appointed emissaries of Paris, many of them mere birds of passage who are anxious to pass on to more prestigious and lucrative posts.

The third factor which strengthens many of the local *notables* in their relations with state officials is the phenomenon of *cumul des mandats* – the accumulation of offices. These offices may be purely local: most departmental councillors are also mayors and chairpersons of a number of local associations. But frequently the offices are national in character. Most national political figures feel the need for local roots and stand for local office, and this is seen as eminently desirable by the electors, who view their Senators and Deputies as the spokesmen for local grievances and as intermediaries for extracting favours from Paris. It is significant that the defeated President Giscard d'Estaing began his political come-back by standing in the departmental elections in 1982.

The phenomenon of *cumul des mandats* is widespread: among the candidates in the March 1971 town elections were thirty-six of the forty-one ministers and junior ministers, 379 of the 487 Deputies and 191 of the 283 Senators; in the departmental elections of March 1976 eighteen ministers, 251 Deputies and 174 Senators were elected (others were not up for re-election that year), and in the 1977 town elections thirty of the thirty-seven ministers and junior ministers. Put another way, of the 491 Deputies in 1978 only 102 (or a fifth) held no local office, while only eighteen of the 264 Senators (or 6.8 per cent) were so placed: it should also be noted that some of the deprived had been unsuccessful candidates in the local elections of 1976 and 1977. The Mauroy government formed in June 1981 contained twenty-four mayors (of towns such as Lille, Marseilles, Rennes, Chartres), while in the National Assembly elected that month there were 246 *députés-maires* (Deputies who were also mayors), 249 Deputies who were members of a departmental council and nineteen who were members of the Paris town council. After the 1986 parliamentary elections 46 per cent of the Deputies were also mayors (exactly the same proportion as in 1981) and 47 per cent were departmental councillors (again, exactly the same as in 1981), while others were simply town councillors. Nearly a fifth of the deputies (19.5 per cent) were both mayors *and* departmental councillors. Overall, it has been calculated that, in 1985, 93 per cent of all senators and 82 per cent of all Deputies held at least one local mandate. The situation may be looked at from another angle: in 1985, of the 96 chairpersons of the departmental councils 56 were Deputies or Senators, and of the 22 regional chairpersons 16 were members of parliament. Among the dominant political figures of the Fifth Republic who have held or hold local office are presidents Pompidou, Giscard d'Estaing and Mitterrand, and prime ministers Debré, Messmer, Chaban-Delmas, Chirac, Mauroy, Fabius and Rocard. Some politicians collect posts like some men collect postage stamps: it is both an obsession and an investment. Ex-Premier Jacques Chirac, leader of the Gaullist Party, for example, was at one stage the mayor of Paris, chairman of the departmental council of the Corrèze and deputy of the *département*, member of the regional council and president of many local organizations. Edgar Faure, ex-minister and ex-president of the National Assembly and hence a Deputy, was chairman of the regional council of Franche-Comté, vice-president of the departmental council of the Doubs, local councillor in Pontarlier (he was mayor until 1977), and chairman or vice-chairman of a host of other national or local associations. The case of Maurice Faure (no relative of the former) who is uncontested seigneur of the *département* of the Lot merely reflects the situation in many rural *départements*. The Communist Party also has its *cumulards*: in 1978 sixty-nine of its eighty-six Deputies held local office. Typical of the *grand notable communiste* is Raymond Maillet who in 1981 was mayor, member of the local departmental council, Deputy of the *département* of the Oise and chairman of the regional council of Picardy. Now it is clear that the relationship between a state official and a local *notable* is bound to be affected by the national notoriety of the *notable*. Put at its most extreme, no state official is likely to make life difficult for the mayor of a tiny commune if that mayor happens to be the minister in charge of his administration. Certainly there was never any doubt during Pompidou's presidency that the most influential man in the *département* of the Morbihan was not the prefect but Marcellin, Mayor of Vannes, chairman of the departmental council . . . and Minister of the Interior (the prefect's hierarchical head). These *grands notables*, local political bosses with extensive Paris contacts, expect and invariably receive deferential and preferential treatment from the state officials. Even influential members of the opposition (especially as they might be influential members of the government in the near future) must be treated with courtesy, concern and consideration (however discreetly): for instance, even before May 1981 only the most imprudent prefect could forget that François Mitterrand, Mayor of Château-Chinon and member of the local departmental council, was the political boss of the *département* of the Nièvre. No prefect appointed by the Left could function successfully in the Western Loire region without the compliance of Olivier Guichard, a Gaullist baron, and the political boss of the region.

The interpenetration of local and national elites which is one of the most distinctive features of the French system completely distorts the formal relationship between certain *notables* and the state officials: official subservience underlined by the texts may become, in practice, domination. There were many demands to abolish or at least curtail the *cumul des mandats*, and the Socialists promised to reduce the number of offices anyone could hold at any one time. The March 1982 Act made no reference to the phenomenon. However, in December 1985 a law was passed which limits to two the number of politically important posts to be held by any individual. The list of such posts comprises Senators and Deputies, membership of the European Parliament, regional and departmental councillors, mayors of towns of over 20,000 inhabitants and deputy mayors of towns of over 100,000 inhabitants. After the 1988 elections many newly elected Deputies had to resign from all but one of the other posts they were holding. It is unclear what the long-term impact of the reform will be. At present it would appear that the local barons are simply placing loyal supporters in the vacated posts. It is unlikely that the interpenetration of national and local elites will be seriously placed on the list of endangered species.

The power of the prefects has always been exaggerated and its nature misunderstood

Before the decentralization reforms of Gaston Defferre, a prefect exercised, in theory, regulatory and discretionary powers which enabled him closely to supervise the activities of local authorities. In practice, however, his power was always circumscribed by several important factors:

- Paradoxically, the extension of his formal *powers* throughout the nineteenth and twentieth centuries had led to a diminution of his *power*, for he was trapped in a network of roles and regulations which frequently hampered his freedom of manoeuvre by restricting his area of initiative and discretion – the real basis of his influence.
- There was a gradual weakening of the formal control he was able to exercise over the local authorities: even before 1982, for example, his control over local budgets had virtually disappeared.
- An elaborate system of administrative law had evolved under the guardianship of the Council of State which set judicial limits to prefectoral action.
- Prefectoral control over the activities of the field services was always tenuous, and there were some legendary clashes between prefects determined to establish their authority and the heads of the field services resolved to rule alone. If there was necessarily a great deal of co-operation between the generalist prefect and the specialist field services there was also chronic tension and intermittent conflict. Generally, the prefect had neither the time, the technical expertise, the qualified staff nor the inclination to supervise the work of the field services. The March 1964 reforms which were designed to strengthen prefectoral authority as the "overlord" of the departmental administration proved largely ineffective, and many, including the prefects themselves, are doubtful whether the Defferre Act, which reasserts the overall administrative leadership of the prefect at departmental level, will be any more effective.
- The local prefect had little control over many pressure groups or big industrial concerns, which had their headquarters in

the capital and which negotiated directly with the Paris bureaucracy.

● His monopoly in the distribution of local patronage was quickly expropriated by the *notables*, particularly those who also sat in parliament: the prefectoral monopoly became a parliamentary oligopoly. In the absence of a strong party system, governments in Paris bought parliamentary favour by granting individual Deputies and Senators the right to distribute local manna to their consituents.

● From the Restoration Monarchy (1815-30), and especially from the July Monarchy (1830-48), it became the practice of governments to consult Deputies and Senators over the appointment, promotion and dismissal of prefects in their constituencies – a fact that few prefects were allowed – or were likely – to forget. Members of parliament (local figures holding several offices), who could make or break a prefect, supplanted the prefects during the Third and Fourth Republics as the most influential decision-makers in the *départements*, and in spite of the decline in the power of the French parliament since 1958 its members remain very influential at local level.

● A prefect's own career ambitions were frequently prejudicial to his success in controlling local government. In practice, promotion was related to mobility; shortly after moving to a particular *département* a prefect was assailed by desires to be transferred to a more important, more lucrative and more prestigious prefecture. Prefectoral instability was a real source of weakness for the corps, and the problem was particularly acute in the small rural *départements*, far from Paris and inhabited by the uncultured and the unwashed. Moreover, prefects already disappeared with the inevitability of Puccini heroines (they were sacked or transferred on the slightest pretext). On average a prefect spent two to three years in a particular *département*, although the average hid wide disparities. Prefectoral instability may be seen in the fact that during the period of the Giscard d'Estaing presidency (1974-81) ninety-one of the ninety-six *départements* saw at least three prefects. The Socialists celebrated their historic victory in May to June 1981 by sacking a handful of prefects and reshuffling most of the others in a massive *valse de préfets*. Therefore, the prefects' own *wanderlust* merely aggravated an acute problem. In many *départements* prefects had little time to become acquainted with the people or the problems, and their authority was lessened in their relations with local politicans and certain officials who had firmer local roots.

● With the growth of the big towns and the creation of the urban communities prefectoral control was considerably weakened, and in some cases totally eliminated.

As noted above, the Defferre decentralization reforms involved a reduction in the role of the prefect: his *a priori* judicial and budgetary control over the activities of the local authorities was abolished; he lost his role as the chief executive officer of the departmental council, and his monopoly over the services of the *département*; certain powers were transferred from the state to the local authorities. However, in many respects, the reform merely formalized the *de facto* situation. He has retained his role as principal representative of the state, the government and the Ministry of the Interior and, as such, retains potential influence. Moreover, the reforms strengthened his position relative to the various state services, and gave him an *a posteriori* right to refer illegal acts to an administrative tribunal or a defective budget to the regional court of accounts. The reformers also insisted that one of his roles should be to prevent any type of local authority from asserting preeminence over another. More important, they assured the prefects that they would continue to have a "*rôle moteur*" in economic and social affairs: key economic committees such as the CODEFI (*comités départementaux des problèmes de financement des entreprises*) and the CORRI (*comités régionaux de restructuration industrielle*) were to be chaired by the prefects. The prefectoral administration was, therefore, weakened by the reforms of the 1980s, but it still retains leverage, particularly in the rural areas and small towns which were not greatly affected by the reforms.

The prefect holds a precarious and vulnerable position, and his success depends on the goodwill and co-operation of people over whom, in principle, he exerts his "tyranny". The main role of the prefect, in practice, is as departmental troubleshooter. Helped by his subprefects, his police and the staff of the prefecture (many of them local men) and in daily contact with the *notables*, he is quickly confronted with the conflicts and tensions of the *département*. He can no longer impose solutions in authoritarian fashion: the *préfet à poigne* (the mail-fisted prefect of popular folklore who was defined as a man who would not hesitate, if ordered, to execute an opponent twice) no longer exists. The present prefect listens, persuades, cajoles gently and rarely bullies. He conciliates rather than coerces, and his main weapons are tact and common sense and not the panoply of formal powers at his disposal. A good prefect can enjoy great influence by careful use of his innate prestige, but a bad prefect can destroy his prestige by careless abuse of his influence. The prefect is a politician, an administrator, a priest, a policeman, a peacemaker, a safety valve and a scapegoat. He performs the most demanding, the most difficult and the most delicate job in the French administration.

His relationship with the local *notables*, far from being a dominant one, is one based on "complementarity and interdependence" (Jean-Claude Thoenig). The links of mutual dependence which bind the prefect and the mayor, for example, are numerous and strong: their nature has been summarized by Mark Kesselman as follows:

● Each needs to lean on the other to strengthen his own legitimacy. The prefect reinforces his position *vis-à-vis* Paris by underlining his privileged *rapports* with the mayors, and the mayors reinforce their standing with their own electors by pointing to their strategic bargaining position with the local prefect.
● Each needs the other to ensure local peace and harmony. Each is anxious to *éviter les histoires*, to avoid being embroiled in politically compromising and personally damaging conflicts.
● Each needs the other as a scapegoat to explain *lack* of success.
● Their active collaboration is frequently required to carry out specific projects.
● They share similar defensive roles especially in their relations with the field services, the pressure groups and the Paris bureaucracies.

The traditional relationship between the *notables* and the prefect was closely symbiotic, each buttressing the other against those outside elements which seemed so keen to undermine both. The Socialist reforms are unlikely to impinge upon that relationship, for it is too embedded in the fabric of local government.

The financial dependence of the local authorities, though real, should not be overestimated

The financial control exercised by the centre over the provinces through the allocation of grants of various types is unquestionably strong. But its extent should not be exaggerated. Indeed, the whole question invites several brief comments.

● While it is true that the budgets of the local authorities represent only a fifth of the total budget of the state, compared with 50 per cent in Sweden, Denmark and Great Britain and 80 per cent in the German Federal Republic, it must be emphasized that local authorities in those countries are paying for many more services imposed upon them by the state: the actual degree of financial autonomy based on *real disposable income* is much less than implied by the above figures.

- There is no *necessary* correlation between the extent of financial dependence and local autonomy: indeed, historically, increasing central aid has often *increased* local autonomy by enabling poorer areas to develop services or implement projects the cost of which was beyond their limited resources. What, in practice, matters is how the centre distributes its manna; what strings it attaches to the grants it allocates. There is no doubt that the bewildering maze of specific grants gives the central administrations considerable leverage in imposing their norms. But several attempts (notably in 1972, 1979 and 1982-83) have been made to shift state subsidies in a more general or "block" way (*globalisation des subventions*): in other words, block capital grants have increasingly replaced specific grants. The Socialists were to retain the same operating costs block grant principle (based on a repayment of 16.25 per cent of the value added tax paid by the local authorities for work carried out by them) as their Right-wing predecessors,and they have promised to "globalize" even further the grant system.
- The financial problems of certain localities have been created by their own imprudence or by deliberate choice, or were the fault of neighbouring communes. A commune often has to provide services for neighbouring communes which have the supermarkets, factories or nuclear power stations which provide them with a healthy local tax base.
- The localities often grumble not about the principle of going to the state for money than about the cumbersome and time-consuming methods involved. Here, too, an effort was made in the 1970s to simplify and to localize procedures: hence, the regional and departmental officials were given a greater say in deciding grants, while the *Caisse des Dépôts* was "regionalized" – only demands for very big loans were decided in Paris.
- As the result of the reforms of Defferre's predecessor, Bonnet, the communes were given the right to determine the rate of the four local taxes. In other words, throughout the 1970s there was an uninterrupted effort to globalize, to rationalize, to simplify and to decentralize the financial arrangements and relationship between the state and the localities.

The basic principles which underlie the financial relationship between the centre and the local authorities are unlikely ever to be radically altered (the reform of local finances is being treated with great caution by the Rocard government appointed in June 1988). This is not only because the centre would be unwilling to give greater autonomy to a periphery which is or might be dominated by its political opponents, or because it would be reluctant to lose control over public sector spending – two points already made. But it is because the vertical nature of the relationship (i.e. the state allocates to the local base) is imposed by the existence of 36,000 communes, ninety-six *départements* and twenty-two regions of very different size and tax capacity. A localized tax system without central intervention would lead to greater disparities, with the rich getting richer and the poor poorer. The problem of financing local government thus underlines the inherent problem of combining efficiency, equality and liberty.

There has been an increase in the number, the size and the autonomy of big towns

In 1975 68.8 per cent of the French population was defined as urban – the percentage represented by the rural population in 1872. Writing in 1976 Crozier and Thoenig noted that "the urban exception is already more important than the rural rule". Of particular significance for local government has been the increase in the number and size of the big towns: according to the last census there were thirty-nine towns with a population of over 100,000 and 107 with a population of over 50,000. By March 1977 there were 221 towns with more than 30,000 inhabitants, compared with 193 in 1971 and 159 in 1965 . . . and forty-seven at the beginning of the Third Republic, when the Act which largely defined the powers of local authorities was passed.

The relations between the big towns and the centre are, in practice, totally different from those which obtain between the vast majority of communes and the centre:

● There has always been a tradition of jealous autonomy in certain big towns such as Toulouse, Lyons and Marseilles: their independence was facilitated by distance and often fed by political enmity.
● The big towns have big and powerful bureaucracies led by a general secretary who is frequently of very high calibre.
● They have their own technical services which rival those of the state.

- Although they are, like all communes, financially dependent upon the state, they nevertheless enjoy some degree of financial autonomy.
- They have greater scope of initiative in important areas such as town planning (by the judicious use of building permits and land expropriation), housing and public transport, the creation of industrial zones, social and cultural matters.
- In certain big towns, notably those held by the Communists, the local authority is helped by a well organized party machine which provides technical expertise and advice.
- They frequently enjoy the dynamic leadership of a powerful, long-serving, full-time and paid mayor. Defferre in Marseilles, Chaban-Delmas in Bordeaux, Crépeau in La Rochelle, Dubedout in Grenoble, Pradel in Lyons, Pflimlin in Strasburg, Fréville in Rennes until his retirement in 1977, Médecin in Nice, Mauroy in Lille, Lecanuet in Rouen and Duromée in Le Havre were or are among the many important mayors who determined the programmes and shaped the priorities of their towns, often giving them a particular image: Strasburg and Grenoble have the reputation of being havens of culture (and by French provincial standards they are); La Rochelle is the "ecological town" in which free bicycles were made available to the inhabitants; Angoulomê pioneered the idea of putting factories in pleasant rural surroundings; Lyons under Mayor Pradel covered itself with concrete. A recent study has pinpointed the key roles played by Fréville, Mayor of Rennes and "an elected autocratic monarch", and by Médecin, Mayor of Nice, in forging the destinies of their towns. Jacques Chirac, who was elected Mayor of Paris in 1977, created for himself a powerful political base in the capital by his enterprising and dynamic style of leadership and by the implementation of projects and policies which elicited, on balance, more praise than criticism.

The relative autonomy of the big towns has been attested to by several studies: it has even been claimed that a patient and determined mayor can do virtually anything he wishes. Jérôme Milch has shown in his study of Montpellier and Nîmes (the former ruled by a Centrist mayor, the latter run by a Communist-dominated council) that they developed different policies in at least three distinct areas: the stifling uniformity which Paris is supposed to impose on local authorities was far from being the dominant characteristic of the two towns' policy outputs. It is also clear that Left-wing municipalities generally spend a greater proportion of their budgets (which are generally bigger) on public housing and public transport than Right-wing municipalities: many have also managed to renovate their town centres without expropriating the homes of the poor (who in Paris and Lyons have been forced to move to the inconvenient suburbs). The innovative role of the Communist Party in local politics (it is powerfully entrenched in many French cities) has long been suspected, and it has recently been confirmed in the perceptive work of Martin Schain. Variations in the policies and styles of the cities and major towns suggest some degree of independence in their relations with Paris. Some authors even refer to the emergence of a totally different model of the centre–periphery relationship in these towns.

Some concluding remarks

The Defferre reforms of March 1982 are likely to introduce more changes that effect real change, since they build upon, rather than profoundly modify, the practices and reforms of his predecessors: the *ordonnances* of January 1959 on communal collaboration; the creation of new towns; the slow emergence of the region in the 1960s and 1970s; the reform of 1975 which gave Paris power comparable with that of any other commune; the financial reforms of the late 1970s and 1980s. It might be argued that the Defferre reforms passed so smoothly because they were based in a growing consensus on the subject. Nor have the Socialist reforms really tackled many of the central issues: the national character of most important local actors; the centralization of most private financial and economic agents; the "nationalization" of politics and political parties which has taken place during the Fifth Republic; the retention, for a variety of reasons, of centralized control of the economy. France will remain a unitary and centralized state, albeit an attenuated one.

It has been claimed by the critics that the French centralized state is *inefficient, insensitive to local needs, stultifying, and un-democratic.*

It is inefficient because it multiplies time-consuming procedures. Jean Lecanuet, Mayor of Rouen, once complained that it took him thirteen years before getting permission to rebuild one of the main squares of the town because an obstructionist Paris bureaucracy rejected successive plans (the final result suggests that Paris should have persisted). More seriously, because of the proverbial slowness of Paris it may take up to twenty years between a local decision to build a hospital and its completion, and Paris has been known to block the building of secondary schools for up to ten years. But decentralizing decision-making does not necessarily speed up the process: the Bouvard Senatorial Report of 1976 concluded that the measures of administrative decentralization decreed in March 1964 led to "growing complexity [of procedures] which increased delays and increased administrative costs'. It must also be conceded that many decisions on certain plans are, and have to be, *intrinsically* time-consuming, for they have not only major financial and technical implications but also wide-ranging social and political "externalities". The decision of one town, for example, to build a new hospital may drain doctors from other towns which are already medically deprived.

The centralized system is also denounced as insensitive to local needs, since it applies uniform policies by its rules, regulations, directives, instructions, recommendations and warnings: areas with differing needs are treated to rigidly similar policies. The criticism merits three main observations. First as already noted, different areas and towns have been able to pursue differing policies. Second, much of the uniformity that does exist springs from the electors, who demand minimum standards in a whole range of social services. Finally, lack of uniformity in certain areas such as defence and foreign affairs would be manifestly absurd and that is readily admitted. But in other areas, too, it would lead to absurd anomalies: for example, allowing practising Catholic regions to have separate legislation on abortion would merely lead to weekend coachloads of Basques and Bretonnes with unwanted pregnancies and sufficient financial means leaving for the more socially tolerant clinics of Paris. Furthermore, decentralizing economic decision-making might lead to greater regional disparities, with the poor getting poorer and the rich richer. Champions of decentralization frequently forget that "malevolent" Paris has sometimes used its powers to ensure greater equity.

The third accusation levelled against the centralized system is that it is stultifying, since it kills local initiative and leads to a spirit of resignation and lassitude among local officials. The evidence for such an assertion is decidedly slim, and the dynamism, the resolution and the imagination of many mayors who have transformed their towns must raise doubts about the accusation.

Finally, the system is denounced as undemocratic, for decisions are made by non-elected Paris bureaucrats or their field services who ride rough-shod over the aspirations of locally elected officials. Again, a number of observations are called for. In the first place, national exigencies and local requirements frequently coincide because both are shaped by similar electoral pressures and by professional networks whose members at national and local level have often been educated and trained in the same institutions and share a common ethos. Second, for the numerous complex reasons outlined in this chapter, the centre is often sensitive to local needs expressed by the *notables*. Third, the present system with its mosaic of small communes ensures that at least 36,000 mayors and some of the 465,000 local councillors play some part – however marginal in some cases - in decision-making. In no other country in Europe is it easier for the ordinary citizens to locate an *identifiable* and *accessible* articulator and transmitter of a grievance than in France: the existence of 36,000 mayors and 465,000 local councillors may be inefficient to the protagonists of economic rationalism, but it is a source of immense strength for local democracy. Fourth, transferring decision-making to the local authorities may involve handing over increased powers to self-perpetuating political cliques. In France certain areas are impregnable bastions of the Right and others are rotten boroughs of the Left, where minority rights may be catered for less well than on the national level, where a small swing in any election may produce a change in government. The final point is that, however deplorable it may seem to the decentralizers, most of the local elites are generally content with the present system, as several official inquiries have demonstrated. It may be that some prefer the dictatorship of the distant and impersonal centre to the closer and more oppressive tyranny of other local potentates. But the reason for the general contentment of the local elites springs from their appreciation of the practical possibilities of a system which is inflexible only in appearance.

If locally elected decision-makers have so few powers it is tempting to ask why local elections are fought with such passion and why the electors turn out in such large numbers to vote for such "impotent" elites (Table 16).

Given the "tyrannical" nature of Paris control over the provinces, it is also curious that the reform of local government, willed by successive governments of the Fifth Republic, was so "piecemeal and gradualist" (Jack Hayward): the reform of local finances, announced in early 1959, was *commenced* only fifteen years later and is far from complete; the 1974 promises of President Giscard d'Estaing to introduce regional reforms were discreetly shelved; the 1982 reforms left many delicate problems unresolved. The reluctance to touch the structures of local government must be attributed to the unwillingness to upset key parts of the administration (especially the prefects) and most of the local elites who, whatever their public protests, find the system generally so satisfactory that they resist all attempts to change it. Those elites are well represented in the French parliament and are grouped in influential bodies such as the *Association des Maires de France*, which have good contacts with the Ministry of the Interior.

Table 16 Abstention rate in national and local elections 1946–88

General elections	Abstention (per cent)	Local elections	Abstention (per cent)
November 1946	21.9	October 1947	23.2
June 1951	19.8	April 1953	20.4
January 1956	17.3	March 1959	25.3
November 1958	22.9	March 1965	21.8
November 1962	31.3	March 1971	24.8
March 1967	19.7	March 1977	21.2
June 1968	19.9	March 1983	32.2
March 1973	19.1		
March 1978	17.2		
June 1981	29.1		
June 1986	21.5		
June 1988	34.3		

There are several models of centre–periphery relations:

● There is the juridical model which is based on a reading of the texts, which suggest a hierarchy of decision-makers, with the locally-elected elites firmly entrenched at the bottom.

● There is the Marxist model: so-called "local power' is relative, for local political institutions are firmly integrated into the state machine and function within a framework firmly fixed by the central state. According to the Marxists, the relative autonomy of local actors is one means by which the hegemonic class ensures the alliance or support of other classes or factions: local actors are allowed some initiative, provided that its use does not conflict with the interests of the hegemonic class. The Marxist model raises, however, more questions than it answers (on matters such as the definition of class at local level and the relationship between key groups and certain classes – however defined), and it fails to encompass the wide variety of centre–periphery relationships.

● There is the Crozierian model, based on the principles of Michel Crozier but perfected by his disciples Jean-Pierre Worms, Pierre Grémion and Jean-Claude Thoenig. The last scholar has elaborated a model which depicts the various actors as inextricably linked in a "honeycomb structure", characterized by mutual interdependence and "conflictual complicity". None of the actors holds all the cards, and it is only through conciliation and compromise that each can fulfil his aims. The system also calls for constant intervention and arbitration by actors at a higher level: it is thus underpinned by a centralist logic.

No one disputes that France is a unitary state, in which most major decisions are taken in Paris. But it is important to know not only where decisions are *taken* but from where they *emanate* and where they are *shaped*, and it has been shown in this chapter that in answering those two questions the weight of the provinces fully emerges,and that relations between Paris and the provinces are immensely subtle and complex. Relations between Paris and the provinces are all too frequently presented as antagonistic when, in reality, there is often a large measure of agreement between them. They are also locked into a system of mutual interdependence. Often they are pursuing common objectives which are defined, in large measure, by electoral pressures to which both are equally sensitive. In the 1950s and 1960s both were involved in encouraging industrialization and both were trying to satisfy the explosion of socio-economic expectations. Both were active agents in extending the net of the welfare state. Both are now frantically concerned with improving the "quality of life" under pressure from the increasingly popular environmentalists. It is unlikely that political decentralization will lead to any dramatic change in policy direction in key areas. Interdependence is rooted not only in the pursuit of common objectives; it is also embedded in mutual self-interest. While many decisions made in Paris automatically affect the provinces it is frequently forgotten that local decisions may have national repercussions. For instance, the policies of the big towns towards immigrant workers have not only local but also national and even international consequences. It is also clear that if the local authorities need the financial assistance of the state, the state frequently calls upon the financial help of the provinces.

Behind a highly centralized formal system lurks a complex and highly personalized web of "parallel powers" (Michel Crozier): Parisian bureaucrats and their provincial agents, prefects and locally elected officials are condemned to live together in a chaos of surreptitious bargaining, illicit agreements, hidden collusion, unspoken complicity, simulated tension and often genuine conflict. The present system of tempered or attenuated centralization is sustained by the customary combination of inertia, apathy and self-interest. There is also a touch of hypocrisy, with Paris and the provinces exploiting each other as the scapegoat responsible for its own deficencies.

The exact nature of the relationship between Paris and a locality depends on a range of factors: the size of the commune and the quality of its technical and financial resources; the relations of the local *notables* with the field services, the prefect and the Paris bureaucrats; the dynamism and leadership of the mayors of the big town; the general sensitivity of state officials to local needs; the prevailing economic situation; the electoral impact of particular issues. Simply to view decision-making in France as completely dominated by power-hungry Jacobins impervious to the demands of frustrated and impotent provincial *notables* is to misunderstand the complexity and subtlety of the relations which exist between a fragmented power structure in the capital and the splintered power structure in the provinces.

13 Conclusion: public policy-making under the Fifth Republic: the constrained polity

The political aims of the founders of the Fifth Republic were clearly stated: to destroy the weak and despised régime of the Fourth Republic which had been undermined by a defective constitution, by unstable and short-lived governments, by a parliament which was omnipotent in theory but impotent in practice, by divided and undisciplined parties, by a ubiquitous and powerful administration, by a resentful and disobedient army and by overactive pressure groups. The new Republic was to be both strong and respected, underpinned by a constitution which strengthened the powers of the executive and which ensured presidential pre-eminence (if not predominance), and in which parliament, the parties, the army, the administration and the pressure groups were relegated firmly to their proper – and subordinate – place. In some important respects, the founders have proved successful in the fulfilment of their basic aims: diplomatically, France is no longer the subject of international derision as she was before 1958; also, in contrast with the situation before 1958, successive opinion polls indicate a high level of satisfaction with the régime, governments now give the appearance of stability, and prime ministers enjoy longer periods of office; the powers of parliament have been effectively curbed; small and undisciplined parties no longer dominate the political scene; the army – 'the state within the state' during the previous régime – has been reduced to silent obedience to the civil authorities. Perhaps the most important, and certainly the most striking, change after 1958 was the emergence of the presidency as the major focus of political decision-making in France. The reasons for the growth of presidential power have been analysed at length in this book: the desire of successive presidents to extend the scope of their powers; their careful use and abuse of the 1958 constitution; the strengthening of their electoral legitimacy by the referendum of October 1962; the reinforcement of the presidential private office; the transformation of ministers into presidential servants; the backing in parliament of a sympathetic and disciplined party coalition; the weakness and divisions of the political opposition; the exploitation of propitious political circumstances. Personal, constitutional and political factors combined, therefore, to ensure presidential supremacy. Before March 1986 that supremacy was demonstrated on innumerable occasions. For instance, President de Gaulle's unilateral decision not to devalue the franc in the autumn of 1968 was matched by Giscard d'Estaing's personal decision to halt the extension of the Paris Left-bank motorway in the summer of 1974, and Mitterrand's personal decision to withdraw the Savary Bill in 1984. Moreover, the general guidelines of important policy areas bear the unmistakable personal imprint of successive presidents: the foreign, European and defence policies of France were shaped by General de Gaulle; the country's industrial policy bears the Pompidou hallmark; the liberalizing measures in the social field taken between 1974 and 1976 owed much to the personal determination of President Giscard d'Estaing; the spate of reforms (industrial and financial, nationalization, territorial decentralization and political liberalization) of 1981-3 were very much inspired by the preferences and priorities of Mitterrand. In some respects, therefore, it was not totally misleading to describe the French political system as 'presidential'. Certainly, the presidency was *perceived* as the major focus of decision-making by the general public, by the political and administrative elite and by the pressure groups. Yet the President of the Republic even before March 1986 was not omnipotent. His powers were considerable, but they were not unlimited, for he was enmeshed in a complex web of personal, historical, constitutional and political restrictions.

The first type of restriction upon presidential power was – and remains – constitutional and judicial in character. There are things that the president cannot do, since he is specifically prevented from doing so by the constitution. For instance, he may not dissolve the National Assembly more than once a year. It should also be recalled that many of the constitutional provisions which limited presidential power and which fell into abeyance after 1959 were always likely to be invoked in the event of an election of a politically hostile National Assembly. The president was, in fact, in a peculiarly vulnerable position, for some of his power rested upon an ambiguous constitution which could be quoted against him and upon several controversial conventions which could be rejected. He was also dependent upon the goodwill and co-operation of the prime minister, the government and parliament – a goodwill which could disappear after any election. And after the March 1986 elections it did so. For the following two years of so-called *cohabitation*, executive power in domestic policy-making, was claimed and exercised by the prime minister who was backed by a majority in parliament. The president was left with his ceremonial duties, his powers in defence, European and foreign affairs, his ability temporarily to obstruct legislation, and his right to advise, to warn and to criticize – a right he exploited with telling effect.

The second – and perhaps most obvious – restriction upon the president's power was, and is, the limited time at his disposal. As official head of state, he is inevitably involved in time-consuming ceremony and travel, and, conscious of the need for support for his policies, he has to spend a great deal of time in political management. The time left for policy-making is fairly limited, and he has, therefore, to delegate many of his powers to his prime minister and other ministers, who, in turn, are obliged to devolve authority on to an army of civil servants.

The third major restriction upon presidential power lies in the efficiency of the administrative instruments at the disposal of his office. The Elysée has been expanded and strengthened compared with the situation under the Fourth Republic, but it is still small relative to the *gros village* which works for the prime minister. The president is entirely dependent upon the Matignon for the implementation of his policies. The president's own perception of his role provides the fourth major constraint upon his power. That perception is shaped not only by the personality and the tastes of the president but also by political calculation. There are a number of reasons why a president may voluntarily, if sometimes unconsciously, impose limitations upon his policy-making role.

- By becoming totally absorbed in the minutiae of legislation he may disqualify himself as the impartial arbiter and as the judge of its wider political implications.
- Too intimate an involvement in making policy, some of which is bound to be politically controversial, may damage his image as the statesman above the political battle, the embodiment of the unity of the nation, the guide to its future action and the guardian of its basic interests. Opinion polls clearly reveal that the more politically active the president becomes the more his popularity declines.
- The President of the Republic is elected for seven years – a very long time in politics – and an over-interventionist role may become physically crushing.
- The over-concentration of political power in the hands of the president may lead to public identification of the president with the régime itself – an identification assiduously fostered by de Gaulle himself in his dire warnings to the electors of *après moi le chaos*, but which was not without its dangers.

When de Gaulle was absent or indecisive during the turbulent days of May1968 there was a power vacuum, with certain members of the government and the top civil service displaying the sense of purpose and direction of freshly decapitated chickens. A similar power vacuum, though less apparent, was no less real during the last year of Pompidou's period of office when the president was suffering from the appalling and enervating disease which was to kill him. The sense of drifting was equally evident during the summer of 1976 when inflation was increasing and the value of the franc was decreasing: ministerial procrastination was attributed to the absence of the president who was hunting big game in Africa. The vacillation of President Mitterrand over macro-economic policy in 1983 encouraged squabbles within the government and created that uncertainty which industry so much dislikes.

For a combination of these reasons Mitterrand after 1984 and again after 1988 voluntarily withdrew from most domestic policy-making. But there may be deeper, if subconscious reasons for presidential self-effacement, and that is the growing awareness of the limits to public policy-making. Being held responsible for policies over which he exercised little control was a situation which the wily Mitterrand rightly perceived as politically damaging. In a highly constrained polity a low profile is advisable.

General constraints on public policy-making

In analysing the constraints upon public policy-making, it is essential to distinguish between those that are inherent in all public policy-making, those evident in most advanced West European societies and those specific to France and the Fifth Republic.

Included in the first category – those inherent in all public policy-making – are the crudeness and unreliability of any nation's statistical and forecasting instruments. This became all too apparent in 1981 and 1982 when the over-optimistic assumptions of the newly elected Left-wing government were based on inaccurate forecasts. But the overproduction of doctors, the building of vast science faculties for non-existent students, and the chronic deficits of the social security system also illustrate the point. France also shares with all other countries the problem of a machinery of government which is overloaded, defective and inefficient: it has been given tasks that it is incapable or unwilling adequately to fulfil: the balancing of the state budget (all the 'balanced' budgets between 1974 and 1977 ended in substantial deficit), the controlling of the money supply (an important factor in inflation), the prevention of the illegal flow of French capital to safer political havens abroad, the prevention of the entry of illegal immigrants into the country, the suppression or even reduction of massive tax evasion. In other important policy areas its control is tenuous or non-existent: for instance, it has no effective method of controlling the 'irrational' behaviour of the foreign exchange markets or of effectively influencing the investment programmes of most big profit-making companies. Studies by Zysman, by McArthur and Scott and by Cohen and Bauer have underlined some of the powerful constraints upon French governments in industrial policy-making. Finally, French governments, like their counterparts elsewhere, are confronted with problems which many consider insoluble: drug-taking, increasing violence and crime, AIDS, a falling birth-rate (which is a French obsession), racialism and loneliness, which are among the major social problems of the day.

The lag which exists between policy implementation and policy impact, and the dependence upon an array of private actors for both implementation and ultimate effect provide two further examples of the inherent constraints of policy-making. But perhaps the biggest constraint of this nature is the past: yesterday's commitments are today's priorities; yesterday's mistakes are today's preoccupations. It is a banality worth reiterating that the biggest decision-maker in any political system is the past. The Fifth Republic, in spite of claims to the contrary by its apologists, inherited a great deal from its predecessor. After May 1958 the upper part of the political superstructure may have been modified, but there was no upheaval in the social, economic and political substructure. Nor did basic cultural traits disappear with the waving of a Gaullist wand. The same social forces remained intact, the same economic interests continued to strive for superiority, the same administrative machine still functioned, and no one dismantled the vast and complex web of committees, commissions and councils which had proliferated since the end of the Second World War. The Fourth Republic bequeathed much to its successor: *a booming economy and a rapidly changing occupational structure; a vague, yet pervasive ideology rooted in a not always consistent series of traditions* such as the primacy of universal suffrage, 'republican legality', the independence of the judiciary, the legitimacy of governmental interventionism within the framework of a mixed economy, the respect for free speech and association; *its basic institutional framework; most of its political and administrative elite* (more than twenty years after the fall of the Fourth Republic, the two leading contenders in the May 1981 presidential elections were Giscard d'Estaing and Mitterrand, who had been colleagues in the last parliament of the Fourth Republic); *a jumble of political norms and conventions* (such as the desirability of *cumul des mandats* described in Chapter 12) that could be transgressed only with the utmost caution; *a wide-ranging series of domestic, diplomatic and defence commitments* (for example, to an extensive system of social welfare, to the North Atlantic Alliance, to the European Common Market); *a tangle of social and economic expectations* (full employment and steadily rising living standards were taken for granted); *a welter of established rights and privileges* involving many powerfully placed groups; *a number of seemingly intractable problems* such as the Algerian war, which dominated and poisoned the politics of the early years of the Fifth Republic. In many policy areas (housing, health, education, energy ...) the advent of the Fifth Republic was not a watershed, but a largely irrelevant political event.

The second category of constraints are those evident in most industrialized West European societies. They are of both an 'imported' or outside and an internal nature. Outside pressures take both a social and economic form. Imported social pressures include the growing demands for higher education, better welfare services, greater public participation in decision-making and for sexual and gender liberation, the questioning of traditional morality and of organized religion – all of which are the results of the processes of cultural homogenization due to increased geographical mobility and the internationalization of the media. The ever-sensitive French leaders have watched helplessly over the Americanization of French culture and the importation of new social demands. Equally, the 'distributional coalitions' which have created, extended and consolidated the welfare state are as present in France as anywhere in Western Europe, and only the most foolhardy government attempts radically to interfere with the welfare benefits of its citizenry: the *machine égalitaire* (Alain Minc) has an engine difficult to slow down and impossible to stop.

All West European governments have also witnessed the growth of external economic constraints, such as the *multinationalization* of major firms which has gathered pace since the 1960s. Many such firms now employ more people abroad than at home. Furthermore, foreign investment in France though smaller than in the United Kingdom, West Germany or Italy, is making significant inroads into the ownership patterns of industry in France. The welcoming of foreign capital since the 1970s has been motivated by the need to create employment, but it has penetrated French industry to such an extent that as early as 1977 the Cotta Report could warn the French government that key sectors of the French economy (such as petroleum, shipbuilding, pharmaceuticals and electronics) were effectively controlled by foreigners: a quasi-monopoly in the construction of nuclear power stations in France was enjoyed by the Belgian-dominated Empain-Schneider group between 1963 and 1981. This does not signify that the state is helpless against such firms (it has many weapons at its disposal – loans, subsidies, public purchasing policy and even nationalization), but it does mean that the already complex task of running the economy is rendered even more difficult.

The growing internationalization of industry has clearly had a constraining effect on national governments, by creating new networks of interdependence and dependence. The 'technology gap', which is the source of so much concern in Brussels, has long affected West European countries: for instance, France's much vaunted computer and civil nuclear energy programmes in the 1960s and 1970s were heavily dependent upon American expertise. The extent of this technological dependence fully emerged during the 1981-82 negotiations between the French government and certain firms it wished to nationalize.

But it is in the area of finance that the processes of internationalization are producing their greatest constraints upon national decision-making. As Charles Kindleberger has recently argued in a brilliant little book, *International Capital Movements*, four financial revolutions have been taking place simultaneously since the mid-1970s. In the first place, exchange rates have been allowed to float. Second, the falling costs of electronic communication are dissolving geographical boundaries between what were once distinct markets. Third, banks and other institutions are creating scores of new financial instruments. And fourth, deregulation is dismantling the barriers that governments deliberately or accidentally placed in the way of traders in international money. Combined, these four revolutions have been a disruptive force, and all are closely inter-related: it is no accident that these accelerating trends have occurred at the same time. Deregulation, for instance, has helped to foster innovation in banking, while international trade in financial services (prompted by cheaper, faster communications) has done much to create the demand for deregulation. The world financial markets are, for Kindleberger, inherently volatile, and he argues that this volatility will be eased only if countries rebuild the barricades against capital flows. But this is now unthinkable. However improbable, the logical outcome of the present situation is a single financial market, with one currency, one supranational monetary authority and one monetary policy: exchange-rate uncertainty would disappear by abolishing exchange rates. This is not the place to discuss the direction in which the financial world is moving. Suffice to note that Kindleberger's four revolutions have clearly had their impact on all European countries and on France perhaps more so than most. It has gradually dismantled its financial barriers, and this has occurred during Left- and Right-wing governments: at present almost all capital controls have gone.

The globalization of the financial circuits has transformed the French financial market: the stock exchange, once one of the sleepiest in Europe, has been revolutionized; French domestic securities firms have become multinational investment banks with some making half their profits abroad; French government bonds are now traded on the New York stock exchange; the major French banks belong to international banking clubs such as Ebic and Ebercor, and carry out many of their foreign exchange transactions in London. It is revealing that the Socialists who nationalized most of what was left of the private banking system in 1981 were soon criticizing state bank managers for acting like private bankers. But they quickly came to recognize that the managers had little choice. If Paris wishes to become a major financial centre – and currently it is not – any French government must fully embrace the logic of internationalization. The signs are that they are doing so.

The internationalization of the financial circuits and their development has been taking place at a time when the real economy – in goods and services – is relatively stagnant, with the result that exchange rates have become much more vulnerable to purely *financial* flows. Since the mid 1980s the difficulty of controlling the international monetary and financial circuits has been fully demonstrated. Now France is in a peculiarly vulnerable position in this respect, and for two essential reasons. First, it is especially sensitive to shifts in the value of the dollar – the cornerstone of the international monetary system: 37 per cent of all French imports are paid in dollars, and so, too, are most foreign debt repayments. Three-fifths of its imported energy (and France is still, after Italy, the most energy-dependent country in Western Europe) are also dollar-denominated. If the effects in France of the first oil crisis were attenuated by the fall in the dollar, those of the second oil crisis after 1979 were aggravated by the rise in the American currency. It has been calculated that this rise reduced the French growth rate by 1 per cent in 1982, pushed up unemployment, inflation and the public sector deficit. The hectic gyrations of the American dollar of the mid-1980s made French financial and monetary management inherently difficult. Thus the slide in the value of the American currency in the autumn of 1986 helped to slow down the Right-wing government's liberalization programme, because investors and speculators shifted their money into a safe currency – the D-mark – and the French franc is pegged to the value of the D-mark in the European Monetary System.

France is especially vulnerable in the current situation for a second reason: that is its chronic trade deficit – itself dependent on the value of the dollar, the state of the oil market, and international commodity prices. It is also clearly dependent on the state of the international economy, especially on the German economy which absorbs 16-17 per cent of total French exports, and on the American and Japanese economies which together account for almost two-fifths of gross world product. France has also been living through a period of increased import penetration and a decline in its exporting capacity. As successive OECD reports have indicated, the French record on trade and competitiveness is not good. France is losing exports at a faster r ite than can be explained by the geography of its markets, product mix, relative prices or exchange rates. If the experts of the OECD are to be believed, what is to be blamed is 'the slowness of industry to adapt to changing patterns of demand'. Any moderate growth sucks in imports, leads to a deterioration in the trade balance, incites investors and speculators to sell the franc, and leads to inflationary pressures through devaluation or interest rate increases. The experience of 1981-1982 is very revealing in this respect. When the newly elected Socialist government attempted to buck the world deflationary trend by opting for a Keynesian-type expansion the result was rising inflation, a yawning current account deficit, mounting public debt, and three politically damaging devaluations of the franc. After a heated debate within the government and the Socialist Party, Mitterrand changed economic course, and from 1983-84 there was a great 'U-turn' as a result of what the Right condescendingly described as the *'apprentissage du réel'* – an apprenticeship in reality. But it was unlike British U-turns of the 1960s and 1970s in that it was radical, coherent, enduring and sincere. From 1983-84 France fully accepted the logic and discipline of the international market. It also more fully accepted the logic and discipline of the Europeanized market.

Clearly, *'François Mitterrand a découvert l'Europe'* as one of his ministers remarked, and he has come fully to integrate the European dimension into his thinking. In his New Year's Eve message in December 1987 he declared: *'La France est notre patrie, l'Europe est notre avenir'*. He has become arguably Europe's leading statesman – and this was not always the case: only after a prolonged bout of agonising did he agree in 1983 that France should remain in the European Monetary System and accept the disciplines that the system imposed. Thereafter, he emerged as one of the great conciliators at the European level and played a key role in the entry of Greece, Portugal and Spain into the EEC. It was thanks to Mitterrand's personal concessions in 1984 at Fontainebleau that the vexed problem of British contributions to the Community budget was solved.

The European constraint has, of course, been present since the establishment of the Community by the Treaty of Rome in 1957. And by the early 1970s some policy areas (such as agriculture) were already essentially determined in Brussels. Since the mid 1970s, however, France has become well and truly enmeshed in the thicket of Europeanization. A series of factors has led to a tightening of the Community constraint. First, the enlargement of the EEC (the United Kingdom and Eire and Denmark joined in 1972, Greece, Portugal and Spain some ten years later) has made decision-making much more complex and less manageable for the French. The second factor has been the redesigning of the industrial, financial and technological map of Europe by firms and major groups: this process is taking place *at the base* – not as a result of political decisions – but of industrial and financial ones. It is a process of subterranean or even surreptitious Europeanization. Since the early 1980s there has been a slow restructuring of European industry and banking as the result of acquisition and mergers. The titanic battle of 1987-88 for control of the *Société Générale* – Belgium's biggest industrial and financial empire – was but the most spectacular of many other examples. The industrial barons of Europe are on the move, creating transnational European firms, or industries on a European scale. Of course, there are limits to these developments imposed by nationalism and national restrictive practices, but the European Commission is now actively pursuing a policy of encouraging the creation of 'European' firms whose strategies will escape the control of national governments. The third major factor constraining France in a European sense has been the impact of the European Monetary System which was established in 1979, with three specific purposes:

● To facilitate trade by creating a zone of monetary stability in Europe.
● To co-ordinate monetary and exchange rate policies towards the rest of the world.
● To prepare the way for the birth of a European Monetary Fund, making the Ecu or European currency unit a reserve currency and a means of settlement, and eventually moving towards full European union.

Without doubt the most effective part of the EMS has been the *exchange rate mechanism* – a system for managing exchange rates within certain bands – it limits each European currency to fluctuations of 2.25 per cent against the others. In practice, the system is very much in the grip of the D-mark – in other words in the hands of the *Bundesbank*. When the French decided to remain in the EMS in 1983 it thereby accepted the ferocious monetary discipline imposed by the West Germans. There have been several French complaints about West German stringency but to no avail. In order to achieve greater exchange stability there has been pressure for convergence in macro-economic and labour-market policies, and this in turn requires policy co-operation, especially on interest rates. A further move in the direction of co-operation was the creation in January 1988 by France and West Germany of a joint Finance and Economic Council which involves their Finance Ministers meeting four times a year to co-ordinate Franco-German policy. There have even been discussions about the creation of a central European Bank, with the Ecu as a reserve currency, although both ideas fell foul of Mrs. Thatcher's handbag. Nevertheless, it is revealing that the French were in the forefront of the discussions.

The final constraining factor at European level has been the impact of the Single European Act of July 1987. It has both policy and institutional dimensions. In effect, the Act represents a binding commitment on the part of the EEC countries to create a unified internal market by the end of 1992 – all barriers to trade, people and capital are to be removed completely in a *Europe sans frontières*: a market of 320 million people (as many as Japan and the USA combined) untrammelled by any barrier.

No doubt this '*Europe sans frontières*' will not be created by 1992: "1992" is part myth, part rhetoric, part exhortation. But there is no doubt that the Single European Act has set up pressures for deregulation and liberalization which the French have fully accepted. It has also triggered off pressures for fiscal harmonization: by 1988 European countries were locked into protracted negotiations over harmonizing, to some extent, the rates of their respective sales taxes (VAT). Since France raises more tax receipts through such taxes than any other West European country, any lowering of the rates – and it looks probable – will have to be compensated, either by cutting government expenditure or by raising direct income taxes – or both, and both are fraught with political difficulties. Harmonization of fiscal and monetary policies raises important and delicate issues: for instance, subsidies to depressed regions or to lame-duck industries will not be tolerated by a country's European neighbours and will be denounced as trade-distorting unfair practices. Already France has had several proposed subsidy programmes refused by the European Commission. Naturally, France, like most of her Community partners, has attempted to avoid the constraints of Europe by the non-implementation of decisions and the violation of the rules. But the capacity to escape Community constraints is being slowly eroded. Thus free capital flows between European countries will automatically penalize any country which steps out of line and adopts counter-cyclical policies, and no country will be equipped to avoid the penalties. Free capital flows also aggravate the problem of tax evasion which is already rife in France – if not quite the national sport that it is in Italy. The result is that there is talk of greater co-operation between the tax gatherers of Europe and of disclosure of all foreign transactions: integration seems to call forth further integration.

There is also an institutional dimension to the Single European Act, since the Act permits more simple majority decisions in Brussels, and it involves the delegation of enhanced executive power to the European Commission. This easing of the decision-making processes and the strengthening of the supra-national element may well have durable consequences for national sovereignty.

As a result of pressures from the international and European environments the major French parties have been squeezed into an involuntary consensus. The policies of the Socialist administration after 1983 were very revealing: there was emphasis on company profits, on the control of public expenditure, the de-indexation of wages, the reduction in the number of civil servants, the shedding of labour and the cutting of capacity in overmanned and inefficient industries, the dismantling of exchange controls, the expansion of the stock exchange. *Modernisation* became the key phrase in the Socialists' vocabulary: if post-1984 French socialism was not 'Thatcherism with a human face' it was a recognition of the brutal realities of the international and European market place. It is significant that in May 1988 after the re-election of Mitterrand to the presidency, shares on the *Bourse* rose an average 2.5 per cent: in May 1981 after his initial election, the value of shares fell so fast that trading had to be suspended.... The Right when it came to power merely extended the policy of liberalization and deregulation of the Socialists.

It is, of course, notoriously difficult to assess the effects of economic interdependence since it involves complex calculations relating to import–export ratios, the dependence of certain home industries on foreign parts, the extent of the investment of foreign (largely American and European Community) firms with holding companies in France, the investments of French firms abroad, the viability of home industries without an international market. Yet it certainly raises questions about a state's capacity to manage its own economy: certainly 'the transnational character of late capitalism' poses problems for states such as France which are very sensitive about autonomy and independence. Again, the events of 1981 to 1983 may be used to illustrate the limits to national sovereignty imposed by the multinationalization, internationalization and Europeanization of the economy. The French government lost control of the leading foreign banking subsidiary of Paribas, the French banking empire it was then nationalizing, because of the ruthless organization of international banking interests; it was powerless to bring down American interest rates which it saw as one of the major obstacles to trade expansion and one of the principal causes of a rapidly appreciating dollar – with which oil had to be purchased. It was virtually helpless to combat the money markets which forced three devaluations of the franc in October 1981, June 1982 and March 1983 (the rate of devaluation was negotiated not within the French Council of Ministers but in Brussels with the other members of the European Monetary System); it had to accept continuing foreign stakes in certain nationalized industries because they were dependent on foreign expertise; it had to concert its effort with its European Community partners to bring pressure on an American administration which had imposed quotas on steel imports; it did the same in order to defy President Reagan's decision, in June 1982, to forbid the supply to Russia of oil and gas equipment by the foreign subsidiaries of American companies (for the building of the pipeline from Siberia to West Europe).

Public policy-making under the Fifth Republic takes place, therefore, within limits imposed by the constraints inherent in all public policy-making and by those of an economy locked into Europe and open to the world. It is also shaped by the domestic political, administrative and constitutional environment.

Domestic constraints upon policy-making

Within the limits defined by history and by the outside world public policy decisions emerge as the result of the interaction – or non-interaction (for mutual avoidance may be profitable) – of a chaos of decision-makers who function at national, regional and local level. Power is diffused among a host of bodies – the executive (which itself resembles a huge Byzantine court riddled with feuding factions), parliament, the political parties (including those of the opposition), the pressure groups, the banks, industrial firms and insurance companies – all of which are fragmented and divided. Even bodies such as the nationalized banks and industries and the administration, although nominally servants of the state, are badly divided, with each part generating and protecting its own corporate interests. Policy co-ordination in this compartmentalized world is peculiarly difficult, but given the web of overlapping jurisdictions it is vital. Any major policy requires the intervention of many state actors. Thus, steel policy-making in the 1980s required the intervention of the President of the Republic, the Prime Minister, the Finance Minister, the Labour Minister, the Minister for Social Affairs, the Minister for European Affairs, and a host of public bodies at national and local level. The Lemoine Report of 1983 indicated that in the state information technology sector there were no fewer than thirty public agencies involved, and none had 'the strength, the authority or the legitimacy' to define and impose a coherent programme. As noted in the Chapter on the public administration, some co-ordinating bodies complicate, rather than facilitate, policy co-ordination, while some rarely if ever meet: of the thirty-three interdepartmental committees in existence in December 1986, three had not met for nearly ten years, and between 1981 and 1985 only eighteen met more than once. The situation in France uncannily conforms to Hanf's general description of public policy-making: 'the problem-solving capacity of governments is disaggregated into a collection of sub-systems with limited tasks, competences and resources, where the relatively independent participants possess different bits of information, represent different interests, and pursue separate, potentially conflicting courses of action'. Decision-making is, therefore, *éclaté*, complicated and messy. It is also prolific (because there are few overall frameworks – save its own specific one – to contain it) but inevitably incoherent. The multiple and conflicting roles of the state are, therefore, reflected in a multiplicity of conflicting decisions.

Outside the state machine relations between the decision-makers – when they exist – range from noisy confrontation to quiet collusion, from the parasitic to the symbiotic, from the permanent to the sporadic. Often the real point of decision-making is difficult to locate, for it is hidden from the public gaze. Analysing the political process in France – as in any complex industrial society – is rather like peering down a dimly-lit kaleidoscope held in a gently inebriated hand: after a while it is possible to distinguish some of the more significant pieces, but the pattern is ever-changing and is sensitive to the slightest shudder. Furthermore, there are pieces that remain in obstinate obscurity.

To ask the question, 'Where does power lie in the Fifth Republic?' is to invite the obvious rejoinder, 'Power to do what?'

It was a President of the Republic who decided to withdraw France from NATO, who decided that Britain could enter the EEC and who decided to liberalize the divorce, abortion and contraception laws. But it was a small group of Communist-led workers, grouped in closed shops, who shut down the port of Le Havre for several weeks and who, on several occasions between 1975 and 1987, brought the Paris press to a complete standstill. It was a powerfully organized Catholic lobby which forced the Socialist government in 1984 into withdrawing its offending legislation. It was the massive protests of the students in the streets of Paris which forced the Right-wing government into radically revising its social and educational programmes. Both the Left and the Right in the 1980s discovered that radical policy-making requires the compliance of affected groups, and such groups are invariably wedded to the *status quo*. That a Left-wing government should be pushed into abandoning its reformist ambitions is nothing new in French history, but that a Right-wing administration should also be forced to declare a 'pause' was an indication of the limited freedom of manoeuvre available to any modern French government.

The power of some strategically placed veto groups is often manifest and easy to assess, but how is it possible accurately to measure the effect of the spiritual power of the church, the impact of the mass media, the agenda-setting influence of the extreme Right, the electoral influence of the old-age pensioners? Clearly, there are different 'unofficial' types of power: the *innovatory* or *pedagogical* power of groups such as the Young Farmers of the 1960s, the CFDT and the ecologists, certain political clubs, the Communist Party at local level; the *intimidatory* power of certain groups whose turbulent and often violent activities are tolerated by apprehensive governments; the *inhibitory* power of bodies such as the Council of State and the Constitutional Council which, by their measures or suspected reactions, have exerted a constant and arguably increasing pressure on French governments.

It might be argued that the emergence of the Constitutional Council as a significant political actor in the 1980s constitutes a major constitutional innovation. The Council's judicial self-restraint of the 1960s and 1970s has disappeared, and the Council has even articulated the doctrine, in its decision of 23 August 1985, that the constitution [which it interprets] is superior to legislation passed by parliament – that 'the law expresses the general will only in so far as it respects the Constitution'. This doctrine represents a fundamental break with Republican tradition according to which the general will is expressed by a sovereign parliament whose legitimacy is based in election. Traditionally, a constitution was viewed not as a sacred text, but merely as a mechanism for defining the rules of the political game. That view has now changed. Between 1981 and 1984 under a Left-wing government and again between 1986 and 1987 under the Right, the Council played a key role in determining the parameters of certain domestic policy areas: for instance, it made important decisions on the nationalization and decentralization programmes of the Left and on the privatization proposals of the Right, and on subjects as equally politically sensitive as the electoral system, the budget, higher education, citizenship requirements, and the mass media. The politicians have not always welcomed the interventions of the Council which they denounce as 'government by judges' but they have never hesitated to resort to it, in order to annul or modify their opponents' actions. For some observers the Council is creating an *État de droit*, a *Rechtstaat*, an overall framework of legal rules, stipulations and norms within which political decision-makers are forced to cast their proposals. For others, however, the Council plays the role of judicial *amortisseur* or defuser of explosive issues in periods of high political polarization: it defines the basic ground rules rather than deeply affects the legislation. Whatever the nature of its present development it is clear that it has gone beyond the mission confided in it by the constitution, and in so doing it has come to constitute yet another constraint upon public policy-makers.

If the power of the Constitutional Council is difficult to assess (and its decisions have given rise to careful analysis) how much more difficult it is to measure the influence of bodies such as the EDF (the nationalized electricity industry), the Atomic Energy Authority, the French administration, the Ministry of Finance, Elf-Aquitaine (the French-owned petrol group), the *Caisse des Dépôts*, the FNSEA (the principal farmers' union). They are very disparate groups, but each of them has been described as 'a state within the state'. There is also the problem of assessing the power of what François Dupuy calls the 'intermediary systems of action of a geographical or sectoral nature', each self-regulating, self-governing and each rooted in a culture or environment which respects its particularism: the agricultural community; the Communist Party in the industrial belt of Paris; the world of the primary school teachers; the medical profession; the universities. Such organizations or institutions or communities are linked with, and many are *ultimately* dependent upon, the state, yet they are structured and function outside the official system. Here we are touching upon, but by no means fully revealing (since there are other important agents of human regulation such as the church and the family) the banal yet crucial distinction between state and society – crucial because vast areas of human experience are regulated outside the confines of 'the political system'. Such bodies secrete their own rules, norms, constraints, politics, structures, hierarchies, elites, which are of as much importance to their members as those of the state.

Measuring power by assessing resources is also a futile exercise, for mere possession does not constitute power: resources have to be mobilized, exploited, or their use threatened or promised, willingly or reluctantly. And this requires judgement and skill in perceiving the propitious moment or the appropriate circumstances. Power is sometimes fluid and variable (compare the situation of Mitterrand before and after May 1981 or the CGT during the 1970s and the 1980s), vulnerable and fleeting. And sometimes it is stable, structured, apparently invulnerable and durable. Sometimes it is personal, sometimes institutional. It may be manifested sporadically or exercised persistently. Certainly the power configuration in any modern state, and France is no exception, is multifaceted, complex and evanescent.

Governments, therefore, are inevitably enmeshed in a concatenation of competing and contradictory forces: they are hemmed in by historical, social, administrative, political and constitutional factors. And if they are not always the helpless spectators of the fate of their country (for they can make or encourage adjustments to the *status quo* by creating a climate which favours certain groups or policies) their freedom of action is often singularly limited.

It has been claimed by the apologists of the present régime that, because of greater governmental powers, stability and authority, decision-making is more 'efficient' and more 'rational' than during the Fourth Republic. Certainly, the Fifth Republic has *attempted* to improve the procedures of decision-making: constant reforms of the machinery of government at national, regional and local level, efforts to improve the administrative co-ordination and implementation of policies; the introduction of RCB (the French equivalent of PPBS); the improvement of statistical and forecasting techniques. The régime has also produced ambitious long-term programmes in order, for example, to restructure the steel industry, to create a national computer industry, to combat monopolies and restrictive practices, to provide the country with nuclear energy, to encourage industrial decentralization and to iron out regional disparities. Yet, compared with the Fourth Republic, the overall picture does not suggest any greater coherence in a system of decision-making which still bears as much the stigmas of fitful and supine incrementalism as the marks of thoughtful rationality. In truth, successive governments of the Fifth Republic have been torn between the competing and often conflicting needs of *national grandeur* (hence Concorde), *rationality* (hence the nuclear energy programme), *electoral opportunism* (hence the totally 'irrational' handouts to the farmers and the steel industry, and the benevolent attention afforded industrial ducks which were not only lame but in some cases totally crippled), and *social consensus* (hence the financial help to Corsica). In the conduct of economic affairs they have lurched between an authoritarian *dirigisme* and a casual liberalism, with reassertion of state authority punctuated by acts destined to undermine it. The general lack of direction in French economic decision-making led one critic, Jacques Chirac, to describe the system as '*dirigisme* without direction'. In other areas, too, 'coherence' has been manifestly lacking, with governments changing the policies of their predecessors with unnerving readiness and alacrity, or members of the same government acting in totally conflicting fashion; in the 1960s the policy of the development of the Paris region was accompanied by measures of industrial decentralization to the provinces; industrial policy involved giving money to expanding industries such as cars and electronics and to declining industries such as textiles and leather, making massive grants to the steel industry in the name of national independence but allowing nuclear energy to fall into the hands of the Belgians; one part of the state machine manufactures cigarettes and another part treats cancer; the Haby Secondary Education Act of 1975 was the fifteenth such Act since 1958, while the Barre anti-inflation programme of 1976 was preceded by innumerable similar programmes. It is, of course, possible to point to major policy options which have been consistently and successfully pursued. President Pompidou's obsessive drive to modernize the French economy is frequently quoted in that respect. Yet it is legitimate to ask whether its success was due to deliberate policy, or whether it was the consequence of other factors: the end of the economically and financially ruinous colonial wars; the impetus of the Common Market; the zeal of the business community, which made huge profits; the weakness of the opposition Left, which in France used to be always good for business; the preparedness of the French to work longer hours than any other Western European people in order to improve their standard of living. Certainly, the policy of vigorous growth has not survived the death of Pompidou. More fairly, it is justifiable to point to the social reforms of the Giscard d'Estaing presidency, and to the territorial and political reforms of the Mitterrand presidency which left France a more civilized, humane and pluralistic polity. But it is significant that the reforms were enacted in the early years of each presidency, before the constraints became too apparent.

The response of the political elites to the politics of constraint has been at three levels: discourse, policy and institutions. At the level of *discours* there has been a systematic attempt to sensitize the electors to the limits of state action. As in the United Kingdom under Thatcher there is a pervasive message: the state cannot do everything. The attempt to reduce peoples' expectations may also be seen in the paucity of election promises. Thus, the 110 specific election proposals of Mitterrand in 1981 were replaced in 1988 by a series of vague and unadventurous general banalities, and the programmes of his principal opponents were disarmingly similar. There is accumulating poll evidence that the electorate is less 'statist' in its disposition and more sceptical about the capacity of the state to solve basic economic problems. At the level of policies there is the strategy of self-constraint, through increased deregulation and liberalization, through the demotion of planning and *dirigisme*, and through the pursuit of modest policy objectives. Finally, at the level of institutions it is possible to discern a number of developments: responsibility for domestic policy-making is being transferred by the president to the government, and from the government downwards. In some cases the delegation is to subordinate state agents (for example, the nationalized industries now have much greater freedom of action *vis-à-vis* the state than some major *private* industries in the early 1970s). In other cases the delegation of powers is to semi-autonomous individuals or groups. A number of contentious issues are now being passed to relatively depoliticized and relatively independent bodies. Thus, the extremely controversial and highly emotive problems of the financing of the social security system and the reform of the nationality laws were handed over to *comités des sages* – to committees of wise people, with the government carefully taking its distance, and the guardianship of the media (once a jealously protected political domain) has been transferred to a non-partisan (though politically sensitive) body. Accompanying this delegation of authority has been a major programme of territorial decentralization undertaken since 1981.

We note, therefore, an official diffusion and decentralization of authority and responsibility. This does not, of course, mean the end of the state, which retains a very powerful presence in French society, but it does imply a redefinition of its role. De Gaulle once said that '*il n'y a France que grâce à l'État*' and it is true that the state has always been viewed as powerful, hegemonic, intrusive – the principal instrument of national creation, consolidation, and modernization. However flawed that might be as history the state may certainly be attributed a key role in French society. The signs are, however, that that role is becoming more *modeste*, to use Michel Crozier's word, more circumspect. It has fewer pretensions and fewer illusions. Its leaders have become increasingly aware that 'dynamic' policy-making is dangerous, 'coherent' policy-making is intrinsically difficult, and 'rational' policy-making a chimera. In this respect, at least, '*la France se banalise*' – France is becoming more and more like its European neighbours.

Appendix 1
Regions and départements

Paris region

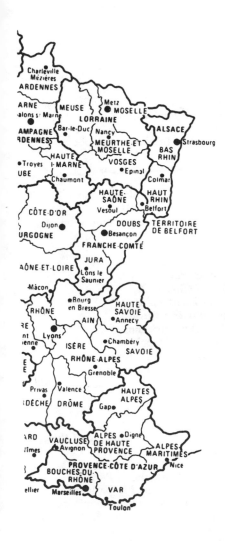

● departmental prefecture

⬤ regional préfecture

—— departmental boundaries

▬▬ regional boundaries

Appendix 2
Chronological table of main events from the Revolution to the collapse of the Fourth Republic

1789	July	Fall of the Bastille.
	August	Abolition of all feudal rights.
1792	August	Fall of the Monarchy.
	September	Establishment of the First Republic
1793	January	Execution of Louis XVI.
1799	November	Bonaparte becomes First Consul.
1804	May	Establishment of First Empire
1814	April	First abdication of Napoleon I and restoration of Louis XVIII
1815	June	Battle of Waterloo, second abdication of Napoleon and a second monarchical restoration.
1824	September	Charles X succeeds Louis XVIII.
1830	July	Revolution in Paris, abdication of Charles X, accession of Louis-Philippe.
1848	February	July Monarchy overthrown, Second Republic proclaimed
	December	Election of Louis Napoleon to the Presidency of the Republic
1851	December	*Coup d'état* by Louis Napoleon.
1852	December	Proclamation of the Second Empire, Napoleon III proclaimed Emperor
1870	July	Outbreak of the Franco-Prussian War.
	September	Battle of Sedan, collapse of the Second Empire and proclamation of the Third Republic
1871	January	Armistice.
	March–May	Revolutionary Commune in Paris.
1875	January–December	Constitutional laws voted in parliament.
1877	May–June	Dissolution of the republican-dominated Chamber of Deputies by President MacMahon.
	October–December	Victory of the Republicans in the elections.

1879	January	Resignation of the President of the Republic, republican victory in the senatorial elections, foundation of the "Republican Republic".
1887	November–December	Wilson scandal, leading to resignation of President Grévy.
1887-1889		Republic threatened by General Boulanger and his supporters.
1892-1893		Panama scandal.
1894	June	President Carnot assassinated.
1897		Beginning of the Dreyfus affair, which dragged on for seven years.
1903-1905		Anti-clerical legislation culminating in the separation of church and state.
1914	July	Assassination of Jaurès, socialist leader.
	August	Outbreak of the First World War.
1918	November	Armistice.
1919	June	Versailles Treaty signed.
1920	December	Tours Congress, foundation of the French Communist Party.
1923	January	French occupation of the Ruhr (until 1930).
1934	February	Violent Right-wing demonstrations in Paris.
1936	March	German re-militarization of the Rhineland.
	April–May	Victory of the Left-wing Popular Front in the elections.
	June	Popular Front government under Léon Blum.
	October	Spanish Civil War began.
1937	June	Collapse of the Popular Front government.
1938	September	Munich.
1939	March	Germany occupied Czechoslovakia.
	September	Outbreak of the Second World War.
1940	May–June	France invaded, Pétain became head of government, de Gaulle to London, armistice. Half of France occupied.
1941	June	Germany invaded Russia.
1942	November	Allied invasion of north Africa, the whole of France occupied.
1944	June	Allies landed in Normandy.
	August	Paris liberated.
	September	General de Gaulle set up government.
1945	May	End of the Second World War.
	October	French voted by referendum to end the Third Republic.
1946	January	General de Gaulle withdrew from the government.

1946	May	France voted against first proposed constitution.
	November	Constitution of the Fourth Republic accepted by referendum, and outbreak of the war in Indo-China.
1947	January	Election of Auriol as President of the Republic.
	April	Foundation of the first mass Gaullist movement – the RPF.
	May	Communists left the government.
	June	Marshall speech on financial aid to Europe.
	November–December	Wave of political strikes.
1949	April	North Atlantic Treaty signed.
1951	April	Coal and steel agreement between France, Germany, Italy and the Benelux countries.
	June	General election.
1952	March–December	Pinay prime minister.
1953	January	Official end of the RPF.
	August	Sultan of Morocco deposed.
	December	Coty elected President of the Republic.
1954	May–July	Dien-Bien-Phu, end of war in Indo-China negotiated by Premier Mendès-France.
	November	Outbreak of the Algerian war.
1956	January	General elections in France, Poujadists fared well.
	February	Demonstrations in Algiers against Premier Mollet.
	March	Independence of Tunisia and Morocco.
	October	Anglo-French intervention in Suez.
1957	March	Treaty of Rome establishing European Economic Community.
1958	May	Revolt by Algerian settlers in Algiers.
	June	General de Gaulle became head of government.
	September	Referendum on the Constitution of the Fifth Republic.

Appendix 3
Chronological table of main events from the foundation of the Fifth Republic until the re-election of Mitterrand to the presidency in 1988

1958	September	Referendum on the Constitution of the Fifth Republic; 79.25 per cent voted in favour.
	October–November	Creation of the Gaullist UNR, general elections, big Gaullist gains.
	December	General de Gaulle elected president by 78.5 per cent of the votes of the electoral college.
1959	January	De Gaulle proclaimed President of the Republic, Michel Debré appointed prime minister.
1960	January	Uprising in Algeria.
	April	Creation of the PSU.
1961	January	Referendum ratifying de Gaulle's policy of self-determination in Algeria: 75.26 per cent voted in favour.
	April	Army coup in Algeria against French Government.
1962	March	Evian agreements on Algeria. Pompidou becomes prime minister.
	April	Referendum ratifying Évian peace settlement with Algeria: 90.7 per cent of voters in favour.
	August	Unsuccessful attempt on de Gaulle's life at Le Petit Clamart.
	October	Motion of censure passed against Pompidou government, parliament dissolved. Referendum for direct election of President of the Republic: 61.75 per cent in favour.
	October–November	General elections, big gains for government.
1963	March–April	Miners' strike, government obliged to climb down.

1965	September	Creation of the FGDS (*Fédération de la Gauche Démocrate et Socialiste*) of Socialists, Radicals and Left-wing clubs.
	December	De Gaulle elected President of the Republic at the second ballot against Mitterrand.
1966	February	France withdrew from NATO.
1967	March	General elections: narrow victory for the government.
	November	Creation of the Gaullist UDVe.
1968	May	The "Events" - student revolt and general strike, National Assembly dissolved.
	June	Big victory of the government in the general elections.
	July	Couve de Murville replaced Pompidou as prime minister.
	November–December	Collapse of the FGDS, Mitterrand withdrew temporarily from political life.
1969	April	Referendum on the Senate and on regional reforms: de Gaulle resigned after 53.1 per cent voted against.
	June	Pompidou elected President of the Republic at the second ballot against Poher. Chaban-Delmas appointed prime minister.
	July	Creation of the CDP and of a new Socialist Party under the leadership of Alain Savary.
1970	November	Death of General de Gaulle.
1971	June	Creation of the new Socialist Party: Mitterrand became first secretary.
1972	April	Referendum ratifying enlargement of the Common Market to include Great Britain, Ireland and Denmark: 67.7 per cent in favour.
	June	Joint Programme of Government signed between the Socialists and the Communists.
	July	Messmer replaced Chaban-Delmas as prime minister.
1973	March	General elections: victory for the government, but with much reduced majority.
1974	April	Death of President Pompidou.
	May	Election of Giscard d'Estaing to the presidency at the second ballot against Mitterrand.

	June	Jacques Chirac became prime minister.
	October	Many leaders of the PSU joined the Socialist Party.
1976	February	Congress of the Communist Party.
	March	Departmental elections: big gains for the Left.
	August	Chirac replaced as prime minister by Raymond Barre.
	December	Creation of the RPR headed by Chirac.
1977	March	Local elections: sweeping victory for the Left.
	May	Creation of the Republican Party (ex-Independent Republicans).
	September	Breakdown of negotiations between the Communists and the Socialists.
1978	February	Creation of the *Union pour la Démocratie Française* (UDF), electoral alliance grouping non-Gaullist parties of presidential coalition.
	March	General elections: victory for the government by comfortable majority.
1979	March	Violent demonstrations in north and east to protest against government's economic policies
	March	Departmental elections: Left-wing gains.
	June	European elections.
1980	September	Senatorial elections: socialist gains.
	November	Mitterrand announces candidacy for presidency.
	December	Law and order bill, "*Sécurité et Liberté*" adopted.
1981	April	First ballot of presidential election.
	May	Election of Mitterrand to the presidency. Resignation of prime minister Barre who is replaced by Mauroy. National Assembly dissolved.
	June	"Historic victory" of Socialists in legislative elections. Mauroy forms second government which includes four Communists.
	October	Devaluation of the franc.
	November	Unemployment reaches two million.
	December	Nationalization Law voted.
1982	January	Constitutional Council rejects several articles of the Nationalization Law.
	February	New Nationalization Law voted.
	March	Defferre Act on decentralization voted. Elections to departmental councils: Right-wing successes.

	June	New devaluation of the franc and austerity programme.
	November	Reform of electoral system for town councils.
1983	January	FLNC dissolved.
	March	Elections for municipal councils: Left loses 31 towns of more than 30,000 inhabitants. Mauroy forms his third government. Second austerity programme and new devaluation of the franc.
	April	Violent farmer's demonstration in Brittany.
	May	Doctor's strike.
	June	Demonstrations by police.
	August	French intervention in Chad.
	September	By-election at Dreux: extreme Right does well. Senatorial elections: gains for Right-wing opposition.
1984	January	Several Communist attacks against government policies.
	February	Lorry drivers block motorways.
	March	Demonstration by Catholics against Savary Bill. PCF denounces restructuring of the steel industry.
	April	Demonstration by Lorraine steel-workers in Paris: leaders of Communist Party participate.
	June	Elections to European Parliament: defeat of Left; extreme Right wins 11 per cent of poll. More than one million demonstrate in Paris against Savary Bill.
	July	Mitterrand withdraws Savary Bill. Mauroy resigns as prime minister; replaced by Laurent Fabius. Communists refuse to enter government.
	September	Press Law voted.
	October	Unemployment reaches 2.5 million.
	November	Mitterrand meets Col. Quadahfi in Crete.
1985	February	XXV Congress of PCF.
	March	Elections to departmental councils: new gains for Right.
	April	Michel Rocard resigns from the government.
	May	Central Committee of PCF critical of government.
	June	Rocard announces candidacy for 1988 presidential elections. Electoral system for legislative elections changed.
	August	Rainbow Warrior Affair.

	September	Charles Hernu, Defence Minister, resigns as result of Rainbow Warrior Affair.
	October	PS Congress at Toulouse: Rocard faction wins 28.5 per cent of votes.
1986	February	Three terrorist explosions in Paris. New French intervention in Chad.
	March	Legislative elections: Left defeated; small majority for moderate Right; *Front National* wins 35 seats; further decline of PCF. Regional elections: Right wins 20 of 22 councils. Chirac appointed prime minister. Series of bomb explosions in Paris.
	April	Right-wing programme presented to National Assembly: included wide-ranging privatization and changes in nationality laws. CERES abandons Marxism and changes title to *Socialisme et République*.
	June	Mitterrand criticises government's proposals on reform of nationality laws.
	July	Mitterrand refuses to sign ordonnance on privatization.
	September	Senate elections. Left loses ground.
	October	Mitterrand refuses to sign ordonnance on electoral constituencies. Electoral law for legislative elections: pre-1986 system re-introduced.
	November	Mitterrand again expresses disagreement with government over reform of nationality laws. Mitterrand publicly disapproves of Bill destined to privatize part of prison service.
	December	Student demonstrations in Paris: Higher Education Bill withdrawn. Public sector strikes.
1987	January	Mitterrand receives delegation of railway workers. Mitterand expresses his disapproval of government policies in New Caledonia.
	March	Demonstration by 30,000 against proposed changes in nationality laws. Demonstration by 200,000 in Paris to defend social security system.
	April	Lille Congress of PS. Extreme Right organizes demonstrations in Marseilles against immigrants.
	May	André Lajoinie selected by PCF as candidate for 1988 presidential election.

	October	Pierre Juquin, dissident Communist, announces candidacy for presidential elections.
1988	January	Jacques Chirac announces candidacy for presidential election.
	February	Raymond Barre officially announces candidacy for presidential election.
	March	Mitterrand officially announces candidacy for presidential elections.
	April	First ballot of presidential elections: Mitterrand and Chirac go through to the next round; Le Pen wins 14 per cent of votes. Lajoinie does badly.
	May	Re-election of Mitterrand as President. Michel Rocard appointed prime minister. National Assembly dissolved.
	June	Election to National Assembly: PS biggest party but no overall majority. Rocard reappointed Prime Minister.

Appendix 4
Presidents and prime ministers of the Fifth Republic

Presidents

Charles de Gaulle from 8 January 1959 to 28 April 1969
Georges Pompidou from 20 June 1969 to 2 April 1974
Valéry Giscard d'Estaing from 21 June 1974 to 21 May 1981
François Mitterrand from 21 May 1981

Prime Ministers

Michel Debré from 8 January 1959
Georges Pompidou from 14 April 1962
Maurice Couve de Murville from 10 July 1968
Jacques Chaban-Delmas from 20 June 1969
Pierre Messmer from 5 July 1972
Jacques Chirac from 27 May 1974
Raymond Barre from 25 August 1976
Pierre Mauroy from 21 May 1981
Laurent Fabius from 17 July 1984
Jacques Chirac from 20 March 1986
Michel Rocard from 13 May 1988

Appendix 5

Results of the referenda of the Fifth Republic

Date	Subject	Abstentions	Votes cast in favour (per cent)
28 September 1958	New constitution	15.4	79.3
8 January 1961	Self-determination for Algeria	23.5	75.3
8 April 1962	Independence for Algeria	24.4	90.7
28 October 1962	Direct election of president	22.8	61.8
27 April 1969	Senate and regional reforms	19.4	46.8
23 April 1972	EEC enlargement	39.6	67.7
6 November 1988	Statute for New Caledonia	62.7	80.0

Appendix 6

Results of the presidential elections of April to May 1988

First ballot (24 April)	Voters	% of registered voters	% of votes cast
Registered voters	38,128,507	100	
Abstentions	7,100,535	18.62	
Voters	31,027,972	81.37	
Spoiled votes	621,934	1.63	
Valid votes	30,406,038		100
Mitterrand	10,367,220	27.19	34.09
Chirac	6,063,514	15.90	19.94
Barre	5,031,849	13.19	16.54
Le Pen	4,375,894	11.47	14.39
Lajoinie	2,055,995	5.39	6.76
Waechter	1,149,642	3.01	3.78
Juquin	639,084	1.67	2.01
Laguiller	606,017	1.58	1.99
Boussel	116,823	0.30	0.38

Second ballot (8 May)			
Registered voters	38,168,869	100	
Abstentions	6,083,798	15.93	
Voters	32,085,071	84.06	
Spoiled votes	1,161,822	3.04	
Valid votes	30,923,249		100
Mitterrand	16,704,279	43.76	54.02
Chirac	14,218,970	37.25	45.98

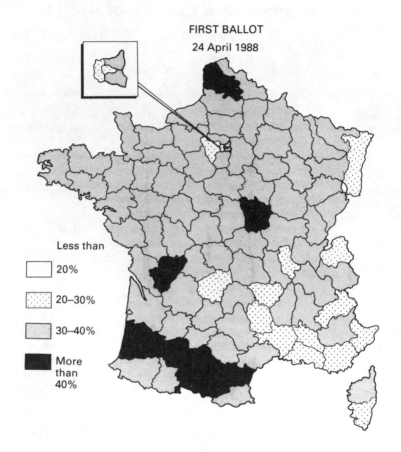

FIRST BALLOT
24 April 1988

Less than

20%

20–30%

30–40%

More
than
40%

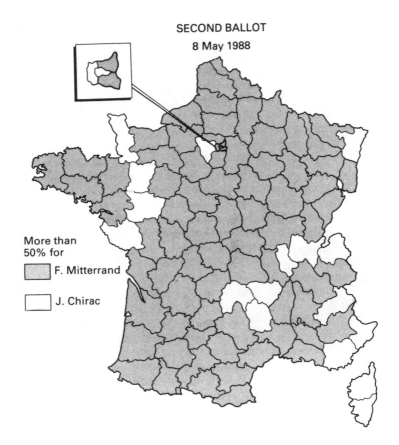

SECOND BALLOT

8 May 1988

More than
50% for

F. Mitterrand

J. Chirac

Appendix 8 (A)

Voting behaviour in the April–May 1988 Presidential elections

First ballot (percentage of votes, BVA exit poll)

Bar+Ch+LP	B,L,J	Laj	Mit	W	Bar	Ch	LP	Total
Total	4	7	34	4	17	20	14	51
Men	6	9	31	3	15	19	17	51
Women	4	5	37	5	18	21	10	49
Age Range								
18–24 years	4	5	35	5	19	17	15	51
25–34	6	9	39	6	16	13	11	40
35–49	4	7	36	4	15	17	17	49
50–64	3	6	29	2	17	29	14	60
65+	1	9	29	1	17	31	12	60
Profession								
Farmers	5	2	20	3	16	36	18	70
Shopkeepers, small businessmen	4	2	15	2	23	23	31	77
Liberal professions	0	0	24	3	16	36	21	71
Business executives	3	1	31	2	22	27	14	63
Teachers and social workers	7	4	47	8	16	12	6	34
Middle management	5	7	33	4	17	18	16	51
Clerical workers	4	7	43	5	15	15	11	41
Commercial employees	5	3	34	3	21	13	21	55
Workers	7	17	43	3	7	7	16	30
Employment Group								
Public sector employee	6	11	41	5	11	13	13	37
Private sector employee	5	6	36	3	19	17	14	50
Self-employed	2	1	20	4	17	32	24	73
Unemployed	6	9	40	6	10	10	19	39
Inactive	4	7	33	3	18	23	12	53

Key:	B	=	Boussel	L	=	Laguiller
	LP	=	LePen	Bar	=	Barre
	J	=	Juquin	Ch	=	Chirac
	Laj	=	Lajoinie	Mit	=	Mitterrand
	W	=	Waechter			

Appendix 8 (B)

Second ballot (percentage of votes, BVA exit poll)

		Mitterrand	Chirac
	Total voters	54	46
Sex			
	Men	54	46
	Women	54	46
Age			
	18–24 years	56	44
	25–34	65	35
	35–49	57	43
	50–64	46	54
	65+	43	57
Profession			
	Farmers	29	71
	Shopkeepers, small businessmen	37	63
	Liberal professions	42	58
	Business executives	46	54
	Teachers and social workers	70	30
	Middle management	58	42
	Clerical workers	60	40
	Commercial workers	58	42
	Workers	74	26
Employment group			
	Public sector employee	74	26
	Private sector employee	59	41
	Self-employed	31	69
	Unemployed	62	38
	Inactive	46	54
Religious practice			
	Practising Catholic	33	67
	Non-practising Catholic	56	44
	No religion	74	26
	Other religion	69	31

Appendix 9

Results of the legislative elections of June 1988 (first ballot)

	Number of candidates		% registered	% valid votes
Registered voters		37,945,582	100	
Abstentions		13,000,790	34.26	
Votes cast		24,944,792	65.74	
Spoilt votes		512,697	2.05	
Valid votes		24,432,095		100
PCF (Communists)	575	2,765,761	7.28	11.32
Extreme Left	77	89,065	0.23	0.36
PS (Socialists)	581	8,493,702	22.38	34.76
Other pro-Mitterrand	55	676,006	1.77	2.76
Total non-Communist Left	713	9,258,773	24.38	37.88
Total Left	1,288	12,024,534	31.66	49.20
RRP (Gaullists)	320	4,687,047	12.35	19.18
UDF (Moderate Right and Centrists)	312	4,519,459	11.91	18.49
Other Moderate Right	220	697,272	1.83	2.85
Total moderate Right	852	9,903,778	26.09	40.52
National Front	553	2,359,528	6.21	9.65
Other extreme Right	107	32,445	0.08	0.13
Total extreme Right	660	2,391,973	6.29	9.78
Total Right	1,512	12,295,751	32.38	50.30
Ecologists	51	86,312	0.22	0.35
Regionalists	25	18,498	0.04	0.07

Appendix 10
Voting in legislative elections of 1986 and 1988
(per cent of votes cast)

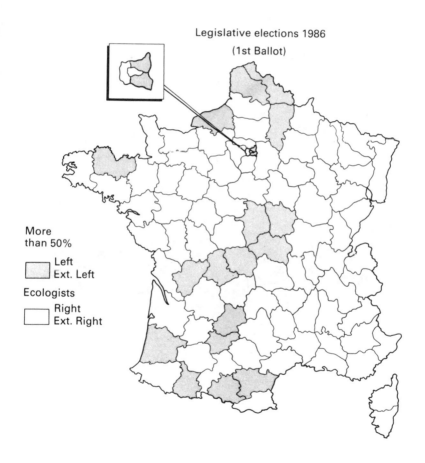

Legislative elections 1986
(1st Ballot)

More
than 50%

Left
Ext. Left

Ecologists

Right
Ext. Right

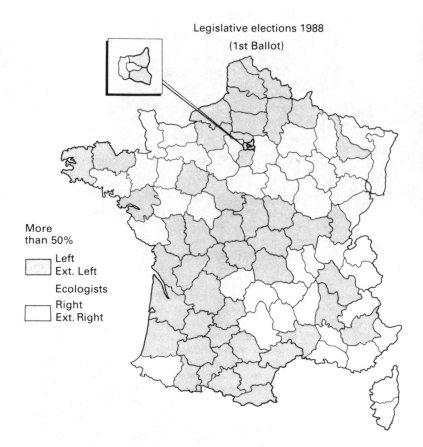

Legislative elections 1988
(1st Ballot)

More
than 50%

Left
Ext. Left

Ecologists

Right
Ext. Right

Appendix 11

Political groups in the French parliament on 1 July 1988 (members and apparentés)

National Assembly		Senate	
Socialists and allies	275	Socialists and Left-wing Radicals	64
Communists	27	Communists	15
Gaullists	130	Gaullists	77
UDF	90	Union des Républicains et Indépendants	54
UDC (Centrists)	41	Union Centriste	70
National Front	1	Democratic Left	35
No group	10	No group	4

Selected further reading

To keep themselves fully informed of developments in French politics readers may find the following useful:

Contemporary France: A Review of Interdisciplinary Studies, an annual review edited by Jolyon Howorth and George Ross, London.

French Politics and Society which is produced by the Center for European Studies at Harvard University.

Modern and Contemporary France which is the review of the Association for the Study of Modern and Contemporary France.

West European Politics which contains an article on French politics in most issues.

Pouvoirs, which is a French review that contains an invaluable *"chronique constitutionelle française"*.

General historical background

Anderson, R.D., *France 1870-1914: Politics and Society*, London 1977.
Brogan, Denis, *The Development of Modern France 1870-1939*, 11th edn, London 1967.
Bury, Patrick, *France 1814-1940*, 4th edn, London 1969.
Cahm, Eric, *Politics and Society in Contemporary France (1789-1971)*, London 1972.
Caron, François, *An Economic History of Modern France*, London 1979.
Cobban, Alfred, *A History of Modern France*, 3 vols, London 1965.
Dupeux, Georges, *French Society 1789-1970*. London 1976.
Earle, Edward M. (ed.), *Modern France*, Princeton 1951.
Goguel, François, *La Politique des partis sous la IIIe République*, 3rd edn, Paris 1958.
Jackson, J.H., *A Short History of France*, 2nd edn, Cambridge 1974.
Larkin, Maurice, *France since the Popular Front: Government and People 1936-1987*, Oxford 1988.
Prost, A., *Petite Histoire de la France au XXe siècle*, Paris 1979.
Rémond, René, *La Vie politique en France depuis 1789*, 2 vols, Paris 1973-4.
Thomson, David, *Democracy in France since 1870*, 5th edn, London 1969.
Trotignon, Yves, *La France au XIXe siècle*, 2 vols, Paris 1980.
Wright, Gordon, *France in Modern Times*, Chicago 1962.
Zeldin, Theodore, *France 1848-1945*, 2 vols, London 1973-7.

The Fourth Republic

Avril, Pierre, and Vincent, Gérard, *La Quatrième République*, Paris 1988.
Barsalou, Joseph, *La Mal-Aimée*, Paris 1964.
Courtier, P., *La Quatrième République*, 3rd edn, Paris 1983.
Elgey, Georgette, *La République des Illusions 1945-1951*, Paris 1965.
Elgey, Georgette, *La République des Contradictions*, Paris 1968.
Fauvet, Jacques, *La Quatrième République*, Paris 1959.
Fauvet, Jacques, *The Cockpit of France*, London 1960.
Fontvielle-Alquier, François, *Plaidoyer pour la IVe République*, Paris 1976.
Goguel, François, *France under the Fourth Republic*, Ithaca 1952.
Macrae, Duncan, *Parliament, Parties and Society in France 1946-1958*, New York 1967.
Pickles, Dorothy, *France: The Fourth Republic*, London 1955.
Priouret, Roger, *La République des partis*, Paris 1947.
La Quatrième République: *Bilan trente ans après la Promulgation de la Constitution du 27 octobre 1946*, Paris 1978.
Rioux, J.P. *La France de la Quatrième République*, 2 vols, Paris 1982-3.
Rioux, J.P., *The Fourth Republic, 1944-1958*, Cambridge 1987.
Williams, Philip, *Crisis and Compromise: Politics in the Fourth Republic*, London 1964.
Wright, Gordon, *The Reshaping of French Democracy*, New York 1948.

General political and social background

Andrews, William G., and Hoffmann, Stanley, *The Impact of the Fifth Republic on France*, New York 1981.
Ardagh, John, *France in the 1980s*, London 1982.
Aron, Raymond, *The Elusive Revolution: Anatomy of a Student Revolt*, London 1969.
Ashford, Douglas, *Policy and Politics in France*, Philadelphia 1982.
Birnbaum, Pierre, *Les Sommets de l'État*, Paris 1977.
Birnbaum, Pierre, Barucq, Charles, and Bellaiche, Michel (eds), *La classe dirigeante française*, Paris 1978.
Birnbaum, Pierre *et al*, *Les élites socialistes au pouvoir*, Paris 1985.
Bredin, Jean-Denis, *La République de M. Pompidou*, Paris 1974.
Brown, Bernard E., *Protest in Paris: Anatomy of a Revolt*, New Jersey 1974.
Cahm, Eric, *Politics and Society in Contemporary France, 1789-1971*, London 1972.
Carmoy, Guy de, *The Foreign Policies of France, 1944-1968*, Chicago 1979.
Cerny, Philip G., *The Politics of Grandeur*, London 1980.
Cerny, Philip G. (ed.), *Social Movements and Protest in France*, London 1982.
Cerny, Philip G., and Schain, Martin A., *French Politics and Public Policy*, London 1982.

Chevallier, Jacques *et al.*, *Discours et Idéologie*, Paris 1980.
Chevallier, Jacques *et al.*, *I.'Institution*, Paris 1981.
Colas, Dominique, *L'Etat et les corporatismes*, Paris, 1988.
Crozier, Michel, *La Société bloquée*, Paris 1970.
Duclaud-Williams, Roger H., *The Politics of Housing in Britain and France*, London 1978.
Duhamel, Alain, *La République giscardienne. Anatomie politique de la France*, London 1980.
Duhamel, Alain, *La République de M. Mitterrand*, Paris 1982.
Duverger, Maurice, *La Monarchie Républicaine*, Paris 1974.
Duverger, Maurice, *Échec au Roi*, Paris 1978.
Dyer, Colin, *Population and Society in Twentieth Century France*, London 1978.
Estier, Claude, and Neiertz, Véronique, *Véridique histoire d'un septennat peu ordinaire*, Paris 1987.
Fabius, Laurent, *La France inégale*, Paris 1975.
Favoreu, Louis, and Philip, Loic, *Le Conseil Constitutionnel*, Paris 1978.
Feigenbaum, H.B., *The Politics of Public Enterprise: Oil and the French State*, Princeton 1985.
Feldman, Elliot J., *Concorde and Dissent: Explaining high technology project failures in Britain and France*, Cambridge 1985.
Ferenczi, Thomas, *Le Prince au miroir. Essai sur l'ordre giscardien*, Paris 1981.
Fournier, Jacques, and Questiaux, Nicole, *Traité du social*, Paris 1976.
Frears, J.R., *France in the Giscard Presidency*, London 1981.
Gaffney, J., (*ed.*), *France and Modernisation*, London 1988.
Hanley, D.L., Kerr, A.P., and Waites, N.H., *Contemporary France: Politics and Society since 1945*, London 1979.
Hoffmann, Stanley, *In Search of France*, Cambridge, Mass. 1963.
Hoffmann, Stanley, *Decline or Renewal: France since the 1930s*, New York 1974.
Horne, Alistair, *A Savage War of Peace: Algeria 1954-1962*, London 1977.
Jobert, Bruno, and Muller, Pierre, *L'Etat en Action: politiques publiques et corporatismes*, Paris 1987.
July, S., *Les Années Mitterrand*, Paris 1986.
Laroque, Pierre, *Les Institutions sociales de la France*, Paris 1980.
Luchaire, François, *Le Conseil Constitutionnel*, Paris 1980.
Marceau, Jane, *Class and Status in France*, Oxford 1977.
Mazey, Sonia, and Newman, Michael, *Mitterrand's France*, London 1987.
Mehl, Dominique, and Dagnaud, Monique, *L'Elite rose*, Paris 1982.
Mendras, H. (ed.), *La Sagesse et le Désordre*, Paris 1980.
Metraux, Rhoda, and Mead, Margaret, *Themes in French Culture: A Preface to a Study of the French Community*, Stanford 1964.
Padioleau, J., *L'Etat au concret*, Paris 1982.
Petifils, Jean-Christian, *La Démocratie giscardienne*, Paris 1981.
Peyrefitte, Alain, *Le Mal français*, Paris 1976.
Poulantzas, N., *La Crise de l'État*, Paris 1976.
Reynaud, J.D. *et al.*, *Tendances et volontés de la société française*, Paris 1966.

Ross, George, Hoffmann, Stanley, and Malzacher, Sylvia, *The Mitterrand Experiment*, Oxford and Cambridge, 1987.
Schwartzenberg, Roger-Gérard, *La Droite absolue*, Paris 1981.
Sfez, Lucien (ed.), *Décision et Pouvoir dans la Société française*, Paris 1979.
Suleiman, Ezra, *Les Élites en France, Grands Corps et Grandes Écoles*, Paris 1978.
Viansson-Ponté, Pierre, *Histoire de la République Gaullienne*, 2 vols, Paris 1970-1.
Wickham, Alexandre, and Coignard, Sophia, *La Nomenklatura Française*, Paris 1986.
Wright, Vincent (ed.), *Conflict and Consensus in France*, London 1979.
Wylie, Laurence, *Village in the Vaucluse*, 2nd edn, New York 1964.
Wylie, Laurence (ed.), *Chanzeaux: A Village in Anjou*, Cambridge, Mass. 1966.

General economic background

Bauchard, Philippe, *La Guerre des Deux Roses: Du Rêve à la Réalité, 1981-1985*, Paris 1986.
Bauchet, Pierre, *Economic Planning: the French Experience*, London 1964.
Bauer, Michel, *Les 200: Comment devient-on un grand patron*, Paris 1987.
Bauer, M., and Cohen, E., *Qui Gouverne les Grands Groupes industriels en France*, Paris 1981.
Bellon, B., *Le Pouvoir financier et l'industrie en France*, Paris 1980.
Carré, J.P., Dubois, P., and Malinvaud, E., *La Croissance française*, Paris 1972.
Coffey, Peter, *The Social Economy of France*, London 1973.
Cohen, E., and Bauer, M., *Les Grandes Manoeuvres industrielles*, Paris 1985.
Cohen, Stephen, *Modern Capitalist Planning: the French Model*, Cambridge, Mass. 1969.
Cohen, Stephen, and Gourevitch, Peter, *France in the Troubled World*, London 1982.
Delorme, Robert, *L'État et l'Économie*, Paris 1983.
Estrin, Saul, and Holmes, Peter, *French Planning in Theory and Practice*, London 1983.
Fourestié, J., *Les Trente Glorieuses ou la Révolution Invisible de 1946 à 1975*, Paris 1979.
Hacket, J., and Hacket, A.M., *Economic Planning in France*, London 1963.
Hall, Peter, *Governing the Economy: The Politics of State Intervention in Britain and France*, Cambridge, 1986.
Hansen, Miles, *French Regional Planning*, Edinburgh 1968.
Hayward, Jack, and Watson, Michael (eds), *Planning Politics and Public Policy*, London 1975.

Holmes, G.M., and Fawcett, P.D., *The Contemporary French Economy*, London 1983.

Hough J.R., *The French Economy*, London 1982.

Kindleberger, Charles, *Economic Growth in France and Britain*, Cambridge, Mass. 1964.

Kuisel, Richard F., *Capitalism and the State in Modern France: Renovation and Economic Management in the Twentieth Century*, Cambridge 1981.

Lamber, V., *The Political Economy of France: from Pompidou to Mitterrand*, London 1983.

Levêque, Jean-Maxime, *En Première Ligne*, Paris 1986.

McArthur, J.H., and Scott, Bruce R., *Industrial Planning in France*, Boston 1969.

Machin, H., and Wright V., *Economic Policy and Policymaking under the Mitterrand Presidency*, London 1985.

Muet, P-A., *La Gauche face à la Crise*, Paris 1985.

Parodi, Maurice, *L'Économie et la société française*, Paris 1981.

Sagou, M'Hamedn, *Paribas. Anatomie d'une puissance*, Paris 1981.

Saint-Geours, Jean, *Pouvoir et finance*, Paris 1979.

Sheahan, John, *Promotion and Control of Industry in Post-war France*, Cambridge, Mass. 1963.

Shonfield, Andrew, *Modern Capitalism*, London 1965.

Tuppen, J., *France under Recession, 1981-1986*, London 1987.

Ullmo, Yves, *La Planification en France*, Paris 1975.

Zysman, John, *Political Strategies for Industrial Order: State, Market and Industry in France*, London 1977.

Political institutions of the Fifth Republic – general

Avril, Pierre, *Le Régime politique de la Ve République*, 2nd edn, Paris 1967.

Avril, Pierre, *La Cinquième République: Histoire politique et constitutionnelle*, Paris 1987.

Berger, Suzanne, *The French Political System*, New York 1974.

Blondel, Jean, *The Government of France*, 2nd revised edn, London 1974.

Chapsal, Jacques, *La Vie politique en France depuis 1940*, 2 vols, 3rd edn, Paris 1987.

Dreyfus, Françoise, and d'Arcy, François, *Les Institutions politiques et administratives de la France*, Paris 1985.

Duhamel, Olivier, and Parodi, Jean-Luc, *La Constitution de la Cinquième République*, Paris 1985.

Duverger, Maurice, *La Cinquième République*, 5th edn, Paris 1974.

Duverger, Maurice, *Le Système politique en France*, 19th edn, Paris 1986.

Ehrmann, Henry, *Politics in France*, 5th edn, Boston 1985.

Favoreu, Louis, and Philip, Loic, *Le Conseil Constitutionnel*, 3rd edn, 1985.

Goguel, François, and Grosser, Alfred, *La Politique en France*, 8th edn, Paris 1984.

Guillaume-Hofnung, M., *Le Référendum*, Paris 1987.

Hamon, Léo, *Une République présidentielle?*, 2 vols, Paris 1975-7.

Hayward, Jack, *Governing France*, 2nd edn, London 1983.
Lavroff, Dmitri-Georges, *Système politique de la Ve République*, Paris 1979.
Portelli, H., *La Politique en France sous la Cinquième République*, Paris 1987.
Quermonne, Jean-Louis, *Le Gouvernement de la France sous la Ve République*, Paris 1980.

Executive and legislative powers

Antoni, P., and Antoni, J.-D., *Les Ministres de la Ve République*, Paris 1976.
Baecque, F. de, *Qui gouverne la France?*, Paris 1976.
Barrillon, Raymond *et al.*, *Dictionnaire de la Constitution*, Paris 1986.
Bouchardeau, Huguette, *Le Ministère du Possible*, Paris 1986.
Cayrol, R., Parodi, J.-L., and Ysmal, Colette (eds), *Le Député français*, Paris 1973.
Claisse, Alain, *Le Premier Ministre de la Ve République*, Paris 1972.
Cohen, Samy, *Les Conseillers du Président*, Paris 1980.
Cohen, S., *La Monarchie Nucléaire*, Paris 1986.
Colombani, Jean-Marie, and Lhomeau, Jean-Yves, *Le Mariage Blanc*, Paris 1987.
Debré, Jean-Louis, *Les idées constitutionnelles du Général de Gaulle*, Paris 1974.
Debré, Jean-Louis, *La Constitution de la Ve République*, Paris 1975.
Decaumont, Françoise, *La Présidence de Georges Pompidou: Essai sur le régime présidentialiste français*, Paris 1980.
Delvolvé, P., and Lesguillions, H., *Le Contrôle parlementaire de politique économique et budgétaire*, Paris 1964.
Dupuis, G., Georgel, J., and Moreau, J., *Le Conseil Constitutionnel*, Paris 1976.
Duverger, Maurice, *Le bréviaire de la cohabitation*, Paris 1986.
Duverger, Maurice, *La Cohabitation des Français*, Paris 1987.
L'Entourage et de Gaulle, publication of the Institut Charles de Gaulle, Paris 1979.
Fondation Nationale des Sciences Politiques, *La Présidence de la République de Georges Pompidou: Exercise du pouvoir et pratique des institutions*, Paris 1983.
Fournier, Jacques, *Le Travail Gouvernemental*, Paris 1987.
Gicquel, Jean, *Essai sur la Pratique Politique de la Ve République*, Paris 1967.
Guichard-Ayoub, E. *et al.*, *Études sur le Parlement de la Ve République*, Paris 1965.
Long, Marceau, *Les Services du Premier Ministre*, Aix 1981.
Lord, Guy, *The French Budgetary Process*, Berkeley 1973.
Maout, Jean-Charles, and Muzellec, R., *Le Parlement sous la Ve République*, Paris 1971.

Massot, Jean, *La Présidence de la République en France* 2nd edn, Paris 1986.
Mastiat, Jean, *Le Sénat de la Cinquième République*, Paris 1980.
Maus, Didier, *Le Parlement sous la Cinquième République*, Paris 1985.
'Le parlement français sous trois présidents, 1958-1980', *Revue Française des Sciences Politiques*, 31(1) February 1981, special issue.
Pfister, Thierry, *L'Hôtel Matignon, au temps de l'Union de la Gauche*, Paris 1985.
Pfister, Thierry, *Dans les coulisses du pouvoir: la comédie de la cohabitation*, Paris 1986.
Pour Connaitre le Sénat, Paris (Documentation française) 1976.
Prate, Alain, *Les batailles économiques du Général de Gaulle*, Paris 1978.
Py, Roseline, *Le Secrétariat Général du Gouvernement*, Paris 1985.
Quermonne, Jean Louis, *Le Gouvernement de la France sous la Cinquième République*, 3rd edn, 1987.
Rials, Stéphane, *Le Premier Ministre*, Paris 1981.
Rials, Stéphane, *La Présidence de la République*, Paris 1981.
Rivoli, Jean, *Le Budget de l'État*, Paris 1975.
Schifres, M., and Sarazin, M., *L'Élysée de Mitterrand: Secrets de la Maison du Prince*, Paris 1985.
Szafran, Maurice, and Katz, Sammy, *Les Familles du Président*, Paris 1982.
Verrier, Patrice, *Les Services de la Présidence de la République*, Paris 1971.
Williams, Philip, *The French Parliament: Politics in the Fifth Republic*, London 1968.

Parties and elections – general

Bon, Frédéric, *Les Élections en France, Histoire et Sociologie*, Paris 1978.
Borella, François, *Les Partis politiques dans la France d'aujourd'hui*, 3rd edn, Paris 1977.
Braud, Philippe, *Le Comportement électoral en France*, Paris 1973.
Campbell, Peter, and Cole, Alistair, *French Electoral Systems and Elections since 1789*, 3rd edn, London 1988.
Capdevielle, Jacques et al., *France de gauche, vote à droite*, Paris 1981.
Charlot, Jean, *Les Français et de Gaulle*, Paris 1971.
Charlot, Jean, *Quand la gauche peut gagner*, Paris 1973.
Charnay, P., *Le Suffrage politique en France*, Paris 1965.
Dupoirier, Elisabeth, and Grunberg, Gérard, (eds), *Mars 1986: la drôle de défaite de la gauche*, Paris 1986.
Gaxie, Daniel (ed.), *Explication du Vote: Un bilan des études électorales en France*, Paris 1985.
Goguel, François, *Modernisation économique et comportement politique*, Paris 1969.
Lancelot, Alain, *Les Attitudes politiques*, 3rd edn, Paris 1969.
Lancelot, M. T., and Lancelot, Alain, *Les Élections en France*, Paris 1978.

Lancelot, A., *Les élections sous la Cinquième République*, Paris 1983.
Lancelot, Alain, (ed.), *1981: les élections de l'alternance*, Paris 1986.
Levy, C., *Les Trois Guerres de Succession*, Paris 1987.
Meynaud, J., and Lancelot, A., *La Participation des Français à la Politique*, 3rd edn, Paris 1971.
Michelat, Guy, and Simon, Michel, *Classe, religion et comportement politique*, Paris 1977.
Penniman, Howard R. (ed.), *France at the Polls: The Presidental Election of 1974*, Washington 1978.
Penniman, Howard R. (ed.), *The French National Assembly Elections of 1978*, Washington 1980.
Rémond, René *et al.*, *Forces religieuses et attitudes politiques dans la France contemporaine*, Paris 1965.
Williams, Philip, *French Politicians and Elections, 1951-1969*, London 1970.
Wilson, Frank, *French Political Parties under the Fifth Republic*, New York 1982.
Ysmal, Colette, *Le comportement électoral en France*, Paris 1986.

Parties of the Right

Anderson, Malcolm, *Conservative Politics in France*, London 1974.
Avril, Pierre, *UDR et Gaullistes*, Paris 1971.
Calderon, D., *La Droite Française*, Paris 1985.
Charlot, Jean, *Le Gaullisme*, Paris 1970.
Charlot, Jean, *The Gaullist Phenomenon*, London 1971.
Colliard, J.C., *Les Républicains Indépendants*, Paris 1971.
Crisol, P., and Lhomeau, J.-Y, *La Machine RPR*, Paris 1977.
Debré, Michel, and Debré, Jean-Louis, *Le Gaullisme*, Paris 1977.
Desjardins, Thierry, *Les Chiraquiens*, Paris 1986.
Dreyfus, François G., *De Gaulle et le Gaullisme*, Paris 1982.
'Le Giscardisme', *Pouvoirs*, 9, 1979, special issue.
Hartley, A., *Gaullism; The Rise and Fall of a Political Movement*, London 1972.
Irving, R.E.M., *Christian Democracy in France*, London 1973.
Lecomte, Bernard, and Sauvage, Christian, *Les Giscardiens*, Paris 1978.
Lorien, Joseph, Critou, Karl, and Dumont, Serge, *Le Système Le Pen*, Paris 1985.
Nordmann, Jean-Thomas, *Histoire des Radicaux, 1820-1973*, Paris 1974.
Petitfils, Jean-Christian, *Le Gaullisme*, Paris 1977.
Petitfils, J.C., *L'Extrême droite*, Paris 1983.
Plenel, Edwy, and Rollat, Alain, *L'Effet Le Pen*, Paris 1984.
Rémond, René, *Les Droites en France*, Paris 1982.
Roussel, Eric, *Le Cas Le Pen*, Paris 1985.
Seguin, Daniel, *Les Nouveaux giscardiens*, Paris 1979.
Touchard, Jean, *Le Gaullisme 1940-1969*, Paris 1978.
Viansson-Ponté, Pierre, *Les Gaullistes*, Paris 1963.

Ysmal, Colette, *Demain la Droite*, Paris 1984.

Parties of the Left

Ayache, Georges, and Fantoni, Mathieu, *Les Barons du parti socialiste*, Paris 1977.
Barillon, Raymond, *La Gauche française en mouvement*, Paris 1967.
Bell, D.S., and Criddle, B., *The French Socialist Party, Resurgence and Victory*, 2nd edn, Oxford 1988.
Bizot, Jean-François, *Anatomie du parti socialiste*, Paris 1975.
Blackmer, Donald L.M., and Tarrow, Sidney G., *Communism in Italy and France*, Princeton, NJ 1975.
Bon, Frédéric *et al.*, *Le Communisme en France*, Paris 1969.
Brunet, Jean-Paul, *Histoire du PCF*, Paris 1982.
Buffin, Didier, and Gerbaud, Dominique, *Les Communistes*, Paris 1981.
Caute, David, *Communism and the French Intellectuals*, London 1964.
Chevènement, Jean-Pierre, *Les Communistes, les socialistes et les autres*, Paris 1976.
Dreyfus, François-Georges, *Histoire des gauches en France*, Paris 1975.
Elleinstein, Jean, *Le Parti Communiste*, Paris 1976.
Fauvet, Jacques, *Histoire du parti communiste*, 2nd edn, Paris 1977.
Fizbin, Henri, *Les Bouches s'ouvrent*, Paris 1980.
Guidoni, Pierre, *Histoire du nouveau parti socialiste*, Paris 1973.
Hincker, François, *Le Parti communiste au carrefour*, Paris 1981.
Hurtig, Christiane, *De la SFIO au nouveau parti socialiste*, Paris 1970.
Johnson, R.W., *The Long March of the French Left*, London 1981.
Judt, Tony, *Marxism and the French Left*, Oxford 1986.
Kergoat, J., *Le Parti Socialiste*, Paris 1983.
Kriegel, Annie, *The French Communists*, London 1972.
Laurens, André, and Pfister, Thierry, *Les Nouveaux communistes au pouvoir*, Paris 1973.
Lavau, Georges, *A Quoi sert le p.c.f.?*, Paris 1981.
Lichteim, George, *Marxism in Modern France*, New York 1966.
Ligou, Daniel, *Histoire du socialisme en France 1871-1961*. Paris 1961.
Nania, Guy, *Un Parti de la gauche, le PSU*, Paris 1966.
Nugent, Neill, and Lowe, David, *The Left in France*, London 1982.
Pfister, Thierry, *Les Socialistes*, Paris 1977.
Poperen, Jean, *L'Unité de la Gauche 1965-1973*, Paris 1975.
Programme commun de gouvernement, Paris 1972.
Robrieux, Philippe, *Histoire intérieure du parti communiste*, 3 vols, Paris 1980-2.
Roucaute, Yves, *Le PCF et les sommets de l'État*, Paris 1981.
Roucaute, Yves, *Le Parti Socialiste*, Paris 1983.
Tiersky, Ronald, *French Communism, 1920-1972*, London 1974.
Touchard, Jean, *La Gauche en France depuis 1900*, Paris 1977.
Verdier, Robert, *PS-PC: une lutte pour l'entente*, Paris 1976.
Wilson, Frank, *The French Democratic Left, 1963-1969*, Stanford 1971.

Wohl, Robert, *French Communism in the Making, 1914-1924*, Stanford, Calif. 1966.

Pressure groups

Adam, Gérard, *Le pouvoir syndical*, 2nd edn, Paris 1985.
Ambler, J.S., *Soldiers against the State; The French Army in Politics 1945-1962*, 2nd edn, New York 1968.
Aubert V. *et al.*, *La forteresse enseignante: La Fédération de l'Éducation Nationale*, Paris 1985.
Barjonet, André, *La CFDT*, Paris 1968.
Barjonet, André, *La CGT*, Paris, 1968.
Barral, Pierre, *Les Agrariens français de Méline à Pisani*, Paris 1968.
Berger, Suzanne, *Peasants against Politics, Rural Organisations in Brittany 1911-1967*, Cambridge, Mass. 1972.
Bergounioux, Alain, *Force Ouvrière*, Paris 1975.
Brizay, Bernard, *Le Patronat*, Paris 1975.
Capdevielle, Jacques, and Mouriaux, René, *Les Syndicats ouvriers en France*, Paris 1973.
Clark, James, *Teachers and Politics in France*, Syracuse, New York 1967.
Colas, Dominique (ed.), *L'État et les Corporatismes*, Paris 1988.
Ehrmann, Henry, *Organized Business in France*, Princeton, NJ 1957.
Faure, M., *Les Paysans dans la société française*, 2nd edn, Paris 1967.
Fields, A.B., *Student Politics in France: A Study of the Union nationale des Étudiants de France*, New York 1970.
Frazer, W.R., *Education and Society in Modern France*, London 1968.
Girardet, Raoul, *La Crise militaire française, 1945-1962*, Paris 1964.
Harmel, Claude, *La CGT*, Paris 1982.
Keeler, John T.S., *Neocorporatism in France: Farmers, the State, and Agricultural Policy-making in the Fifth Republic*, Oxford 1987.
Kelley, George A., *Lost Soldiers; The French Army and Empire in Crisis, 1947-1962*, Cambridge, Mass. 1964.
Kesselman M. and Groux, G. (eds), *Le Mouvement Ouvrier Française: Crise économique et changement politique*, Paris 1984.
La Gorce, P.M. de, *La République et son armée*, Paris 1963.
Landier, Hubert, *Les Organisations syndicales en France*, Paris 1980.
Landier, Hubert, *Demain, quels syndicats?*, Paris 1981.
Martin, J.M., *Le CNPF*, Paris 1983.
Mendras, H., and Tavernier, Y. (eds), *Terre, paysans et politique*, Paris 1969-70.
Meynaud, Jean, *Les Groupes de pression*, Paris 1958.
Meynaud, Jean, *Nouvelles études sur les groupes de pression*, Paris 1962.
Mouriaux, René, *La CGT*, Paris 1982.
Mouriaux, René, *Les Syndicats dans la société française*, Paris 1983.
Mouriaux, René, *Le syndicalisme face à la crise*, Paris 1986.
Nelkin, Dorothy, and Pollak, Michael, *The Atom Besieged; Extra-parliamentary Dissent in France and Germany*, Cambridge, Mass. 1982.
Rand-Smith, W., *Organizing Class Struggle in France: Grassroots Unionism in the CGT and CFDT*, London 1986.

Rand-Smith, W., *Crisis in the French Labour Movement*, London 1987.
Reece, Jack E., *The Bretons against France: Ethnic Minority Nationalism in Twentieth-Century Brittany*, Chapel Hill, North Carolina 1977.
Reynaud, Jean-Daniel, *Les Syndicats en France*, 2 vols, Paris 1975.
Ross, George, *Workers and Communists in France: From Popular Front to Eurocommunism*, Berkeley, Calif. 1982.
Segrestin, Daniel, *Le Phénomène corporatiste: essai sur l'avenir des systèmes professionnels fermés en France*, Paris 1985.
Shackleton, Michael, *The Politics of Fishing in Britain and France*, Aldershot 1986.
Suleiman, Ezra N., *Les Notaires: les pouvoirs d'une corporation*, Paris 1987.
Tavernier, Yves, *La FNSEA*, Paris 1965.
Tavernier, Yves, *Le CNJA*, Paris 1966.
Tavernier, Yves, *Le Syndicalisme Paysan*, Paris 1969.
Vernon, Raymond, *Big Business and the State*, Cambridge, Mass. 1973.
Weber, Henri, *Le Parti des Patrons: Le CNPF 1946-1986*, Paris 1986.
Wilson, Frank L., *Interest Group Politics in France*, Cambridge 1987.
Wright, Gordon, *Rural Revolution in France*, Stanford 1964.

The public sector and administration

Armstrong, John A., *The European Administrative Elite*, Princeton, NJ 1973.
Baecque, F. de, *L'Administration centrale de la France*, Paris 1976.
Baecque, F. de, *Qui gouverne la France?*, Paris 1976.
Baecque, F. de, and Quermonne, J.-L. (eds), *Administration et Politique sous la Cinquième République*, Paris 1982.
Belorgey, Gérard, *Le Gouvernement et l'administration de la France*, 2nd edn, Paris 1970.
Billy, Jacques, *Les Technocrates*, Paris 1975.
Bodiguel, Jean-Luc, *Les Anciens élèves de l'ENA*, Paris 1978.
Bodiguel, J.L., and Quermonne, J.L., *La Haute Fonction Publique sous la Cinquième République*, Paris 1983.
Brachet, P., *L'État entrepreneur, théorie et réalité*, Paris 1975.
Brown, L. Neville, and Garner, J.F., *French Administrative Law*, London 1967.
Catherine, Robert, *Le Fonctionnaire français*, 2nd edn, Paris 1973.
Catherine, Robert, and Thuillier, Guy, *Introduction à une philosophie de l'administration*, Paris 1969.
Chénot, B., *Les Entreprises nationalisées*, Paris 1977.
Chevallier, Jacques, *Les Enterprises publiques en France*, Paris 1979.
Closon, F.L., and Filippi, J., *L'Économie et les finances*, Paris 1968.
Crozier, Michel, *The Bureaucratic Phenomenon*, Chicago, 1964.
Crozier, Michel, and Friedberg, Erhard (eds), *Où va l'administration française?*, Paris 1984.
Darbel, Alain, and Schnapper, Dominique, *Morphologie de la haute administration française*, 2 vols, Paris 1969-72.

Debbasch, Charles, *L'Administration au pouvoir*, Paris 1969.

Delion, André, and Durupty, Michel, *Les Nationalisations de 1982*, Paris 1982.

Deroche, Henri, *Les Mythes administratifs*, Paris 1966.

Dreyfus, Françoise, *L'Interventionisme économique*, Paris 1971.

Dupuy, François, and Thoenig, Jean-Claude, *Sociologie de l'Administration française*, Paris 1983.

Dupuy, François, and Thoenig, Jean-Claude, *L'Administration en miettes*, Paris 1985.

Eck, François, *L'État emprunteur et prêteur*, Paris 1971.

Eck, F., *La Direction du Trésor*, Paris 1986.

Escoube, P., *Les Grands corps de l'État*, 2nd edn, Paris 1977.

Fanachi, Pierre, *La Justice administrative*, Paris 1980.

Fougère, Louis, *La Fonction publique*, Paris 1966.

Fourneret, Pierre, *L'Administration économique*, Paris 1972.

Freches, José, *L'ENA. Voyage au centre de l'État*, Paris 1981.

Freedman, Charles E., *The Conseil d'État in Modern France*, New York 1961.

Friedberg, E., and Desjeux, D., *Le Ministère de l'Industrie et son environnement*, Paris 1973.

Friedberg, E., and Desjeux, D., *Les Systèmes d'intervention en matière industrielle*, Paris 1973.

Gournay, Bernard, and Kesler, Jean-François (eds), *Administration publique*, Paris 1967.

Gournay, Bernard, *Introduction à la science administrative*, Paris 1978.

Gouyou-Beauchamps, Xavier, *Un État dans l'État? Le Ministère de l'Économie et des Finances*, Paris 1976.

Grémion, Catherine, *Profession: décideurs*, Paris 1979.

Kesler, Jean-François, *Sociologie des fonctionnaires*, Paris 1980.

Kesler, Jean-François, *L'ENA, la Société, l'État*, 1985.

Kessler, Marie-Christine, *Le Conseil d'État*, Paris 1968.

Kessler, Marie-Christine, *La Politique de la haute fonction publique*, Paris 1978.

Kessler, Marie-Christine, *Les Grands Corps de l'État*, Paris 1986.

Kosciusko-Morizet, Joseph A., *La 'Mafia' polytechnicienne*, Paris 1973.

Langrod, G., *L'Administration consultative*, Paris 1972.

Leca, Dominique, *Du Ministère des Finances*, Paris 1966.

Letourneur, M., Bauchet, J., and Meric, J., *Le Conseil d'État et les tribunaux administratifs*, Paris 1970.

Lochak, D., Chevallier, J. et al., *La Haute Administration et la Politique*, Paris 1986.

Maillet, Pierre, and Maillet, Monique, *Le Secteur public en France*, Paris 1970.

Mamou, Y., *Une machine de pouvoir: La direction du Trésor*, Paris 1987.

Milloz, Pierre, *Le Mal Administratif*, Paris 1987.

Negrin, J.P., *Le Conseil d'État et la vie politique en France depuis 1956*, Paris 1968.

Pfister, Thierry, *La République des fonctionnaires*, Paris 1988.

Rémond, René et al., *Quarante ans de cabinets ministériels*, Paris 1982.

Rigaud, Jacques and Delcros, Xavier, *Les institutions administratives françaises*, Paris Vol. I 1984, Vol II 1986.
Schifres, Michel, *L'Enaklatura*, Paris 1987.
Suleiman, Ezra, *Politics, Power and Bureaucracy in France*, London 1974.
Superstructures des administrations centrales, Cahier de l'Institut Français des Sciences Administratives, Paris 1973.
Thoenig, Jean-Claude, *L'Ère des technocrates*, Paris 1973.
Thuillier, Guy, *Regards sur la haute administration en France*, Paris 1979.
Thuiller, Guy, *Les Cabinets Ministériels*, Paris 1982.

Local governments

Administration des grandes villes, Cahier de l'Institut Français des Sciences Administratives, Paris 1977.
Ashford, Douglas, *British Dogmatism and French Pragmatism*, London 1982.
Becquart-Leclerq, Jeanne, *Paradoxes du pouvoir local*, Paris 1976.
Belorgey, G., *La France décentralisée*, Paris 1984.
Bernard, Paul, *Le Grand Tournant des communes de France*, Paris 1969.
Bernard, Paul, *L'État et la décentralisation: du préfet au commissaire de la République*, Paris 1983.
Besson, Jean François, *Les interventions économiques des collectivités locales*, Paris 1981.
Biarez, S. *et al.*, *Les Élus locaux et l'aménagement urbain dans l'agglomération grenobloise*, Grenoble 1970.
Biarez, S. *et al.*, *Institutions communales et pouvoir politique*, Paris 1973.
Castells, M., *La Question urbaine*, Paris 1972.
Castells, M., and Godard, F., *Monopolville: l'entreprise, l'État, l'urbain*, Paris 1974.
Chapman, Brian, *Prefects and Provincial France*, London 1955.
Chevallier, J., Rangeon, F. and Sellier M., *Le Pouvoir régional*, Paris 1982.
Detton, H., *L'Administration régionale et locale en Franec*, 2nd edn, Paris 1963.
Dion, Stéphane, *La Politisation des Maires*, Paris 1986.
Flory, T., *Le Mouvement régionaliste français*, Paris 1966.
Frège, Xavier, *La Décentralisation*, Paris 1986.
Gontcharoff, G. and Milano, S., *La Décentralisation: nouveaux pouvoirs, nouveaux enjeux*, Paris 1982.
Graziani, P., *Le Nouveau Pouvoir: essai sur la décentralisation*, Paris 1985.
Grémion, Pierre, *La Structuration du pouvoir au niveau départemental*, Paris 1969.
Grémion, Pierre, *Le Pouvoir périphérique*, Paris 1976.
Grémion, Pierre, and Worms, J.P., *Les Institutions régionales et la société locale*, Paris 1969.
Gruber, Annie, *La décentralisation et les institutions administratives*, Paris 1986.

Kesselman, Mark, *The Ambiguous Consensus: A Study of Local Government in France*, New York 1967.

Kukawka, P., *Les Théories du pouvoir local*, Grenoble 1973.

Laborie, J.P., and Lugan, J.C., *Le Système politique des petites villes françaises*, Toulouse 1975.

Lacorne, Denis, *Les Notables rouges*, Paris 1980.

Lagroye, Jacques, *Société et Politique: Jacques Chaban-Delmas à Bordeaux*, Paris 1973.

Lagroye, Jacques, and Wright, Vincent (eds), *Local Government in Britain and France*, London 1979.

Lanversin, J. de, *La Région et l'aménagement du territoire*, Paris 1979.

Lavau, Georges, *La Région et la réforme administrative*, Paris 1964.

Lojkine, J., *La Politique urbaine dans la région lyonnaise*, Paris 1974.

Lojkine, J., *La Politique urbaine dans la région parisienne*, Paris 1976.

Longepierre, Michel, *Les Conseillers généraux dans le système administratif français*, Paris 1971.

Mabileau, Albert (ed.), *Les Facteurs locaux de la vie politique nationale*, Paris 1972.

Mabileau, Albert (ed.), *Les Pouvoirs locaux à l'épreuve de la décentralisation*, Paris 1983.

Machin, Howard, *The Prefect in French Public Administration*, London 1977.

Madiot, Y., *L'Aménagement du territoire*, Paris 1979.

Marchand, Marie-Hélène, *Les Conseillers généraux en France depuis 1945*, Paris 1970.

Mény, Yves, *Centralisation et décentralisation dans le débat politique français 1945-1969*, Paris 1974.

Moderne, Franck, *Les Nouvelles Compétences locales*, Paris 1985.

Muret, J.P. *et al.*, *Le Conseil Régional*, 2nd edn, Paris 1986.

Ollivaux, J.P., *La région et l'aménagement du territoire*, Paris 1986.

Perrineau, Pascal (ed.), *Régions: le baptême des urnes*, Paris 1987.

Pontier, Jean-Marie, *L'État et les collectivités locales*, Paris 1987.

Ravanel, Jean, *La Réforme des Collectivités locales et des Régions*, Paris 1984.

Reece, Jack, *The Bretons against France. Ethnic Minority Nationalism in Twentieth Century Brittany*, Chapel Hill, North Carolina 1977.

Schain, Martin, *Communists in Power*, Paris 1980.

Simonet, A., and Leger, J.M., *De la Coopération intercommunale au regroupement des communes*, Paris 1975.

Souchon, Marie-France, *Le Maire, élu local dans une société en changement*, Paris 1968.

Tarrow, Sidney, *Between Centre and Periphery*, London 1977.

Terrazzoni, A., *La Décentralisation – à l'épreuve des faits*, Paris 1987.

Thoenig, Jean-Claude, *L'Ère des technocrates: le cas des Ponts-et-Chaussées*, Paris 1973.

Vié, Jean-Emile, *La décentralisation sans illusion*, Paris 1982.

Useful biographies, autobiographies and works by prominent politicians

Amouroux, H., *Monsieur Barre*, Paris 1986.
Aron, Robert, *An Explanation of de Gaulle*, New York 1966.
Barre, Raymond, *Questions de Confiance*, Paris 1988.
Bassi, Michel, *Valéry Giscard d'Estaing*, Paris 1968.
Borzeix, Jean-Marie, *Mitterrand lui-même*, Paris 1973.
Bunel, Jean, and Meunier, Paul, *Chaban-Delmas*, Paris 1972.
Buron, Robert, *Le Plus beau des métiers*, Paris 1963.
Chaban-Delmas, Jacques, *L'Ardeur*, Paris 1976.
Chénot, Bernard, *Etre Ministre*, Paris 1967.
Clessis, Catherine *et al.*, *Jacques Chirac ou la République des cadets*, Paris 1972.
Daniel, Jean, *Les religions d'un Président: Regard sur les aventures mitterrandistes*, Paris 1988.
Debré, Michel, *La Mort de l'État Républicain*, Paris 1947.
Debré, Michel, *Ces Princes qui nous gouvernent*, Paris 1957.
Debré, Michel, *Au Service de la nation*, Paris 1963.
Debré, Michel, *Sur le Gaullisme*, Paris 1967.
Debré, Michel, *Une Certaine idée de la France*, Paris 1972
Deligny, Henri, *Chirac ou la fringale du pouvoir*, Paris 1977.
Gaulle, Charles de, *Discours et messages*, Paris 1970.
Gaulle, Charles de, *Memoirs of Hope*, 2 vols, London 1971.
Giesbert, Franz-Olivier, *François Mitterrand ou la tentation de l'histoire*, Paris 1977.
Giesbert, Franz-Olivier, *Jacques Chirac*, Paris 1987.
Giroud, Françoise, *La Comédie du pouvoir*, Paris 1977.
Giscard d'Estaing, Valéry, *La Démocratie française*, Paris 1976.
Giscard d'Estaing, V., *Le Pouvoir et la vie*, Paris 1988.
Guichard, Olivier, *Un Chemin tranquil*, Paris 1975.
Jobert, Michel, *Mémoires d'avenir*, Paris 1974.
Jouary, J.-P., Pelachaud, G., and Spire, A. (eds), *Giscard et les idées: Essai sur la guerre idéologique*, Paris 1980.
Lacouture, Jean, *De Gaulle*, London 1970.
Lacouture, Jean, *De Gaulle*, 3 vols, Paris 1984, 1985, 1986.
La Fournière, Xavier de, *Giscard d'Estaing et nous*, Paris 1976.
La Gorce, Paul-Marie de, *De Gaulle entre deux mondes*, Paris 1964.
Lagroye, Jacques, *Chaban-Delmas à Bordeaux*, Paris 1973.
Lancel, François, *Valéry Giscard d'Estaing*, Paris 1974.
Lande, David, *François Mitterrand*, Paris 1974.
Malraux, André, *Les Chênes qu'on abat*, Paris 1971.
Marcellin, Raymond, *L'importune Vérité*, Paris 1978.
Marchais, Georges, *Le Défi démocratique*, Paris 1973.
Marchais, Georges, *Parlons franchement*, Paris 1977.
Mendès-France, Pierre, *A Modern French Republic*, New York 1963.
Mitterrand, François, *Le Coup d'État permanent*, Paris 1964.
Mitterrand, François, *Ma Part de vérité*, Paris 1969.
Mitterrand, François, *La Paille et le grain*, Paris 1975.

Mitterrand, François, *La Rose au poing*, Paris 1975.
Mitterrand, François, *Politique*, Paris 1977.
Mitterrand, François, *Ici et maintenant*, Paris 1980.
Mollet, Guy, *13 mai 1958–12 mai 1962*, Paris 1962.
Monnet, Jean, *Mémoires*, Paris 1976.
Pautard, André, *Valéry Giscard d'Estaing*, Paris 1974.
Pisani, Edgard, *Le Général indivis*, Paris 1974.
Pompidou, Georges, *Le Noeud Gordien*, Paris 1974.
Pompidou, Georges, *Pour rétablir une vérité*, Paris 1982.
Poniatowski, Michel, *Cartes sur table*, Paris 1972.
Poniatowski, Michel, *Conduire le changement*, Paris 1975.
Poujade, Robert, *Le Ministère de l'impossible*, Paris 1975.
Rouanet, P., *Pompidou*, Paris 1969.
Roussel, E., *Georges Pompidou*, Paris 1984.
Servan-Schreiber, Jean-Jacques, *Le Manifeste Radical*, Paris 1970.
Soustelle, Jacques, *Vingt-huit années de gaullisme*, Paris 1968.
Szafran, Maurice, *Jacques Chirac ou les passions du pouvoir*, Paris 1986.
Szafran, Maurice, and Ketz, Samy, *Les familles du Président*, Paris 1982.
Todd, Olivier, *La Marelle de Giscard, 1926-1974*, Paris 1977.
Vallon, Louis, *L'Anti-de Gaulle*, Paris 1968.
Werth, Alexander, *De Gaulle*, London 1965.

List of abbreviations

AGREF	Association des grandes entreprises françaises faisant appel à l'épargne
APC	Association des Patriotes Corses
APEL	Association des Parents d'Élèves de l'Enseignement Libre
ARC	Action pour la Renaissance de la Corse
CAECL	Caisse d'aide à l'équipment des collectivités locales
CAR	Conférence Administrative Régionale
CD	Centre Démocrate
CDP	Centre Démocratie et Progrès
CDS	Centre des Démocrates Sociaux
CERES	Centre d'Études, de Recherches et d'Éducation Socialistes
CFDT	Confédération Française Démocratique du Travail
CFE-CGC	Confédération Française de l'Encadrement-Confédération Générale des Cadres
CFT	Confédération Française du Travail
CFTC	Confédération Française des Travailleurs Chrétiens
CGC	Confédération Générale des Cadres
CGPME	Confédération Générale des Petites et Moyennes Entreprises
CGT	Confédération Générale du Travail
CID-UNATI	Comité d'Information et de Défense–Union Nationale des Artisans et Travailleurs Indépendants
CIR	Convention des Institutions Républicaines
CJP	Centre des Jeunes Patrons
CNIP	Centre National des Indépendants et Paysans
CNJA	Centre National des Jeunes Agriculteurs
CNPF	Conseil National du Patronat Français
CNSTP	Confédération Nationale des Syndicats des Travailleurs-Paysans
CODEFI	Comité départemental des problémes de financement des entreprises
CORRI	Comité Régional de Restructuration industrielle
DATAR	Délégation Générale à l'Aménagement du Territoire
DGRST	Délégation Générale de la Recherche Scientifique et Technique
ENA	École Nationale d'Administration
EDF	Électricité de France

FEN	Fédération de l'Éducation Nationale
FFA	Fédération Française de l'Agriculture
FGDS	Fédération de la Gauche Démocrate et Socialiste
FIAT	Fonds de l'intervention pour l'aménagement du territoire
FLB-ARB	Front de Libération Bretonne–Armée Républicaine Bretonne
FLNC	Front de Libération Nationale Corse
FNAFU	Fonds national de l'aménagement foncier et de l'urbanisme
FNSEA	Fédération Nationale des Syndicats d'Exploitants Agricoles
FO	Force Ouvrière
INSEE	Institut National d'Études Statistiques et Économiques
MDSF	Mouvement Démocrate Socialiste de France
MODEF	Mouvement pour la Co-ordination et la Défense de l'Exploitation Familiale
MONATAR	Mouvement National des Travailleurs Agricoles et Ruraux
MRP	Mouvement Républicain Populaire
PCF	Parti Communiste Français
PPBS	Planning, programming budgeting systems
PS	Parti Socialiste
PSU	Parti Socialiste Unifié
RCB	Rationalisation des Choix Budgétaires
RI	Républicains Indépendants
RPF	Rassemblement du Peuple Français
RPR	Rassemblement pour la République
SFIO	Section Française de l'Internationale Ouvrière
SNES	Syndicat National de l'enseignement secondaire
SNI	Syndicat National des Instituteurs
TPG	Trésorier Payeur Général
UDCA	Union de Défense des Commercants et des Artisans
UDF	Union pour la démocratie française
UDR	Union des Démocrates pour la République
UDT	Union Démocratique du Travail
UDVE	Union des Démocrates pour la Ve République
UGSD	Union de la Gauche Socialiste et Démocrate
UNEF	Union Nationale des Étudiants de France
UNR	Union pour la Nouvelle République
UPC	Union du Peuple Corse

Index